THE TRANSMITTER TO GOD

The Limbic System, the Soul, and Spirituality

Rhawn Joseph, Ph.D.
Neurodynamics, Brain Research Laboratory
Brain-Mind.com

Third Printing

Joseph, Rhawn
The Transmitter to God: The Limbic System, the Soul, Spirituality/ R. Joseph —
1st ed.

Includes bibliographical references

ISBN 09700733313

1. God. 2. Spirituality 3. Soul. 4. Death.
5. Religion. 6. Psychology. 7. Ghosts.
8. Occult. 9. Brain and Neuroscience. 10. Aliens and UFOs

University Press California
San Jose, California

Can a lizard comprehend a man?
Can a man comprehend a god?
Who dares speak for God?
Perhaps…
… Even the gods have gods...

CONTENTS

GAZING FORWARD: LOOKING BACK

It has been declared that god is dead, that spirituality is an "opiate" for the people. And yet, there is a scientific, neurological, and genetic foundation for religious belief, spirituality, and paranormal phenomenon, including the experience of gods, demons, spirits, souls, and life after death. There is historical and scientific evidence demonstrating the participation of "god" in the destruction of previous civilizations, and in the last century, Hitler's rise to power. And there are specific regions of the brain, the limbic system, which serve as a transmitter to god. These tissues of the mind become highly active when dreaming, during trance states, meditation, prayer, or under LSD, and enable us to experience those realms of reality normally filtered from consciousness, including the reality of god, the spirit, the soul, and life after death.

It has been known for thousands of years that dream sleep, trance states, isolation, and food and water deprivation can enhance an individual's ability to experience realms of reality which are normally filtered from conscious awareness. Under these conditions the limbic system will become highly active, and even hyper-activated, such that what is normally filtered out is perceived. Under these conditions some claim to speak with god, others seek to transcend god, to achieve oneness with the spiritually sublime.

Limbic system structures such as the amygdala, hippocampus, and inferior temporal lobe have been repeatedly shown to subserve and provide the foundations for mystical, spiritual, and religious experience, and the perception, including the "hallucination" of ghosts, demons, spirits and sprites, and belief in demonic or angelic possession (Bear 1979; Daly 1958; Joseph, 1996, Mesulam 1981; Penfield & Perot 1963; Schenk &Bear 1981; Williams 1956). When these brain areas are hyperactivated, "religious" experiences are not uncommon.

Of course, there are some who might take this to mean that these experiences are nothing more than hallucinations produced by an abnormal brain. In some instances this is true. However, rather than due to some abnormality, religious experience and the seeking of spiritual nourishment is the norm and not the exception. It is this natural upwelling of spiritual emotion and religiosity which explains why despite decades of terror and suppression, totalitarian states such as Communist China, Cuba, and the former Soviet Union were unable and have been unable to crush spiritual and religious expression in their countries.

Belief in souls, spirits, the haunted house, and angels or demons, and the capacity to have mystical experiences, including the sensation of being possessed by gods or devils or hearing their voices, is world wide (Budge 1994; Campbell 1988, Frazier 1950; Godwin 1990; Harris, 1993; James 1958; Jaynes

1976; O'Keefe 1982; Malinowkski 1948; Smart 1969; Wilson 1951). Humans have been demonstrating a belief in the spiritual world for over 100,000 years (Joseph, 1996, 2000a).

These historical and cross-cultural commonalties in religious and archetypal experience include viewing the sign of the cross with spiritual awe, and the experiences of demons and devils and hearing the voice of "God" or communing with the "Great Spirit," as well as the many vestiges or incarnations of what has been referred to as the personal soul or "ghost."

Figure 1. *Souls ascending to Heaven. From Northwest Africa, Upper Paleolithic. These figures sometimes occur with "wondjina" figures which are the "souls of men.*

Some may argue, however, that from a strictly "scientific" perspective, there is no basis for religious and spiritual belief. And, there is no "god."

According to some scientists, we are but random collections of molecules that emerged from an organic soup following the big bang creation of the universe, and we evolved following the generation of random mutations. There is no room for god or spirituality in these "scientific" equations.

However, it seems curious that humans would have evolved the capacity to experience something that does not exist. Indeed, experience acts on gene selection to activate silent genes and silent traits that exist prior to their selection (Joseph, 1997, 2000b). In the absence of specific experiences, those brain structures and neurons which subserve those experiences, die and atrophy (Casagrande & Joseph, 1978, 1980; Joseph, 1982, 1998a, 1999a). The genes generating these neurons remain silent and suppressed (Joseph, 1997, 2000b).

In this regard we should be forced to conclude that humans evolved the capacity to have religious and spiritual experiences, because these experiences acted on gene selection, thereby enabling humans to evolve specific brain structures which allowed them to more fully participate in and experience the spiritually sublime.

And yet, how do we reconcile spirituality and religiosity with the "big bang," the belief that life originated in an organic soup, and with Darwinian principles of random mutations as the basis of human evolution?

There is no need for a reconciliation, for as we shall see in later chapters, the big bang is a myth, we have no idea as to the age of the universe, the proverbial organic "alphabet" soup was missing all essential ingredients for the creation of life and DNA, whereas the Darwinian theory of evolution is refuted by genetics and the fossil record.

The big bang, organic soup, Darwin's theory, are but myths propagated by the Temple Priests of Science, myths which have replaced previous scientific myths, which replaced those older still.

By contrast, and, as we shall see in later chapters, there is a scientific, genetic, and neurological basis for religious and spiritual experience. The brain has evolved the capacity to act as a transmitter to god. It is this neurological, genetic, as well as this spiritual foundation which explains the historical and cross-cultural commonalty in religious experience.

Presumably because all humans possess a limbic system and a brain that is organized in a similar manner, they have similar religious and mystical experiences, what Jung (1964) referred to as "archetypes." Archetypes are inborn tendencies to dream of, and respond similarly to specific images and symbols, and to experience a personal soul and the presence of god. Humans have similar religious experiences because these experiences are real and are perceived in a similar manner by the same regions of the brain. Each and every human is born with a brain and mind that serves as a transmitter to god.

Indeed, it could be argued that the essence of "God," and of our living soul, may be dwelling within the depths of the ancient limbic lobe which is buried within the belly of the brain. And not just the soul or the Great Spirit, for in the Upanishads and Tao it is said, and as Buddha, Lao Tzu, Chuang Tzu, Jesus, the Sufis, and as Sumerian, Babylonian, Egyptian, Jewish, Arabic, Aryan, Greek, Roman, Indian, Muslim, and Gnostic mystics have proclaimed:

"The kingdom of God is within you."

PALEOLITHIC SPIRITUALITY

DEATH AND THE TRANSMIGRATION OF THE SOUL

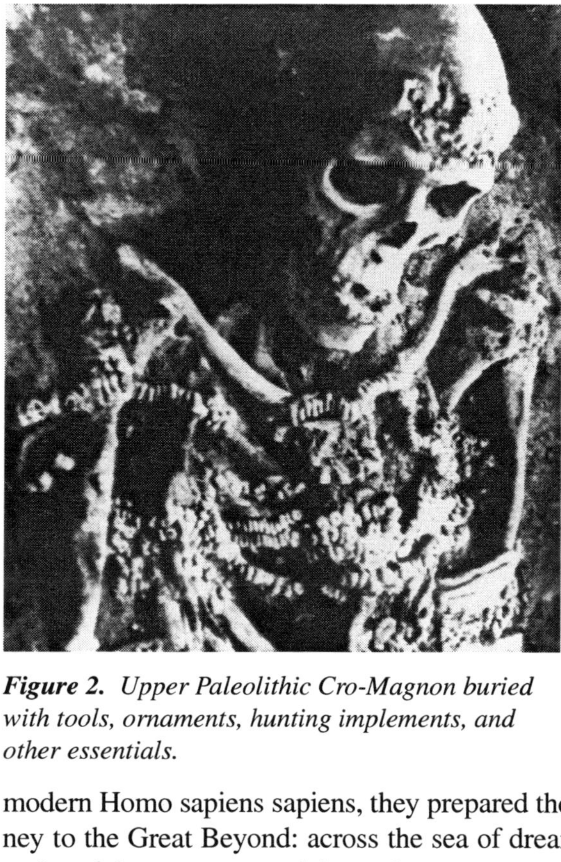

Figure 2. *Upper Paleolithic Cro-Magnon buried with tools, ornaments, hunting implements, and other essentials.*

Belief in the transmigration of the soul, of a life after death, of a world beyond the grave, has been a human characteristic for at least 100,000 years, as ancient graves and mortuary rites attest (e.g., Belfer-Cohen & Hovers, 1992; Butzer, 1982; McCown, 1937; Rightmire, 1984; Schwarcz et al., 1988; Smirnov, 1989; Trinkaus 1986). Despite their small brains and primitive intellectual, linguistic, cognitive, and mental capabilities, primitive "archaic" human beings who wondered the planet over 120,000 years ago, carefully buried their dead (Butzer, 1982; Rightmire, 1984). And like modern Homo sapiens sapiens, they prepared the recently departed for the journey to the Great Beyond: across the sea of dreams, to the land of the dead, the realm of the ancestors and the gods.

Throughout the Middle and Upper Paleolithic it was not uncommon for tools and hunting implements to be placed beside the body, even 100,000 years ago, for the dead would need them in the next world (Belfer-Cohen & Hovers, 1992; McCown, 1937; Trinkaus, 1986). A hunter in life he was to be a hunter in death, for the ethereal world of the Paleolithic was populated by spirits and souls of bear, wolf, deer, bison, and mammoth (e.g., Campbell, 1988; Kuhn, 1955). Moreover, food and water might be set near the head in case the spirit hungered or experienced thirst on its long sojourn to the Hereafter. And finally,

Figure 3. *A Neanderthal seemingly glowers from the grave at those who have disturbed his long slumber. His body had been sprinkled with 7 different types of flowers. Reproduced from R. Solecki. Shanidar: The first Flower people. New York, A.A. Knopf.*

fragrant blossoming flowers and red ocher might be sprinkled upon the bodies (Solecki, 1971) along with the tears of those who loved them.

Given the relative paucity of cognitive, cultural, and intellectual development among Middle Paleolithic Neanderthal and "archaic" humans, and the likelihood that they had not yet acquired modern human speech (Joseph, 1996, 2000a,b,), evidence of spiritual concerns among these Middle Paleolithic peoples may be somewhat surprising if not unbelievable (Gargett 1989).

Neanderthals, archaics, and other peoples of the Middle Paleolithic were not very smart and used simple stones for tools. In fact, they constructed and made essentially the same stone tools over and over again for perhaps 200,000 years, until around 35,000 B.P., with little variation or consideration of alternatives (Binford, 1982; Gowlett, 1984; Mellars, 1989). Neanderthals greatly lacked in creativity, initiative, imagination, and

Figure 4. *Neanderthal tools.*

tended to create simple stone tools that served a single purpose.

As neatly summed up by an ardent defender of Neanderthal cognitive capabilities (Hayden, 1993, p. 139), "as a rule, there is no evidence of private ownership or food storage, no evidence for the use of economic resources for status or political competition, no elaborate burials, no ornaments or other status display items, no skin garments requiring intensive labor to produce, no tools requiring high energy investments, no intensive regional exchange for rare items like sea shells or amber, no competition for labor to produce economic surpluses and no corporate art or labor intensive rituals in deep cave recesses to impress onlookers and help attract labor."

Neanderthals tended to live in the "here and now," with little ability to think about or consider the distant future (Binford, 1973, 1982; Dennell, 1985; Mellars, 1989, 1996); the only notable exception, the future life after death.

This notable dichotomy is in part a function of the differential evolution of the frontal versus the temporal lobes. The frontal lobes are the senior executive of the brain and are responsible for initiative, goal formation, long term planning, the generation of multiple alternatives, and the consideration of multiple alternative consequences (Joseph, 1986a, 1988a, 1999b). The frontal lobes are the source of creativity and imagination, whereas the temporal lobes are the seat of the soul. It is the temporal lobes which were maximally developed in archaic and Neanderthals, whereas the frontal lobe would increase in size by a third in

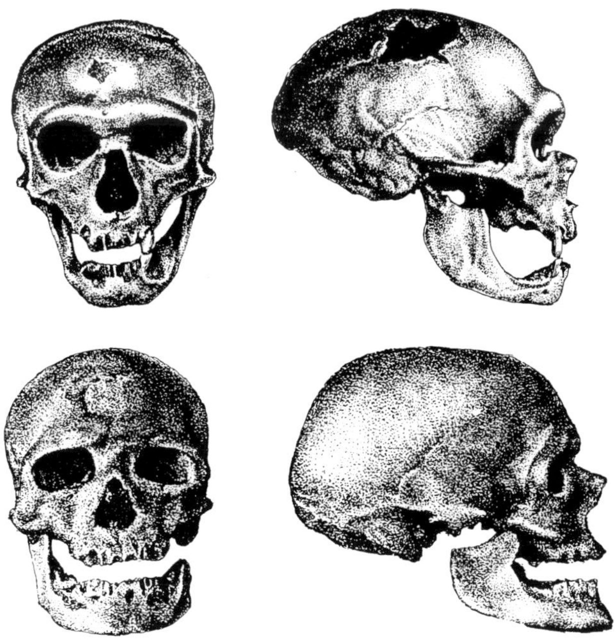

Figure 5. *Neanderthal (top) and Cro-Magnon (bottom) craniums. Note expanded frontal region of skull in Cro-Magnon. The brain of the Cro-Magnon was 30% larger than the Neanderthal brain.*

the transition from archaic humans to Cro-Magnon woman and man.

Based on a gross analysis of the skull and casts made of the inner surface of the skull as well as other evidence some of which will be reviewed here, it is apparent that "archaic" Neanderthal men and women possessed a well developed inferior temporal lobe whereas the frontal lobe is sloped and stunted (Joseph, 1996, 2000a). It is the temporal lobes, and the limbic structures buried within which are directly implicated in the generation of personal, emotional, and religious experience including the ability to from long term emotional attachments and to feel intense love (Gloor, 1997; Joseph, 1992a, 1999b, 2000a; MacLean, 1990).

In fact, Neanderthals provided loving care for friends and family who had been injured or maimed, enabling them to live many more years despite their grievous injuries. For example, the skeleton of one Neanderthal male, who was about age 45 when he died, had been nursed for a number of years following profoundly crippling injuries. His right arm had atrophied, and his lower arm and hand had apparently been ripped or bitten off, and his left eye socket , right shoulder, collarbone, and both legs were badly injured. Obviously someone loved and tenderly cared for this man. He was no doubt a father, a husband, a brother, and son, and someone in his family not only provided long term loving care to make him comfortable in this life, but prepared him for the next life as well.

Neanderthals were unable to fashion complex tools or think complex thoughts, yet they were people of passion who experienced profound emotions and love; made possible by the limbic system and temporal lobe. In fact, it is because they had the limbic capacity to experience love, spiritual awe, and religious concerns, that these expressions of love continued beyond death. Thus the Neanderthals carefully buried their dead, providing them with food and even sprinkling the bodies with seven different types of blooming, blossoming, fragrant flowers.

THE ANTIQUITY OF THE SOUL

MIDDLE PALEOLITHIC SPIRITUALITY

When humans first became aware of a "god" or "gods" cannot be determined. Nevertheless, the antiquity of religious and spiritual belief extends well beyond the course of the last 100,000 years, as it has been well established that Neanderthals and other Homo Sapiens of the Middle Paleolithic (e.g. 150,000 to 35,000 B.P.) and Upper Paleolithic (35,000 B.P. to 10,000 B.P.) engaged in complex religious rituals. These rituals are evident from the manner in which they decorated their caves and the spiritual symbolism associated with death.

Neanderthals (a people who lived in Europe, Russia, Iraq, Africa, and China from around 150,000 to 30,000 B.P.), have been buried in sleeping positions with the body flexed and lying on its side. Some were laid to rest with limestone blocks placed beneath the head like a pillow—as if they were not truly dead but merely asleep.

Sleep and dreams have long been associated with the spirit world, and it is through dreams that gods including the Lord God worshipped by Jews, Christians, and Muslims, have communicated their thoughts, warnings, intentions, and commands. Throughout the ages, and as repeatedly stated in the Old Testament and the Koran, dreams have been commonly thought to be the primary medium in which gods and human interact (Campbell 1988; Freud, 1900; Jung 1945, 1964). Insofar as the ancients (and many moderns folks) were concerned, dreams served as a doorway, a portal of entry to the spirit world through which "God," His angels, or myriad demons could make their intentions known.

It is through dreams, we are told, that one is able to come into direct contact with the spirit world and a reality so magical and profoundly different yet as real as anything experienced during waking. It is through dreams that ancient humans came to believe the spiritual world sits at the boundaries of the physical, where day turns to dusk, the hinterland of the imagination where dreams flourish and grow. And it is while dreaming that one's own soul may transcend the body, to soar like an eagle, or to commune with the spirits of loved ones who reside in heaven along side the gods.

Neanderthals prepared their dead for this great and final journey, by laying their loved ones to rest so that they would sleep with the spirits and dream of heavenly eternity.

Neanderthals have also been buried surrounded by goat horns placed in a circle, with reindeer vertebrae, animal skins, stone tools, red ocher, and in one grave, seven different types of flowers. In one cave (unearthed after 60,000 years had passed), a deep chamber was discovered which housed a single skull which was surrounded by a ring of stones.

Yet others were buried with large bovine bones above the head, with limestone blocks placed on top of the head and shoulders, and with heads severed coupled with evidence of ritual decapitation, facial bone removal, and cannibalism (Belfer-Cohen and Hovers 1992; Binford 1968; Harold 1980; Smirnov 1989; Solecki 1971). In one site, dated to over 100,000 years B.P., Neanderthals decapitated eleven of their fellow Neanderthals, and smashed their faces beyond recognition.

Moreover, Neanderthals buried bears at a number of sites including Regourdou. At Drachenloch they buried stone "cysts" containing bear skulls (Kurten 1976); hence, "the clan of the cave bear."

It therefore seems apparent that Neanderthals not only engaged in complex religious rituals, but they believed in spirits, ghosts, and a life after death. Hence the sleeping position, stone pillows, stone tools and food. They were preparing the departing spirit for the journey to the Hereafter and the land of dreams.

It is also appears that they feared the dead, and were terrified by the prospect that certain souls might haunt the living. They were afraid of ghosts, and frightened by the possibility that just as one might awake from sleep after visiting the land of the dead, the dead might also awake from this death-like slumber. The dead, or at least their personal souls, had to be prevented from causing mischief among the living; especially the dead of dreaded enemies. Hence, the ritual decapitation, facial bone removal, and placement of heavy stones upon the body.

It can be concluded, therefore, that almost 100,000 years ago, primitive humans had already come to believe in ghosts, souls, spirits, and a continuation of "life" after death. And, they also took precautions, in some cases, to prevent certain souls from being released from the body and returning to cause mischief among the living.

Moreover, they appear to have believed in a personal soul, which is why, in the case or powerful enemies, the Neanderthals would cut off heads and hands. They went to great lengths to obliterate all aspects of that dreaded individual's personal identity; e.g., smashing the face beyond recognition.

Of course, the fact that these Neanderthals were buried does not necessarily imply that they held a belief in "God." Rather, what the evidence demonstrates is that Neanderthals were capable of very intense emotions and feelings ranging from murderous rage to love to spiritual and superstitious awe. Although no god is implied, Neanderthals held spiritual and mystical beliefs involving the transmigration of the soul and all the horrors, fears, and hopes that accompany such feelings and beliefs. Although the Neanderthals had not discovered god, they stood upon the threshold.

THE NEANDERTHALS: A CHARACTER STUDY

What is most surprising about the depth of Neanderthal spirituality is the fact that these were an exceedingly violent, murderous people, as the remnants of their skeletons preserved for so many eons attests. Many of their fossils still betray the cruel ravages of deliberately and violently inflicted wounds.

They also appear to have systematically engaged in female infanticide, and displayed a willingness to eat almost anything on four or two legs—including other Neanderthals. In one site, dated to over 100,000 years B.P., Neanderthals decapitated eleven of their fellow Neanderthals, and then enlarged the base of each skull (the foramen magnum) so the brains could be scooped out and presumably eaten. Even the skulls of children were treated in this fashion.

In fact, they would throw the bones and carcasses of other Neanderthals into the refuse pile. In one cave, a collection of over 20 Neanderthals were found mixed up with the remains of other animals and refuse. Presumably,

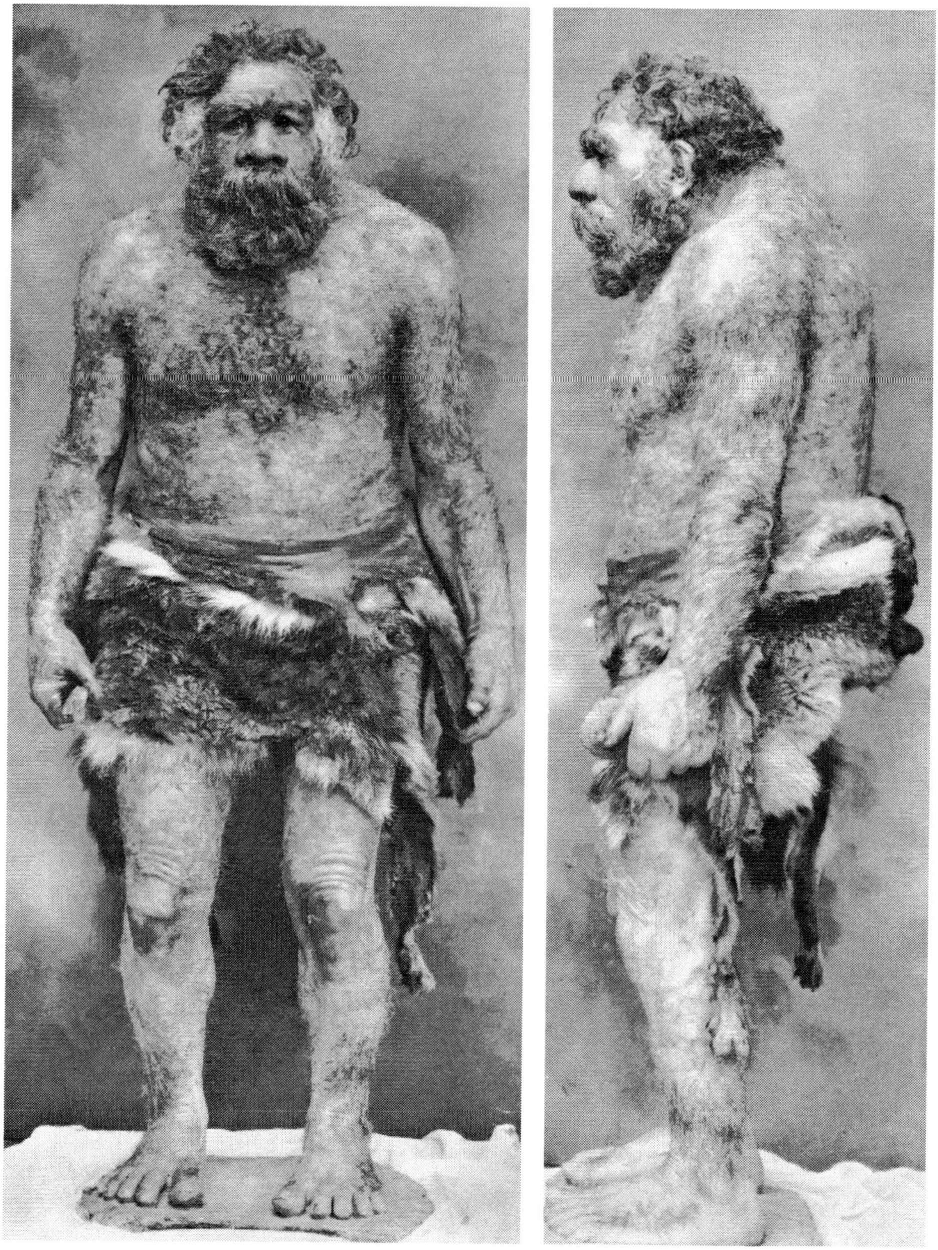

Figure 6. *A stereotypical Neanderthal. From the Chicago Natural History Museum, by Blaschke.*

these were enemies or just hapless strangers, innocent cave dwellers who were attacked and sometimes eaten after being brutally killed.

Hence, with the obvious exception of "friends," mates, and family, Neanderthals often saw one another as a potential meal, and had almost no regard for a stranger's innate humanness. These were a violent, murderous, ritualistic people, and strangers were often killed and eaten.

These characteristics, however, are also associated with religious fervor. Among ancient and present day peoples, violence, murder, ritual cannibalism, and even the sacrifice and murder of children are common religious practices.

Violence and murder are also under the control of the limbic system. And

Figure 7. *The head and torso of a stereotypical Neanderthal man. Reprinted from Howells, 1997. Getting Here. Compass Press, Washington D.C.*

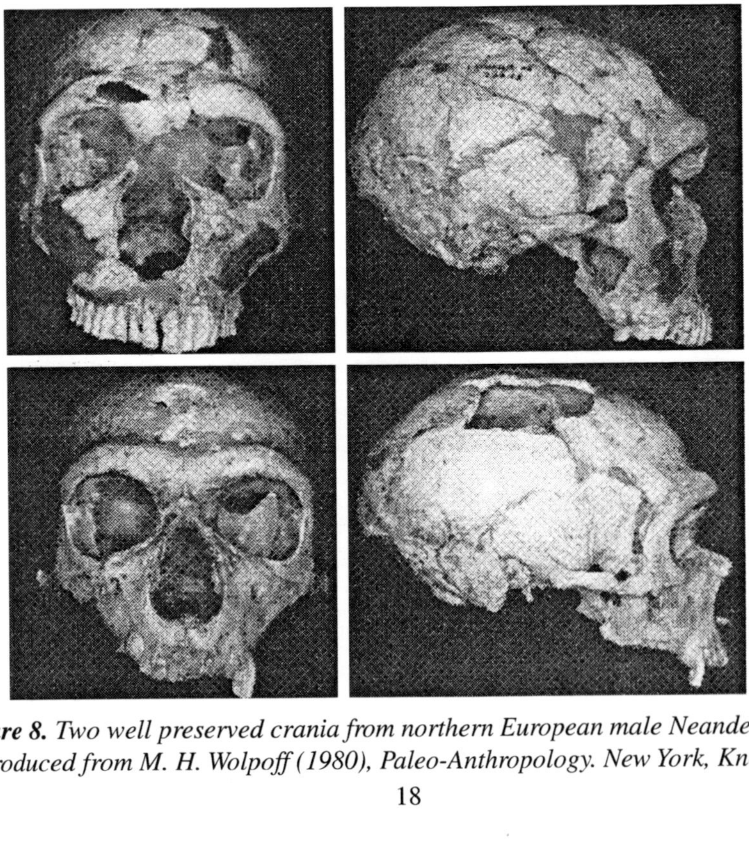

Figure 8. *Two well preserved crania from northern European male Neanderthals. Reproduced from M. H. Wolpoff (1980), Paleo-Anthropology. New York, Knopf.*

it is the limbic system which mediates religious and spiritual experience.

ARCHAIC SPIRITUALITY AND MORTUARY RITUALS

The Neanderthals were not a very intelligent or tidy people. Yet they possessed a well developed limbic system and temporal lobe. In fact, from an examination of fossilized skulls, it appears that other archaic Homo sapiens, including the still primitive "early modern" Homo sapiens of the Middle Paleolithic were well endowed in this regard, though the frontal lobe remained poorly developed (Joseph, 1996, 2000a,b).

Figure 9. Neanderthal burial.

As noted, the temporal lobe began to expand and evolve at a faster and earlier rate than the frontal lobe (Gloor, 1997), which is a characteristic of ontological development as well (Joseph, 1982, 2000a).

It is the expansion of the temporal lobe, this "transmitter to god" which also explains why even earlier species of primitive humanity practiced complex spiritual rituals and mortuary rites. "Early modern," and other "archaic" Homo sapiens commonly buried infants, children, and adults with tools, grave offerings, and animal bones.

For example, archaic H. sapiens and "early moderns" were carefully buried in Qafzeh, near Nazareth and in the Mt. Carmel, Mugharetes-Skhul caves on the Israeli coast over 90,000 to 98,000 years ago (McCown 1937; Smirnov 1989; Trinkaus 1986). This includes a Qafzeh mother and child who were buried together, and an infant who was buried holding the antlers of a fallow deer across his chest. In a nearby site equally as old (i.e. Skhul), yet another was buried with the mandible of a boar held in his hands, whereas an adult had stone tools placed by his side (Belfer-Cohen and Hovers 1992; McCown 1937).

NEOLITHIC MORTUARY PRACTICES

It is unknown if the burial practices of the Paleolithic peoples included burning, as is common in many ancient and present day cultures (e.g. India). There is ample evidence, however, that burning was a widespread custom during the Neolithic. In some cases, only the bones were buried, which indicates that either the body was burnt, or it was only buried after the flesh had rotted away; referred to by anthropologists as a "secondary burial."

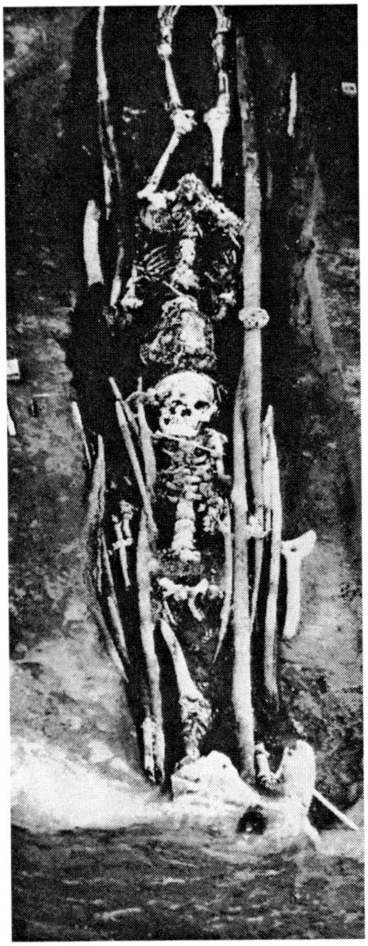

Figure 10. *Two Upper Paleolithic boys buried head to head with grave goods, necklaces, beads, and hunting implements.*

Like those who came before them, the mortuary practices of the Neolithic peoples, such as those living in predynastic Egypt, included the burial of loved ones in sleeping positions, often lying the dead on their left side (Budge, 1900; Hoffman, 1991). The dead "sleeping" body would also be buried with substantial grave goods including surplus wealth.

"The deceased were laid on reed mats and invariably accompanied by grave offerings that reflected their relative wealth and aspects of daily life. These included tools, flint knives, scrapers, arrowheads, ornaments like shell and stone beads, and a bewildering variety of fine, handmade polished red ware jars, backed clay figurines, amulets, and carved ivory plaques" (Hoffman, 1991, p. 110).

Moreover, just as Paleolithic peoples also sometimes took steps to prevent the souls of the dead from returning to haunt the living, or to take up residence in the dead bodies, those of the late Upper Paleolithic and early Neolithic did likewise. For example, the dead might be buried covered with huge stone slabs and with heads, arms, hands and feet missing, and/or impaled with weapons (Budge, 1900).

Mortuary rites and religious rituals have therefore been practiced the world over, from the Middle Paleolithic to the Upper Paleolithic to the Neolithic and beyond to the present. For over 100,000 years humans have buried and weeped over their dead, have believed in spirits and a life after death, and have provisioned their souls for the journey to the Hereafter.

We may be born of the flesh, but we are spiritual beings. Spirituality has been a defining aspect of the human condition for over 100,000 years.

-2-

CRO-MAGNON GENESIS:
The Children of the Gods

Biblical accounts of creation tell us that increasingly complex life forms emerged upon the planet, in a step-wise, "day to day" sequence, beginning with simple creatures and culminating, on day 6, with the creation of woman and man. In fact, this same progression is evident from the fossil record, and was first detailed in the Sumerian and Biblical accounts of Genesis.

Almost 6000 years ago the Sumerians, a cultured people whose cities and civilization eventually gave rise to Babylon, explained that the first humans were exceedingly "primitive" and unsuitable to perform the work required by the gods. The gods required intelligent and skilled workers to tend their farms and gardens.

According to the ancient Sumerians, Enki, the Anunnaki god of science and wisdom, decided to rectify the situation by taking tissue from the gods, mixing it with other substances, so as to create the first true human beings; humans that were fashioned in the image of the gods and provided the spirit, the living soul of god. Enki's emblem was the sign of the double helix, two entwined snakes.

The Biblical account in Genesis echoes the Sumerian account: "And God said, Let us make man in our image, after our likeness. So God created man in his image, in the image of God created he him; male and female he created them."

In the account provided by Genesis there is also a second act of human creation by a "Lord God." This Lord God appears upon the scene after "God ended his work... and rested on the seventh day."

As the men and women created on the sixth day were not suitable to farm the land or manage his herds, the "Lord God" engaged in another act of creation because "there was not a man to till the ground... And the Lord God formed man of the dust of the ground and breathed into his nostrils the breath of life; and man became a living soul. And the Lord God planted a garden eastward in Eden and there he put the man whom he had formed."

Thus we see that the man created after the seventh day differs from the man created on the sixth day, in two important respects. The man created on the sixth day, was created by "God," as part of a natural progression beginning with simple creatures. This first man, however, was unable "to till the land." The man fashioned after the seventh day, after "God" had rested, was created by the "Lord God" after all the natural sequential acts of creation had come to an end. And, this new man, created after the seventh day was able to till the

Figure 11. *The Anunnaki "god" Enki is associated with entwined serpents that form a double helix. reprinted from Sitchin, 1990. Genesis Revisited. Avon, New York.*

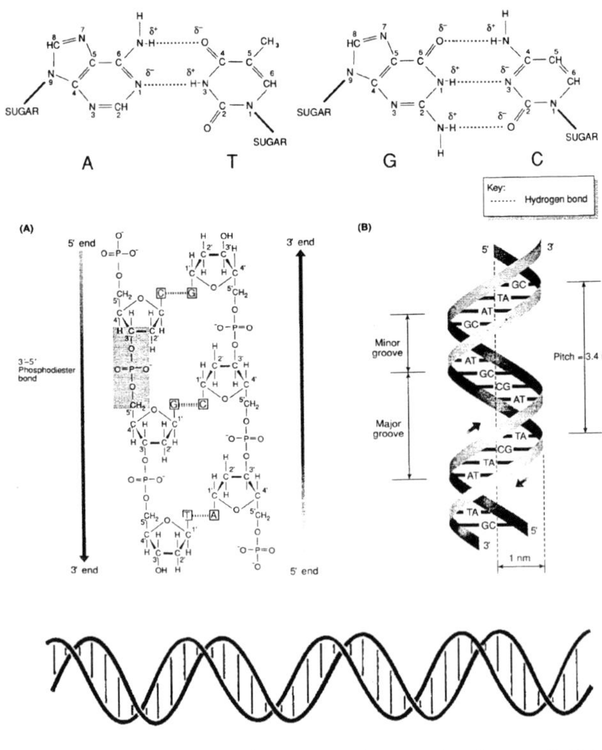

Figure 12. *Molecular and structural organization of DNA.*

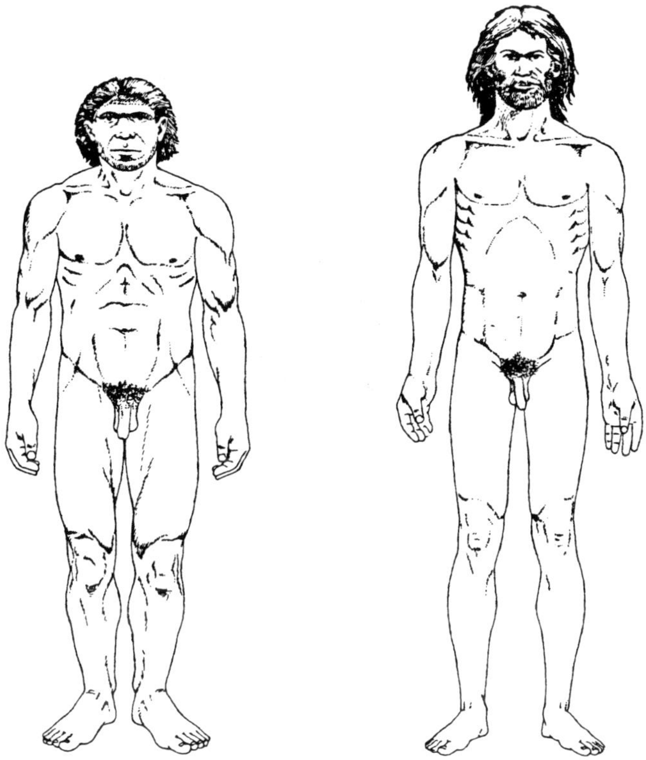

Figure 13. *Depiction of Neanderthal and a Cro-Magnon man. Reprinted from Howells, 1997. Getting Here. Compass Press, Washington D.C.*

gardens, and was provided with a "living soul."

Because the Earth was already swarming with these more primitive humans, Cain (the son of Adam and Eve) worried aloud to the Lord God, that he may be killed: "I shall be a fugitive and a vagabond in the earth; and it shall come to pass that everyone that findeth me shall slay me... And the Lord set a mark upon Cain, lest any finding him should kill him" (Genesis, 4: 14-15).

Thus we may presume that the first men and women did not possess a "living soul," were exceedingly primitive and violent, and lacked the intellectual capability to perform the tasks assigned—at least, as stated by the Sumerians and echoed in Genesis. "There was not a man to till the ground." They were like animals. They had no souls.

By contrast, the second creation resulted in men and women who were not only created in the image of the Gods, but who were highly intelligent, and who received something of God, becoming a "living soul." Unlike the men and women created on the sixth day, this newly created woman and man were so creative, intelligent, and demonstrated such wisdom, that the "the Lord God..." proclaimed "man had become as one of us, to know good and evil."

THE CRO-MAGNON

The Cro-Magnon were a very handsome people with thin hips, broad shoulders, aquiline noses, prominent chins, small even perfect teeth, high rounded foreheads, and with brains almost a third larger than those of the average woman and man today, i.e. 1800 cc vs 1350 ccs. There was nothing ape-like or Neanderthal about these people.

These were a tall and noble looking race. Consider, whereas the average height of a present day male averages (depending on country) from between five foot four to five foot 9 inches, Cro-Magnon men stood 6 foot tall, though the women were somewhat smaller and more delicate. Compared to those who came before or after them, and until the advent of the 20th century, these people were giants and they may well have appeared as "gods;" at least to the Neanderthals who managed to hang on for another 10,000 years after the Cro-Magnons had appeared upon the scene. In fact, it was not until the 20th century and with significant changes in nutrition and diet that people in the Western world grew by almost half a foot in height, the men reaching five feet nine inches on average.

The Cro-Magnon were also intellectual giants. They were accomplished artists, musicians, craftsmen, sorcerers, and extremely talented hunters, fishermen, and highly efficient gatherers and herbalists. When they emerged upon the scene over 35,000 years ago, they carried and fashioned tools and weapons that had never before been seen. They had the know how to make and bake pottery and construct clay figurines as well as construct kilns and burn coal so as to fire and mold their creations.

From the time of Homo Erectus (1.9 million to 500,000 B.P), humans had utilized fire to keep warm, to provide light, to cook their food, and to ward off animals. However, the Cro-Magnon learned over 30,000 years ago how to make fire using the firestone; iron pyrite which was repeatedly struck with a flint thus making sparks which could easily ignite brush.

They also created the first rudimentary blast furnaces which were capable of emitting enormous amounts of heat, so as to fire clay. This was accomplished by digging a tiny tunnel into the bottom of the hearth which allowed air to be drawn in. Indeed, 30,000 years ago these people were making fire hardened ceramics and clay figures of animals and females with bulging buttocks and breasts—which are presumed to be the first goddesses.

Many of these female figurines were shaped so that they tapered into points. Because they were pointed they could be stuck into the ground or into some other substance either for ornamental or supernatural purposes, e.g., household goddesses or as fertility figures and earth mothers. In fact, much of the art produced, be it finely crafted "laurel leafs" or other artistic masterpieces, served ritual, spiritual, and esthetic functions. However, they also created art that was

Figure 14. *"Venus" figurines. Upper Paleolithic Goddesses.*

meant to be looked at, owned and admired, and for trade, as jewelry and household decorations, and as highly prized possessions as well as for religious reverence.

Likewise, the first musical instruments were created by these people some 25,000 years ago. These included wooden drums and tiny flutes and whistles.

These peoples were also the first to weave baskets, and the first to use needle and thread in order to make finely fitted clothes which were carefully and deftly sewn together. Unlike all those who had come before them they decorated their clothes and tools and weapons with elaborate designs and geometric and animal symbols. Within their underground cathedrals they left behind elaborate and complex paintings, some of which were almost 3-dimensional. These peoples demonstrated an esthetic artistic awareness and mastery that was unprecedented and which equals the ability of any living artist today.

Thirty five thousand years ago, Cro-Magnon were painting animals not only on walls but on ceilings, utilizing rich yellows, reds, and browns in their paintings and employing the actual shape of the cave walls so as to conform with and give life-like dimensions, including the illusion of movement to the creature they were depicting. Many of their engraving on bones and stones also show a complete mastery of geometric awareness and they often used the nature contours of the cave walls, including protuberances, to create a 3-dimensional effect.

The drawing or carving often became a harmonious or rather, an organic part of the object, wall, ceiling, or tool upon which it was depicted. The Cro-Magnon drew and painted scenes in which animals mated, defecated, fought, charged, and/or were fleeing and dying from wounds inflicted by hunters. The Cro-Magnon cave painters were exceedingly adept at recreating the scenes of everyday life. Moreover, most of the animals were drawn to scale, that is, they were depicted in their actual size; and all this, 35,000 years ago (e.g. Chauvet, et al., 1997).

Figure 15. *Paleolithic art. Stags, horses, bulls. etc.*

The Cro-Magnon obtained their colors from natural earth pigments, such as ocher, a clay that contains a variety of iron minerals. However, whereas Neanderthals and H. habilis apparently had a fondness for red, the Cro-Magnon learned to separate and mix these pigments creating a variety of hues and colors. In order to mix and to arrive at the correct consistency, a variety of lubricants were employed such as blood, urine, vegetable and fruit juices, animal fat, and the contents of eggs. The separate colors were then mixed in various hollowed out rocks and shells.

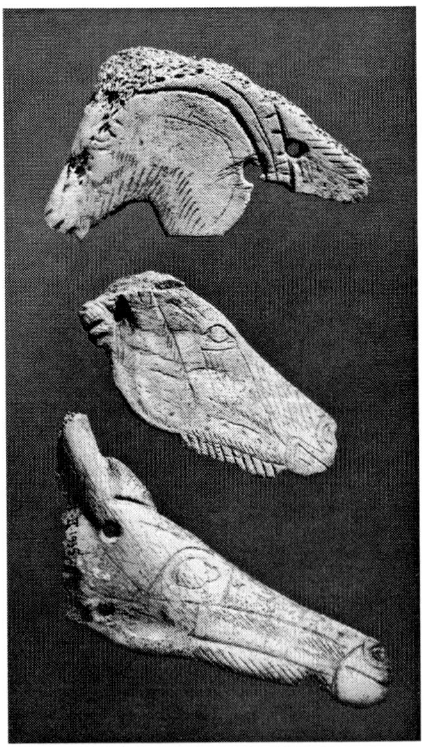

Figure 16. *Paleolithic art.*

The Cro-Magnon artist used a brush, as well as his or her fingers in order to paint. In fact, they used a variety of different brushes which enabled the artist to create different shades and strokes. In some cases the artist simply blew the paint onto the drawing via a tubular bone, thus making a mist-like spray.

The Cro-Magnon artists had also

invented abstract impressionism, as many of their paintings and artworks were exceedingly abstract, surrealistic, or comprised of geometric forms and concentric shapes and ovals which in some cases formed abstract versions of animals or women. Indeed, they displayed an artistic mastery equal to that of any modern master, including Picasso. Awe stuck by these Paleolithic masterpieces Picasso complained that in 30,000 years "we have learned nothing new. We have invented nothing." Indeed, the geometric and angular form of representation employed by these Paleolithic Masters appears again and again throughout history and is found in Egyptian, Sumerian, and even early Greek art (Joseph, 1993, 2000a).

The origins of the Cro-Magnon peoples, however, are completely unknown. There are no transitional forms that link them with Neanderthals or the still primitive "early modern" peoples of the Middle Paleolithic who were decidedly more archaic in appearance. Neanderthals did not evolve into Cro-Magnons, and they coexisted for almost 15,000 years, until finally the Neanderthals disappeared from the face of the Earth, around 30,000 years B.P. (Mellars, 1996). Indeed, the Neanderthals were of a completely different race; and not just physically, but genetically, for when they died out, so too did their genetic heritage and all traces of their DNA (Ovchinnikov et al., 2000).

By contrast although modern human DNA differs significantly from Neanderthal DNA, "modern" human DNA traces its ancestral lineage to female ancestors who lived around 250,000 years ago (Stoneking & Cann, 1989; Vigilant et al. 1991). Likewise, according to the Sumerian Kings' lists, the Anunnaki created the first god-like humans around 240,000 years ago (Roux, 1992) when Enki implanted a mixture into a female goddess who gave birth to the first man.

Thirty thousand years ago, and with the demise of the Neanderthals, the Cro-Magnons gained dominion over the earth. And it is thirty thousand years ago that the ancient Egyptians claim that first kings came to rule Egypt, and that these kings were gods.

In comparison to all those who had come before them, and the Neanderthals who still lived in adjacent lands, the Cro-Magnon were so physically, intellectually, technologically, culturally and genetically advanced, and had such a huge brain, and they appeared so suddenly upon the Earth, that they may well have been created by God and in the image of the Gods... knowing good and evil.

GILGAMESH THE CRO-MAGNON & ENKIDU THE NEANDERTHAL

The Sumerians in fact tell us that these peoples, these titans and heroes of old were two thirds divine, and one-third mortal. Gilgamesh, the Sumerians tell us in the "Gilgamesh Cycles," was one of the divine kings who ruled the predeluvial city of Eresch. And although two thirds god and a great hero, Gilgamesh was still a man and felt love, hate, sadness, joy, hope and despair,

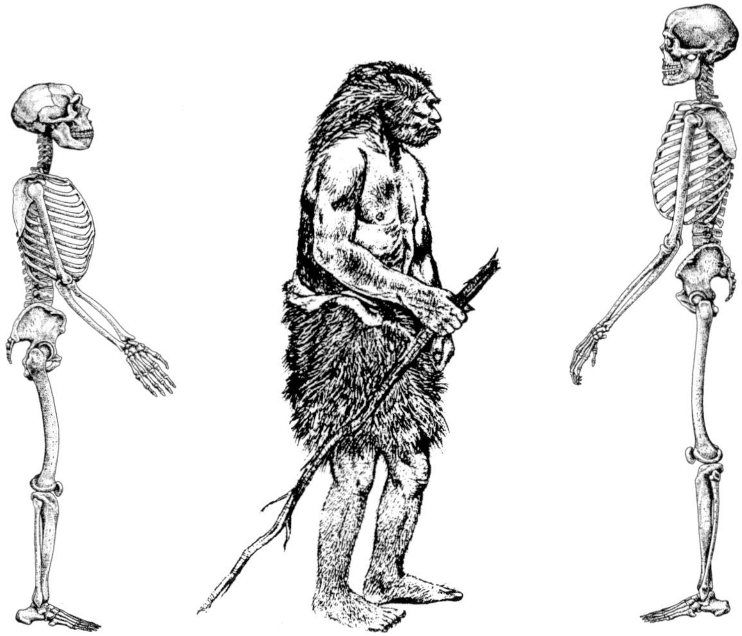

Figure 17. *Neanderthals and a Cro-Magnon.*

and who was forever seeking adventure. It was while on one of these adventures that he came upon a long haired, naked and powerful wild man from the mountains, Enkidu, who was more beast than man.

Gilgamesh (or the Gilgamesh people) at first struggles with, then befriends, and humanizes his half-human half-animal friend Enkidu. And part of the civilizing process involves complete sexual satiation. Unlike the hairy naked beast-women of Enkidu's tribe who have sex cycles similar to animals, the women of Eresch, being part human part goddesses, can have sex at all times.

Enkidu transcends his beastly origins, and through sex becomes wise. He also becomes a more fitting friend for Gilgamesh and together they roam far and wide and undertake a number of heroic adventures.

But then comes the day that Enkidu (or the Enkidu people) grew sick and after a 12 day illness, finally died. Gilgamesh (or the Gilgamesh people) is stunned with grief. Horrified and feeling helpless in the face of death, Gilgamesh goes in search of immortality... the tree of life... And for this and other crimes of knowledge and wisdom, Enlil, the Anunnaki king of the gods, sentences Gilgamesh to die.

CRO-MAGNON UPPER PALEOLITHIC SPIRITUALITY

The spiritual belief systems of the Cro-Magnon and other peoples of the Upper Paleolithic, completely outstripped those of their predecessors in complexity, originality, and artistic and symbolic accomplishments. As the brain and man and woman evolved, so too did their spiritual beliefs. Hence, the Cro-Magnon conception of, and ability to symbolically express the spirit world, became much more complex as well, undergoing what has been described as a "symbolic explosion" (Bandi 1961; Kuhn 1955; Leroi-Gurhan 1964, 1982; Prideaux 1973).

The Cro-Magnon practiced complex religious rituals and apparently were the first peoples to have arrived at the conception of "god." However, it was not a male god who they worshipped but female goddesses who were attended by animals and animal-head shaman.

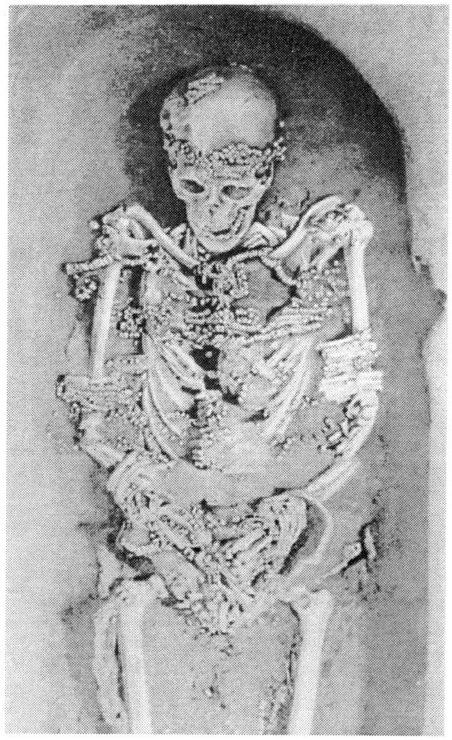

Figure 18. *The open grave of an Upper Paleolithic Cro-Magnon*

By 35,000 years ago the Cro-Magnon were painting, drawing, and etching bear and mammoth, dear and horse, and pregnant females and goddesses in the recesses of dark and dusky caverns (Bandi 1961; Chauvet et al., 1996; Leroi-Gurhan 1964, 1982; Prideaux 1973). The pregnant females include Venus statuettes, many of which were fertility goddesses. The Cro-Magnon were well aware of the differences between a slim sexy woman and a fertility Goddess for they were able to draw both. In fact, these were the first people to paint and etch what today might be considered Paleolithic porno. That is, in addition to pregnant fertility goddesses they drew and painted slim, shapely, naked and nubile young maidens in various positions of repose (Joseph, 1993, 2000a).

It is noteworthy that even 35,000 years ago and continuing for the next 25,000 years, the Cro-Magnon artist often drew and painted over existing drawings, including paintings which were hidden away in deep recesses of dark underground caverns that were extremely difficult to get to. This indicates that the location within the cave was of particular mystical, spiritual, or at least ritualistic significance, particularly in that many paintings were in out of the way places where one had to crawl long distance through tiny spaces and along rather tortuous routes to get to them. In fact, not just the location but the journey to these hidden recesses may have been of ritualistic significance perhaps relating to birth or even rebirth following death.

SPIRITS, SOULS, AND SORCERERS

As is evident from their cave art and symbolic accomplishments, the nether world of the Cro-Magnon and other peoples of the Upper Paleolithic, was haunted by the spirits and souls of the living, the dead, and those yet to be born, both animal and human (Brandon 1967; Campbell 1988; Kuhn 1955; Prideaux 1973).

Upper Paleolithic peoples apparently believed these souls and spirits could be charmed and controlled by hunting magic, and through the spells of sorcerers and shamans. Hence, in conjunction with the worship of the goddess, the Cro-Magnons also relied on shamans and priests.

Hundreds of feet beneath the earth, the likeness of one ancient shaman attired in animal skins and stag antlers, graces the upper wall directly above the entrance to the 20,000-25,000 year-old grand gallery at Les Trois-Freres in southern France (Prideaux1973). Galloping, running, and swirling about this ancient sorcerer are bison, stag, horse, deer, and presumably their spirits and their souls. Oddly, images of an almost identical "sorcerer" appear again in ancient Sumerian and Babylonian inscriptions fashioned four to six thousand years ago.

Figure 20. *A Sumerian/Babylonian god, holding a staff upon which sits a flying solar disc.*

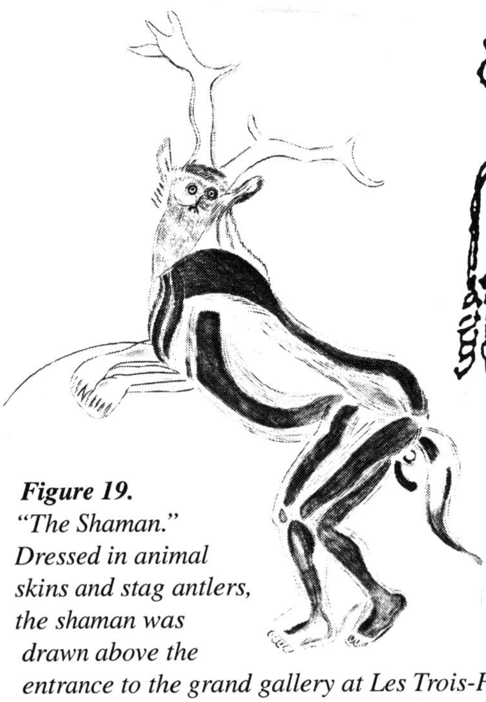

Figure 19. *"The Shaman." Dressed in animal skins and stag antlers, the shaman was drawn above the entrance to the grand gallery at Les Trois-Freres Cave in Southern France. Upper Paleolithic. From a copy made by Abbe Breuil.*

***Figure 21** . The Inca Demi-god, Macoc Apac. The solar disc indicates Divine status. According to the Incas, Macoc Apac was a pre-deluvial god who came from heaven, and who taught humans wisdom and science. Note the resemblance to the Sumerian god, (previous page) who also holds the solar disc in his hand. According to the Sumerians and all ancient peoples, these gods rule the entire Earth, and similar imagery repeatedly appears in ancient cultures separated by oceans and thousands of miles.*

They also believed in and worshipped the goddess who was associated with the fertility of the earth, as well as the moon and the stars. One great goddess was carved in limestone over the entrance to an underground cathedral in Laussel, France, over 25,000 years ago. She was painted in the colors of life and fertility, blood red. Her left hand still rests upon her pregnant belly whereas in her right hand she holds the horned crescent of the moon which is engraved with thirteen lines, the number of moon cycles in a solar year. She was a goddess of life, linked to the mysteries of the heavens and the magical powers of the moon whose 30 day cycle corresponds with the menstrual cycle which issues from a woman's life giving womb. The Cro-Magnon believed in god. God was a woman.

***Figure 22.** A mother goddess, holding in her hand the symbol of the moon with 13 lines, which is the number of lunar cycles in a solar year. Her other hand rests upon her pregnant belly. This goddess was carved outside the entrance to an underground Paleolitic Cathedral.*

UNDERGROUND CATHEDRALS: EMBRACED BY THE LIGHT

In order to view many of these Cro-Magnon paintings and "religious" statues and shrines, one has to enter the hidden entrance of an underground cave, and crawl a considerable distance, sometimes hundreds of yards, through a twisting, narrowing, pitch black tunnel before reaching these Upper Paleolithic underground Cathedrals. Here the Cro-Magnon would light candles and lamps, performing magical and spiritual rituals as the painted animals and spirits wavered in the cave light.

The nature and location of the Cro-Magnon cathedrals, which have been found throughout Europe, and the nature of the tortuous routes to get to them, and the effect of cave light bringing these paintings to life, is significant as it embraces features associated with after death experiences as retold by present day as well as ancient peoples.

In the ancient Egyptian and Tibetan Books of the Dead, and has been reported among many of those who have undergone a "near death" or "life after death" experience, being enveloped in a dark tunnel is commonly experienced soon after death. It is only as one ascends the tunnel that one will see in the decreasing distance, a light, the "light" of "Heaven" and of paradise. Once embraced by the light "the recently dead" may be greeted by the souls of dead relatives, friends, and/or radiant human or animal-like entities (Eadie, 1992; Rawling 1978; Ring 1980).

Figure 23. *The entrance to Heaven. By Hieronymus Bosch, 1500.*

Given the nature of their rituals, shamanic images, and goddess figurines, including the symbolism of flight associated with death, it thus appears that the Cro-Magnon were probably the first people to engage in magic and sorcery and may have been the first to develop notions of heaven and god and goddesses and the first to invent priests and shamans.

And, because the Cro-Magnons obviously believed in an after-life, they buried their dead with food, weapons, flowers, jewelry, clothing, pendants, rings, necklaces, multifaceted tools, head bands, beads, bracelets and so on. The Cro-Magnon were a profoundly spiritual people and they fully prepared the dead for the journey to the spirit world, equipping them so that they could live for all eternity in the land of the gods.

Figure 24. *A dead hunter and a birds head. A disembowled bison stands above him. Presumably this scene depicts the death of a hunter and the flight of his soul as symbolized by the bird. Bird heads were commonly employed by ancient peoples including the Egyptians to depict the ascension to heaven. Eventually, bird heads were replaced by creatures with wings, e.g. angels. Reproduced with permission, Bildarchiv Preubischer Kulturbesitz.*

Figure 25 . *Goddesses with bird heads. From Libya, approximately 10,000 B.P. The bird head symbolizes the capacity for flight and thus the ability to ascend to heaven.*

THE SONS OF GOD HAVE SEX WITH THE DAUGHTERS OF MEN

"And it came to pass when men began to multiply on the face of the earth, and daughters were born unto them, that the sons of God saw the daughters of men, that they were fair, and they took them wives of all which they chose... There were giants in the earth in those days; and also after that, when the sons of God came in unto the daughters of men, and they bare children to them, the same became mighty men which were of old, men of renown." -Genesis 6.1-4.

Figure 26. Upper Paleolithic art.

Six foot tall, with a massive brain and perfect body, the Cro-Magnons strode to and fro upon the Earth, much like gods. As retold in Genesis, they were in fact so god-like, and the women so god-beautiful, that the son's of God descended from the heavens to make love with these ladies and make these women their wives.

Admittedly, these stories may well by myths. And yet, it is obvious and apparent that these intellectual and physical giants had indeed eaten of the fruit of the tree of knowledge.

CRO-MAGNON GODS IN THE GARDEN OF EDEN

MAN THE HUNTER

The achievements of the Upper Paleolithic Cro-Magnon were not merely limited to art, ceramics, music, and spirituality, as they constantly experimented with and created new inventions such as the sewing needle, pointed burins, highly efficient cutters and scrapers, and the spear thrower. This device consisted of a spear that was fitted into a long hooked rod, about 1-2 feet in length.

Via the spear thrower a Cro-Magnon hunter or warrior could toss his weapon an incredible distance and at a tremendous velocity thus greatly enhancing his killing power and range. In effect, the spear thrower acted as an extension of a man's arm and enabled a man to almost double the distance in which he could throw a spear. He could easily impale and kill an animal or another man standing anywhere from 70 to 150 yards away.

Like all their tools, the spear throwers were elaborately decorated with fine carvings, etchings, drawings and paintings of animals such as horses, deer, bison, birds and fish. These tools and weapons were also made from a variety of substances such as reindeer antlers.

These people also realized that a spear covered with barbs, harpoon style, would do much more damage than a smooth point. However, even with barbs, animals often were not killed outright and the mortally wounded beast would sometimes run for miles before falling down and dying.The Cro-Magnon, therefore, created blood grooves along side the bone spearheads so that blood could more efficiently gush from the wound thus speeding the process of dying.

In addition, perhaps 20,000 years ago the first bows and arrows apparently came into widespread use and the arrows appear to have been feathered so as to stabilize their flight. With the creation of the bow the hunter could now remain completely hidden for if he missed with his first shot the animal would not even know he was there (so long as he stayed down wind and out of sight).The hunter could now shoot again and again.

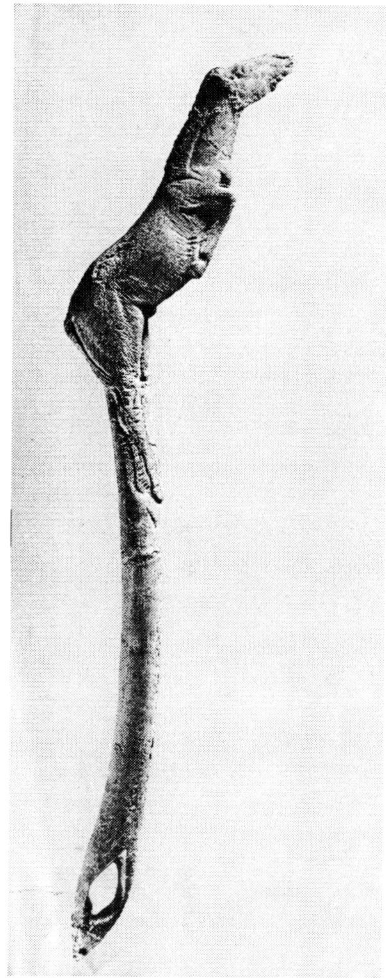

Figure 27. *Upper Paleolithic art. Leaping horse.*

The Cro-magnon were the greatest hunters of their time and unlike those who came before them, they were able to easily kill antelopes, bison, wild horses, reindeer, mammoths, and even lions and bears. They were also good trappers and fisherman and took birds, small animals and fish in abundance. In fact they were the first true fishermen and constantly harvested the abundant game living in the lakes, rivers and seas. These people utilized nets, a trident shaped spear as well as a baited hook which would then become lodged in the throat of the fish.

They also developed the "trap," a rawhide or thick vine noose which was attached to a bent sapling which was tethered to some object such as a huge rock. The noose would be laid where the animal was expected to walk. Any animal or human which tripped the tether that held the sapling would be snared by the loop which would yank the unfortunate creature into the air. There it would hang only to die exposed to the elements or to be later beaten to death.

The Cro-Magnon people likely utilized iron and engaged in metal tool making. Unfortunately such devices would not have withstood the ravages of time and have disappeared from the fossil record. However, the flint points they utilized were in fact superior to iron or steel in their cutting power and can penetrate more deeply when thrown at some unfortunate animal or human. These people also applied some type of solvent to these blades to make them more durable as they tend to be somewhat brittle and can be broken.

Diversity in tool making is the hall mark of the Cro-Magnon. Thirty five thousand years ago, a typical tool kit consisted of well over 125 items, e.g. knives for cutting, whittling, stone saws, chisels, perforators for making holes, needles, scrapers for bone others for skin, pounding slabs, etc.. Many of these tools were attached to wood, bone and antler handles, and/or were made of these materials including ivory. Ivory can also be steamed and bent so that specific shapes can be molded.

In contrast, the Neanderthal and those who came before them, simply knocked two stones together so as to sharpen a rock, or they chipped away flakes from rocks and used these as cutting tools and weapons. The typical Neanderthal tool kit consisted from between 5 to 60 different items, such as horizontal stone scrapers and blunted and doubled edged rock knives.

WOMAN THE GATHERER

Figure 28. *Gatherers (by de Bry). (right) Paleolithic Goddess.*

By the dawn of the Upper Paleolithic hunting had become the center of religious and artistic life for the men. Nevertheless, 60-80% of the Cro-Magnon diet consisted of fruits, nuts, grains, honey, roots and vegetables (Clark, 1952; Prideaux, 1973), which were gathered by females (Joseph, 2000b). Among the hunting and gathering societies in existence during the last few centuries, women have been and are the gatherers and main providers of food whereas spoils from the hunt account for only about 35% of the diet (Dahlberg, 1981; Lee & DeVore, 1968; Martin & Voorhies, 1975; Murdock & Provost, 1973; Zilman, 1981).

Gathering was also a spiritual affair which unlike hunting and the taking of life, celebrated the nurturance and giving of life and life's abundance. These Paleolithic women likely gathered in groups of 7 or more adults. The Cro-Magnon woman did not just gatherer the produce from the Garden of Eden, but she experimented with horticulture, herbology, and the fertility of the Earth.

Man the hunter, woman the gatherer and giver of life, has characterized the psychic and spiritual dichotomy of the human condition since well before the Paleolithic. Yet, with the arrival of the Cro-Magnon, woman became a tool-making, gathering goddess and mistress of the hearth and the hunt. And woman, the first god, was worshipped by woman and man.

THE GODDESS

Whereas hunting was the center of religious life for men, food gathering and herbology served the same purpose for women. Such gathering groups must have commonly been loud, noisy and very gay affairs filled with the talk and singing of the women and the sounds of games and yells of the children. Some women were pregnant or probably carried and nursed infants who might be passed from mother to sister, to aunt, and back again. Children and young adolescents would frolic about and play. The women could talk, sing, celebrate life's abundance, and share and practice their spiritual faith and worship together as they harvested nature's bounty.

Figure 29. *Paleolithic fertility rites. Dancing Paleolithic Goddess surrounded by female dancers.*

Figure 30. *Paleolithic fertility rites. Paleolithic women and men depicted in a dancing frenzy.*

Woman the gatherer worshipped the Great Mother, the Great Goddess, the Lord of Creation, Mother Earth, the Mother of All. And she carried with her ivory and stone engravings of the Great Mother, and amulets and rings, and mother goddess statues that could be stuck into the ground.

And while the men performed their rituals in the deep recesses of caverns and caves, woman worshipped the Great Mother by dawn's early light, and the light of the harvest moon. And whereas the men practiced rituals involving death and the spiritual hereafter, women practiced rituals of fertility that celebrated life's abundance. Dancing, singing, fertility rites, and sex orgies became hallmarks of their rituals.

THE LIFE OF A CRO-MAGNON GODDESS

Whereas the Cro-Magnon hunter invented his own religion and a stockpile of technologically advanced weapons that made him the greatest hunter of all time, woman the gatherer discovered her own unique life giving spirituality and created her own arsenal of tools which made her the greatest artisan of all time. Her creations included statues of female gods, earrings, necklaces, bacelets, pendants, and beads, and complex tools for domestic ease including choppers, scrapers, cleavers with a straight cutting edge on one side (Day, 1996; Righmire, 1990). That these tools were fashioned by a female hand can be deduced by their domestic use (Joseph, 2000a,b). Among hunting and gathering groups it is females and not the males who make and use tools (Niethhammer, 1977), the only exception being hunting implements and weapons of war which females are not allowed to touch (Tabet, 1982).

The responsibilities of the Cro-Magnon woman included the preparation of the food she gathered and any meat which the men brought home from their hunting sojourns. In addition to food preparation, clothes were sewn and fashioned out of hides (Clark, 1952, 1967; Prideaux, 1973), and these too are tasks associated with women (Gusinde, 1961; Lee, 1974; Neithhammer, 1977), including, presumably, the Cro-Magnon females of the Upper Paleolithic.

Thus the duties of the Upper Paleolithic female were much more multifaceted and complex than her predecessors, and included cleaning hides via a scraper, drying and curing the skin over the smoke of a fire, and then using a knife or cutter to make the general desired shape. The Upper Paleolithic female was also employing a punch to make holes in these hides, through which leather straps or a vine could be passed so as to create a garment that could keep out the cold (Clark, 1952, 1967; Prideaux, 1973). They were also weaving and using a needle to sew garments together; "domestic" tasks which are almost exclusively associated with "women's" work (Murdock & Provost, 1973; Neithhammer, 1977).

The women were exceedingly skilled artisans whose abilities easily excel those of any modern woman today. And they were creating beautiful, colorful, intricately designed, embroidered, and tailored clothes over 30,000 years ago.

The Cro-Magnon women dressed their men and their children like woodland gods, fed them the food of the gods, picked fresh daily from the Paleolithic garden of Eden. And they worshipped woman as the life creating and life giving goddess, the Great Mother of All who gave life to the earth and woman and man.

VILLAGES BECOME CITIES, BECOME CIVILIZATIONS

These people and their descendants became so proficient at art, crafts, horticulture and hunting that they were able to settle year round in villages. In fact, the Cro-Magnon built long houses of wood and stone that were large enough to easily provide shelter for up to 20-25 adults and children at a time. These long houses were about 50 feet long and 20 or more feet wide. These were not merely makeshift accommodations that could be moved at whim. The houses were set on stone foundations that were sunk 2-3 feet into the ground. These houses also contained bedrooms, common living areas (or living rooms), kilns and fireplaces, as well as stone storage vaults where meat and other perishables could be easily stored for weeks at a time.

By contrast, the Neanderthals were still living in cold, damp caves.

"Long houses" are associated with matriarchal, female dominated societies. In these societies daughters and the daughters of daughters never leave home but live with their mothers and grandmothers, thus forming extended families living under one roof, the long house. Men marry into these households, and together these households would make up a village or small town which would be governed by the matriarchs. Therefore it can be deduced that Cro-Magnon society was also matriarchal as is also indicated by the widespread religious cult of the goddess.

By 15,000 years ago, they were already living in great cities of thousands of people; cities surrounded by woodland and small farms and fields of wild wheat. Stone sickles and grinding stones were in use 20,000 years ago which allowed for the harvesting and milling of wild and domestic grains. Moreover, they probably made beer from the grain and may well have discovered that wine could be produced from the fermented grape. Hence, the Cro-Magnon people invented civilization over 20,000 years ago; which is exactly what the oldest written records and the ancient Sumerian, Egyptian and Mayan Kings lists patiently explain.

However, not all Cro-Magnon were city dwellers. Many made their homes out of animal skins that were sewn together thus forming tents. The tents were held together by poles and were anchored to the ground by wooden posts.

The massive efficiency by which these people were able to hunt, gather, forage, as well as plant and harvest their own grains not only resulted in a very well rounded and healthy diet but increased leisure time. Indeed, these people may well have arrived at a 3 day work week 35,000 years ago; leisure time that could be devoted to the development of other pursuits and interests, such as the acquisition of material goods and wealth and the seeking of knowledge and spiritual wisdom; wisdom and knowledge not just of this world, but of the next one.

AND THE EARTH BECAME A VOID:

The War in Heaven. The Battle Among the Stars

According to the most ancient written records available to woman and man, a god-like people gained dominion over the Earth tens of thousands of years ago. And these titans and heroes of old built great sparkling cities and developed technologically advanced civilizations that ringed the globe.

THE GREAT SERPENT

And we are told of a war in heaven, of a battle among the stars, where the planet Venus attacked the planet Mars, and then snaked like a fiery comet through the skies and attacked the Earth, shaking the cities, destroying the kingdoms, and washing away the crowns of creation of woman and man.

"And there appeared a great wonder in heaven: A woman clothed with the sun, and the moon under her feet, and upon her head a crown of twelve stars: And she being with child cried travailing in birth and pained to be delivered..."

"And there appeared another wonder in heaven: And behold a great red dragon having seven heads and ten horns and seven crowns upon his head. And his tail drew the third part of the stars of heaven and did cast them to the earth..."

"And there was a war in heaven: Michael and his angels fought against the dragon: and the dragon fought and his angels. And the great dragon was cast out, that old serpent, called the Devil and Satan which deceivith the whole world: He was cast out and his angels were cast out with him..."

"And the serpent cast out of his mouth water as a flood. And the earth opened her mouth and swallowed up the flood which the dragon cast out his mouth. And the dragon was wroth and went to make war..." -Revelation, 12

According to the written records of the Sumerian people, whose own civilization arose 6,000 years ago, the Cro-Magnon peoples and their great cities were destroyed by a cosmic upheaval, when the planet Venus somehow freed herself of Jupiter's grasp, and snaked through the heavens attacking Mars, and then careened close to the Earth, plunging the planet into an icy, watery darkness that was then followed by cataclysmic floods, almost 12,000 years ago.

Indeed, the ancient Sumerians, Babylonians, Hebrews, Mayas, Romans, Greeks, and plain's Indians of the Americas all report that Venus, the wrathful fertility goddess of love, brought evil, catastrophe, flood and misfortune to our planet; and she did so in the guise of the Great Serpent -also known as Satan, the Morning Star, the destroyer of Kingdoms.

"How art thou fallen from heaven, O' Lucifer son of the morning. For thou hast said in thine heart: I will ascend into heaven. I will exalt my throne above the stars of God. I will ascend above the heights of the clouds. I will be like the most High..."

"How art thou fallen from heaven, O' Lucifer star of the morning. Is this the one that made the earth to tremble, that did to shake kingdoms. That made the world as a wilderness, and destroyed the cities..."

But beware and rejoice not because the rod of his that smote thee is broken: for out of the serpents root and of his fruit shall be a fiery flying dragon..." Isaiah, 14

The ancient Sumerians, Egyptians, Hindus, Chinese, Greeks, Romans and the Olmecs, Mayas, Aztecs, and American Plains Indians of the Mississippi and Ohio Valley all refer to this war in heaven, with particular emphasis devoted to Venus and the great serpent. Great serpent mounds, miles in length, sometimes depicting the serpent with a planet in its mouth, dot the landscape throughout the Americas.

The Sumerian and Babylonians associated the serpent with the planet Venus, and with the god Enki, the serpent god of knowledge, wisdom, science, and the bringer of rain.

Similarly the Mayas and Aztecs associated the serpent with Venus, and with Quetzocoatl, a god whose emblem was the sign of the cross and whose temple was shaped like a serpentine planet; i.e. round with a single entrance "carved in the form of a serpent's mouth, diabolically painted with fangs and teeth...it looked like the mouth of hell" (De Gorma, 1964, p. 165).

The ancient Egyptians had a similar god, the Great Serpent, Apep, who was viewed as representing cosmic evil. Apep not only threatened Earth and the other plan-

__Figure 31.__ The Maya and Aztec God, Quetzalocoatl, the bearded and plumed serpent, was associated with the planet Venus; i.e. the bringer of rain, light and knowledge. The sign of the cross was one of his many emblems which is depicted in the center of his shield. Reproduced from Z. Sitchin 1990.

ets, but the sun god, Ra. Ra had to repeatedly battle Apep during his nightly journey through the underworld.

The Mayas and Aztecs also make reference to the flood, the serpent and its battles with the sun, referring to Venus as "she who tears out the eye of the sun" and who plunged the Earth into an icy watery darkness; an event also mentioned in the lore of the ancient Hebrews and Arabs, and which may well have been an account of a total eclipse of the sun by a wayward Venus.

The peoples of ancient Greece and Rome, tell us however, that before attacking the Earth and the sun, that Venus first broke lose from Jupiter's grip. The Sumerians, Babylonians, Greeks, Romans, Mayans, Aztecs, tell us that she then became embroiled in a cosmic war with Mars. There ensued a series of cosmic battles in which the red planet was mortally wounded and ingloriously defeated. Venus stripped Mars of his splendid coat of arms as well as his skin (at least according to the Indians of Mexico and Central America). It was his coat and his skin that Venus dragged triumphantly in her wake as she snaked through the skies toward the Earth to engage in yet one more heavenly battle.

And what is the "coat" and "skin" of a planet? Perhaps the Martian atmosphere and seas? For it is an ocean of water that Venus is said to have deposited upon the Earth, thus causing the deluge and a massive loss of Earthly life.

It is now well established that the red planet was long ago flush with rivers, oceans, lakes and seas, maybe as recently at 10,000 years ago. At one time Mars was probably also enveloped in a oxygen and nitrogen rich atmosphere, perhaps somewhat similar to that of Earth. And then, before the Universe could take a breath, the Martian oceans and atmosphere were stripped away—possibly by a colossal, and wayward planetary body, and so too was its life... leaving behind only distant, difficult to discern shadows and perhaps forgotten memories of towering sandy pyramids and titanic stone faces that stare somberly into the abyss.

As per Venus assuming a new orbit after breaking free of Jupiter's grasp, there is now evidence to suggest that the planets Uranus and Neptune may have long ago orbited Jupiter, as planet-sized moons. However, for reasons not well understood, these planets broke away and were flung into their current orbits.

Likewise, Venus may have long ago been a planet sized moon of Jupiter which also broke away only to speed toward Mars and Earth. If Venus, which is ten times the size of the red planet, were to sweep by Mars, gravity alone would strip Mars of her seas and atmosphere which would trail behind Venus like a comet's tail—just as our tiny moon can draw up the surface of the oceans and create tides and heavy seas. And as she snaked like a comet toward the Earth, Venus would have looked like a fire breathing serpent due to the reflection of the sun. And if indeed the oceans of Mars trailed in her wake, Venus would have lashed the Earth with her watery tail as the planets crossed orbits; and as she sped onward, she would have caused a temporary total eclipse of the sun which would have sent temperatures plummeting. As she was taken slave by the sun, and assumed her new orbit, and the sun again began to shine, the frozen Martian seas would have begun to melt, inundating the Earth by a second flood that could well have lasted even longer than the first. In fact, two floods are described in Genesis, one that last seven days, and yet another that lasted 40.

THE DELUGE AND THE HISTORICAL RECORD

Sumerians, Babylonians, the ancient Jews, Greeks, and Romans, and in the Western half of the World, the ancient Mayas and Aztecs, and in the Eastern half, ancient China, all tell of an incredible catastrophe that occurred around 12,000 years ago; a cosmic calamity that took on the specter of a horrible war in heaven, a war of the worlds involving Venus—that terrible serpent—and which shook the kingdoms and destroyed the cities and destroyed the crowns of creation of woman and man —a war which was accompanied by earthquakes, volcanic activity, terrible rains, floods, then Arctic cold.

These stories are not exactly myths. The geological evidence and the historical record indicates that around 12,000 years ago temperatures dropped precipitously. The last ice age began and ended quite suddenly. This last instant ice age was initiated by a massive flood, followed by a drastic drop in temperature, followed by a rapid increase in temperatures and terrible floods—floods upon floods that would have washed away not just all signs of civilization, but the top layers of the earth itself, leaving behind only the bedrock of ancient ocean floors from half a million years ago. In fact, sea levels rose by 400 feet such that mountain tops became islands, the valley settlements down below, swallowed by oceans of water. And what was the source of the rising waters?

We also know that some momentous event resulted in the flash freezing of innumerable creatures including the woolly mammoth. Woolly mammoths and other animals, have been found frozen solid, with absolutely no sign of decay and with grass in their mouth and food in their belly—carcasses dated to 12,000 years ago. They had obviously been drenched in an avalanche of water and then flash frozen alive. As is evident from their diet and the food in their mouths, these calamitous events took place in a most inviting environment that just moments before had been lush and teaming with life.

Supporting the possibility of a sudden inundation of water, is the fact that the glaciers from the last ice age were not uniformly established in the way advancing ice sheets would be expected; as if the Earth had swept through an ocean of water drifting in space, leaving some regions high and dry, and others drenched only to flash freeze.

For example, the ice sheets in India were located along the Equator and extended upward toward the Himalayas, rather than from North to South as might be expected. Conversely, the ice sheet in Africa extended from the Equator toward the South pole, which again is the opposite of what might have been expected. In fact, the Americas, Europe, parts of Africa, India and Siberia were covered, whereas the rest of Asia and everything north of Siberia, including the North Pole, was unaffected. There was almost a randomness to it. This is reminiscent of the manner in which some flu viruses spread; which, some scientists have proposed, may be due to the Earth orbiting through regions of contagion and passing through cosmic viral clouds.

However, after a period in which the Earth was tossed to and fro, this last glacial period just as suddenly ended. The melting glaciers released wave upon tidal wave of an ocean of rushing water which not only swept away all in its path, but which resulted in sea levels rising up to 400 feet, creating islands where there were once mountain tops.

THE GOLDEN AGE

Plato, the ancient Greek Philosopher, twice tells a similar tale, of floods and rising seas that destroyed several ancient technologically advanced cities and civilizations, 9,000 years before his own time, almost 12,000 years ago.

And not just the Sumerians, and Plato, but the Egyptians, and the ancient Mayas of Central American, tell similar tales of ancient cities and civilizations ruled by the descendants of the gods. And paralleling the accounts of Plato and the Sumerians, the Mayas and Aztecs tell us that all was destroyed some 10,000 years before their own time, when the planet Venus attacked Mars, and then snaked through the heavens and careened close to our planet, enveloping the Earth in terrible floods.

Indeed, the oldest records and accounts passed down through history all attest of these great kingdoms and city states which were completely inundated and washed away leaving only distant memories of a long lost golden age (Hammerly-Dupuy, 1988; Kramer, 1981; Woolley, 1965); a golden age that included a land of pyramids and sphinx, west of the Garden of Eden.

The Egyptians too, speak of a Golden age that began with a Dynasty of Gods, 32,500 years ago; a dynasty that lasted almost 15,000 years, and which was replaced 17,390 years ago, when the Dynasty of the Demigods began. The first line of kings did not establish rule until 15,400 B.P., at about the time the calendars of Thebes, (deemed ancient 6,000 years ago), are believed to have been first composed (Pochan, 1978). It may well have been 15,000 years ago that the great Sphinx and the three great pyramids of Giza were also first erected.

BEFORE THE DELUGE

Of course, there are those who scoff at these "myths." However, the Egyptians and Sumerians were fully able to distinguish between myth and fact. The

Sumerians always began their tales of the marvelous in the following way: "One upon a time..." The same is not true of Sumerian accounts of five great cities that they claim had been erected thousands of years before the flood. Likewise, the Kings lists were believed to be completely authentic by the ancient Egyptians.

According to the Sumerians, these wondrous marvelous cities included Eridu, Badtibira, Larak, Sippar, and Shuruppak—all completely washed away by the deluge. According to Plato, Atlantis and an ancient, predeluvial Athens were among the great "marvelous" cities lost beneath the rising seas.

In fact, the Sumerians divided history into two periods: "Before the flood" (Lam abubi) and "After the flood" (Arki abubi), with their own civilization, some 6,000 years ago (in what today is Iraq), belonging to the later.

According to the Sumerians these predeluvial civilizations were incredibly scientifically advanced, and were ruled by mighty kings. As stated by the Sumerians, Egyptians, and Mayas, these first kings were descendants of gods, they were men and women created in the images of the gods, a tall and noble people who erected great temples and pyramids guarded by an army of sphinx—temples and pyramids whose predeluvial perfection remained unsurpassed by those civilizations that arose after the deluge.

THE TEMPLES AND PYRAMIDS OF THE GODS

Although badly weathered by water erosion, a great sphinx still stands in a land called Egypt; a great sphinx which is around 13,000 (or more) years in age, and which suffered the bulk of its erosion when inundated by torrential rains and flooding (Schoch,

Figure 32. *The Great Pyramids of Giza. The ancient historical record and their technological perfection suggests that the 3 great pyramids were also erected by a technologically advanced predeluvial culture and civilization. Note in the foreground, the crumbling miniature remnants of the tiny pyramids erected by the ancient Egyptians.*

Figure 33. Weathering studies indicate the Sphinx was likely first erected over 13,000 years ago and suffered most of its erosion when inundated by a massive amount of water.

1992). The great sphinx was constructed thousands of years before the rise of ancient Egypt; erected by a technologically advanced predeluvial civilization.

It has also been claimed that the three pyramids of Giza were also constructed before the deluge, which in turn may explain their utter perfection versus the (comparatively) shoddy nature of those tiny copies erected beginning around 4,000 years ago by the ancient Egyptians. Although there are claims and counter claims regarding who built the three pyramids of Giza, even the ancient kings of Egypt refer to them as being quite ancient. In fact, although the grandest and oldest of them all is attributed to Khufu, Khufu indicates that the Great Pyramid and the Sphinx, had been constructed long before his own time.

Some ancient Arabian historians explain that these first three Pyramids, which exceeds all other pyramids in size and perfection, were created before the great flood:

"Saurid...one of the kings of Egypt prior to the Great Flood, who resided in the great city of Amusus... was the builder of two of the great pyramids... Three hundred years before the Great Flood, Saurid had a dream where the Earth turned upside down with all its people, the people fled in a blind rush, and the stars fell down..."(al-Maqrizi, 1911).

According to al-Maqrizi (1911), all the kings advisors had the same dream and predicted the end of civilization. So, Saurid, the pre-deluvial King of Egypt, decided to build the pyramids in order to serve as a great museum and library where all the worlds knowledge could be preserved. Indeed, the great pyramid itself, was to be a source of knowledge and wisdom, harboring the answers to all questions regarding the cosmos and the creation.

As all who visit or who have studied these grand monuments can attest, the three pyramids are not just the oldest, grandest, largest, and architecturally superior to all those built by the ancient Egyptians, but they are completely un-Egyptian. Unlike all other Egyptian edifices the chambers and inner walls of the three great pyramids of Giza are completely barren of hieroglyphics and are lacking in any markings whatsoever.

Coupled with their incredible size and utter perfection, it is evident that they were built by a different, technologically advanced civilization.

Consider: all authorities agree that these first three giant pyramids were constructed first, well before the erection of all other Egyptian pyramids which were but stunted, lopsided, poorly constructed miniaturizations in comparison.

The base of the Great Pyramid covers 13 acres (5 hectares), and reaches a height of 480 feet (145 meters). The Great Pyramid consists of 2,300,000 stones, each weighing 21/2 tons, measuring 50 by 50 by 28 inches. It has five sides and five corners and a "pyramid inch" is one-fifth of one-fifth of a cubit—what Sir Isaac Newton called sacred and profane cubits. The north side is 755.4 feet long, the west 755.8, the east 755.9, and the south side is 756.1 feet long, indicating an incredible degree of engineering precision that was, in total no more than half a foot off from perfection. Indeed, as the Earth has shook and moved over the eons, the pyramid may well have shifted every so slightly, such that originally all sides were precisely the same.

Moreover, not just the Great Pyramid, but the sides of all three of the Pyramids of Giza are perfectly aligned to the cardinal points of the compass.

As noted, the great pyramid was said by ancient Arabic historians to contain the world's knowledge, wisdom, and the secrets of the cosmos and creation.

The area of the Great Pyramid's base divided by twice its height gives the figure 3.14159+, (pi). Pi is the constant that is multiplied by the diameter of a circle to give its circumferences. Indeed, the Great Pyramids was built in accordance with geometrical and astronomical laws to record the dimensions of the earth and the duration of the solar year.

The builders of the pyramid were well versed in astronomy and knew the relationship of the radius to its circumference. They knew the circumference of the Earth, and the distance of the center of the Earth to the poles. The ratio of the Great Pyramid's altitude to its perimeter is the same as that of the polar radius of the Earth to its circumference: 2 pi. Hence, the Great Pyramid could be used to record the movements of the stars around the heavens in relation to the earth.

In fact, as determined by Charles Piazzi Smyth, the Astronomer-Royal of Scotland, the Great Pyramid incorporates and reveals the distance of the earth from the sun when its height is multiplied by the proportion of its height to its width, that is, ten to the ninth power.

The builders of the Great Pyramid "had determined the shape of the earth which they knew to be a true circle, its size, its precise circumference, the geographical distance from the equator to the poles, the fact that the earth is flattened at the poles, degrees of latitude and longitude to within a few hundred feet, the fact that they were shorter at the equator and longer at the poles, and the exact distance of the Earth from the sun. They had designed the pyramid's base to correspond to the distance the earth rotates in half a second" (Funrneaux, 1987, p 17).

Werner von Siemens, founder of Siemens' Electric, scaled the summit of the Great Pyramid in 1859, and stuck his finger up into the air. As he assumed a triumphant pose, a crack of electricity rang out and he received an electric shock. Later when he brought along a Leyden jar, which stores static electricity, it not only became charged, but generated sparks.

THE LORD GOD SEEKS TO DESTROY THE CHILDREN OF GOD

"There were giants in the earth in those days; and also after that...mighty men, men of renown. And God saw that the wickedness of man was great in the earth, and that every imagination of the thought of his heart was only evil continually." -Genesis 6:4,5.

It is noteworthy that the Bible tell us that the "giants" were "in the earth" and that wickedness was great "in the earth." Could "in the earth" be a reference to the Cro-Magnon underground Cathedrals?

We are also told that the Lord God considered the use of one's imagination and the acquisition of knowledge to be evil. "Every imagination of the thought of his heart was evil."

The Lord God's first commandment is: thou shalt not know:

"But of the tree of knowledge, of good and evil, thou shalt not eat, for in the day that thou eatest thereof, thou shall surely die." -Genesis 2:17.

But woman and man did eat of the tree of knowledge; they exercised their imagination; they were incredibly intelligent, creative, and beautiful; the daughters of man had sex with the sons of god; and the people began to worship female gods, and they built great towering, marvelous cities. However, according to Plato, some of these cities began to wage war.

"And the Lord said, I shall destroy man... Behold, I bring a flood of waters upon the earth to destroy all flesh...I will cause it to rain upon the earth... and every living thing I will destroy from off the face of the earth... And all in whose nostrils was the breath of life, of all that was in the dry land, died."
-Genesis, 6:7.

The accuracy of these ancient stories are also supported not just by the geological record but ancient records, including those compiled by the Sumerians, Babylonians, Greeks, Mayas and Aztecs. Peoples throughout the world, across divergent and distant cultures all speak in hushed and somber tones about the Great Flood (e.g. Dundes, 1988). This cataclysmic event was so momentous in the history of woman and man that it is detailed by the Greeks, the Mayas and Aztecs, as well as in Genesis and the even more ancient records of the Babylonians and Sumerians (Horcasitas, 1988; Kramer, 1981; Woolley, 1965).

ATLANTIS AND THE DELUGE

Plato wrote two "dialogues" Timaeus and Critias, around 355 B.C. Critias, a historian explains, that there were two great and "wondrous" cities, one of which was located on the continent of Atlantis, far beyond the Pillars of Hercules. The other was ancient Athens, a city of the gods, that had been established over 9,000 years before Plato's time.

Atlantis, Plato explained, was "a great and marvelous power" that extended its reach through much of the world. However, as their power and technology grew, the people of Atlantis began "arrogantly" seeking control over the world and became embroiled in a terrible world wide war with Athens with much suffering and loss of life.

"The Lord saw how great was man's wickedness... The Earth was filled with violence." -Genesis 6:11.

And this global war came to a violent, earthquaking end, when the floods swallowed up Atlantis and the armies of Athens, and the continent of Atlantis sank beneath the rising seas.

"All the fountains of the great deep burst apart, all the floodgates of the sky broke open." -Genesis 7:11

Plato insisted throughout Critias, that the story of Atlantis and Athens was not made up but was "genuine history" and "from the realm of fact". Plato provided considerable ceremonial, engineering, and architectural detail regarding ancient Atlantis, including descriptions of the great harbor, the stadium, the lavish bathrooms, and the ritual sacrifice of the bulls. The capital city of Atlantis, he tells us, was 300 miles across and the continent was divided into ten kingdoms.

Moreover, Plato insists there were other "marvelous" cities and nation states that existed before the flood, including ancient Athens; marvelous cities that rose and fell over 9,000 years before his own time. According to Plato, the goddess of wisdom, Athena, established the city Athens where lived "men of the greatest wisdom." But like Atlantis, the great city was destroyed by the terrible floods.

MU AND THE DELUGE

In 1864, armed with the key to the complex Mayan alphabet, the French Scholar and cleric, Charles-Etienne Breasseur de Bourbourg, began translating the few Mayan manuscripts which had survived destruction by the 16th century Spanish conquistadors. One manuscript told of an ancient land of wise men and women that sank beneath the ocean following a cosmic catastrophe associated with Venus, the bringer of rain.

This ancient continent and city, Charles-Etienne Breasseur de Bourbourg decided, was somehow associated with the mysterious letters: m and u which repeatedly appeared in the manuscript. Hence, he named the lost continent, Mu.

According to Mayan accounts, just prior to the deluge, strife had broken out in the land of Mu between two brothers and their armies. The great civilization and city was at war when Venus struck, sending all beneath the waves of the rising seas.

Like Atlantis, Mu was located in the Atlantic, on a large island, and consisted of 10 separate kingdoms. And, both Atlantis and Mu sunk beneath the waves more than 10,000 years ago.

The Mu and the Atlantians may well have been one and the same; children of the gods, so say the ancients, the survivors seeking safety in distant lands, when their own homes and cities sank beneath the sea.

And yet, even those who survived did not escape this cosmic wrath. The Lord God vowed to hunt down and destroy the children of the gods. He would create an army of his own "godly offspring" to cleanse the lands of the last of the Cro-Magnon, the Anakites, the Nephilim, and would someday completely destroy the last of their cities and their gods.

-4-

THE LIMBIC SYSTEM AND THE SOUL

Spirits, Dreams, and Poltergeists

Middle Paleolithic peoples and those of the Upper Paleolithic buried their dead with grave offerings and with the body placed in sleeping positions. These peoples believed in an afterlife and a spirit world which could be entered through a doorway of dreams. According to the ancients, the soul could exit the body when dreaming and following death.

Because these ancient peoples were capable of experiencing love, fear, and mystical and religious awe, and as they believed in spirits and ghosts, they evolved religious rituals and religious symbolism to help them communicate with and gain control over the spiritual realms. These rites included the development or discovery of signs and symbols which could generate religious awe regardless of time or culture.

For example, in addition to their complex mortuary practices, one of the

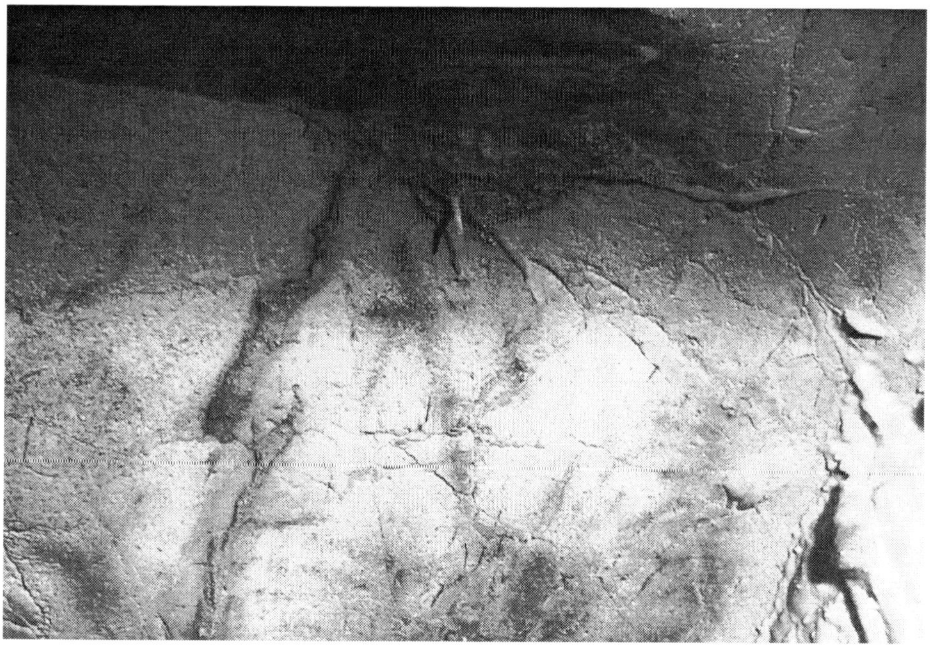

Figure 34. *The entrance to the underground Upper Paleolithic cathedral. The Chauvet cave. Note the sign of the cross. Reprinted from Chauvet et al., (1996). Dawn of Art: The Chauvet Cave. Henry H. Adams. New York.*

first signs of exceedingly ancient religious symbolism is an engraved "cross" that is perhaps between 60,000 to 100,000 years old (Mellars, 1989). Likewise, the underground entrance to the Chauvet cathedral, in France, is marked by a large red cross that was painted 35,000 years ago (Chauvet et al., 1996).

Regardless of time and culture, from the Aztecs, Mayans, American Indians, Romans, Greeks, Africans, Christians, Cro-Magnons, Egyptians (the key of life), and so on, the cross consistently appears in a mystical context, and/or is attributed tremendous cosmic or spiritual significance (Budge ,1994; Campbell, 1988; Joseph, 2000a; Jung, 1964; Sitchin, 1990).

The "sign of the cross" is found in almost all cultures and generally signifies religious or cosmic significance, e.g. the four corners of the cosmos. The sign of the cross was the ideogram of An, the Sumerian giver of all life from which rained down the seeds of life on all worlds including the worlds of the gods. An of the cross gave life to the gods, and to woman and man.

The symbol of the cross is in fact associated with innumerable gods and goddesses, including Anu of the ancient Egyptians (who is identical to An), the Egyptian God Seb, the Goddess Nut, the God Horus (the hawk), as well as Christ and the Mayan and Aztec God, Quetzocoatl. For example, like the Catholics, the Mayas and Aztecs adorned their temples with the sign of the cross. Quetzocoatl, like Jesus, was a god of the cross.

In China the equilateral cross is represented as within a square which

Figure 35. *(left) The God Seb supporting the Goddess Nut who represents heaven. Note the repeated depictions of the key of life; i.e. a ring with a cross at the end.(right) Quetzocoatal.*

represents the Earth, the meaning of which is: "God made the Earth in the form of a cross." It is noteworthy that the Chinese cross-in-a-box can also be likened to the swastika—also referred to as the "gammadion" which is one of the names of the Lord God: "Tetragammadion"

Figure 36. *The sign of the cross appears appears across cultures, e.g., the Maya, Aztecs, Chaldeans, Hindus, Persians, Paleolithic American Indians, Chinese. In China the equilateral cross is represented as within a square which represents the Earth, the meaning of which is: "God made the Earth in the form of a cross." It is noteworthy that the Chinese cross-in-a-box can also be likened to the swastika—also referred to as the "gammadion."*

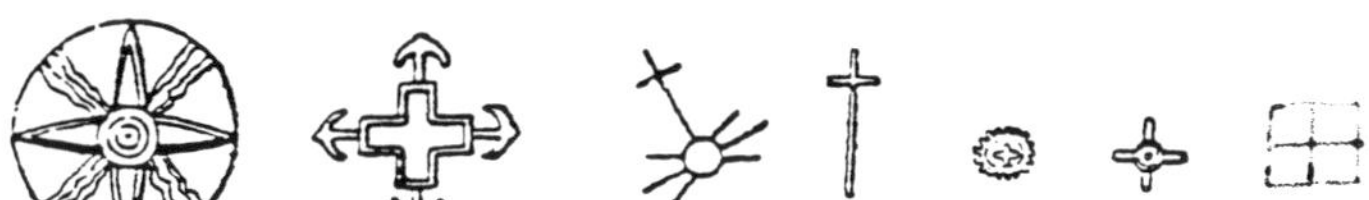

SOLAR CROSSES.[1]

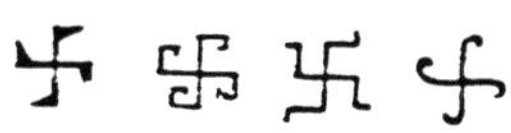

VARIETIES OF THE GAMMADION.

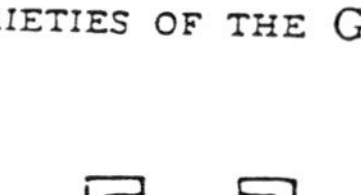

GAMMADIONS.

Swastikas, the crooked cross, also appear across cultures and is associated with the gods, with the heavens, with the creation of the Earth, e.g., the four corners of the Earth, and the four corners of the heavens; and with sexuality, the fertility of the Earth. The swastika is a sex symbol. Four men or women lying together on their sides engaged in mutual masturbation and oral-anal sex.

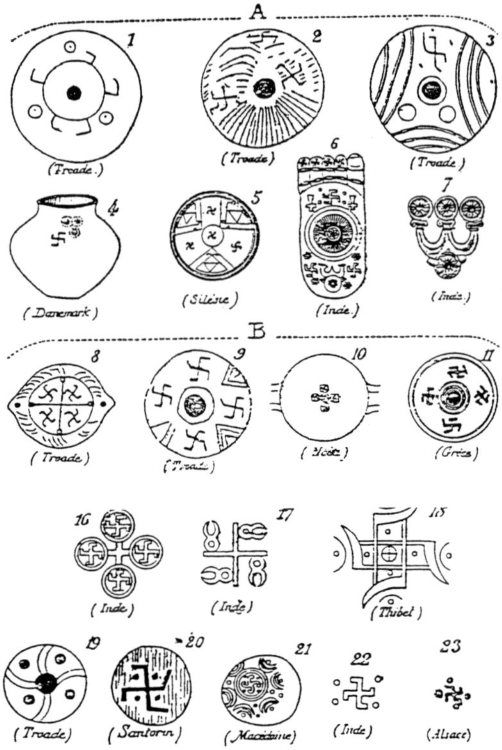

Figure 37. *Swastikas across cultures and is associated with the gods, with the heavens, with the creation of the Earth, the four corners of the Earth and the four corners of the heavens.*

The commonalty in religious significance associated with the cross may have to do with the "four corners" of the world and the heavens. As ancient priests and shamans turned their eyes to the heavens, seeking to peer beyond the mystery that separated this world from the next, the "four corners" may

Figure 38. *The swatiska is a sex symbol and associated with sexuality; i.e., four people laying side by side performing felatio or cunnilingus upon one another*

have been a common astronomical deduction, a way of dividing the divine circle into four equal parts for navigation, localization, and calculation. And there may have been stars that were aligned together like today's southern cross, and these constellations may have also been observed by priests and shamans as they turned their eyes to the heavens, and who viewed these celestial symbols as having heavenly significance.

Yet another factor may be due to the shared commonalty of the limbic system, which contains feature detecting neurons sensitive to geometric stimuli including the sign of the cross. The brain structures of the limbic system, e.g., amygdala and hippocampus, and inferior temporal lobe, have been repeatedly implicated in the generation of fear, love, intense emotions, and religious and spiritual beliefs (Bear 1979; Daly 1958; d'Aquili and Newberg 1993; Gloor 1986, 1992; Halgren 1992; Horowitz et al. 1968; Jaynes 1976; Joseph 1992a, 1998a; MacLean 1990; Mesulam1981; Penfield and Perot1963; Rolls 1992; Schenk and Bear 1981; Slater and Beard 1963; Subirana and Oller-Daurelia, 1953; Trimble 1991; Weingarten, et al. 1977; Williams 1956).

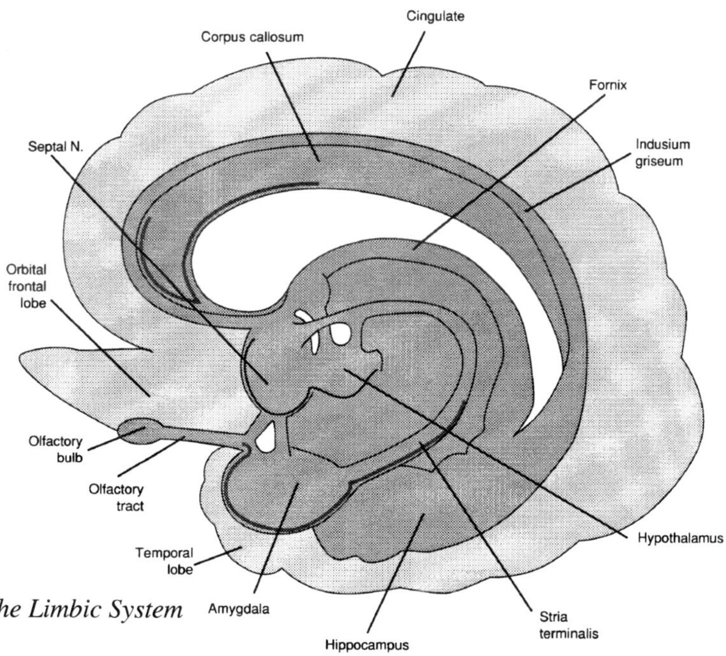

Figure 39. *The Limbic System*

The amygdala is able to receive, process and integrate multiple signals from all the sensory modalities simultaneously. The amygdala enables us to hear "sweet sounds," recall "bitter memories," or determine if something is spiritually significant, sexually enticing, or good to eat (Gloor 1986, 1992, 1997; Halgren 1992; Joseph 1992a, 1996; Kling et al., 1987; O'Keefe and Bouma 1969; Rolls 1992; Ursin and Kaada 1960).

The amygdala enables us to experience the spiritually sublime, is concerned with the most basic animal emotions, and allows us to store emotional and personally significant experiences in memory.

The amygdala also makes it possible for us to reexperience these memories when awake or during the course of a dream in the form of visual, auditory, or religious or spiritual imagery (Bear 1979; d'Aquili and Newberg 1993; Gloor 1986, 1992, 1997; Halgren, 1992). It is the amygdala which enables an individual to experience emotions such as love and religious rapture, as well as the ecstasy associated with orgasm, and the dread and terror associated with the unknown. It also appears to generate religious and spiritual significance when presented with the sign of the cross.

CROSS-RECOGNITION NEURONS

The inferior temporal lobe, and thus the amygdala and hippocampus, appears to have been well developed in "archaics," and Neanderthals, comparable, grossly, to the temporal lobes of Upper Paleolithic and present day peoples (Joseph, 1996, 2000a). It is these cerebral structures which have made it possible to experience as well as to attribute spiritual or religious significance to certain actions and geometric signs and stimuli.

Along the neocortical surface of the inferior temporal lobe and the amygdala are dense neuronal fields that contain neurons that fire selectively in response to visual images of faces, hands, eyes, and complex geometric shapes, including crosses (Gross et al. 1972; Hasselmo, Rolls and Baylis, 1989; Morris et al., 1996; Richmond, et al. 1983, 1987; Rolls 1984, 1992). These neurons are sometimes referred to as "feature detectors." The ability to recognize faces, geometric shapes, and social emotional nuances are dependent on these specialized temporal lobe and amygdala feature-detecting neurons (Gross, et al. 1972; Hasselmo et al. 1989; Morris et al., 1996; Richmond, et al. 1983, 1987; Rolls 1984). Together these structures interact to create complex neural networks that respond selectively to these stimuli, such that, when perceiving a face or a cross the amygdala and temporal lobe become activated.

If the amygdala and overlying temporal lobe were destroyed, the individual would lose the ability to perceive faces or complex geometric stimuli. They would also lose the capacity to feel love or affection, or to recognize family or friends. Isolation would be preferred. They would also cease to experience emotional or spiritual awe in reaction to religious symbols, such as the sign of the cross.

THE AMYGDALA AND SPIRITUAL SYMBOLISM

Neurons in the amygdala and inferior temporal are multimodally responsive, receiving and integrating signals from all sensory association areas simultaneously (Gloor 1986, 1992, 1997; Halgren 1992; Joseph 1992a, 1996; Kling et al., 1987; O'Keefe and Bouma 1969; Rolls 1992; Ursin and Kaada 1960). Because these structures contain feature detectors and subserve almost all aspects of emotion, including religious feeling, it is possible for faces, hands, eyes, and geometric symbols to become infused with, or to stimulate, mystical and religious feeling, including for example, the "evil eye." The amygdala located in the right temporal lobe in fact becomes exceedingly excited when it detects that someone is gazing directly at them.

Abnormal activation of the amygdala-temporal lobe is also associated with the experience of frightening hallucinations—due to the activation of these feature-detecting neurons (Gloor, 1997; Joseph, 1992a, Halgren, 1992). The emotion is aroused in response to the hallucination, but is also generated internally even in the absence of a hallucination; fear being the most common reaction associated with amygdala activation (Davis et al., 1997; Gloor, 1997; LeDoux, 1996).

Moreover, as these nuclei respond selectively to stimuli such as crosses or when being stared at, heightened emotional activity within these limbic nuclei could result in feelings of fear, foreboding, or religious awe which is attributed to objects such as "crosses" or the "evil eye." Crosses, eyes, faces, and related emotions may also be hallucinated if the related feature-detecting neurons are also activated.

Similar explanations could be offered in regard to the spiritual significance attributed to triangles (i.e. pyramids), circles, hands, and eyes. The amygdala and overlying temporal lobe also become activated in response to these perceptual stimuli. In fact, crosses, triangles and circles were etched on Cro-Magnon cave walls over 35,000 years ago (Chauvet et al., 1996), whereas hands, and eyes repeatedly appear in mystical contexts.

Figure 40. *A Kumeyaay shaman ("Native American"). Photo by TT. Waterman, 1898. Note hands painted on his chest and solar disc on his belly.*

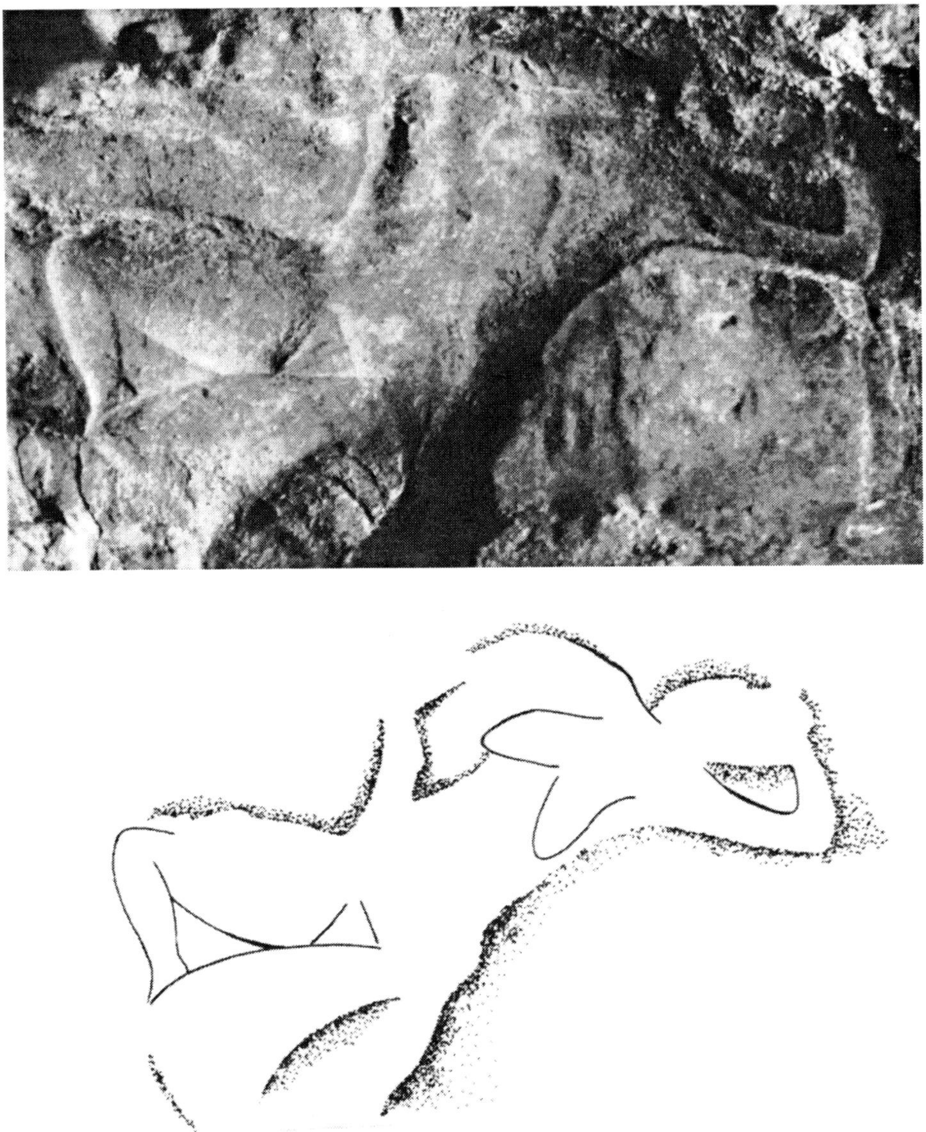

Figure 41. *The pyramid/triangle often appears in a mystical context and is associated with the life giving attributes of the Great Goddess, the Mother of All. Specifically, the pyramid/triangle is associated with a woman's vagina, the source of new life.*

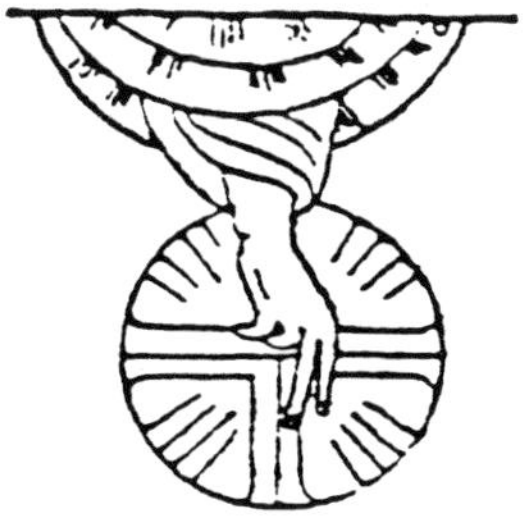

***Figure 42.** The hand of "god" emerging from a cloud, with the finger tips emitting rays of light, as if the hand were "a living sun." 9th Century. Paris.*

However, as to the triangle (which is also the shape of a pyramid), this had long been a sex symbol, and a symbol of fertility, as long ago as the Upper Paleolithic. The triangle is associated with the outer shape of a woman's vagina—the gateway to the womb, the source of life. And, the amygdala is not only responsive to tri-

***Figure 43.** Aton, the sun God. Note rays of sunlight becoming caressing hands.*

***Figure 44.** The all-seeing eye of God. Painting by Jan Provost, 15th century.*

angles, but it is one of the primary structures responsible for generating sexual arousal (Joseph, 1992a).

Hence, it can be assumed that "cross" and "pyramid" neurons as well as "mystical/religious" feeling neurons (or neural networks) had probably evolved by 35,000 and perhaps 100,000 years ago—possibly in reaction to repeated exposure to a woman's naked body, and the experience of "cross-like" stimuli in nature. One need only rise their arms horizontally or walk in the forest to spy dead trees that take the form of a "cross," or look upward to view birds with extended cross-like wings soaring through the skies. The sign of the cross is not uncommon and when staring at a cross the temporal lobes and the amygdala are activated.

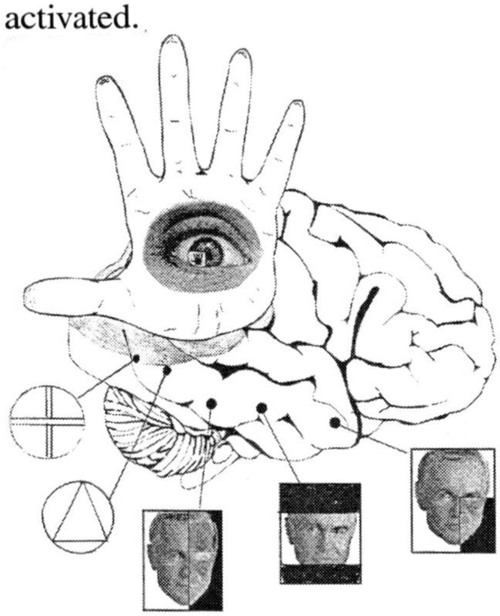

Figure 45. *The parietal lobe has been referred to as a "lobe of the hand." Neurons within the inferior temporal lobe respond to foveal and the upper visual field, and contain "facial" and "feature" detection neurons.*

Likewise, a woman with her legs spread, or in the act of giving birth, would have also generated extremely intense emotions, ranging from sexual arousal in reaction to her triangular-shaped vagina, to the dread and fear associated with the life creating potential of the womb and the great unknown.

SPIRITS AND THE SOUL

The amygdala enables us to hear "sweet sounds," recall "bitter memories," or determine if something is spiritually significant, sexually enticing, or good to eat. The amygdala also makes it possible for us to store personal, sexual, spiritual, and emotional experiences in memory and to recall and reexperience these memories when awake or during the course of a dream in the form of visual, auditory, or religious or spiritual imagery (Bear 1979; d'Aquili and Newberg 1993; Gloor 1986, 1992, 1997; Halgren, 1992; Joseph, 1982, 1996, 2000a).

The amygdala, in conjunction with the hippocampus, contributes in large part to the production of very sexual as well as bizarre, unusual and fearful mental phenomenon including out-of-body dissociative states, feelings of depersonalization, and hallucinogenic and dream-like recollections involving threatening men, naked women, sexual intercourse, religion, the experience of god, as well as demons and ghosts and pigs walking upright dressed as people (Bear 1979; Daly 1958; d'Aquili & Newberg 1993; Gloor 1986, 1992; Halgren 1992; Horowitz et al., 1968; Jaynes 1976; MacLean 1990; Mesulam1981; Penfield & Perot1963; Rolls, 1992; Schenk & Bear 1981; Slater & Beard 1963; Subirana & Oller-Daurelia 1953; Taylor, 1972, 1975; Trimble, 1991; Weingarten et al., 1977; Williams, 1956).

The amygdala also makes it possible to experience not just spiritual and religious awe, but all the terror and dread of the unknown. Indeed, the amygdala can generate feelings of hellish, nightmarish fear

And yet, it is also the amygdala which is responsible for the capacity to transcend the known, this reality. It is also the amygdala which assists in maintaining this reality through the inhibition and filtering of most of the sensory signals bombarding the brain and body. If not for this sensory filtering, a color might have taste and its own particular texture, whereas sounds might provoke smells, warmth, light, colors, tastes, and feelings of weight. Hyperactivation of the amygdala, and overlying temporal lobes removes these sensory filters, and what is concealed is revealed, sometimes in overwhelming confusing majesty.

Neurosurgical patients have reported communing with spirits or receiving profound knowledge from the Hereafter, following depth electrode amygdala stimulation or activation (Penfield and Perot 1963; Subirana and Oller-Daurelia, 1953; Williams 1956). Some have reported hearing even the singing of angels and the voice of "God."

THE LIMBIC SYSTEM: SPIRITUALITY AND EMOTION

According to d'Aquili and Newberg (1993) mystical states may be voluntarily or involuntarily induced and are dependent upon the differential stimulation of limbic system nuclei, including the hypothalamus, hippocampus, and amygdala, as well as the right frontal and right temporal lobe. However, it appears that these brain areas differentially contribute to religious and emotional experience.

For example, the hypothalamus is concerned with all rudimentary aspects of emotion, homeostasis such as food and water intake, and controls the hormonal and related aspects of violent behavior and sexual activity. The amygdala also plays a highly significant role in sexual and violent behavior, and, in conjunction with the temporal lobe and hippocampus, enables a human to have religious, spiritual and mystical experiences (Bear 1979; Daly 1958; d'Aquili and Newberg 1993; Horowitz et al. 1968; Mesulam1981; Penfield and Perot1963; Schenk, and Bear 1981; Slater & Beard 1963; Subirana & Oller-

Daurelia 1953; Trimble 1991; Weingarten, et al. 1977; Williams 1956). These religious experiences, however, may also involve violent behavior or sexual activity, due to limbic involvement.

As we shall see in later chapters, many religious customs and rituals involve violence and sexuality, which in turn is due to the activation of this limbic system transmitter to god.

The amygdala and hypothalamus subserve the capacity to experience feelings of intense sexual arousal, fear or, conversely, euphoria, including an orgasmic feeling of rapture, or the "nirvana" of a heroin "high." This is because the hypothalamus and amygdala are major pleasure centers, and contain opiate-producing neurons and opiate (enkephalin) receptive neurons, thus generating feelings of numbness and a narcotic high. Large concentrations of opiate receptors and enkephalin-producing neurons are located throughout the amygdala (Atweh & Kuhar 1977ab; Uhl et al., 1978).

In response to pain, stress, shock, fear, or terror, the amygdala and other limbic nuclei begin to secrete high levels of opiates which can eventually induce a state of calmness as well as analgesia and euphoria (Joseph, 1998a, 1999a). It is this heroin high that explains why an ox, deer, and other animals will simply give up and lie still while they are devoured and eaten alive. It is this amygala-induced heroin high which also contributes to feelings of religious rapture and the ecstasy associated with life after death and the attainment of Nirvana.

THE AMYGDALA, HIPPOCAMPUS AND HALLUCINATIONS

Whereas the amygdala and hypothalamus interact in regard to pleasure, rage, and sexuality, the amygdala and hippocampus interact to subserve and mediate wholly different aspects of experience, including memory, dreaming, and hallucinations. The hippocampus in particular appears to be responsible for certain types of "hallucinations" such as the visualizations of astral projection or seeing oneself floating above the body (Joseph 1996, 1999b, 2000a). Some patients report not only floating, but of being embraced by a light and taken to a vast realm of fantastic proportions where they are given access to knowledge of the nature of life and death.

The amygdala, hippocampus, and temporal lobe are richly interconnected and appear to act in concert in regard to mystical experience, including the generation and experience of dream states and complex auditory and visual hallucinations, such as may be induced by LSD (Broughton 1982; Goldstein et al. 1972; Gloor 19861992; Hodoba 1986; Horowitz, et al. 1968; Joseph, 1992a; Meyer et al. 1987; Penfield and Perot 1963; Weingarten, et al. 1977; Williams 1956). If these neurons are hyperactivated, such as occurs during dream states,

Figure 46. *The Transfiguration. Raphael.*

seizures, physical pain, terror, food deprivation, social and sensory isolation, and under LSD (which disinhibits the amygdala by blocking serotonin) an individual might infuse their perceptions with tremendous religious and emotional feeling. Hence, under these conditions the individual may hallucinate, and ordinary perceptions, objects or people may be perceived as spiritual in nature or endowed with special or religious significance.

Intense activation of the temporal lobe, hippocampus, and amygdala has been reported to give rise to a host of sexual, religious and spiritual experiences; and chronic hyperstimulation can induce an individual to become hyper-religious or to visualize and experience ghosts, demons, angels, and even "God," as well as claim demonic and angelic possession or the sensation of having left their body (Bear 1979; Gloor 1986, 1992; Horowitz et al. 1968; MacLean 1990; Mesulam1981; Penfield & Perot1963; Schenk, and Bear 1981; Weingarten, et al. 1977; Williams 1956).

In some instances the individual may come to believe he or she is hearing, seeing, and interacting with gods, angels and demons when in fact they are hallucinating. These false beliefs are accentuated further because they are excessively emotionally and religiously aroused and are experiencing an "enkephalin" high and feelings of rapture or "nirvana."

In many cases, however, the individual is not hallucinating. Rather, their eyes have been opened, and they suddenly see as gods... knowing good and evil.

LSD, LIMBIC SYSTEM FILTERING AND HALLUCINATIONS

The amygdala is capable of processing visual, tactile, auditory, gustatory, olfactory, and emotional stimuli simultaneously. Amygdaloid neurons are multimodally responsive. Normally much of this data is suppressed and filtered so as to prevent the tasting of colors, the visualization of sound, and so on.

Under conditions of hyperactivity, limbic sensory acuity is increased and in many respects what is perceived is not necessarily a hallucination but instead represents the perception of overlapping sensory qualities that are normally filtered out. Colors may be felt and tasted, music may be observed as well as heard, the molecular composition of ceilings, floor and walls may be parted so that one can see through the spaces between where molecules join together. And the pulse of life may be experienced as it ebbs and flows in a leaf one holds between their finger tips.

Consider, for example, a description of someone's first LSD "trip."

"It was 1966... Jimi Hendrix was singing about purple haze, and that is exactly what we scored up in Haight Ashbury—mixed by the master himself, Stanley Osley..."

"About half an hour after I'd taken it, I was walking toward the park to meet and trip with my fellow tripsters when I began to notice the incredible clarity and vividness of my surroundings. Colors were brighter, plants seem to sparkle...and I stopped and touched a leaf...I could feel its energy, its life... I could taste it through my fingers...And when I got to the park I was so overwhelmed with the colors, the tastes, the smells, the incredible vividity and clarity that I felt almost overwhelmed and sat down to take it all in..."

"And then I heard a jet somewhere in the distance, and I looked into the sky but couldn't see it but my ears led my eyes to one of the mountains surrounding the valley, and oh my god, I could see right through the mountain. It was like the molecular composition of the mountain was parting into separate molecules. I could see the spaces between the molecules which were all in a frenzy of activity... it was as if I had achieved X-ray vision, and there were these crystal blue holes—like bubbles—and I could see right through the mountain and I could see the sky on the other side, including the jet. I could see the jet on the other side of the mountain by looking right through the mountain, by looking right through those gaps in the spaces between the molecules which were zipping along in their own unique pattern. And then the jet flew over the top of the mountain and instead of one jet I could see ten, then a hundred, and a kaleidoscope of jets in the sky."

"I raised my hand to point to this incredible sight, and instead of one hand, there were these trails of hands. And I did that again, waved my hand and there were these hand-arm trails of hands-hands-hands catching up and then merging... and it was then that I realized I could see through my hand. So I gazed at it for closer inspection. It was as if my eyes became a tunneling microscope—and this was 10 years before they invented tunneling microscopes."

"At first I could see the incredible cellular structure of the skin, and then the molecular structure...the pulsating molecules themselves... and then I could see between the spaces where the molecules joined together... my sight penetrated the skin and I could see the blood vessels, and then my eyes penetrated the blood vessels and I could see inside the blood vessel, I could see the blood platelets and the white corpuscles as they swirled through the vessel—and I kept thinking: How come I never noticed this before? I had forgotten that I had taken LSD."

Hallucinogens, of course, are an age-old means of obtaining access to alternate realities, including the realities of "god." Hallucinogens are said to enable an individual to peer between the space that separate this reality from all other realities, such that what is concealed is suddenly revealed. It is the amygdala, hippocampus, and temporal lobe which are responsible for these complex hallucinations, and it is the amygdala which normally filters much of this information so that it remains hidden. Hence, by hyperactivating these structures, in essence, one is also activating the transmitter to god.

SOULS, SPIRITS, DREAMS, AND POLTERGEISTS

TO KNOW FEAR IS TO KNOW GOD

"Fear the Lord your God." -Deuteronomy 10:12.

Priests, prophets, shamans and many others who encounter "god" or His "angels" not uncommonly experience tremendous fear. Fear is the most common emotion associated with the amygdala (Gloor, 1997; Halgren, 1992; LeDoux, 1996; Williams, 1956), with some patients experiencing horrifying, hellish, and nightmarish fear, sometimes coupled with hellish hallucinations.

We are repeatedly told in the Bible, that to know fear is to know god. Indeed, even a committed atheist may feel compelled to cry out and pray to god if sufficiently terrified. Terror is also an emotion associated with the amygdala... as well as with the Lord God.

Yet others experience awe and rapture when confronted by the divine. As noted, amygdala hyperactivation is also associated with feelings of extreme joy and ecstasy.

According to d'Aquili and Newberg (1993; p. 194) "a combination of the experience of both fear and exhalation" is "usually termed religious awe." These feeling states are "almost always associated with religious symbols, sacred images, or archetypal symbols" which flow "from the inferior temporal lobe" and which "appear sometimes as monsters or gods". Indeed, angels, demons, and poltergeists may be experienced.

Most people find these experiences quite terrifying. They also frequently believe their perceptions are completely real and are not hallucinations.

SPIRITS AND POLTERGEISTS

"Cindy," a 22 year old college student, was plagued by demons and ghosts for months until her abnormal right inferior temporal lobe was surgically removed.

Prior to her brain injury, Cindy had never been very religious, and had certainly never seen a ghost; that is, until following her auto accident. She had been thrown over 50 feet through the windshield of her car and suffered a fracture of the right temporal region of the skull and developed a subdural hemotoma, a blood clot, which was pressing on the temporal lobe inducing herniation. Burr holes were drilled into her skull and the clot was surgically evacuated. Although her brain and temporal lobe had been injured, over the following weeks she seemed to quickly recover.

It was several days after her release from the hospital when she was startled while watching television. The arms, legs, hands, feet, and heads of the various actors began protruding from the screen into the living room where she sat.

Cindy said that at first she thought the television was broken and turned it off. But, as she stared back at the blank screen she saw what looked like her dead father staring back at her (which was probably her own reflection). As she backed away, the figure emerged from the television. He beckoned to her, and then behind him ghostly spooks and wraiths began to stream from the picture tube.

Terrified and crying for her mother she raced for the bathroom and locked herself in. Yet, even as she hid within the inner sanctum of the washroom, spirits, sprites and poltergeists streamed from the bathroom mirror and swirled about her. Crying and stumbling, she raced back into the living room and was horrified to see a spirit enter and take possession of her mother. Her mother was transformed before her eyes.

Panicked and terrified, Cindy ran into the street crying for help. A police officer, after investigating the scene, brought her to the local hospital and psychiatry unit. She was medicated and kept there on a 72 hour hold.

Later she decided what she had experienced were ghosts and lost souls of people who had been buried in an old, almost completely forgotten cemetery on the other side of the hill from where she lived. She also thought they were the ghosts of Indians who had been entombed beneath her house as there are numerous Indian burial grounds in the county.

Once she was released from her 72 hour psychiatric hold, she stopped taking her medication, and over the course of the next several weeks, she claimed to see "animal spirits." She reported that the "secret souls" of her mother's house plants were watching and observing her and that she could sometimes see filmy, soul-like entities traveling to and fro across the room and between different plants.

After several more hospitalizations, and an EEG, it was determined that she was suffering from excessive activity, seizure activity in the damaged temporal lobe. The inferior temporal lobe and the underlying amygdala were surgically ablated and destroyed, and she ceased to "hallucinate."

DREAMS, ANIMAL SPIRITS AND LOST SOULS

Across time and culture, people have believed that not just humans and animals, but plants and trees were sensitive, sentient, intelligent, and the abode of spirits including the souls of dead ancestors (Campbell 1988; Frazier 1950; Harris, 1993; Jung 1964; Malinowski 1948). Before felling a tree, the spirit sometimes had to be conjured forth so as to not harm it (Campbell 1988; Frazier 1950). Be it animal or plant, souls were also believed capable of migrating to new abodes.

Among the ancients and many so called primitive cultures, it was believed that souls are reflected in shadows, in streams, and pools of water (Campbell, 1988; Frazier, 1950; Harris, 1993; Jung, 1964; Malinowkski, 1948).

Figure 47. *(Left) The souls of young women who had drowned beckon to passing men, luring them to their deaths. (Above) A female tree spirit.*

Because ghosts or demons sometimes attempt to abduct souls, this required that one's shadow and reflection be protected. Even water spirits might try to capture a person's soul, so staring into reflecting ponds and lakes was to be avoided.

Moreover, the ancients believed that the shadows and reflections of oth-

Figure 48. *Wondjina figure with plum tree at its side. Wondjinas are spirits. Above the Wondjina are the "children of the wondjinas" which are the souls of men.*

ers had to be avoided so that one did not come into contact with the soul of a witch, sorcerer, or a demon. It was believed that one's soul could be abducted by demons and witches as well as the recently departed. This is also why in some cultures people turn mirrors to the wall after a death and lay down pictures of the recently departed (Frazier 1950). This insures that living souls are not stolen by the souls of the dead who are leaving this world for the next one.

The belief in the persistence of the soul after death gave rise to ancestor worship in some ancient cultures, including China. Oracle Bones were believed to contain the souls of the dead and were employed for divinatory purposes in ancient China over 4,000 years ago. The earliest Oracle Bones so far discovered are covered with pictograms including a man with a large ghostly distorted head (Brandon, 1967). This pictogram also denotes the word kuei, which means, soul. Oracle bones also included characters signifying the words "she, shen, and tsu." "Tsu" means dead ancestor, "she" is a protective fertility deity of the soil, and "shen" are divine beings connotating phallic significance.

The ancient Chinese practiced a religious ritual which was intended to prevent the soul from departing the body at death. The orifices would be stopped up to keep the kuei safely inside the body. So long as the soul remained tethered to the body, the body would not undergo its final fatal disintegration. These beliefs gave rise to the ritual of "calling back of the soul," a ritual also performed for the living as the souls were believed able to wander forth from the body, such as during sleep, exposing the living body to death and extinction (Brandon, 1967).

The ancient Chinese believed that the kuei represented by the yin-soul, was associated with the body since conception. By contrast, a yang-soul was associated with the individual personality and the person's unique mental qualities.

The alternating and competing principles of the yin-soul and the yang-soul are directly related to the concepts of ying and yang. They also gave rise to ancestor worship as the ancient Chinese believed that the life force, the energy associated with the soul, this *substance familiale,* lay buried beneath the ground as *une masse indistincte*. "This energy was represented above ground at any given moment, only by the living members of the family, which constituted the individualized portions of that *substance familial*. It followed, accordingly, that each birth within the family represented the reincarnation of a portion of that subterranean *substance familial*, while each death meant the return of a part of this individual family substance familial to the *masse indistincte in* the ground below" (Brandon, 1967, p. 180).

SOULFUL DREAMS

Souls were also believed by ancient humans to wonder about while people sleep and dream (Brandon 1967; Frazier 1950; Harris 1993; Jung 1945, 1964; Malinowkski 1990). That is, among many different cultures and religions the soul is believed to sometimes escape the body via the mouth or nostril during sleep. Moreover, during a dream the soul may wonder away from the body and may engage in certain acts or interact with other souls including those of the dear but long dead and departed.

Sometimes the soul is believed to take on another form, such as a bird, or deer, fox, rabbit, wolf, and so on. The spirit and the soul could also hover about in human-like, ghostly vestiges, at the fringes of reality, the hinterland where day turns into night (Campbell 1988; Frazier 1950; Jung 1964; Malinowski 1954; Wilson 1951). The souls of animal's such as a wolf or eagle, could also leave the body and take on various forms including that of a woman or Man. Not just men but animals too had souls that had to be respected.

Even after death souls continued to interact with the living, and every living being possessed a soul. Hence, the ancients believed that these souls could be influenced, their behavior controlled, and, in consequence, a good hunt insured or with the assistance of a soul, or by performing magical rituals aimed at the soul, enemies could be defeated and an evil man could be easily slain.

Because animals and plants had souls, and as some gods would also take up residence within an animal or plant as a temporary or permanent abode, this gave rise to animal worship and animal sacrifice, as well as the avoidance of certain animals or plants which were not to be killed or eaten, or killed or eaten only in a certain ritualized manner (Campbell 1988; Frazier 1950; Malinowkski 1948; Smart 1969).

Over the course of human cultural and cognitive evolution, these beliefs became increasingly complex and required specialists to interpret and minister the rituals and rites (Armstrong 1994; Brandon 1967; Campbell 1988; Frazier 1950; Smart 1969; Wilson 1951). Soon priests, prophets, and even the Gods evolved.

DREAMING OF GOD

Priests and prophets as well as the common people, often experienced God as well as animal spirits and the souls of the dead, during the course of a dream (Campbell 1988; Frazier 1950; Jung 1945, 1964; Malinowkski 1954).

Dreams have their source in the amygdala and hippocampus and inferior temporal lobe (Joseph, 1988, 1992a, 1996, 2000a). Although mediated by brainstem nuclei, activity within the amygdala may in fact trigger the first phase of dreaming (REM), which is signified by the buildup of PGO (pontine-geniculate-occipital) waves. REM (dream) sleep is heralded and then accompanied by what has been referred to as PGO waves. That is, the amygdala is active not only during REM, but amygdala activity triggers PGO waves (Calvo, et al. 1987) which then leads to dream sleep. The amygdala produces the dream, and dreams the dream, and the dream may consist of fragmentary memories, hallucinatory imagery, and emotional extremes.

In addition to amygdala activity during REM, the hippocampus begins to produce slow wave, theta activity (Jouvet 1967; Olmstead, Best, and Mays 1973; Steriade and McCarley 1990). Presumably, during REM, the hippocampus and amygdala act as a reservoir from which various memories, images, emotions, words, and ideas are drawn and incorporated into the matrix of dream-like activity being woven by the right (and left) hemisphere (Joseph 1982, 1988, 1996, 2000a). The hippocampus and amygdala also serve as a source from which material is drawn during the course of a daydream.

Yet, as also noted, these limbic structures also normally acts to inhibit the perception of most of the stimuli impinging on the body. This information is filtered so that one reality is maintained and to prevent the individual from being overwhelmed with competing streams of input. In other words, just as a channel selector on a television or radio permits the select reception of information from a single source (a single reality), these brain structures perform likewise. However, just as there are a multitude of channels, and just as one can change from channel to channel in order to receive a wealth of data, images, sounds, and information from a variety of sources (a variety of realities), likewise, the limbic system can also become tuned to other sources of information which are not normally perceived.

And, once the Doors of Perception are opened, all appears as it is...infinite.

DREAMS, SPIRITS AND REALITY

"I the Lord will make Myself known to him in a vision, and will speak with him in a dream." -Numbers 12.6

When the limbic system becomes hyperactivated it is not at all uncommon for an individual to dream. Dreams, it has been proclaimed, are the royal road to the unconscious (Freud, 1900).

It is also via dreams that gods and spirits speak to women and men (Campbell, 1988; Jaynes, 1976; Jung, 1945, 1964). It was via dreams that hunter-gatherers and ancient humans were able to gain access to the domicile of the soul and the spirit world of the hereafter (Frazier 1950; James 1958; Neihardt and Black Elk1989). Indeed, it has been argued that dreams (and thus the limbic system) enable an individual to come into contact with a different reality; the same reality shared and experienced by our ancestors and the gods—the ultimate reality of the Great Spirit.

DREAMS AND MULTIPLE REALITIES

Our ancient human ancestors lived in two realities, that of the physical and of the spiritual, both of which were undeniable and experienced by enemies and friends alike (Frazier, 1950; Jung, 1945, 1964). One need only spend a night alone in the forest among the trees and the elements to become quickly convinced that one is not alone, but is being watched by various entities both alive and supernatural, animal and spirit, benevolent and unkind.

Like modern day humans, the ancients had dreams by which they were transported or exposed to a world of magic and untold wonders. It is as if one had been transported to a different world and a reality which obeyed its own laws of time, space, and motion.

It is through dreams that humans came to believe the spiritual world sits at the boundaries of the physical, where day turns to dusk, the hinterland of the mind where imagination and dreams flourish and grow (Frazier, 1950; Jung, 1945, 1964; Malinowkski, 1954); hence the tendency to bury the dead in a sleeping position even 100,000 years ago.

It is also via dreams that humans came to know that spirits and lost souls populated the night. The dream was real and so too were the Gods and demons who thundered and condemned and the ghosts and phantoms that hovered at the edge of night. Although but a dream, like modern humans, our ancient ancestors experienced this through the senses, much as the physical world is experienced. Both were real and were taken seriously.

Dreams are the royal road to the unconscious realms of the mind and to realities that lie just beyond conscious awareness. And it is through the amygdala, hippocampus, and temporal lobe, that dreams emerge and flow. The limbic neurons subserving spiritual experiences also give rise to dreams. Thus the link between the world of dreams and the spirit land of gods and demons is the limbic system; i.e. the "transmitter to god."

RIGHT TEMPORAL LOBE HYPERACTIVATION & DREAMING

The amygdala and the neocortex of the temporal lobe are interactionally involved in the production of religious and hallucinatory experiences including dream states (Broughton, 1982; Gloor, 1997; Goldstein et al., 1972; Hodoba, 1986; Humphrey & Zangwill 1961; Kerr & Foulkes 1978; Meyer et al., 1987); the right temporal lobe and amygdala in particular (Joseph, 1988a, 1992a).

Similarly, d'Aquili and Newberg (1993) argue that the right hemisphere (and right amygdala) is more involved than the left in the reception and production of religious imagery. This is likely as the right hippocampus and amygdala, and the right hemisphere in general (Broughton, 1982; Goldstein et al., 1972; Hodoba, 1986; Humphrey & Zangwill 1961; Joseph, 1988, 2000a; Kerr and Foulkes 1978; Meyer, Ishikawa, Hata, and Karacan 1987) also appear to be involved in the production of hallucinations, dream imagery as well as REM during sleep. Indeed, like the limbic system, the right hemisphere is not only associated with dreams, but the unconscious mind (Joseph, 1982, 1988a,b, 1992ab).

Electrophysiologically the right temporal lobe becomes highly active during REM, whereas, conversely, the left temporal region becomes more active during dreamless sleep, i.e., NREM (Goldstein et al. 1972; Hodoba 1986). Similarly, measurements of cerebral blood flow have shown an increase in the right temporal regions during REM sleep. Right temporal lobe blood flow also increases in subjects who upon wakening report visual, hypnogogic, hallucinatory and auditory dreaming (Meyer et al. 1987). Abnormal and enhanced activity in the right temporal and temporal-occipital area will also provoke dreaming and acts to increase the length and amount of dreaming and REM sleep for an atypically long time (Hodoba 1986).

As noted, LSD induces its "hallucinatory" effects by disinhibiting the amygdala. That is, LSD blocks the sensory filtering and perceptual inhibitory activity of a neural transmitter, serotonin. In consequence multi-sensory qualities that are normally suppressed are suddenly perceived such that what was hidden is revealed; sounds have color and colors and sounds can be tasted, as the bounds of this reality melt away thus revealing the supernatural reality of the otherside.

Conversely, LSD induced hallucinations are significantly reduced when the right but not the left temporal lobe has been surgically ablated (Serafintides1965). Similarly, it has been reported that dreaming is abolished with right but not left temporal lobe destruction (Bakan, 1978). Hence, it appears that there is a specific complementary relationship between REM sleep, hallucinations, LSD, mystical experiences, and right temporal (and thus right amygdala and hippocampus) electrophysiological activity. By contrast, the left half of the brain appears to be the domain of the more logical and nonintuitive aspects of conscious experience.

Whereas the right hemisphere is dominant for all aspects of emotion, and is the domain of the more visual and imaginal aspects of the mind, the left hemisphere is dominant for language, math, and the temporal sequential aspects of consciousness. It is the right hemisphere which dreams the dream, and it is the left hemisphere which not only passively observes but which forgets the dream upon waking (Joseph, 1988a). It is the more unconscious realms associated with the right hemisphere which are directly in tune with these alternate realities, such as conveyed through dreams, and it is the left hemisphere which dismisses and rationally explains away these experiences as nonsense.

DAY DREAMS AND FORESEEING THE FUTURE

During dream states we see and experience events which are normally filtered from the conscious mind. We can also gain insight into problems which have plagued us, or gain access to knowledge of events which occurred in the past or which will occur in the future (Joseph, 1988a, 2000a; Jung 1945, 1964)—just as we can think about the future or the past and make certain deductions and predictions.

Consider the day dream. In addition to its images and memories, the fantasy produced also consists of anticipations regarding the future, and in this respect, the day dream could be considered an imaginal means of preparation for various possible realities. Interestingly, daydreams appear to follow the same 90-120 minute cycle that characterize the fluctuation between REM and NREM periods, as well as fluctuations in mental capabilities associated with the right and left hemisphere (Broughton 1982; Kripke and Sonneschein 1990). That is, the cerebral hemispheres tend to oscillate in activity every 90-120 minutes. This cycle corresponds to the REM-NREM cycle and the appearance of day and night dreams, and the right hemisphere also appears to be the source of day dreams.

According to the ancients, day and night dreams both contained important information, not just regarding the past or the world of souls and spirits, but the future. As possible harbingers of the future, the intentions of the gods, and the future of self, friends and family, it has long been believed that dreams should be observed most carefully and could be used to foretell the future (Campbell 1988; Frazier 1950; Freud 1900; Jung 1945, 1964; Malinowkski 1954). It was pharaoh's dream which foretold that seven years of famine would follow seven years of plenty.

In fact, among the ancients, the American Indians, and even the highly cultured Romans, every once in a while someone would have what is called "a big dream." The big dream was of great importance to the whole clan, tribe, city, or nation. Often, the man or woman having the dream would gather the others together and announce it. And more often than not, it would be a woman who would have the big dream, for women have always been said to be more in touch with the "irrational," and throughout history it is women who have predominantly served as oracles.

THE TRANSMITTER TO GOD

Given that dreams reflect mental activity, it is thus not terribly surprising that dreams may also contain meaningful information that is not otherwise available to the conscious mind. Since the right hemisphere and limbic system which are responsible for dreaming dreams also "speak different languages" and attend to and process unique types of information, this data cannot always be transferred to and understood by the left hemisphere (Joseph, 1986a, 1988a,b; Joseph et al., 1984). From the perspective of the temporal sequential language dependent mind, these impressions remain unconscious.

The conscious mind is often denied information and social-emotional nuances that may be unconsciously conveyed by others but which may be perceived within the right hemisphere and limbic system (Joseph, 1982, 1988a, 1992b, 2000a; Joseph et al., 1984). This is because the information attended to and the manner in which this data is analyzed by the limbic system and right hemisphere is so different from that normally received and processed by the left hemisphere.

Nevertheless, sensory and emotional stimuli, which are normally ignored or filtered out by the language-dependent left hemisphere during waking are nevertheless perceived and analyzed by other regions of the brain so that a variety of conclusions may be arrived at, albeit unconsciously; and the same occurs during dream sleep.

During dream states, serotonin levels diminish (similar to what occurs under LSD) and multimodal neurons begin to fire such that the brain becomes in tune with, and is sometimes overwhelmed by sensory and ideational events which are normally filtered before reaching consciousness. However, during dreaming, this information may be recalled, integrated, assimilated, and certain conclusions arrived at; that is, by the right hemisphere and limbic system. And this information may then be conveyed to the language dependent left half of the brain which is at a low level of arousal during dream sleep and thus cannot prevent its reception. The left hemisphere observes the dream, which, however, it may forget upon waking.

Because the limbic system and right temporal lobe are hyperactivated during dream states, not only does the brain become freed of inhibitory restraint, but one is presumably able to gain access to dream-like alternate realities, including, perhaps, the spiritual reality of the Hereafter. Presumably the same occurs when fasting, isolated, in pain, under LSD, in trance, or in the throes of religious ecstasy, all of which activates the limbic system thus increasing channel capacity, so that what is concealed is revealed.

-5-

DREAMS OF DAMON WELLS:
Son of the Devil

"Witchcraft" and any and all "paranormal" capabilities, including "ESP" or divining by dreams, has been condemned as "unnatural" by many (but not all) religions throughout the ages including the ancient Jews and the Catholic Church.

"Witchcraft is a sin." I Samuel 15: 23

Of course, the "god" Yahweh would communicate with his prophets through visions and dreams. However, the unauthorized use of these same capacities was also condemned and outlawed, and those possessing these "unnatural" attributes killed.

"I will gather you and blow upon you the fire of my wrath, and ye shall be melted in the midst therefore... for... They prophesy falsely and divine deceitfully. They have profaned what is sacred to me... I am profaned in their midst" (Ezekiel, 22:23).

The Lord God declared religious war against and condemned to death all witches and all those who could commune with the dead, speak with spirits, conjure ghosts, or communicate with devils (Exodus 22: 18, Samuel 15: 23; Ezekiel 22:23).

"You know... how he has cut off those familiar with ghosts and spirits and wizards. So wherefore then layest thou a snare for my life, to cause me to be killed." -I Samuel 28:8-10.

Likewise, the Medieval Catholic Church burnt witches, warlocks, and dreamers, and all those suspected of communing with devils. According to Church and religious authorities, these practices were the work of the Devil, Satan, the fallen angel, the fallen god, the serpent also known as the god of the snake.

These "supernatural abilities" were viewed as a threat for they could be employed to divine the future, to influence and cast spells on other humans, or to communicate with the dead or even with other gods including the devil. Hence, those who saw the future through trance states or via dreams, or who demonstrated what might be described as "ESP," although venerated by some, were condemned by others as "unnatural" and sinful.

"Thou shall not suffer a witch to live." Exodus 22:18

DREAMING THE FUTURE

It is said that Mary Lincoln dreamed of President Lincoln's assassination, and saw his dead body laid out with the bullet wound to his head. If that story is true, it could be said that Mary Lincoln gained advance access to information that already existed in the future, in some distant realm of space. Because time is a function of movement through space and distance, it could be assumed that Mary Lincoln was able to see what lay up ahead whereas others, being more "near sighted" were unable to perceive these events until they were upon them.

Yet another possibility is that she somehow deduced what might transpire, and then it did come to pass. Therefore what she dreams was a well reasoned prediction, rather than a form of extra-sensory perception.

Yet another possibility is that the murder of Lincoln, the actual intention of killing him, had been communicated to her; that is, through her dreams and perhaps the dreams of Mr. John Wilkes Booth or one of his co-conspirators. That is, she may have received this information through the commingling of dreams, or perhaps, through the interaction of souls which some believe can leave the body during sleep and interact with the souls of others.

Anecdotal evidence abound to support the possibility that people can communicate with one another while dreaming. Some studies suggest that a dreamer can even tap into the thoughts of those awake.

Consider, for example, studies performed in the Sleep Laboratory of Mimonides Medical Center in New York, by Dr. Williams Erwin. In these studies, participants were introduced, and then later, while one subject slept and when it was determined he had entered REM sleep, the other would begin looking at particular paintings and prints. He would then attempt to project these images into the mind of the sleeper.

In one experiment, when the test subject entered REM, the "sender" opened a package which contained an art print of the Mexican and Indian followers of the Mexican revolutionary Emiliano Zapta, i.e. Zapatistas, by Romero. When the test subject entered REM, the other began gazing at the picture and attempted to project it to the dreamer. The dreamer was immediately awakened when the REM episode had ceased and was asked to describe his dream: "...a feeling of memory... of New Mexico... a lot of mountains...Indians, Pueblos" (reviewed in Broughton, 1991; see also Child, 1985; Devereuz, 1953; Ullman & Krippner, 1989).

Or, consider some of the unusual aspects of a Santa Clara County murder case which I reviewed and investigated by examining all court, psychiatric, police, and investigative records, and which I followed up through interviews with many of the principles directly involved.

DAMON WELLS — "SON OF THE DEVIL"

District Attorney (D.A.): "Did you join the United States Army in 1980?"

Witness (Stephen M): "Yes, sir."

D.A.: "You were stationed in Germany?"

S.M.: "Yes."

D.A.: "And while in Germany, did you come to know a person by the name of Damon Wells?"

S.M.: "Yes, sir."

D.A.: "Do you recall when you first met Damon Wells?"

S.M.: "Yes. It was 1981."

D.A.: "How did he introduce himself?"

S.M.: "He said, 'My name is Damon Wells, son of the devil."

D.A.: "Did you become friends with Damon Wells?"

S.M.: "We were both soldiers, and it was a pretty isolated site. Pretty secluded on top of a mountain, so I had a lot of contact with him."

D.A.: "What type of duties did you perform?"

S.M. "I was a satellite technician. Wells was a mechanic, a motor mechanic."

D.A.: "What kind of worker was he?"

S.M. "He was a fantastic worker. One of the best mechanics we ever had up there. He'd fix vehicles and the electric generators which powered our site. We didn't have any electricity up there."

D.A. "Did you ever notice anything odd about Damon?"

S.M. "Sure. Many times."

D.A. "Such as?"

S.M. "Sometimes he would stop what he was doing and would say, The voices are here. Can you hear them?"

D.A. "Anything else?"

S.M. "Damon used to sit for hours on top of this mountain, looking down into the valley. It was totally remote and isolated and heavily forested, but sometimes you could see him from the communications tower. Sometimes he would meditate by these ruins on the side of this mountain.

"He'd sit for hours, like in a trance. His legs would be crossed. He'd be rocking, and chanting, mumbling about demons and angels from Hell. Even when it began to rain, or even snow, Damon would just sit there, trance-like. He'd be soaking wet or freezing, sometimes in just shirt sleeves. I had to go get him a few times."

D.A. "Did Damon ever show you a cave?"

S.M. "Yes, he did. He had found this cave, hidden deep in the woods, on the back side of a mountain across the valley. I don't know how he ever found it. He had a rope tied to a tree on the mountain top, and you had to climb, to rappel down the rope in order to get to this cave. It was really kind of creepy."

D.A. "Did you ever go inside this cave?"

S.M. "Yes, I did. There was a large stone slab, and some candles and gun powder, and a knife and some books inside. It was obvious he had spent a lot of time there."

D.A. "Did Damon ever tell you why he visited this cave?"

S.M. "Yeah. He told me he went there to talk to the voices. The voices, from his point of view, came from the devil. He said he could communicate with the devil, and that the devil would appear in this cave and speak with him."

D.A. "Did he every talk to you about sacrifices?"

S.M. "Yes, he did. Especially after I pointed out what looked like animal bones, and blood stains on this big slab of rock. In fact, he showed me this book of black magic and it had a picture of a naked woman lying spread eagle on a rock. Standing over her was a hooded man with a big knife. Damon said that was how the devil would sacrifice his victims. Damon said, that since he was a slave of the devil, he was supposed to sacrifice victims the same way, on this rock."

D.A. "And what did you tell him after he said and showed these things to you?"

S.M. "I told him he had a serious problem, that he needed help. In fact, I suggested a few times that maybe he should see a psychiatrist or a priest."

D.A. "And what did he say when you told him he should see a priest?"

S.M. "He laughed and began talking about voodoo and demons. About how he could project his thoughts, and with the help of the demons, he could harm his enemies. He said that priests were enemies of the devil, they couldn't help him. Besides, he said, I have everything under control. The Demons do as I tell them.'"

D.A. "Did Damon ever tell you he had committed a serious crime? That he had sacrificed anyone to the devil?"

S.M. "Yes sir, he did. A few months later. He said he picked up a hitchhiker, drove her to the woods, and then killed her because the devil had told him to. He said the devil took control over him, and he killed her and had sex with her."

D.A. "Did you believe him?"

S.M. "No. He was really mixed up, confused like he was two people. He seemed possessed. I thought he was flipping out. When I asked if he had really killed someone, he just said, They're taking me over, Steve. They are taking me over."

Damon Wells claimed to have sacrificed a number of women, some in Germany. However, his trial in Santa Clara County was for the murder of Tanya Z. On the afternoon of the murder, Damon had been communing with the Devil and had taken several "tabs" of LSD—Orange sunshine—what he referred to as the "flesh of the Devil." At the direction of the Devil, he was going to search for a woman to sacrifice; that woman would be Tanya Z.

As Damon, hallucinating and mumbling to himself, made his way to his car, Tanya, a very attractive, dark haired, young woman, was just getting off work at a Santa Cruz bank. She was accompanied to her car by a female friend and coworker and was chattering away and showing her friend a birthday card and explaining that she was going shopping for a birthday present for her fiancee. However, first she would have to drive over the Santa Cruz mountains, on Highway 17, to stop at her house.

As Damon walked to his car intent on finding a sacrificial victim, he could hear the voice of the Devil, urging him on, explaining what to do. It was then that a neighbor happened to walk by, and overhearing Damon mumbling, he asked: "What?" Damon looked at him: "Don't you hear them?"

"What?"

"The voices are here. You can't hear them?"

"Hear who?"

"The Devil," Damon replied. He got into his car and drove into the Santa Cruz mountains.

Tanya had just made it over the summit when her car began to stall, and then it died. She pulled over to the side of the busy highway, and then repeatedly attempted to get it to start, but to no avail. She had run out of gas.

It was then that Damon drove by. According to Damon, the voice of the Devil told him that this woman was to be the sacrifice that He required. Damon pulled up and offered to help.

Damon had been hearing the voice of the Devil since late childhood, beginning when he, along with his highly religious family, were living on a huge ranch owned by his grandparents, located in the heavily forested and mountainous regions of the Northern California, Nevada border. His aunt and uncle, and several of his cousins also lived on the ranch, in their own cabins.

Damon was perceived by other family members as strange and odd. At times he seemed withdrawn and preoccupied, and at other times he became strangely mystical and self-confident and had a look in his eyes that frightened people. Throughout his life people would comment on the intensity of his eyes. His personality seemed to rapidly change, and at times he acted as if he were two different people. Sometimes he would talk to people that no one else could see.

Damon was also experimenting with voodoo and devil worship, and would frequently talk about demons and black magic at home and at high school. He claimed to hear the devil's voice and claimed he could read other peoples thoughts. He made several voodoo dolls which he would use to hurt people, one of which depicted a bully from school. His school mates tended to avoid him, except this bully, an older boy in the 12th grade, who would delight in teasing him.

According to investigative records, years later Damon sought revenge against this particular tormentor. He took the bully's picture from their highschool yearbook, created a special voodoo doll, and repeatedly casts spells and called upon the Devil to destroy him. Coincidentally this bully is reported to have stabbed and killed his pregnant wife, finally turning the knife upon himself. He claimed to have been possessed by the devil.

Damon's only friend was his pretty little cousin, Rose. Damon confided in Rose, told her about the voices and his power, and induced her to participate in his strange ceremonies. Soon Rose claimed that she too could hear the voices, including the voices of demons and the devil.

Because they spent so much time together, his other cousins would taunt them: "Your babies are going to be deformed... Your babies will be monsters." Likewise, his aunt did not approve of their close relationship. Their relationship thus came to an abrupt end when Rose's mother intervened and forbid further contact. Soon thereafter, cousin Rose and her family moved away.

Damon was enraged. He began practicing voodoo and casting spells on his aunt and uncle. Soon thereafter, his uncle tried to commit suicide, and his aunt began hearing voices. Four suicide attempts later, Damon's uncle complained of hearing voices of demons and killed himself in front of his family. Damon's aunt soon began having similar hallucinations and had to be hospitalized.

Back on the ranch, Damon and his cousin, Rose, were briefly reunited, and she confided in him that she was ill. According to Rose, Damon's face became angry and evil looking. A strange light seemed to shine from his eyes. He said in a scary, deep voice: "You're pregnant," and he acted so threatening that she ran away. Later, she discovered she was in fact pregnant.

In 1977, Damon Wells met a 15 year old girl who claimed to be a witch. Together they performed magic spells and sexual rituals, and practiced mind reading and astral projection, and attempted to communicate with one another while asleep and dreaming.

Damon later claimed that he and this girl captured a young man, wrapped him in chains, and then stabbed him to death as part of a black magic ceremony.

This young woman soon broke off their relationship, and Damon became enraged. According to Damon he began dreaming of killing her and began plotting demonic revenge. A few weeks later, she was brutally raped and savagely murdered. Years later he claimed responsibility for her death.

As noted, Damon joined the Army, and became a motor mechanic. He was stationed on a remote mountain top in an isolated, heavily wooded and mountainous region of Germany.

Damon spent much time hiking in the mountains and discovered an old cave that contained a huge slab of rock, the perfect altar for human sacrifice. According to Damon, the Devil told him in voices and dreams that he must perform human sacrifices here. Damon equipped the cave accordingly, and killed and sacrificed a number of animals including dogs and cats.

However, according to Damon, the Devil kept demanding human sacrifice. As he would hear these demands while awake and dreaming, Damon decided to sacrifice a woman.

During his free time he sometimes traveled to the nearest village and hung out at the local bar looking for victims. However, he insisted they had to have the mark of the devil. According to Damon, he found a prostitute who was perfect and he beguiled her into accompanying him to his car where he savagely beat and knocked her unconscious. Damon claimed that he took her to his cave where he had sex with her and then performed a bloody sacrifice with a knife. Afterwards he said he cut up and discarded the body. The next day, however, he wondered if it was all a dream.

In 1984, Damon was discharged from the Army and moved into the Santa Cruz mountain home of his father. It was there that he discovered a photo of his cousin, Rose. It was a picture of her and her husband and baby. According to Damon, he began brooding over this picture and then created several voodoo dolls which represented Rose and her family. He claims that he practiced voodoo and called upon the devil to destroy her. He states he was so upset and angry, that he repeatedly dreamed of her death, of killing her, her husband, and her baby, with a knife.

Coincidentally, Rose began suffering severe psychiatric problems during this time, and began hearing voices, including the devil's voice which urged her to kill her husband and son. According to Rose, the voice was chanting: "Do it, do it, do it." So she picked up a knife intent on killing her family, and then herself. However, she was so startled when her son said he saw a ghost, that she dropped the knife and was subdued by her husband. She was subsequently hospitalized in a locked psychiatric ward.

One night while driving through the heavily forested Santa Cruz Mountains, Damon claims to have had an encounter with a warlock. Damon claimed that he was compelled, against his will to accompany the man. According to Damon a spell was cast on him and he was taken to a ramshackle cabin in the woods, where he participated with this warlock and several witches in the sacrifice and murder of a baby and its young mother. After the sacrifice, however, the warlock turned his attention to Damon, and raped and sodomized him.

According to Damon, it was after this experience that he began to lose control over the forces of darkness. That is, rather than controlling the demons, he felt he was being controlled by these demons as well as the Devil, and was losing his free will, his very soul. He became so panicked that he called his friend, Steve, who still resided in Germany and cried out "They're out to get me, Steve. They're out to get me." Then he hung up.

According to Damon, it was because these demons and the Devil took control over him, that he went in search of a sacrificial victim on the afternoon of 8/27/84. And it was while listening to the voice of the Devil and hallucinating from the effects of LSD that he came upon the quite attractive, 21 year old Tanya Z. whose car has run out of gas. After introducing himself and offering to help, but then failing to start her car, Damon says he offered her a ride to the nearest phone. Instead, he took her deep into the mountains, attacked her, dragged her body down a heavily wooded mountain side, laid her out sacrificial style upon a large rock, killed her, sexually assaulted her, and then left the dead body lying on the rock.

That evening Tanya's father and fiancee began searching for her. They found only the abandoned car. They contacted the police, who, however, could find no evidence of a crime. There was no body. No blood. No signs of a struggle. Just an abandoned car.

That evening, Damon kept thinking about and visualizing the murder. He says he dreamed of her that night. According to Damon he dreamed of the murder and kept seeing images of the victim who appeared in his dream and would stand and accuse him.

That same night a woman named "Sunshine" had a dream and a vision where she saw and essentially witnessed (that is, in dream time) portions of the murder. "Sunshine" was a nudist and lived in a nudist colony, Lupin Lodge, situated in the Santa Cruz Mountains (and no I did not make this up!). According to "Sunshine" the dead woman, Tanya, appeared in her dreams.

Throughout the ages women have always been thought to be the more intuitive sex, and more closely in touch with the "irrational;" and this in turn is due to her greater social-emotional sensitivity, her more emotional nature, and possibly the fact that the limbic system is sexually differentiated. Indeed, that area associated with emotion, religious experience, and dreaming, the female amygdala, contains neurons which are more numerous and more densely packed than those of the male (Bubenik & Brown, 1973; Nishizuka & Arai, 1981) which in turn enhances their ability to become hyperactivated.

Because of her association with the goddess, and because of her supernatural abilities, the Popes and the Catholic Church proclaimed woman a witch and declared war against women. Indeed, in a series of Papal bulls on sorcery and witchcraft, including the notorious Super illius specula (issued in 1322) and the Bull Summis desiderantes affectibus (issued in 1484), the Catholic Popes not only condemned women in general, but demanded the death of these women due to their propensity for communicating with demons and devils and for her use of dreams and enchantments to destroy men's lives.

In any case, over the next several evenings following the murder Damon was continually beset by visions and horrible nightmares in which Tanya appeared and accused him. He dreamed of the murder over and over.

Over the next several days, as the local media covered the story and friends and others searched for Tanya, Damon was plagued by nightmares of demons, warlocks, and Tanya.

And while Damon was dreaming his nightmares of Tanya Z. Sunshine was also having dreams in which Tanya appeared and in which the entire murder was revealed to her.

According to Sunshine, Tanya showed her the road off highway 17 where Damon had taken her. Tanya then showed Sunshine the spot where Damon had parked his car and attacked her. Next she led Sunshine down a rather steep incline, and then along a trail, and pointed out her body, lying spread eagle on this huge slab of rock.

The next morning, on 9/15/84 Sunshine contacted members of Tanya's family, and led them and the police to the spot Tanya had showed her in the dream. They climbed down the steep incline, and then found the trail. But, there was no body.

That night Sunshine had another dream and this time Tanya took her to the same spot, down the same trail, then pointed at and emphasized a little trail that forked off to the right and which led directly to the body. The next day, Sunshine and the family searched again, climbed down the incline, and took the trail to the right, where they found Tanya's body which was laid out exactly as revealed to Sunshine when dreaming. The police and media swarm to the scene.

The murder remained unsolved, however, until 2/7/88 when Damon Wells, beset by horrible nightmares, sought psychiatric treatment. He confessed in a desperate attempt to find redemption in confession and judgment, so as to escape the dreams and visions which tormented him.

JUDGMENT DAY AND THE SECOND DEATH

There are a variety of conditions which can hyperactive the limbic system, including death. The anticipation of death, the terror and dread of impending death, are also made possible by the limbic system. The limbic system can anticipate, and it can feel fear and anxiety in response to the unknown.

Archaics, Neanderthal, Cro-Magnon, and peoples of the Neolithic practiced mortuary rituals because they could also see beyond death, beyond one's personal demise, which is why these earthen graves contained tools, food, and ornaments. The souls of the dead would need these items in the next world.

The dead, therefore, were believed to survive the experience of dying. It was believed that they would retain a personal identity, in the form of a personal soul, which would ascend to the heavens and join the abode of the spirits and the gods.

The ancients were exceedingly concerned about what happened after death, and what trials and tribulations they may experience in the hereafter. And they worried about evil spirits, and the behavior of those souls who when alive had committed evil on Earth.

To protect the living, the enemy dead were sometimes decapitated, their hands and legs removed, and their eyes sewn shut and faces smashed, so that their souls would be unable to rise from the dead and cause mischief in the afterlife. In this regard, the ancients did not necessarily believe that every soul would immediately ascend to heaven, but may remain tethered to the earth below.

Those souls that remain earth bound were often believed to be evil spirits, undeserving of a place among the gods. As detailed in the Egyptian and Tibetan Books of the Dead, however, it was also believed that some souls could lose their way, and thus remained earthbound.

Yet others, such as the priesthood of the Roman Catholic Church, believed that souls almost never immediately ascended to heaven. Instead, the souls of the dead were believed to spend at least part of eternity in a realm called purgatory.

PURGATORY

Some conceive "purgatory" as a spirit-like world that exists between this reality and the reality of God. During the middle ages many Catholic theologians came to believe that the length of time a soul might remain in purgatory would depend on the nature and extent of their sins. Purgatory was like a jail sentence, and once sufficient punishment had been doled out, the soul was free to ascend to heaven.

Likewise, some of those of the Buddhist faith believed "that at death, the self, the Atman, departs to another world, where it works out the consequences of its karma. Some of these worlds were pleasant, others were hells where retribution was suffered for evil deeds. When the consequences of its karma was worked out, the self was reincarnated (Brandon, 1967, p.171).

Others of the Christian faith, however, also came to believe that upon death the soul merely goes to sleep; that sleep is the fate of the soul following death until a second awakening at the time of the final judgment.

According to John Calvin "the souls of the faithful, after completing their term of combat and travail, are gathered into rest, where they await with joy the fruition of their promised glory; and thus all things remain in suspense until Jesus Christ appears as the Redeemer."

The Koran endorses certain aspects of this view, such that the dead will have no knowledge of the time that has elapsed since their death. And when these soul awake to experience judgment day, they will think they have just awakened from sleep. Hence, the soul was believed to be unconscious while the body decayed, and is awakened by the trumpet heralding the last judgment.

The ancients, however, believed that the soul could depart the body during sleep, and that death was the final liberation of the soul. The soul did not sleep. Again, the soul could remain earth bound and observe all that took place below, or ascend to heaven where it would be embraced by the light.

However, as pointed out by the Egyptian and Tibetan Books of the Dead, the soul might also be embraced by darkness, or they may lose their way and could be harried for all eternity by demons and devilish monstrosities in the darkness of the underworld.

SUBTERRANEAN HELL

As the dead were buried in the earth, it was believed by some that the soul may descend into the earth womb, into the subterranean realms of the spirits and gods of the dead.

The ancient Greeks believed that at death and with the dissolution of the unity of the body, thymos—the conscious self— was released into the air, and psyche —the life principle— was transformed into a wraith, a shadowy image of the living person, known as the eidolon. It was the life principle, psyche, which descended into Hades, which was a huge subterranean pit deep beneath the ground. There the life principle became a wraith, and existed with other eidolons, but devoid of self-consciousness in a state of perpetual and eternal gloom.

Figure 49. *Devils and demons. 17th century.*

Greek thought was in some respects basically identical to that of the Sumerians, Akkadians, Baby-lonians, and Israelites who believed that the spirits of all the dead dwelled for all eternity in a dreary, lightless, subterranean abode. According to the Sumerians and Akkadians death involved a horrible transformation where the dead became a diseased, decaying, grisly being which descended to the underworld, "the land of no return."

According to the Hebrews, this terrible realm of darkness was called She'ol.

She'ol, was where kings and peasants, rich and poor, good and evil, existed in a state of equal and horrible wretchedness. Hades and the Hebrew She'ol are identical. The good and the wicked, rich and poor, kings and peasants, all descended into hell and assumed this wraith-like existence in the realm of the dead.

Yet others preached that only the evil go to this subterranean hell. The righteous, the just, and the good, ascend to heaven and live in bliss for all eternity. However, if one went to heaven or hell depended on how one had lived their life, and how they were judged by the gods.

JUDGMENT DAY

Figure 50. *(Above) Sinners cast into hell (Blake). Jesus presiding over the judgement of those cast into hell (by Hans Memlinc).*

Some souls would go to heaven, others would spend eternity in hell. The determination of which soul would go where, thus gave rise to the concept of being judged. The nature of one's afterlife depended on how one was judged and the nature of one's good and evil deads. Death, therefore, also became a final judgment day where the wicked were punished, and the good rewarded with eternal heavenly bliss.

We do not know if the Cro-Magnon believed in hell or a final judgment. The ancient Sumerians, Babylonians, and Egyptians, as well as the ancient peoples of the Indus valley, and ancient China clearly believed that a final judgment awaited man after death.

For example, in the Rig-Veda we are told that the good are invited to live in heaven, whereas the wicked are hurled by the deities Soma and Indra into an eternally dark prison from whence their is no return.

According to the ancient Egyptians, the woman and man who respected and maintained maat—that is, truth, justice, and righteousness—would achieve a state of eternal beatitude, whereas those who did not could expect to suffer in a dreary Hellish underworld where the enemies of the sun god Ra would burn for all eternity—roasted by the burning rays of the sun. Indeed, most of these ideas were laid out in considerable detail in the Egyptian Book of the Dead, the Pyramid Texts.

The Pyramid Texts were composed and compiled by the priests of Heliopolis, to help the dead pharaohs achieve eternal bliss in the afterlife. Only the morally just could expect to enter heaven. Nevertheless, the dead, both good and evil, would have to defend themselves against every accusation. Life in the afterworld could be easily imperiled by accusations of those who had been wronged.

Yet, in ancient Egypt, it was believed that the chief accuser would be memory, the dead's own memories, and the dead's own heart would recount and remember their good or evil deeds. Indeed, it would be hell to be plagued for all eternity by every bad memory and all associated feelings of guilt and psychic pain.

This same belief is recounted in the Tibetan Book of the Dead: "You are now before Yama, King of the Dead. The mirror in which Yama seems to read your past is your own memory, and also his judgment is your own. It is you yourself who pronounces your own judgment, which in turn determines your rebirth."

However, whereas the Tibetan Buddhists believed that the souls of the dead passed judgment on themselves, the ancient Egyptians believed that the Great God Osiris would pass judgment. Osiris, would hold and weigh the scales of justice.

Figure 51. *The Archangel Michael weighing the souls of the dead. Detail from the Last Judgement (by Hans Memlinc.)*

Figure 52. *Anubis, Egyptian God of the Dead (top), weighing the souls of the dead (bottom).*

Figure 53. *Ani and his wife Thuthu entering the Hall of Judgement.*

***Figure 54**. Anubis testing the balance upon which sits a feather (right) and the heart (in container, left).*

Figure 55. *Thoth recording the judgement. The Devourer of the dead crouches behind him.*

Figure 56. *Horus leading Ani into the presence of Osiris.*

Figure 57. *Ani kneeling before the thron of Osiris (next page).*

Figure 58. *Osiris upon his throne. Behind him are the gods Isis and Nephyths.*

JUDGMENT

The Great God of the ancient Egyptians did not pass judgment alone, for in this he was assisted by a council of 12, a tribunal of the Great God. As detailed in the Book of the Dead, the jackal-headed god of death, Anubis, adjusts the scales of justice which will determine one's fate; to his right stands Thoth, the ibis-headed god of wisdom—the divine scribe who records the final verdict. And behind Osiris crouches a horrible hybrid monster, the eater of the dead.

"The council which judges the deficient, thou knowest that they are not lenient on the day of judging the miserable, the hour of doing their duty. It is woe when the accuser is one of knowledge. Do not trust in length of years, for they regard a lifetime as but an hour. A man remains after death, and his deeds are placed beside him in heaps. However, existence yonder is for eternity, and he who complains of it is a fool. But as for him who reaches it without wrongdoing, he shall exist yonder like a god, stepping out freely like the lords of eternity." -Egyptian Book of the Dead.

Not only is it futile for the guilty to proclaim their innocence, but the consequences, the manner in which the balance sways depends on one's own heart and memories, which will testify against the dead. According to the ancient Egyptians, the heart will be laid upon the scales and weighed against the lightness of a feather and balanced against Maat; Maat being truth.

"Thou cannot protect thyself from the god of mysterious form, whose two eye brows are the two arms of the balance, who can cast his lasso over the wicked and toss him into the abyss, who annihilates souls, in that day evil is assessed, in the presence of the Master of All." -Egyptian Book of the Dead.

Chapters 30 and 125 of the Book of the Dead are particularly concerned about this post-mortem trial and judgment and the weighing of the heart and one's good and evil deeds, against truth, Maat. It is also pointed out, however, that even if one has been a sinner, if the good outweighs the evil, salvation would be at hand, for it could be expected that "the offenses of which thou art accused will be eliminated, thy fault wiped out by the balancing of the balance, in the day of the evaluation of qualities; thou causes the weighing to be made as Thoth." -Egyptian Book of the Dead.

As noted, according to the ancient Egyptians the final judgment is listed into a book. Jewish, Christian and Islamic faith also involves a book in which the final judgment is listed.

"And I saw the dead, great and small, standing before the throne, and books were opened. Also another book was opened, which is the book of life. And the dead were judged by what was written in the books, by what they had done." -R.S.V. 10:11-15.

However, according to the ancient Hebrews, a sinner might have his name erased from the book: "who ever sins against me, I will blot out of my book." —Exodus 33:33. And with this erasure, by having one's name blotted out, the soul of the dead would be condemned for all eternity, forgotten, never to be remembered even by the Lord God.

THE LIFE REVIEW: HEART OF A MEMORY

The notion of being judged and a weighing of one's sins is a common belief that recurs throughout history. The ancient Chinese, although practicing ancestor worship, also believed that sinners would roast in hell. The souls of the ancient Chines were judged by officials of the underworld which was comprised of 10 tribunals. The soul would typically kneel before these judges next to whom would stand officers with books with the records against which the soul would be judged.

Similar beliefs were held by the ancient Greeks. For example, after Odysseus met with the ghost of Achilles in Hades he states that: "I saw Minos, the glorious son of Zeus, golden scepter in hand, giving judgment to the dead from his seat, while they sat and stood about the king through the wide-gated house of Hades."

According to the ancient Egyptians, the chief prosecutor and the witness against the accused, would be the accused themselves. That is, the dead, their heart, would be forced to testify against themselves. Memories, both good and bad, would be recalled involuntarily. That is, the dead would undergo a life review.

Hence, in pictures of judgment day, we see that on the scales rest the hieroglyphic sign of the heart, the ib, and a feather. And before the balance stands the dead. If the dead soul has lived a righteous life, his heart will detail his good deeds which are then weighed against truth. If he has done evil, he implores his heart not to witness against him. He struggles not to remember. But to no avail.

Death, to the ancients, therefore, involved a life review, where one's memories are recalled and one's life is judged on the scale of good and evil, on the balance of truth.

Although we now know that the amygdala, in conjunction with the hippocampus becomes particularly active when recalling personal and emotional memories (Halgren, 1992; Heath, 1964; Penfield & Perot, 1963), the ancients believed these memories were stored in the heart which served as one's conscience. Whereas we localized the transmitter of god to the limbic system, the ancient Egyptians believed that the heart was "the god which is in man." On the other hand, the amygdala directly affects cardiovascular functioning and thus the beating of the heart.

The ancient Egyptians experienced a considerable degree of apprehension about judgment day and the fact that their hearts would witness against them. The Egyptians were painfully aware that they might be condemned to the hell of eternally by their own evil memories. These same concerns also appear in the Tibetan Book of the Dead.

"You are now before Yama, King of the Dead. In vain will you try to lie, and to deny or conceal the evil deeds you have done. The Judge holds up before you the shinning mirror of Karma, wherein all your deeds are reflected. But again you have to deal with dream images, which you yourself have made, and which you project outside, without recognizing them as your own work. The mirror in which Yama seems to read your past is your own memory, and also his judgment is your own. It is you yourself who pronounces your own judgment, which in turn determines your rebirth." -Tibetan Book of the Dead.

The weighing of the heart and undergoing a final judgment is not shared by all religions. However, judgment day has been a common belief among many different religions since the Neolithic, including Christian, Greek, Roman, Christian and the apocryphal writings of the Jews:

"The spirits of the dead shall be separated. A division has been made for the spirits of the righteous, in which there is a bright spring of water. And such has been made for sinners when they die and are buried in the earth and judgment. Here their spirits shall be set apart in great pain."-Book of Enoch

THE SECOND DEATH

"So I prophesied as I was commanded: and as I prophesied, there was a noise, and behold, a rattling; and the bones came together, bone to its bone. And as I looked, there were sinews on them, and flesh had come upon them, and skin had covered them; but there was no breath in them. Then he said to me, Prophesy to the breath, prophesy, son of man, and say to the breath, Thus says the Lord God: Come from the four winds, O breath, and breathe upon these slain, that they may live. So I prophesied as he commanded me, and the breath came into them, and they lived, and stood upon their feet, an exceedingly great host." -Ezekial.

Yahweh, Ezekial tell us, has the power to resurrect the dead, to join together even disarticulated bones, and turn them into human bodies, giving them life. This is the second life after death. And there is a second death that awaits all sinners.

"Then Raphael answered, one of the holy angels who was with me, and said unto me: These hollow places have been created for this very purpose, that the spirits of the souls of the dead should assemble therein, ye that all the souls of the children of men should assemble here. And these places have been made to receive them till the day of their judgment and till the appointed time period till the judgment comes upon them."-Book of Enoch

In later Vedic literature, including the Brahmanas, we are told of a second death. All souls would suffer a penalty that would be paid in the form of dying again and again, possibly for all eternity. This is called samsara, the transmigration of the soul. Thus according to the ancient peoples of the Indus Valley, after one dies, they could suffer a second death, and then a third death, and so on, for all eternity, each subsequent life determined by one's character and behavior in previous lives.

Although the Greeks thought it possible to achieve a state of blissed eternal beatitude, they also believed that some souls fall from their primal state of beatitude and undergo a series of incarnations, beginning in insect or bestial form, and that they then have to live and die ten thousand deaths before regaining a human state. Only enlightened souls can escape this endless cycle of birth and death.

According to the Jewish and modern Christian faiths, the dead also suffer a second death, which may be more horrible than the first. That is, after the soul awakens from purgatory: "The Son of man will send his angels, and they will gather out of his kingdom all causes of sin and all evildoers, and throw them into the furnace of fire; there men will weep and gnash their teeth. Then the righteous will shine like the sun in the kingdom of their father." -R.S.V. 13:41-43.

"Then I saw a great white throne and him who sat upon it; from his presence earth and sky fled away, and no place was found for them. And I saw the dead, great and small, standing before the throne, and books were opened. Also another book was opened, which is the book of life. And the dead were judged by what was written in the books, by what they had done. And the sea gave up the dead in it. Death and Hades gave up the dead in them, and all were judged by what they had done. Then Death and Hades were thrown into the lake of fire. This is the second death, the lake of fire; and if any one's name was not found written in the book of life, he was thrown into the lake of fire." -R.S.V. 10:11-15.

"The cowardly, the faithless, the polluted, murderers, fornicators, sorcerers, idolaters, and all liars, their lot shall be the lake that burns with fire and brimstone, which is the second death." -Revelation of St. John, II:184, 4356-457.

"Do you not know that the unrighteous will not inherit the kingdom of God? Do not be deceived; neither the immoral, nor idolaters, no adulterers, nor homosexuals, nor thieves, nor the greedy, nor drunkards, nor revivlers, nor robbers, will inherit the kingdom of God."-Paul, Galatians, V 22-23.

And yet, there is a second salvation.

Idolaters, adulterers, homosexuals, thieves, the greedy, drunkards, revivlers, and robbers... And such were some of you! But you were washed, you were sanctified, you were justified in the name of the Lord Jesus Christ and in the Spirit of our god." -Paul, Galatians, V 22-23.

Hence, it was also believed possible to escape the second death if one had lived a life free of sin, or if one repented for their sinful ways. And this same belief is held by those of the Hindu and Buddhist faith. That is, if the consequences of one's Karma could be worked out by the self, the Atman before the next reincarnation, the soul would not have to be born again only to die again and yet again.

As to those who failed to work out the consequences of their Karma, or those who had lived a life of the utmost evil, their lot would become an eternal hell.

HELL: JUDGMENT AND PUNISHMENT

Although the Sumerians and ancient Hebrews and Greeks initially believed that both good and evil, rich and poor, would descend to hell, some also believed that She'ol, Hades, and Hell, were places of judgment, where punishments were doled out to the wicked.

"Upon the termination of life they were brought to trial; and, according to their sentence, some go to prison-houses beneath the earth, to suffer for their sins, while others, by virtue of their trial, are borne lightly upwards to some celestial spot, where they pass their days in a manner worthy of the life they lived." -Plato, Phaedrus.

In ancient Chinese religion, the realm of the dead was believed to consist of seven Hells where the evil would roast for all eternity. Likewise, in ancient Egypt, Greece, the Middle East, and Catholic Rome, punishment for the wicked, for the enemies of god, became eternal hell fire and all manner of demonic horrors.

"And I" the Apostle Peter "saw also another place very squalid; and it was a place of punishment, and they that were punished and the angels that punished them had their raiment dark, according to the air of the place. And some there were hanging by their tongues; and those were they that blasphemed the way of righteousness, and under them was laid fire flaming and tormenting them... and there were others, women, hanged by their hair above that mire which boiled up; and these were they that adorned themselves for adultery... And in another place were gravel-stones sharper than swords or any spit, heated with fire, and men and women clad in filthy rages rolled upon them in torment... and others being cast down from a great precipice to the rocks below..."

"For those who have disbelieved... shall roast in fire... and their bellies and skin shall be melted. To them it is said: Taste the punishment of the Burning." -Koran

-7-

AFTER-DEATH,OUT-OF-BODY, ASTRAL PROJECTION

The Book of the Dead

"The Book of the Dead" is the title given to the great collection of mortuary texts, also referred to as Pyramid texts, which the ancient Egyptian theologians composed for the benefit of the dead. However, they were first called the "book of the dead" or "a dead man's book" by tomb robbers, as these texts were commonly found in the dead man's coffin. By the sixth Dynasty, the common name for the Book of the Dead was "manifested in the light" or "embraced by the light."

According to E.A. Wallis Budge, Late Keeper of the Egyptian and Assyrian Antiquities of the British Museum, these texts were already quite ancient by the rise of the first dynasty, over 6,000 years ago, as even the predynastic Egyptians "were quite certain that men did not perish when they died, but that some part of a man departed after death to some place where he would renew his life in some form, according to the dictates of some divine being" (Budge, 1994, p. 4).

According to the Book of the Dead, at death the spirit-soul of the deceased would arise from the body, and although translucent and transparent to the living, this spirit-soul would at first hover above and look upon the body and could see and hear what was taking place below (chapter CLXXVII). The spirit-soul may then depart, only to return to visit the body (e.g. chapter LXXXIX: The Soul Visiting the Body which Lies on a Bier), sometimes even reanimating the body (chapter XCII), such that the dead might live again in this world.

Like their Paleolithic predecessors, the walls of all Egyptian tombs and all but three of the hundreds of pyramids that dot the land, were graced with paintings of all manner of animal life and realistic scenes of the every day life to which they were accustomed. And within these tombs dwelled the ka, a spirit-like force which resided in a ka-statue of the dead person. These statues were exact replicas of the dead, that is, when they were alive.

It was the ba, the soul of the dead, which the Egyptians believed ascended to heaven. The ba would sometimes be depicted in flight, as a human-headed bird. Upon entering heaven the dead achieved the status of an akh—a "glorified being" that had reached completeness of attainment.

However, as detailed in the Egyptian Book of the Dead, prior to entering heaven (Anu), the spirit-soul of the deceased might "fly through the air" (chapter XCII) "pass over the earth" (chapter IV), such that it could move freely from place to place, before entering a tunnel or realm of darkness, and then arising into the sky to the abode of the gods in heaven at which point they bask in "a shining, glorious light" (Budge, 1994).

Similarly, according to Book I, of the Bardo, Tibetan Book of the Dead, following death the deceased will be enveloped with a "Clear Light" of "Wisdom and the Knower will experience the shining, dazzling, glorious, Radiance of the Clear light of Pure Reality, the All Good. Thine own consciousness, shining, void, and inseparable from the Great Body of Radiance, hath no birth, nor death, and is the Immutable Light—Buddha Amitabha."

Likewise, according to the Egyptian Book of the Dead, the soul ascends into the sky to the abode of the gods in heaven at which point the dead bask in "a shining, glorious light" and are led into the presence of dead relatives and brethren, and finally to the divine being Osiris, who is said to have made "men and women to be born again" and where they then dwell in bliss for all eternity having achieved everlasting life: "My soul is God. My soul is eternity" (Budge, 1994).

It is noteworthy that the soul, at first, usually does not know it is dead, that the body has died. According to the Tibetan Book of the Dead: "When the consciousness-principle gettest outside the body, it sayeth to itself, Am I dead, or am I not dead? It cannot determine. It can see that the body is being stripped of its garments. It seeth its relatives and heareth the weepings and wailings of friends and relatives, and although it seeth them and heareth them calling upon him, they seeth him not."

OUT-OF-BODY AND AFTER-DEATH EXPERIENCES

The notion of a soul leaving the body following death is a common belief among almost all religions. Again, some believe that the soul may fall asleep, whereas others believe it will either ascend to heaven or descend into hell. And, as noted, we are also told that the soul of the dead may linger upon the Earth, may remain tethered to the body, or may even return to visit the dead body, sometimes hovering above it, and in rare instances, somehow reanimating the body, such that the dead come back to life.

Likewise, among modern day people, some children and adults who have been declared "clinically" dead have returned to life. And many of those who subsequently return to life, have reported that after "dying" they left their body and floated above the scene (Eadie 1992; Rawling 1978; Ring 1980). And, at first, many do not realize they are dead.

According to modern accounts, typically they become increasingly euphoric as they float above their body, after which they may float away, become enveloped in a dark tunnel and then enter a soothing radiant light. And later, when they come back to life, they may even claim conscious knowledge of

Figure 59. *Jesus. The Ascension.*

what occurred around their body while they were dead and floating nearby.

"Lisa" for example, was a 22 year old college coed with no religious background or spiritual beliefs, who was badly injured in an auto accident when the windshield collapsed and all but completely severed her arm. According to Lisa, when she got out of the car her was blood spraying everywhere and she only walked a few feet before collapsing. Apparently an ambulance arrived in just a few minutes. However, the next thing she noticed was that part of the time she was looking up from the ground, and part of the time she was up in the air looking down. From above she could see the ambulance crew working, picking up her body, placing it on a gurney and into the ambulance.

According to Lisa, during the entire ride to the hospital it was like she was half in and half out of the ambulance, as if she were running along outside or just extending out of the vehicle watching the cars and trees go by. When they got to the hospital she was no longer attached to her body but was floating up and down the halls, watching the doctors and nurses and attendants. One doctor in particular drew her attention because he had a big belt buckle with his name written on it. She could even read it and it said "Mike."

According to Lisa, she was "tripping out, bobbing up and down the halls, just checking everything out" when she noticed a girl lying on a gurney with several doctors and nurses working frantically. When she floated over and peered over the shoulder of one of the doctors to take a look she suddenly realized the girl was her and that her hair and face were very bloody and needed to be washed. At that point she realized she was floating well above her body and the doctors, and that she looked to be "dead." However, according to Lisa she did not feel afraid or upset, although the fact that her hair was bloody and dirty bothered her.

She soon floated up and outside the Emergency room and was enveloped in a total blackness, "like I was passing through a tunnel at the end of which was a light which became brighter and more brilliant, radiating outward." The light soon enveloped her body which made her feel exceedingly happy and very warm. A few moments later she heard the voice of her grandmother who had died when Lisa was a young girl. Although Lisa had no memory of this grandmother, she nevertheless recognized her and felt exceedingly happy. However, her grandmother very sorrowfully told her it was "too soon" she would have to "go back." Lisa didn't want to go back, but had no choice. She was drawn away from the light and felt herself falling only to land with a painful thump in her own body. At this point she moved her hand which alerted one of the emergency room staff that Lisa was no longer dead.

It is noteworthy that Lisa had no religious training and had never heard of "near death experiences" (she was injured in 1982). After returning to life she only reluctantly explained what had happened when she was questioned by one of her doctors.

Lisa also claimed that while she was dead and floating about the emergency room that she saw, heard and upon coming back to life was able to recall everything that occurred in the emergency room up to the point when she was enveloped in darkness. She was able to accurately describe "Mike" (who in fact wore a belt buckel engraved with "Mike"), most of the staff who attended her, as well as the conversations that occurred around her as well as some of the other patients.

Similar "after death" claims of leaving and floating above the body, and seeing everything occurring below, are common (Eadie 1992; Moody 1977; Rawling 1978; Ring 1980; Sabom 1982; Wilson 1987), and, as noted, are even reported in the 6,000 year old Egyptian Book of the Dead (Budge 1994), as well as the Tibetan Book of the Dead (the Bardo Thodol) which was composed over 1,300 years ago (Evans-Wentz 1960). Approximately 37% of patients who are resuscitated report "out of body" experiences (Ring 1980).

Consider for example, the case of Army Specialist J. C. Bayne of the 196th Light Infantry Brigade. Bayne was "killed" in Chu Lai, Vietnam, in 1966. He was simultaneously machine gunned and struck by a mortar. According to Bayne, when he opened his eyes he was floating in the air, looking down on his crumpled, burnt, and bloody body, and he could see a number of Vietcong who were searching and stripping him:

"I could see me... it was like looking at a mannequin laying there... I was burnt up and there was blood all over the place... I could see the Vietcong. I could see the guy pull my boots off. I could see the rest of them picking up various things... I was like a spectator... It was about four or five in the afternoon when our own troops came. I could hear and see them approaching... I could see me... It was obvious I was burnt up. I looked dead... they put me in a bag... transferred me to a truck and then to the morgue. And from that point, it was the embalming process."

"I was on that table and a guy was telling a couple of jokes about those USO girls... all I had on was bloody undershorts... he placed my leg out and made a slight incision and stopped... he checked my pulse and heartbeat again and I could see that too...It was about that point I just lost track of what was taking place… [until much later] when the chaplain was in there saying everything was going to be all right… I was no longer outside. I was part of it at this point" (reported in Wilson, 1987, pp 113-114; and Sabom, 1982, pp 81-82).

Some surgery patients, although ostensibly "unconscious" due to anesthesia, are also able to later describe conversations and related events that occurred during the operation (Furlong, 1990; Kilhstrom, et al. 1990; Polster, 1993). Hence, the notion that those who are "clinically dead" or near death may also recall various events that occurred while they were ostensibly "dead" should not be dismissed out of hand. Moreover, some surgery patients also claim to "leave their bodies" while they were "unconscious" and claim to recall seeing not just the events occurring below, but in one case, dirt on top of a light fixture (Ring 1980). "It was filthy. And I remember thinking, 'Got to tell the nurses about that."

Did the above surgical patient or Lisa or Army Specialist Bayne really float above and observe their bodies and the events taking place below? Or did they merely transpose what they heard (e.g. conversations, noises, etc.) and then visualize, imagine, or hallucinate an accompanying and plausible scenario? This seems likely, even in regard to the "filthy" light fixture. On the other hand, not all those who have an "out of body" hear conversations, voices, or even sounds. Rather, they may be enveloped in silence.

"I was struck from behind...That's the last thing I remember until I was above the whole scene viewing the accident. I was very detached. Everything was very quiet. This was the amazing thing about it to me...I could see my shoe which was crushed under the car and I thought: Oh no. My new dress is ruined... I don't remember hearing anything. I don't remember anybody saying anything. I was just viewing things...like I floated up there..." (Sabom, 1982; p. 90).

Moreover, even individuals born blind experience these "near death" hallucinations. And although blind, while dead they will see for the first time.

However, whereas many who experience life after death find the experience exhilarating, others respond with feelings of extreme dread and terror. Death is not a pleasant experience.

FEAR AND OUT-OF-BODY EXPERIENCES

The prospect of being terribly injured or killed in an auto accident or fire fight between opposing troops, or even dying during the course of surgery, are often accompanied by fear. It is also not uncommon for individuals who experience terror to report perceptual and hallucinogenic experiences, including dissociation, depersonalization and the splitting off of ego functions. They may feel as if they have separated from their bodies and floated away, or were on the ceiling looking down (Campbell 1988; Courtois 1995; Grinker and Spiegel 1945; James 1958; Neihardt and Black Elk 1932/1989; Noyes and Kletti 1977; Parson 1988; Southard 1919; Terr1990). Consider the following accounts:

"The next thing I knew I wasn't in the truck anymore; I was looking down from 50 to 100 feel in the air." "I had a clear image of myself... as though watching it on a television screen." "I had a sensation of floating. It was almost like stepping out of reality. I seemed to step out of this world" (Noyes and Kletti 1977).

Or as a close friend described his experience:

"I was shooting down the freeway doing about 100 or more in my Mustang when a Firebird in the middle lane up ahead suddenly cut me off. As I switched lanes to avoid him, he also switched lanes at which point I hit the breaks and began to lose control. The Mustang began to slide and spin... I felt real terror... I was probably going to be killed... I was trying to control the Mustang and avoid turning over, or hitting any of the surrounding cars or the guard rail... time seemed to slow down and then I suddenly realized that part of my mind was a few feet outside the car looking all around; zooming above it and then beside it and behind it and in front of it, looking at and analyzing the respective positions of my spinning Mustang and the cars surrounding me. Simultaneously I was inside trying to steer and control it in accordance with the multiple perspectives I was suddenly given by that part of my mind that was outside. It was like my mind split and one consciousness was inside the car, while the other was zooming all around outside and giving me visual feedback that enabled me to avoid hitting anyone or destroying my Mustang."

HIPPOCAMPAL PLACE NEURONS: ASTRAL PROJECTION

Feelings of fear and terror are mediated by the amygdala, whereas the capacity to cognitively map, or visualize one's position and the position of other objects and individuals in visual-space is dependent on the hippocampus (Nadel, 1991; O'Keefe, 1976; Wilson and McNaughton, 1993).

The hippocampus contains "place" neurons which are able to encode one's position, place, and movement in space. Specifically, O'Keefe, Nadel, and colleagues, found that hippocampal pyramidal cells were able to become attuned to specific locations within the environment, as well as to particular objects and their location in that environment, thereby creating cognitive maps of visual space. Moreover, they discovered that as the subject moves about in that environment, entire populations of cells would fire but only when in a particular spot, whereas other cells would fire when in a different location.

Some cells respond not just when moving about, but in reaction to the speed of movement, or when turning in different directions. Moreover, some cells are responsive to the movements of other people in that environment and will fire as that person is observed to move around (Nadel, 1991; O'Keefe, 1976; Wilson and McNaughton, 1993).

The hippocampus, therefore, can create a cognitive map of an individual's environment and their movements and the movement of others within it. Presumably it is via the hippocampus that an individual can visualize themselves as if looking at their body from afar, and can remember and thus see themselves engaged in certain actions, as if one were an outside witness (Joseph, 1996, 1998b, 1999b, 2000a).

Under conditions of hyperactivation (such as in response to extreme fear) it appears that the hippocampus may create a visual hallucination of that "cognitive map" such that the individual may "experience" themselves as outside their body, observing all that is occurring and/or hallucinate themselves as moving about in that environment such as flying above it.

In fact, it has been repeatedly demonstrated that hyperactivation or electrical stimulation of the amygdala-hippocampus-temporal lobe, can cause some individuals to report they have left their bodies and are hovering upon the ceiling staring down (Daly 1958; Jackson and Stewart 1899; Joseph, 1996; Penfield 1952; Penfield and Perot 1963; Williams 1956). That is, their ego and sense of personal identity appears to split off from their body, such that they may feel as if they are two different people, one watching from above, the other being observed down below.

As described by Penfield (1952), "it was as though the patient were attending a familiar play and was both the actor and audience."

Presumably abnormal activation due to extreme fear or direct electrical stimulation induces an individual to think they are seeing themselves from afar because the hippocampus is transposing and "hallucinating" one's image; similar to what occurs during normal remembering.

As noted, however, many patients who are diagnosed as "clinically dead" and then return to "life" report that after leaving their body they enter a dark tunnel and are then enveloped in a soothing radiant light. The same is reported in the Egyptian and Tibetan Books of the Dead.

Presumably, in that the hippocampus, amygdala, and inferior temporal lobe receive direct and indirect visual input and contain neurons sensitive to the fovea and upper visual fields, hyperactivation of this region also induces the sensation of seeing a radiant light. The massive release of opiates (due to physical trauma leading to "death") would account for the immediate loss of fear and the experience of tranquillity and joy. Continued activation of these brain regions would also account for the hallucinations of seeing dead relatives, that are commonly reported by those who have "died," as well as the life review, in which one's past life flashes before their eyes.

At death, the amygdala and hippocampus would begin to remember, and memories that were emotional and personal, and all accompanying emotions, such as guilt, would be experienced as part of death. That is, not just the memory, but the awful feeling of the memory would be reexperienced. These structures, therefore, account for the feeling of floating above the body, the life review, and the judgment imposed on the self by their guilty or guilt-free conscience.

The hyperactivation of these limbic structures, therefore, explains why those who have near death experiences report feelings of peace, rapture and joy as they were "bathed by the light" and stood in the all knowing presence of "God" or other divine beings including friends and relatives who had previously passed away. Indeed, these exact same feelings and experiences can be induced by electrically stimulating the inferior temporal lobe and amygdala-hippocampal complex.

EXPERIMENTAL AND SEIZURE INDUCED OUT-OF-BODY, HEAVENLY AND OTHER WORLDLY EXPERIENCES

Some individuals suffering from temporal lobe epilepsy also report "out of body experiences." Penfield and Perot (1963) describe several patients who during a temporal lobe seizure claimed they could see themselves in different situations. One woman stated that "it was though I were two persons, one watching, and the other having this happen to me," and that it was she who was doing the watching as if she was completely separated from her body.

One patient had a sensation of being outside her body and watching and observing her body from the outside. Another neurosurgery patient alleged that while outside her body she was also overcome by feelings of euphoria and eternal harmony.

Other patients claim to have quite pleasant auras and describe feelings such as elation, security, eternal harmony, immense joy, paradisiacal happiness, euphoria, completeness. Between .5 and 20% of such patients report these feelings (Daly 1958; Williams 1956).

A patient of Williams (1956) claimed that his attacks began with a "sudden feeling of extreme well being involving all my senses. I see a curtain of beautiful colors before my eyes and experience a pleasant but indescribable taste in my mouth. Objects feel pleasurably warm, the room assumes vast proportions, and I feel as if in another world."

A patient described by Daly (1958) claimed his temporal lobe seizure felt like "a sunny day when your friends are all around you." He then felt dissociated from his body, as if he were looking down upon himself and watching his actions.

Williams (1956) describes a patient who during a seizure-induced aura reported that she experienced a feeling of being lifted up out of her body, coupled with a very pleasant sensation of elation and the feeling that she was "just about to find out knowledge no one else shares, something to do with the link between life and death."

Subirana and Oller-Daurelia (1953) described two patients who experienced ecstatic feelings of "extraordinary beatitude" or of paradise as if they had gone to heaven. Their fantastic feelings also lasted for hours.

Other patients suffering from temporal lobe seizures have noted that feelings and things suddenly become "crystal clear" or that they had a feeling of clairvoyance, or of having the truth revealed to them, or of having achieved a sense of greater awareness such that sounds, smells and visual objects seemed to have a greater meaning and sensibility. Similar claims are made by those who have "died" and returned to tell the tale.

One woman I evaluated claimed she not only would float on the ceiling, but could float outside and could see everything that was going on, including on one occasion, a friend who was coming up the walkway. She also reported that by having a certain thought, she could propel herself to other locals including the homes of her neighbors.

EMBRACED BY THE LIGHT

"The heavens were opened and the whole creation which is under heaven shone... I saw a light, and a child in the light... And while I looked he became an old man. And he changed his form again… and I saw... an image with multiple forms in the light." -Apocryphon of John.

Betty J. Eadie reports in her 1992 book, "embraced by the light" that after dying and then communing with three "ancient" men who appeared at her side and who "glowed" she suddenly thought of her husband and children who she wanted to visit. "I began to look for an exit" and discovered that "my spiritual body could move through anything...My trip home was a blur. I began moving at a tremendous speed... and I was aware of trees rushing below me. I just thought of home and knew I was going there... I saw my husband sitting in his favorite armchair reading the newspaper. I saw my children running up and down the stairs... I was drawn back to the hospital, but I don't remember the trip; it seemed to happen instantaneously" (pp. 33-35).

BLACK ELK

Compare Eadie's description with that of Black Elk (Neihardt and Black Elk, 1932/1989), a Lakota Sioux Medicine Man and spiritual leader (born in 1863). During a visit to England (he was part of Buffalo Bills Wild West Show) he suddenly fell out of his chair as if dead, and then experienced himself being lifted up. In fact, his companions thought he had died.

According to Black Elk: "Far down below I could see houses and towns and green land and streams... I was very happy now. I kept on going very fast...Then I was right over Pine Ridge. I looked down (and) saw my father's and mother's teepee. They went outside, and she was cooking... My mother looked up, and I felt sure she saw me... then I started back, going very fast...Then I was lying on my back in bed and the girl and her father and a doctor were looking at me in a queer way...I had been dead three days (they told him)...and they were getting ready to buy my coffin" (pp. 226-228).

This was not Black Elk's first out of body experience, however. Black Elk demonstrated numerous behaviors and symptoms suggestive of temporal lobe epilepsy. Beginning even in childhood Black Elk repeatedly experienced "queer feelings" and heard voices, had visions, and suffered numerous instances of sudden and terrible fear and depression accompanied by weeping, as well as trance states in which he would fall to the ground as if dead.

Black Elk also had other visions similar to those reporting "life-after-death" experiences, including the following incident that occurred during one of his trance and out-of-body states: "Twelve men were coming towards me, and they said, Our father, the two-legged chief, you shall see... There was a man standing. He was not Wasichu (white) and he was not an Indian. While I was staring at him his body began to change and became very beautiful with all colors of light, and around him there was light..." (p. 245).

Similar accounts, including descriptions of a tribunal of 12 are detailed in the Egytian Book of the Dead.

Ms. Eadie (like many others who have experienced "life after death") came upon a man standing in the light which "radiated all around him. As I got closer the light became brilliant...I saw that the light was golden, as if his whole body had a golden halo around it, and I could see that the golden halo burst out from around him and spread into a brilliant, magnificent whiteness that extended out for some distances" (pp. 40-41).

ASTRAL ANTIQUITY

Muhammed reports that while sleeping and dreaming he was lifted into the air and transported by the angel Gabriel from Arabia to the Temple Mount in Jerusalem. There he was greeted by three men, who he believed to be Abraham, Moses, and Jesus, as well as a crowd of other prophets. He was then lifted up and entered a divine sphere and came upon the garden of promise and, according to the Koran, saw a "lote-tree veiled in a veil of nameless splendor."

In Hinduism, the lote tree symbolizes the limit of this reality and rational thought.

St. Augustine reports that he was "lifted up by an ardent affection towards eternal being itself... we climbed beyond all corporate objects and the heaven itself, where sun, moon, and stars shed light on the earth."

Some individuals (and their followers) claim to be able to voluntarily leave their body (Monroe, 1994), this includes any number of "mystics," and New Age spiritualists, as well as some priests, prophets and shaman. Indeed, Monroe (1994) founded an Institute to study this phenomenon, and claims that others can learn this technique. Monroe, however, notes that when he had his first out-of-body experience he had felt extremely frightened.

That so many people, regardless of culture or antiquity, have similar experiences (or hallucinations) while in trance states, or dreaming, or after "dying," of leaving their body, is presumably due to all possessing a limbic system and temporal lobe that is organized similarly.

The fact that although ostensibly similar, many of these experiences are also colored by one's cultural background, can in turn be explained by differences in experience and cultural expectations and thinking patterns. As explained in the Tibetan Book of the Dead: "It is quite sufficient for you (the deceased) to know that these apparitions are [the reflections of] your own thought forms."

DEATH AND THE LIMBIC SYSTEM

Presumably conditions such as dreaming, trance states, depth electrode activation, extreme fear, traumatic injury, or temporal lobe epilepsy, result in hyperactivation of the amygdala and hippocampus and overlying temporal lobe. These structures create an image of the individual floating or even soaring above familiar or bizarre surroundings, and will trigger memories, hallucinations, brilliant lights, as well as secrete opiate-like neurotransmitters which induce a state of euphoria and thus eternal peace and harmony.

Given that similar experiences are reported by those who have experienced depth electrode stimulation of these structures, and by those declared "clinically dead" also raises the possibility that the hippocampus and amygdala may be the first areas of the brain to be effected by approaching death, as well as one of the last regions of the brain to actually die.

That is, as one approaches death and even after medical death, the amygdala and hippocampus may continue to function briefly and not only become hyperactivated, but produce a feeling of eternal peace and tranquillity and a hallucination of floating outside the body and of meeting relatives and other religious figures; like a dream.

On the other hand, it is curious that so many individuals have basically a very similar "dream" and only under conditions of death. Moreover, it is exceedingly difficult to reconcile these experiences with the Darwinian notion of evolution.

What is the "evolutionary" adaptive significance of so many members of the human race having a dream of the "Hereafter" after they die.

Indeed, as noted, and as will be detailed in a later chapter, this reality is only one of many, and the perception of these alternate realities, and all associated manifestations of extra-ordinary psychic abilities, are normally inhibited and suppressed. Under conditions of hyperactivity, the limbic system may not only hallucinate, it may also begin to process this information, and gain access to and engage in alternate modes of thinking, perceiving, and communicating, such that what is normally concealed is revealed to the receptive mind.

-8-

HELL AND ALIEN ABDUCTIONS

Life after death and near death experience, are in some respects similar to the experience of having undergone an alien abduction. For example, in addition to a feeling of being lifted, enveloped in light, and entering a room of vast proportions, many abductees claim to have undergone a religious theophany at the conclusion of the abduction—as do most of those who die only to return to life (Bullard, 1987; Mack, 1994; Ritchie, 1994). However, just as some who die report that the experience was hellish, so too do many of those who claim to have been abducted.

Many "abductees" also claim a sequence of perceptual experience similar to those who have died and returned to tell the tale. Abductees report the presence of a bright light, or a strange illumination which may envelop them in a beam or halo of light. They feel drawn upward toward the light, and they feel and see themselves as floating in the air (Bullard, 1987; Mack, 1994; Ritchie, 1994).

Similar to those who have "experienced" life after death, abductees report going on voyages through the air, where they rapidly fly over the land or sea, to destinations including the Egyptian pyramids, New York City, and the North pole (Bullard, 1987; Mack, 1994; Ritchie, 1994).

Over the course of the last fifty years there have been numerous reports of alien abductions (Bullard, 1987; Mack, 1994; Ritchie, 1994). Typically they are "abducted" while asleep or dreaming, or just upon wakening in the middle of the night -which raises the specter of hallucination and temporal lobe limbic system activation as these structures become exceedingly active during dream sleep.

Others claim they were abducted while driving late at night, while tired and under conditions where the head lights, moon light, and oncoming lights may flicker past (Bullard, 1987; Mack, 1994; Ritchie, 1994) -thus inducing possible seizure activity.

However, the religious experience of some abductees is often hellish, and the aftermath includes prolonged feelings of depression, and horror and despair. "Abductees" frequently report that once they were drawn up toward the light, they felt overwhelmed with terror and that once they "arrived" they were subjected to painful and agonizing procedures (Bullard, 1987; Mack, 1994; Ritchie, 1994).

Women often report that they were stripped naked and their legs spread, and that they were sexually molested, raped, or painfully probed.

Figure 60. *Alien-devils probing abductees. 17th century woodcut.*

Male and female abductees frequently report undergoing painful and invasive physical exams by alien monstrosities who loom demonically, probing vaginas, wombs, the anus, the eyeballs, and the viscera, with needle-like devices, or with twisting wires, or sharp, painfully cold lance-like instruments that may deliver electric, burning, or shock like sensations (Bullard, 1987; Mack, 1994; Ritchie, 1994).

Like those who experience life after death, some abductees report undergoing a "life review." They may see themselves or others on a viewing screen, usually engaged in sexual or violent activity. Similar sexual flashbacks are not uncommon with direct amygdala stimulation (Gloor, 1990, 1997; Halgren, 1992).

Once they return to earth and/or awake in their beds, many abductees are initially amnesic for the experience, though they may be troubled by fleeting, horrifying images and flashbacks (Bullard, 1987; Mack, 1994; Ritchie, 1994). Likewise, hyperactivation of the hippocampus can induce a temporary amnesia (Joseph, 1998a, 1999b).

They also suffer from depression, sleeplessness, anxiety and panic attacks; which again are suggestive of limbic system and temporal lobe abnormalities as well as post-traumatic stress disorder.

It is noteworthy, however, that some of those who undergo life-after-death also report exceedingly unpleasant experiences. This includes feelings of terror, sensations of terrible physical pain, the presence of demonic monstrosities, or hallucinations of people crying, moaning, screaming, and burning in flames.

"For those who have disbelieved... shall roast in fire... and their bellies and skin shall be melted. To them it is said: Taste the punishment of the burning." -Koran

THE EVOLUTION OF HELL

"Jesus said: There is a light within a man of light, and it lights up the whole world. If he does not shine, he is darkness." -Gospel of Thomas.

In contrast to the light and bliss of "heaven," Hell has commonly been associated with darkness and the underworld. In part, the notion of an underworld is a direct consequence of burial practices, and perhaps the belief that sinners will fail to rise to heaven but instead will be condemned to a bleak existence deep beneath the Earth.

The belief in an underworld where sinners burn in hell, is also related to the worship of the sun as god. That is, during the day the sun god rules the Earth, but each evening it must pass through the underworld where it may be attacked by the demons of darkness. Every night, therefore, the sun god would have to fight these demons, and would do so with the rays of the sun. That is, the sun-god would burn the enemies of god with the fire of the sun's rays. Hence, Hell also became associated with fire, such that, as these beliefs evolved, sinners and enemies of god would be sent to hell where they would not only be attacked by devils and demons, but would burn in flames for all eternity.

The belief in Hell and in demons and devils is world wide and vivid descriptions of a hellish underworld and its demonic denizens are also described in the Egyptian and Tibetan Books of the Dead. Indeed, these books were written so as to inform believers as to the mysteries of death and the trials and tribulations one might experience following death so that demons and other devilish monstrosities and misfortunes might be avoided.

For example, priests or relatives of the recently departed were expected to read various hymns, litanies, magical formula, spells, and incantations from the Egyptian Book of the Dead which would help protect the dead from the multitude of devils and fiends that would seek to devour and destroy the spirit-soul. "These powers of evil had hideous and terrifying shapes and forms, and their haunts infested the region through which the road of the dead lay when passing from this world to the Kingdom of Osiris" (Budge, 1994). Moreover, according to the ancient Egyptians, the gods were basically powerless to protect the souls from these demons which could inflict horrible suffering upon the spirit souls for all eternity.

"Then the Lord of Death will place around thy neck a rope and drag these along; he will cut off thy head, tear out thy heart, pull out thy intestines, lick up thy brain, drink thy blood, eat thy flesh, and gnaw thy bones; but thou will be incapable of dying. Even when the body is hacked to pieces, it will revive again and thy will be tortured for all eternity."-Tibetan Book of the Dead.

However, these evils can also be avoided which is the purpose of these texts. In this regard, these texts actually educate the reader as to "The Art of Dying" so that an undesirable and hellish death can be avoided.

Unfortunately, or so say these texts, many are condemned to Hell for all eternity. According to the Tibetan Book of the Dead, a hellish death is due to the "power of accumulated evil Karma." Likewise, according to the Egyptian Book of the Dead, spirit souls may be judged and condemned to hell for all eternity if they had behaved in an evil and unjust manner when living. Hence, both texts warn of a judgment day and a life review and warn that those who have committed evil acts will be judged, found guilty, and then condemned.

Hence, it can be deduced that by 6,000 years ago, that in addition to a heaven and hell, a moral-religious spiritual conscience and moral-consciousness has evolved. This is reflected by the religious conviction that the just and the unjust would be rewarded and punished in the next world after they had died; their good deeds often weighed against the bad.

As is now well established, a sense of morality and a personal conscience (as in: Let your conscience be your guide) is directly associated with the functional integrity of the frontal lobe (Joseph, 1986a, 1999a). The frontal lobes are concerned with anticipating consequences and serve to inhibit or redirect unacceptable impulses in order to avoid punishment.

It also appears that the frontal lobe had fully evolved and reached its peak levels of development and expansion during the Upper Paleolithic. In this regard, although there is no physical evidence to indicate that Upper Paleolithic peoples had also evolved a moral conscience or a concern that the spirit soul would be punished for past misdeeds, Budge (1994) argues that the Book of the Dead and the beliefs that permeate the pyramid texts, were already quite ancient by the rise of the first Dynasty, and thus have pre-dynastic, and therefore, Upper Paleolithic origins.

It is noteworthy that although the Tibetan (and Egyptian) Book of the Dead warn of a judgment day, and describe all manner of Hellish devils and demons, this text repeatedly reminds the reader that these demonic entities are a product of one's own mind. They are illusions erupting from the depths of the primeval unconscious which is freed of the suppressive restraints of the every day reality and the illusions of this world.

According to this text, different demons and hells are not only associated with the unconscious but issue from specific regions of the brain, including, according to descriptions in these texts, tissue of the mind that appear to be associated with the temporal lobes, the right temporal lobe in particular ("eastern regions of the brain"). That is, when facing north, the frontal lobes are the northern part of the brain, the occipital lobes the southern, and the left and right temporal lobes the western and eastern portions of the brain.

FEAR AND HELLISH DEPRESSION

The temporal lobes consists not only of neocortex, but primary limbic system structures, the amygdala and hippocampus. As repeatedly emphasized, these structures are directly associated with religious and hallucinatory experiences, and with the maintenance of a personal identity and personal emotional memories that possibly may be maintained and reexperienced after death. Moreover, just as exceedingly positive emotions are associated with limbic system activation, exceedingly negative emotions are also commonly triggered following direct activation or seizure activity. These include fear and/or feelings of depression so painful that sufferers contemplate or seek to end their lives to escape the awful misery.

Patients with temporal lobe abnormalities may believe they are the most horrible person on earth, deserving of the worst of punishments—feelings which could conceivably continue after death, such that their after death experience would be hellish.

As noted, according to the Egyptian Book of the Dead, it is one's own heart, one's own personal memories which will testify against the sinner, and this fate, the possibility of being condemned to hell, and burning and suffering miserably for all eternity was greatly feared by these people.

The amygdala is also associated with feelings of fear as this is the most common emotion triggered from seizures or direct stimulation (Davis et al., 1997; Gloor, 1992, 1997; Halgren, 1992; Rose and Schulkin, 1998; Scott et al., 1997; Williams, 1956). Patients may also remember or reexperience horrifying and traumatic memories, as well as rising epigastric sensations, chest sensations, nausea, heart palpations, and feelings of extreme cold or warmth including burning sensations.

Death is frightening, and so too might be the experience of an alien abduction. Both experiences may also be subserved by the same region of the brain, including the torments associated with hell or an alien physical examination.

Fear is also most likely to arise following right temporal lobe activation. For example, Gloor et al. (1982) in their depth electrode study of five individuals with seizure disorders, found that all feelings of fear and displeasure were associated with right temporal, right amygdala, or right hippocampal activation. These findings are consistent with the observations of Slater, Beard and Glithero (1969), Bear and Fedio (1977), Flor-Henry (1969) and others who have noted an association between right temporal seizures and affective disorders.

Other reports, however, have been less clear cut — presumably due to the fact that seizures originating in the amygdala/temporal lobe can quickly spread from one hemisphere to another (via the anterior commissure), and the failure to employ depth electrodes to pinpoint the seizure foci. Hence, in some instances, emotions such as fear seem to arise regardless of which hemisphere is involved (Strauss et al., 1982). Nevertheless, even in these cases an emotional dichotomy is apparent.

For example, Herman and Chambria (1980) have described cases with right temporal foci who developed terrifying, "death-like" and "nightmarish" feelings of fear, whereas an individual with a left temporal foci developed specific fears of certain individuals and situations. Similarly, Weil (1956) reports that the majority of his patients with right sided foci developed intense sometimes horrifying, hellish fears, though they were unable to describe what they were afraid of.

Moreover, in addition to nightmarish fear, right temporal seizures have been reported to cause paroxysmal attacks of weeping, with lacrimation, the making of mournful sounds, including sobbing and crying (Offen et al., 1976). It is thus noteworthy that some individuals who have died and then returned to life, have also reported hearing crying, sobbing, and weeping, and have described the experience as nightmarish and hellish.

Likewise, feelings of religious awe may be based on fear (d'Aquili and Newberg, 1993) as well as rage, extreme hunger, sexual arousal. Extreme fear might induce a committed atheist to cry out to god.

These religious-fear reactions can be so overwhelming that the victim becomes almost catatonic, that is, petrified with fear—due to amygdala hyperactivation of the striatum and medial frontal lobes (Joseph, 1999a). Even in the absence of any religious feeling, under conditions of extreme terror there may be a complete loss of will, the victim surrendering to their fate in almost a trance-like fashion. "Surrender" is also a feature of many religions. It is through surrender that one opens themselves up to the presence of god, and the spiritual hereafter.

"The beginning of wisdom is the fear of the Lord." -Proverbs 1:7, 9:10, 15:33.

Likewise, the "Lord God" Yahweh depends on overwhelming fear to reveal his presence and power; a condition which directly activates the limbic system and amygdala—also known as the transmitter to god.

LIMBIC BLOOD LUST: MURDER, GENOCIDE, AND RELIGIOUS EXPERIENCE

THE HYPOTHALAMUS, SEX, AND EMOTION

The nuclei of the ancient limbic system include the hypothalamus, amygdala, cingulate gyrus, septal nuclei, and hippocampus (e.g. Gloor 1992, 1997; Halgren 1992; Joseph 1982, 1992a, 1998a, 1999b; Ledoux, 1996; MacLean 1969; 1990; Rolls 1992). It is these limbic system nuclei which are primary in regard to memory, the production of visual imagery, sexuality, and the expression and perception of most aspects of emotion, including love, sadness, grief, depression, fear, aggression, rage, pleasure, happiness, elation, and even sexual and religious ecstasy.

However, different limbic system nuclei, such as the hypothalamus, are more ancient and more primitive in emotional expression as compared to structures such as the more recently evolved amygdala (e.g. Halgren 1992; Joseph, 1992a, 1998a; MacLean 1969; 1990; Rolls 1992). For example, the hypothalamus mediates the expression of very intense, rudimentary and transient emotional states that are common to most creatures, including reptiles, amphibians, fish and even sharks (Joseph 1992a; MacLean 1969; 1990). The hypothalamus monitors internal homeostasis, and mediates and controls the desire to eat, drink, attack, or have sex; i.e. the four F's: Feeding, fighting, fleeing, and fornicating.

In addition to aggression, sexuality and pleasure and the avoidance of pain are of the utmost concern to the hypothalamus, and it is capable of generating orgasmic sensations of great intensity (Joseph, 1992a; Olds and Forbes 1981; MacLean 1969, 1990) via the release of naturally occurring opiates (Atweh and Kuhar 1977ab; Uhl, Kuhar and Snyder 1978).

LIMBIC LUST, MURDER, AND RELIGIOUS EXPERIENCE

The amygdala and hypothalamus often act in a highly coordinated manner in reaction to an exceedingly important emotional stimulus, or in response to a specific limbic need, such as hunger, thirst, rage, or sexual desire (Joseph, 1992a, 1996; MacLean 1969, 1990). For example, in response to hypothalamically monitored needs (hunger, sexual desire), the amygdala may scan the environment until it determines that a particular food item or person, has the necessary attributes (Gloor 1992; Joseph 1992a,b, 1996; Kling et al., 1987; O'Keefe and Bouma 1969; Ursin and Kaada 1960). In response to urgent hypothalamic desires, the amygdala might even assign sexual attributes to an individual that normally might not be viewed as sexually enticing.

It is also through hypothalamic and amygdala activity that a particular item or object (e.g. a banana) might be viewed as both a food item and sexual object. Or conversely, why certain individuals may be viewed as sexual as well as aversive and hateful (e.g. one's husband or wife). Indeed, because the hypothalamus and amygdala are so concerned with sex, rage, fear, and hunger, not only may these attributes be assigned to one individual, animal, or object simultaneously (e.g. fear of the beast one is going to enjoy killing and eating; hunger, guilt, and aversion regarding a high caloric treat; hatred for a loved one) but these conflicting emotions may be combined so as to give rise to exceedingly intense, albeit abstract emotional states; e.g. religious awe.

THE AMYGDALA, FEAR, AND THE LORD

"And now Israel, what does the Lord your god require of you, but to fear the Lord your god." -Deuteronomy 10:12.

The amygdala in particular is exceedingly important in generating feelings of fear (Davis et al., 1997; Gloor, 1992, 1997; Halgren, 1992; Rosen & Schulkin 1998; Scott et al., 1997; Williams 1956) as well as sexuality, rage, and hunger. In this regard, feelings of religious awe may be based on fear (d'Aquili and Newberg 1993), rage, extreme, hunger, or sexual arousal. Fear, however, is often the most potent means of eliciting religious feeling, for again, even a committed atheist when confronted with the possibility of a horrifying death may cry out to god. The "Lord God" Yahweh, in fact, depends on fear, and glories in terrifying his subjects in order to reveal his presence and power.

"The beginning of wisdom is the fear of the Lord." -Proverbs 1:7, 9:10, 15:33.

"And now, Israel, what does the Lord your god require of you, but to fear the Lord your god." Deuteronomy 10:12.

"God has come... in order that the fear of Him may be ever with you so that you do not go astray." -Exodus 20:17.

THE FRONTAL-TEMPORAL LOBES

In addition to the amygdala, temporal lobe and hippocampus, d'Aquili and Newberg (1993) point out that the right frontal lobe also plays a significant role in the generation of mystical experience. It is thus noteworthy that the right frontal lobe can pray, swear, and curse "God" even when the (speaking) left cerebral hemisphere has been severely damaged and the patient is aphasic and can no longer speak (Joseph, 1982, 1988a, 1999a).

The right frontal and temporal lobe, hypothalamus, and amygdala also interact in regard to sexual arousal (Freemon & Nevis 1969; Joseph, 1986a, 1988a, 1992a, 1999a; MacLean 1969, 1990; Remmillard et al. 1983; Robinson & Mishkin 1968; Spencer et al., 1983). This is a very important relationship, and in part explains why (although there are exceptions), religions tend to be quite sexual and/or exceedingly concerned with sexual mores and related activity. As is well known, female pregnancy and matters pertaining to birth control and abortion are of extreme concern to most modern as well as ancient religions (Campbell 1988; Frazier 1955; Parrinder 1980; Smart 1969).

However, the limbic system as well as the frontal and temporal lobes are also highly concerned with acting on or inhibiting aggression and murderous rage reactions which also arise in the limbic system (Joseph 1986, 1988, 1992a, 1996). This may also explain why many religious sects are so "righteously" belligerent and hateful and have employed torture, human or animal sacrifice, and sanctioned if not encouraged the murder of non-believers: What could be referred to as limbic-religious blood lust.

"Shed man's blood, by man your blood be shed." -Genesis 9:6.

SHED MAN'S BLOOD

The "Lord God," Yahweh, repeatedly required that the ancient Israelites undergo a bloody ritual of submission (e.g. Exodus 24:1-14), and in fact proscribed a ritual of incredible bloodyness for the investiture of his priests (Exodus 29: 1-46). This "Lord God" also required the slaughter and sacrifice of living creatures whose blood is splashed on his alter, and on his priests.

For example, upon the ratification of the covenant, twelve oxen were drained of their blood, one oxen for each of the 12 tribes of Israel, and as it is splashed on the people, Moses says" This is the blood of the covenant that the Lord now makes with you concerning these commands" (Exodus 24:8). In yet another bloody ritual a bull is slaughtered then a ram, then yet another ram, and their blood is splashed and smeared on the altars, on the priests, and on the people, and climaxes with those who are being ordained as priests holding up bloody pieces of the body (Exodus 29: 10-28).

King Solomon slaughtered 22,000 oxen and 22,000 sheep as an offering to this "Lord God" whose loves meat, but not his vegetables.

In fact, as this "Lord God" is apparently a meat eater, this may explain why he criticized Cain, a tiller of the soil, and rejected his first harvest offering of fruit and vegetables that he had grown with his own hand (Genesis, 4).

Figure 61. *Sumerian "gods" were meat eaters and supervise a Sumerian king as he hunts.*

"And in the process of time it can to pass that Cain brought of the fruit of the ground and offering until the Lord. And Abel, he also brought of the firstlings of his flock and the fat thereof. And the Lord had respect unto Abel and to his offering: But unto Cain and to his offering he had not respect." -Genesis 4.3-5.

For ancient hunters, aggression and the killing of animals (and other humans) was a way of life. Hunters often employed hunting magic and related religious rituals to insure success. Religion and murder, like religion and sex, are linked to the limbic system and evolved accordingly. Consequently, when in the throes of religious excitement, torture and murder may even receive the blessing or might be actively encouraged by one's "God."

Indeed, in the case of the "Lord God" He enjoys killing people, and informs Moses that even those who wish to convert should be slaughtered: "You shall make no covenant with them... " and "I will blot out their memory... The Lord will be at war with Amalek throughout the ages" (Exodus 17:14-16). This Lord God, will in fact engage in widespread ethnic cleansing and genocide, and will also impose a rein of terror on His own people (e.g., Exodus 32: 26-29, 35). The Lord God loves to spill the blood of innocent and guilty alike.

On the other hand, the blood sacrifice is also related to the worship of the goddess, the Great Mother of All. It is menstrual blood which issues from the womb, the source of all life, and the rites of the goddess cult involved sanctifying and splashing menstrual blood on the altar. Hence, many ancient patriarchal religions appear to have adopted this practice, with the notable exception that instead of using the blood to celebrate life, the purpose of these bloody rituals was to evoke the power to take life which would be sacrificed to a warring, meat eating, God.

WARRIOR GODS: FEAR AND PANIC

Throughout history, many of the patriarchal Gods have been aggressive, jealous, conquering, angry and war-like e.g., Marduk, Mazda, Zeus, Apollo, Mars, and Yahweh "the Lord of hosts." For example, in addition to being described as the "Lord of hosts," Yahweh also means: "The Destroyer."

These warrior gods, including Yahweh, were prone to mass murder and extremely violent rages. Yahweh repeatedly threatened and engaged in the slaughter of enemies and believers alike, without mercy or regard for women and children. Terror, war, and murder: the Lord God's middle names.

"Terror, and the pit, and the snare are upon you, O inhabitant of earth (Isaiah 24:17). And as the Lord took delight in doing you good and multiplying you, so the Lord will take delight in bringing ruin upon you and destroying you (Deuteronomy 26:63). The Lord will bring a nation against you from afar, from the end of the earth, which will swoop down like the eagle... a ruthless nation, that will show the old no regard and the young no mercy (Deuteronomy 28:47-50). It shall devour the offspring... you shall eat your own issue, the flesh of your sons and daughters... until He has wiped you out... leaving you nothing... until it has brought ruin unto you..." (Deuteronomy 28:50-55).

"In the Name of God... by the Troops shall the unbelievers be driven towards Hell, until when they reach it, its gates shall be opened... for just is the sentence of punishment on the unbelievers… " -Koran, XXXIX

"Behold I send an angel before thee, to keep thee in the way. Beware of him and obey his voice, for I will be an enemy unto thine enemies, and an adversary unto thine adversaries, and I will cut them off… .I will send my terror before thee, and will destroy all the people to whom thou shalt come… . and I will drive them out from before thee, until thou be increased and inherit the land." -Exodus 23:20-30

"...when you approach a town, you shall lay seizure to it, and when the Lord your god delivers it into your hand, you shall put all its males to the sword. You may, however, take as your booty the women, the children, the livestock, and everything in the town—all its spoils—and enjoy the spoil of your enemy which the Lord your god gives you… In the towns of the people which the Lord your god is giving you as a heritage, you shall not let a soul remain alive." -Exodus 20:15-18; -Deuteronomy 20:12-16

"When Israel had killed all the inhabitants of Ai… and all of them, to the last man had fallen by the sword, all the Israelites turned back to Ai and put it to the sword...until all the inhabitants of Ai had been exterminated... and the king of Ai was impaled on a stake and it was left lying at the entrance to the city gate." -Deuteronomy 8:24-29.

In fact, the Lord God condemned even his most loyal followers if they dared to show even the slightest mercy even to animals (e.g., I Samuel 28:18-19). The Lord God, as described in the Old Testament, had what might best be described as a hair trigger temper, such that at the slightest sign of murmuring he would pounce and kill men, women, and children, the innocent and guilty alike including those of his own people. As is evident, for example, in the story of Exodus, the people were His prisoners, and He killed or insured that every adult who exited Egypt would die in the desert, including even Moses for making but one small mistake in following His orders: Instead of ordering a rock to give water, Moses tapped it with his cain.

LIMBIC AND RELIGIOUS MASS MURDER

ETHNIC CLEANSING, AND GENETIC GENOCIDE

Led by Moses, and their "Lord God" the ancient Hebrews/Israelites murdered untold numbers, perhaps hundreds of thousands of innocent men, women, children, including even their livestock. These atrocities were committed against all manner of innocent peoples not because they had sinned, but because they happened to be along the path to the "promised land" and because they had the misfortune of living on land and possessing property that the "Lord God" wanted to give to his people.

"When the Lord they God shall bring thee into the land, and shall cast out many nations before thee, the Hittite, and the Gergashite, and the Amorite, and the Canaanite, and the Perizzite, and the Hivite, and the Jebusite... and the Lord thy god shall deliver them up before thee, and thou shalt smite them, then thou shall utterly destroy them."-Deuteronomy 7:1-2.

"Of the cities of these peoples, that the Lord they God giveth thee for an inheritance, thou shalt save alive nothing that breathest." -Deuteronomy, 20:16.

Moreover, "God" gloried not only in the murder of innocent women and children, but took special satisfaction in the theft of their property—the spoils of a godly-genocidal war. The Lord God believed that theft and injustice was a testament to his glory as a conquering warrior god.

"Great and goody cities, which thou didst not build and houses full of all good things which thou didst not fill, and cisterns hewn, which thou didst not hew, and vineyards and olive-trees, which thou didst not plant, and thou shalt eat and be satisfied." -Deuteronomy 6:10-11.

Yahweh, the Lord of Hosts, the "Destroyer," apparently so enjoyed the spectacle of mass murder, that once he began to kill He found it difficult to stop, killing everything and everyone, the guilty and the innocent, the righteous and the wicked, and even their animals. Apparently only blood and more blood, the signs of death, could protect the innocent, and cool his ardor for indiscriminate mass murder, which is why He explains to Moses that the only way to protect himself and the Jewish people from slaughter was by painting their doors red with blood: "When I see the blood" He informs Moses, "I will pass over you, and there shall be no plague upon you to destroy you, when I smite the land of Egypt" (Exodus 12:12-13).

In fact (if the Bible is to be believed), it was only the sight of blood which prevented Yahweh from killing Moses almost immediately after informing him that he was to lead the Israelites out of Egypt.

"And the Lord said unto Moses...Go... And it came to pass by the way in the inn, that the Lord met him and sought to kill him. Then Zipporah" (the wife of Moses) "took a sharp stone and cut off the foreskin of her son, and cast it at his feet, and said, Surely a bloody husband art though to me."

Why would the "Lord God" seek to kill his prophet? There are many possibilities, all of which may have provoked "Lord God's" inherent murderous nature. For example, Moses dilly dallied and did not go directly to Egypt as he had been commanded. In addition, the "Lord God" may have been provoked to rage because Moses had failed to circumcise his son. Moses, in fact (if the Bible is to be believed) never did escape the wrath of the "Lord" for the "Lord God" kills Moses just as he and the Israelites are on the verge of entering the promised land.

THOU SHALT KILL AND KILL AND KILL

Despite the commandment "thou shall not kill" Yahweh kills and murders the innocent and guilty alike and encourages and in fact orders the Israelites to murder even babies and women with children.

"And they warred... as the Lord commanded and slew all the males. And they slew the Kings... and they took all the women and their little ones... and they burnt all their cities wherein they dwelt, and all their goodly castles with fire... And Moses was wroth...and said unto them. Have ye saved all the women and the little ones alive? Now therefore kill every male among the little ones, and kill every woman that hath known man by lying with him." (Numbers, 31).

As repeatedly detailed in Exodus, the "Lord God" purposefully and repeatedly "hardened Pharaoh's heart" simply as an excuse for murdering innocent Egyptians, so that He could glory in the carnage.

"I will harden Pharaoh's heart that I may multiply My signs and marvels in The land of Egypt. When the Pharaoh does not heed you, I will lay My hand upon Egypt." -Exodus 7:3.

Moreover, it is not just Egyptians or the hapless innocents who the Israelites and their Lord God murder in their 40 years of wondering, but tens of thousands if not hundreds of thousands of Jews. The Lord God kills them for rebelling, He kills them for "murmuring," He kills them for complaining, He kills them for questioning. And He kills their wives, brothers, fathers, mothers, and children: "Go forth and slay brother, neighbor, and kin" (Genesis, 32:26-29).

For example, when Moses ascended the Mountain to meet with the Lord God, the Israelites grew impatient with the hardships and murders they were forced to endure, and they turned again to worshipping the scared goddess, as represented by the golden calf. In reaction, Yahweh thunders and his prophet Moses proclaims that innocent and guilty alike shall be murdered: "Put ye every man his sword upon his thigh and slay every man...his brother, and every man his companion, and every man his neighbor and kin" (Genesis, 32:26-29).

When Moses proclaimed the Israelites a "nation of priests," some of the Israelites then dared to ask: if "Every member of the community is holy and the Lord is among them all... Why do you set yourselves up above the assembly of the Lord?" The response? Those who dared to ask questions are killed, including their wives, children, brothers and neighbors: "And the Earth opened her mouth and swallowed them" (Numbers, 16:32).

The ancient Israelis not only received special permission from their "Lord God" to murder wayward Jews, non-Jews and Jewish non-believers, including women and children whom they slaughtered without mercy (e.g. Numbers, 3115-18; Numbers 34, 50-53), but even Jewish babies. Indeed, it was a Hebrew religious-tradition to kill and slaughter not only non-Jewish males in general and first born Jewish sons (a custom until the time of Moses, e.g. Bergmann 1992).

SACRIFICIAL MURDERS

Human sacrifice was a common feature of many ancient religions, and serves as one of the founding stones of Christianity: The Lord God's sacrifice of his son, Jesus, on the Cross. Hence, it is said that "Christ died for your sins." Christ was sacrificed as an offering to the Lord God, so as to wash away the sins of the masses—or so claims the Roman Catholic Church.

The Lord God showed a particular fondness for killing first born sons, including the first born of the ancient Egyptians, as well as his own people.

"A blessing on him who seizes your babies and dashes them against rocks." -Psalm 137:9).

"I polluted them with their own offerings, making them sacrifice all their first-born, which was to punish them, so that they would learn that I am Yahweh." -Ezekiel 20:25-36; 22:28-29.

This "Lord God" even required the death of the first born son of King David and his wife Bethsheba, this despite the fact that He claimed to have loved David most dearly. However, by killing this little boy, "God" in effect pardoned King David for repeatedly breaking two of His commandments, i.e., murder (of Bethsheba's husband) and adultery. Thus, the son of David was sacrificed by the Lord God so as to cleanse David of his sins, including, perhaps his sinful propensity for having sex with other men's wives (e.g. Abigail wife of Nabal, and Michal wife of Paltiel). However, David the murderer and adulterer, was also a fierce warrior who had killed tens of thousands, including even tens of thousands of Jews—and this "Lord God" loved him most dearly.

Sacrificial murder, therefore, is a way of indicating atonement, and for obtaining favor from one's god, including the Lord God. For thousands of years it has been a world wide religious custom to sacrifice captured warriors, young virgins, and especially children.

In some ancient societies children were killed because they were "pure" and precious. Thus the death of these innocent children could be considered a true sacrifice. Moreover, the ancient gods, including Yahweh, required that those murdered in their glory, be pure and without blemish. Children, and virgins, therefore, were a natural choice.

First born sons in particular were singled out for this honor as many ancient religions held to the belief that the first born was the offspring of a god who had opened the womb and impregnated the mother. This belief may even have caused the Lord God some consternation, for he not only required the killing of the first born, but he repeatedly shows favor to second born sons, e.g., Abel over Cain, Isaac instead of Ishmael, Jacob instead of Esau, Ephram over Manasseh, Soloman the second born son of David and Bethsheba, and so on.

It was also believed by many pagan groups that because a god may have impregnated the mother, the god also lost some of his lifeforce in the process. Hence, the first born would be killed to liberate that energy which could then be absorbed by the god.

It may well have been because of these beliefs that other gods were absorbing this life force, that the Lord God, although at first demanding the sacrifice of first born sons, later changed His mind, and condemned the practice.

"This very day you defile yourselves in the presentation of your gifts by making your children pass through the fire of all your fetishes." -Ezekiel 20:31.

CHRISTIAN HOLY WARS

KILL THEM ALL: GOD WILL RECOGNIZE HIS OWN

It was upon these images of the murdering warrior God, the Lord of Hosts, that Pope Urban II proclaimed that war for the sake of God was holy. In fact, acting under the religious delusion they were serving Jesus Christ, the Catholic Church ordered the murder of hundreds of thousands of men and women. However, a reading of scripture will reveal that the Church was not adhering to the preaching of Christ, but were following the philosophy of Paul (who spent the first half of his life harassing Christians) and the dictates of Peter whom Jesus repeatedly castigated as "Satan" e.g. St. Matthew 16: 23; Matthew 17: 24-25; Mark 8:33: "But he turned and said unto Peter, "Get thee behind me, Satan, thou art an offense unto me; for thou savourest not the things that be of God, but those of men." Indeed, Christ never, never, encouraged murder. Murder and mass murder is the way of the Lord God.

Thus, the Catholic Popes instigated numerous Crusades and inquisitions. In consequence hundreds of thousands of Moslems, Jews, and women and children, were sexually tortured, slaughtered, spitted, and roasted alive, and their cities and villages pillaged and set ablaze. All in the name of the Lord God. So intense was their limbic blood lust that even Christians were murdered.

For example, in the 13th Century an army of some thirty thousand Christian knights and Crusaders descended into southern France and attacked the town of Beziers in search of heretics. Over thirteen thousand Christians flocked to the churches for protection. When the Bishop, one of the Pope's representatives, was informed that the army was unable to distinguish between true believers and heretics, he replied, "Kill them all. God will recognize his own."

However, in order to recruit those worthy of such a glorious and murderous undertaking, the Pope had to appeal to murderers, rapists, molesters of children, and those who enjoyed the prolonged torture of their victims.

"You oppressors of orphans, you robbers of widows, you homicides, you blasphemers, you plunderers of others' rights... If you want to take counsel for your souls you must go forward boldly as knights of Christ..." so proclaimed the Pope who offered "indulgences" and forgiveness to all those who would commit blasphemies and murder women and children in the name of the Lord God and Jesus Christ.

As summed up by Henry Charles Lea: "Protestants and Catholics rivaled each other in the madness of the hours… Christendom seemed to have grown delirious, and Satan might well have smiled at the tribute to his powers seen in the endless smoke of the holocaust which bore witness to his triumph over the Almighty."

Again, however, although "Lord God" of the "Old Testament" repeatedly approved of mass murder and rape, and in fact employed these practices against His own people, Jesus Christ obviously did not preach mass murder, torture, rape, pedophilia, and the castration of young boys: "But love ye your enemies and do good and lend, hoping for nothing and your reward shall be great. Be ye merciful...judge not, and ye shall not be judged: condemn not and ye shall not be condemned: forgive and ye shall be forgiven" (Luke, 7: 35-37); "For the Son of man is not come to destroy men's lives, but to save them" (Luke 10: 56; however, see Matthew 10:16 vs 34-35).

Nevertheless, despite the teaching of Christ, the Catholic Church fully approved of castration, mass murder, and the most horrible of tortures. Indeed, as is well known, the Spanish and Catholic missionaries, acting at the behest of the Catholic Popes (and their Spanish/Catholic Sovereigns), continued these Satanic practices once they invaded the America's during the 1500's and up through the 19th century.

As the Catholic Dominican Bishop Bartolom de Las Casas reported to the Pope: the Aztec and Indian natives were hung and burnt alive "in groups of 13... thus honoring our Savior and the 12 apostles." However, because some of the various victims managed to live throughout the night, the Dominican priests ordered that sticks be shoved down their throats so the soldiers and priests would not be kept awake at night by their cries and moans.

Figure 62. *According to Catholic Dominican Bishop Bartolom de Las Casas, the Indian natives were hung and burnt alive "in groups of 13... thus honoring our Savior and the 12 apostles." Because some of the victims managed to live throughout the night, the Dominican priests ordered that sticks be shoved down their throats so the soldiers and priests would not be kept awake at night by their cries and moans. Woodcut by De la Bray, 15th century.*

Of course the Aztecs did not practice a benign form of worship, for they tore the beating hearts from their victims in order to please their God (Carrasco 1990) and they killed thousands if not hundreds of thousands in so doing.

Figure 63.*The Aztecs regularly practiced human sacrifice by cutting out the hearts of captured warriors in honor of their god. A victim lies dead at the foot of the temple steps, whereas the warrior at top has his chest cut open by the temple priest, which allows his soul to ascend skyward leaving behind a bloody trail.*

Similarly, many Indian tribes of the Mississippi valley practiced human sacrifice as did the ancient Jews, Europeans, and leaders of the Protestant Reformation who urged the killing of anyone and everyone who did not agree with their interpretation of the Bible, including fellow Christians:

"Therefore let everyone who can smite, slay, and stab, secretly or openly, remembering that nothing can be more poisonous, hurtful, or devilish that a rebel. It is just as when one must kill a mad dog; if you do not strike him he will strike you, and a whole land with you. -Martin Luther.

What is the origin of these sadistic religious practices? The human limbic system.

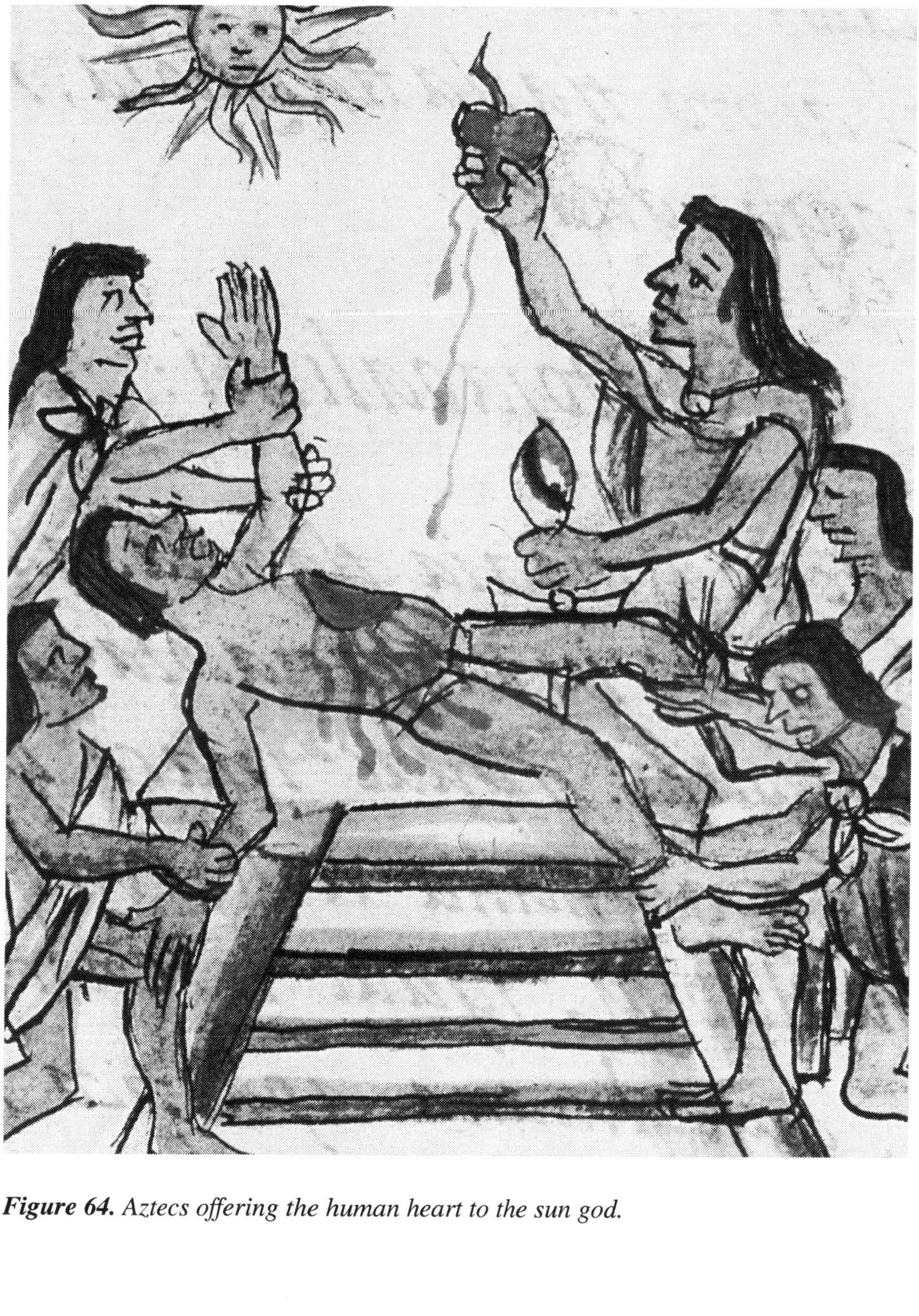

Figure 64. *Aztecs offering the human heart to the sun god.*

MASS SUICIDE AND MODERN RELIGIOUS MURDERERS

Murder of the innocents and the slaughter of infidels and non-believers are not antiquated religious customs. Cults and religious groups regularly arise in various lands and cultures and frequently indulge in similar practices, e.g. the mass suicide of Jim Jones and his followers in "Jonestown" ("People's Temple"), David Koresh and the fiery death of his followers at Waco Texas.

MASS DEATH AT JONESTOWN

On November 18, 1978, the reverend Jim Jones exhorted and then forced his followers to engage in mass murder and mass suicide in Guyana. More than 900 people, many of them children, drank, or were forced to drink cyanide-laced fruit punch. Jones, a charismatic monomaniac who at one time was a favorite of San Francisco's liberal political elite, took a less painful and quicker way out. He died of a bullet to the head.

Jim Jones was born in 1931 and became a "Holy Roller" preacher as a child. As he reached adulthood he developed a creed he called "apostolic socialism" which deified social justice but which downplayed the role of god—hence his appeal to the ultra-liberal San Francisco political elite. Current San Francisco Mayor, and former leader of the California Assembly, Willie Brown, was one of Jones' "biggest cheerleaders." Nevertheless, despite his cult status even among the city's liberal elite, Jones became increasingly paranoid and disillusioned with San Francisco, especially following a negative magazine article in New West magazine. Jones moved his followers to a 3,800 acre plot of land in Guyana's outback, where they raised livestock and grew their own food.

The people's paradise soon became a prison camp. Followers were not allowed to leave, and there were forced beatings and forced sex. Jones who required that his followers refer to him as "father" demanded utter obedience. Incessant screaming and threats were delivered nightly against imagined slights and for faintly perceived faults, with the guilty being beat with "the board of education." Anyone who questioned his authority was placed in "The Box," an underground coffin. Unruly children would be taken to the Jonestown well and hung upside down by a rope tied around their ankles and would be repeatedly dunked and beaten.

Jones became increasingly concerned about the CIA and FBI plotting against him and his paradise, and soon required that his followers practice mass suicide so as to protect them from outside threats: the "White Night" drills. Jones would get on the compound loud speaker at night and begin shouting: "White Night! White Night!" which signaled a coming attack. Followers were required to leap from their beds and assemble at designated spots where they would then drink from huge vats.

However, what triggered the mass suicide was a visit from a California politician, Leo Ryan, who upon leaving invited a number of Jones' followers to come with him. Ryan was murdered and insofar as Jones was concerned, the day of reckoning was at hand. One of those who drank the poison wrote in her suicide note: "We died because you would not leave us alone."

HEAVEN'S GATE

Mass suicide has been practiced by numerous religious cults, both ancient and recent, including, in the 1990s, 74 followers of the "Order of the Solar temple," and 39 members of "The Higher Source," i.e. "Heavens Gate." Many of the male members of the Higher Source, including the leader of the cult, a minister (and son of a Presbyterian minister), Marshall Applewhite (also known as "Do") also had themselves castrated.

In the case of Applewhite, castration was not only a means of achieving purity, but a way to control his rampant homosexuality. In 1970, for example, he was fired from the University of Saint Thomas after it became known that he was having sex with male students. Soon thereafter he apparently began hearing voices, including the voice of god and was awakened to a new form of spirituality which required abstinence from sex. His creed eventually came to include strict rules involving "no human-level relationships and no socializing."

As an aside it is noteworthy that abnormal amygdala activity, or amygdala destruction, can alter sex drive and sexual orientation, and can also induce a loss of social interest. Human-level relationships are avoided (Joseph, 1999b; 2000a).

Soon Applewhite's credo came to include UFOs.

Specifically, Applewhite saw the coming of the Hale-Bopp comet as a heavenly sign that a UFO was coming to take him and his followers to a better place, to "the level above human, to take us home to TheirWorld: Heaven." The cultists, therefore, killed themselves by eating a poison laced pudding, and lay on bunk beds in a standard black uniform and Nike tennis shoes and died.

DAVID KORESH: BEATEN BY THY GOD

David Koresh ("Vernon") of the Branch Dividian cult, also ordered the death of his followers, and they apparently obeyed his wishes, for he had told them he was "god." In fact he first made his announcement on January 30, 1987, when he sent a wedding invitation to the Seventh Adventists Church in southern California, which read in part: "I have seven eyes and seven horns. My Name is the Word of God...Prepare to Meet Thy God."

David Koresh was a sexual sadist. He had sex with the wives of all his many followers, and had sex with and would beat and order the beating of their and his children. According to one of his followers, Marc Breault (Breault & King, 1993) "Children were spanked for any reason; crying during a sixteen hour Bible study, refusing to sit on Vernon's lap, or daring to defy the prophet's wishes."

"Each child had their own special paddle with their name written on it...Some women thought the best way to please their Son of God lover was to be especially severe when dishing out discipline. But sometimes it wasn't easy for the adults to spank the children. They couldn't find a spot on the child's buttocks that wasn't black and blue or bleeding" (Breault & King, 1993).

The women were sometimes subjected to the same treatment. One 29-year old woman who announced that she was hearing voices was imprisoned in one of the small cottages on their property. She was beaten, and repeatedly raped by her "guards."

David Koresh was also a prophet of Doom, and between the months of October 1991 to February 1993, he and his group spent over $200,000.00 on guns. This arsenal included 50-caliber machine-guns and a million rounds of ammunition (Breault & King, 1993). Koresh was not only preparing for Armageddon but was contemplating mass suicide.

On Sunday, February 28, 1993, at 9.55 A.M., in Waco, Texas, a hundred ATF agents began their raid which resulted in a blood bath. A 51 day siege finally ended in a firestorm, and the death of David Koresh, his followers, and their children who burned to death when the compound was set on fire and burned to the ground. It was David's wish, however, for the entire world to go up in flames.

SPIRITUAL BLOOD LUST AND THE LIMBIC SYSTEM

These crazed religious practices are not limited to Americans. Consider, the Japanese religious cult "Aum." Their leader Shoko Asahara and many top cult members were arrested and charged with murder in June of 1995 for releasing the nerve gas Sarin in five subway cars during rush hour injuring over 5,500 Japanese commuters (New York Times, 6/7/95).

Similarly, although the "modern" Islamic, Christian and Jewish religions forbids it, many modern day Middle Eastern and African Islamic, Christian, and Jewish fundamentalists, regularly preach murder and hatred.

For example, "militant rabbis" in Israel had encouraged and condoned the assassination of Israel's Prime Minister, Yitzhak Rabin, and had issued a "pursuer's decree," which in effect morally required that he be killed (New York Times 11/11/95). And, he was murdered by a student of religion, Yigal Amir, who claimed he acted upon "God's" instructions.

Because of this limbic religious blood lust, members of religious sects may turn against one another and commit murder in the name of God, just as Jews would murder Jews, and Christians would murder Christians in the name of God.

For example, on November 29, 1998, six members of the United Pentecostal Church were arrested for kicking to death six people, including three children, "to wipe out the enemies of God." According to Reuters new agency (11/28/98), the killings began two weeks prior, when the pastor of the thirty member sect announced during a sermon that he could hear voices from Jesus Christ" ordering that members of the group be punished. "The pastor, helped by his wife and two other men, began beating, whipping and stamping on the worshipers... followed by more disciplinary torture over several days. Among the dead were two boys, aged three and four."

"Terrorist attacks" by Muslim religious zealots is not uncommon. However, these attacks and calls for the death of infidels, are not always aimed at Jews or Americans, but their "brothers" and "sisters," i.e. fellow Arabs and Muslims.

Consider Algeria. Between 1992 and 1999, over 80,000 Algerians were murdered by Muslim zealots, with the majority of victims consisting of children, girls, and pregnant women who were beheaded, disemboweled, or who had their throats slashed. The reason for these murders and campaign of terror? To establish a holy Islamic state.

In fact, in 1998, on the first holy day of Ramadan—which marks "god's" revelation of the Koran to the Prophet Muhammed—Muslim religious zealots killed and slaughtered more than 400 people, most of them women.

Even Buddhist monks murder and assault one another. For example, in November of 1998, gray-robed Buddhist monks of the Chogye Buddhist order in Korea, spent several weeks assaulting and beating each other with clubs, chairs, and even fire bombs as they battled over religious control of the order's main temple (Associated Press, 11/17/98). In one brawl alone, 37 were seriously injured and five killed.

RELIGIOUS MURDERS AND THE LIMBIC SYSTEM

What is the source of these religious-murderous and sadistic behaviors? The limbic system and the same cluster of nuclei which subserve aggression, sexuality, and spirituality. It is the limbic system which enables humans to respond with irrational and murderous blood lust in the name of "God" and religion and it is the amygdala that can induce a horribly violent and murderous assault with minor provocation—and as we have seen, the Lord God, and numerous religious fanatics, have also murdered at the slightest provocation.

For example, if the amygdala is directly stimulated rage reactions are commonly triggered. The face will begin to contort, the teeth will be bared, the pupils will dilate, the nostrils will flare, and then the animal or human will viciously attack (Egger & Flynn, 1963; Gunne & Lewander, 1966; Mark et al., 1972; Ursin & Kaada, 1960; Zbrozyna, 1963). Amygdaloid activation results in attacks directed at something real, or, in the absence of an actual stimulus, at something imaginary; including, presumably, in the case of religious fanatics, imaginary slights or insults.

There have been reported instances of patients suddenly lashing out and even attempting to attack those close by, while in the midst of a temporal lobe seizure (Saint-Hilaire et al., 1980), and/or attacking, kicking, and destroying furniture and other objects (Ashford et al., 1980). One female patient, during amygdala stimulation, became irritable and angry, and then enraged. Her lips retracted, there was extreme facial grimacing, threatening behavior, and then rage and attack—all of which persisted well beyond stimulus termination (Mark et al., 1972).

Yet another man developed intractable aggression following a head injury and the development of abnormal activity within the amygdala (Schiff et al.,1982). Subsequently, he became easily enraged, sexually preoccupied, and developed hyper-religiosity and psuedo-mystical ideas. He became violently religious.

Indeed, the amygdala is able to overwhelm the neocortex and the rest of the brain so that the person not only forms religious ideas but responds to them, sometimes with vicious, horrifying results. Hence, it appears to be the limbic system, and the amygdala in particular, which not only contributes to religious and spiritual experience, but religious brutality and murder committed in the name of one's god.

-10-

SEX, GOD, AND RELIGION:

Sexual Spirituality and the War Against Women

LIMBIC SYSTEM SEXUALITY

The limbic system is concerned with sex, and in fact, structures such as the amygdala and hypothalamus not only mediate sexual behavior, but they are sexually differentiated and have sex specific patterns of neuronal and dendritic development, (Allen et al. 1989; Blier et al. 1982; Gorski et al. 1978; Nishizuka & Arai, 1981; Rainbow et al. 1982; Raisman & Field, 1971, 1973; Simerly, 1990; Swaab & fliers, 1985).That is, there are "male" and "female" limbic systems, and even "homosexual" limbic systems such that male homosexuals are in possession of a limbic system which is more "female" than "male" in structural organization (Levay, 1991; Swaab, 1990), and in some respects (the anterior commissure) hyper-female in size (Allen, & Gorski, 1992).

Because the limbic system is organized and structured in a unique, sex-specific fashion it also performs different functions depending on if one is a man or a woman, such as, for example, lactation and maternal behavior (Numan, 1985). In fact, dendritic spine density of ventromedial hypothalamic neurons varies across the estrus cycle (Frankfurt et al., 1990) and thus presumably during pregnancy and while nursing.

Likewise, the amygdala is not only sexually differentiated (Nishizuka & Arai, 1981; Simerly, 1990), but the male amygdala is larger than the female amygdala (Breedlove & Cooke, 1999; Filipek, et al., 1994), and contains a greater number of synaptic connections and shows different patterns of steroid activity (Breedlove & Cooke, 1999; Nishizuka & Arai, 1981; Simerly, 1990; Stopa et al., 1991). The number of immunoreactive cells in the female amygdala also fluctuates during the estrus cycle, being highest during proestrus (Simerly, 1990). These "female" immunoreactive cells presumably acts so that if pregnant, the fetus will not be attacked as foreign.

Moreover, activation of these sexually dimorphic structures can trigger male vs female sexual behavior (Hart et al., 1985; Lisk, 1967, 1971). Electrical stimulation of the hypothalamus increases sexual behavior in males, and significantly increases the frequency of erections, copulations and ejaculations, we well as pelvic thrusting followed by an explosive discharge of semen even in the absence of a mate (Hart, et al., 1985; Maclean, 1973). Conversely, lesions to the preoptic and posterior hypothalamus eliminates male sexual behavior and results in gonadal atrophy.

Activation of the amygdala can produce penile erection (Kling & Brothers, 1992; MacLean, 1990; Robinson & Mishkin, 1968; Stoffels et al., 1980) sexual feelings (Bancaud et al., 1970; Remmillard et al., 1983), sensations of extreme pleasure (Olds & Forbes, 1981), memories of sexual intercourse (Gloor, 1986), as well as ovulation, uterine contractions, lactogenetic responses, and orgasm (Backman & Rossel, 1984; Currier et al., 1971; Freemon & Nevis, 1969; Warneke, 1976; Remmillard et al., 1983; Shealy & Peel, 1957).

By contrast, injuries to and/or seizure activity within the amygdala/temporal lobe may result in bizarre sexual changes, such as continuous masturbation and indiscriminate, often hypersexual hetero- and homosexual behaviors including attempts at sex with inanimate objects (Kling & Brothers, 1992; Kluver & Bucy, 1939; Pribram & Bagshaw 1953; Terzian & Ore, 1955). Hypersexuality following amygdala injury has been documented among numerous species, including cats, dogs, and humans (Blumer 1970; Kling and Brothers, 1992).

Humans with an abnormally activated or severely injured amygdala/temporal lobe may expose and manipulate their genitals (Leutmezer et al., 1999), masturbate in public, and attempt to have sex with family members or individuals of the same sex (Blumer, 1970; Kolarsky et al., 1967; Terzian & Ore, 1955). Moreover, heightened activity involving the amygdala and overlying temporal lobe has been associated with hypersexuality (Blumer, 1970) as well as homosexuality, transvestitism, and thus confusion over sexual orientation (Davies and Morgenstern, 1960; Kolarsky et al., 1967). In fact, abnormal- or seizure activity within the amygdala or overlying temporal lobe may induce an individual to engage in "sexual intercourse" even in the absence of a partner.

For example, Currier and colleagues (1971, p. 260) described a female temporal lobe seizure patient who was "sitting at the kitchen table with her daughter making out a shopping list" when she suffered a seizure. "She appeared dazed, slumped to the floor on her back, lifted her skirt, spread her knees and elevated her pelvis rhythmically. She made appropriate vocalizations for sexual intercourse such as: It feels so good...further, further."

THE RELIGIOUS WAR AGAINST WOMEN

Unfortunately, abnormalities in these structures can also provoke extreme sexual violence. In one case, a young man with seizure activity originating in his amygdala and temporal lobe, beat his mother to death and then sexually assaulted the body (Joseph, 2000a).

Thus an abnormal limbic system may abnormally link sex with murder; and among men, the sexual murder or torture of women. Moreover, because the amygdala is clearly linked to religious experience, sexual behavior and religious expression may become linked in a positive or a negative fashion. Augustine, Jerome, Tertullian, and other Catholic theologians absolutely hated women, viewing them as evil temptresses that lead men to hell.

"What is the differences whether it is a wife or mother, it is still Eve the temptress that we must beware of in any woman." -St. Augustine.

"Do you not know that you are each an Eve? The sentence of God on this sex of yours lives in this age: the guilt must of necessity live too. You are the devil's gateway; you are the unsealer of that forbidden tree; you are the first deserter of the divine law; you are she who persuaded him whom the devil was not valiant enough to attack. You so carelessly destroyed man, God's image. On account of you, even the Son of God had to die." -Tertullian, 16th Century

Even the Lord God, Yahweh voiced contempt and hatred for women.

"Because the daughters of Zion are haughty and walk with stretched forth necks and wanton eyes, walking and mincing as they go, and making a tinkling with their feet...The Lord shall wash away the filth of the daughters of Zion... by the spirit of burning." -Isaiah 3:16-26, 4:4.

Women throughout the ages, therefore, were often demeaned and attacked by male and homosexual religious authorities, and their murder was often sanctioned by various gods. Indeed, during the middle ages, the Catholic Church declared war on women who were then systematically tortured and slaughtered by the Catholic authorities after the men had marched off to Catholic Crusades and the women were left unprotected.

FEAR OF FERTILITY

Yet another factor in the religious crusade against women was the fear of the goddess cult by the patriarchal religious authorities. For example, during the Crusades, because the women were temporarily freed of male dominance, some began to practice their own religion and worship their own goddesses, including those pagan goddesses that celebrated female sexuality; e.g., fertility cults—perhaps the oldest and most ancient of "organized religions." In consequence, the leaders of the Catholic Church felt compelled to act. They sought to destroy woman in general, and those women associated in any way with the goddess and her fertility cults. Women, therefore, were suspect if they were in any way sexually attractive, and those who were the most sexually appealing (i.e. fertile) were the first to be murdered by the Catholic Authorities. Her reproductive facility was viewed as supernatural in origin, her menstrual cycle being in tune with the cycles of the moon, and the moon and the blood of her menstruation were believed to have supernatural power. Every woman was not just Eve, but an incarnation of the goddess.

As noted in an earlier chapter, the reproductive and supernatural power of menstrual blood may have contributed to those rituals requiring that animals be drained of blood and their blood splashed on religious altars, including the altars of the Lord God Yahweh. Originally it was menstrual blood that was splashed upon the altar of the goddess.

The ancient Hebrews, and the Catholic authorities, therefore, deemed a menstruating woman as unclean, for menstrual blood had the power of life and that of the supernatural. Women in general, therefore, were subject to attack, with the ancient Jews reciting a prayer thanking god "for not making me a woman." However, it was her reproductive facility, and thus her association with the goddess that was most feared and detested.

As detailed by Robert Briffault in his brilliant text, "The Mothers" (Briffault, 1931) "the supernatural source which magic powers are regarded as being primarily derived is... connected in the closest manner with the functions of women... her... reproductive functions... and a power which is used in a dread-inspiring manner. And by virtue of their natural position and function, the wielder of domestic magic...she had charge of the sacred objects and performed all the religious functions connected with the household."

Yet another factor in the religious persecution of woman, was her facility at speech. Indeed, and as is now well demonstrated, females demonstrate clear language superiorities over males, and they even talk faster as well (Joseph, 2000b). Speech and language, that is, a woman's tongue, is her natural and traditional weapon, which she may use for "pronouncing curses, of casting spells... of bewitching and performing incantations. It was a dreaded power. The curse of a woman is accounted far more potent than the curse of a man" (Briffault, 1931). Women in general, therefore, were considered suspect by the Catholic authorities and during the Middle Ages they were rounded up, sexually tortured, and killed.

THE CATHOLIC CHURCH DECLARES WAR AGAINST WOMEN

Woman has been persecuted by various religious authorities because of the power of her tongue, her reproductive power, her associations with pagan goddesses, and her ability to enchant men with her sexuality.

Woman is biologically predisposed to having multiple orgasms, multiple partners, and to indulging in promiscuity—which does not mean she will necessarily behave promiscuously (Joseph, 2000a,c). Nevertheless, because of her sexual nature and association with fertility, religious rituals of the goddess stereotypically involved sexual orgies and ritual prostitution.

Male authorities, both religious and otherwise, have also attempted throughout the ages to control and yoke female sexuality.

However, in Europe, including Rome, during the 6th through 11th century, female sexuality and her promiscuous nature was openly flaunted, and the worship of pagan goddesses had become widespread and was threatening the authority of the Church.

In fact, as early as the 1st century, the missionary sermons of St. Paul were repeatedly drowned out by women chanting "Diana, Diana, Diana;" Diana being the goddess known since prehistoric times as the Queen of Heaven.

Unable to suppress the goddess cult, and the fertility rites of her worshippers, the Catholic Church finally issued the "Canon Episcopi" in the 10th century: "Some wicked women, reverting to Satan, and seduced by the illusions and phantasms of demons, believe and profess that they ride at night with Diana, on beasts, with an innumerable multitude of women. It would be well if these women, one and all, perished for their infidelities."

HOLY WAR: WOMAN THE WITCH, SORCERESS, AND HEALER

The proclamation, however, had little effect. Hence, in 1252, Pope Innocent IV issued the Ad Exitrpanda, which authorized the execution of heretics (e.g. wealthy landowners) and the seizure of their goods, and the prolonged sexual torture of women who were beautiful, wealthy, or old, ugly, and eccentric and/or who gathered in groups to talk and converse and possibly worship pagan, goddesses. This was followed by the first Papal bull on sorcery, in 1259, and yet another bull, the notorious Super illius specula, in 1322 (by Pope John the XXII), and then the famous Bull Summis desiderantes affectibus, in 1484 (by Pope Innocent VIII), which demanded the death of these women. The Popes and the Catholic Church proclaimed them witches and declared war against women.

Being "true soldiers of Christ," the Dominicans Heinrich Kramer and Johann Sprenger responded to this Papal decree by writing and issuing the Malleus Maleficarum (witch's hammer), thus unleashing a murderous, sadistic, blood lust that demanded the sexual torture and burning of "woman the witch, healer and sorceress" (Achterberg, 1991; Gies & Gies 1978; Lederer 1968). "For she is a liar by nature, so in her speech she stings while she delights us… for her voice is like the song of the Sirens, who with their sweet melody entice the passerby's and kill them..." (Malleus Maleficarum).

These sadistic misogynists were soon seconded by Bishop Bossuet, of France, who believed there was an army of 180,000 witches threatening France and Rome, all of them beautiful and thus bewitching. The Bishop then demanded that they be gathered up in one body and that "all be burned at once in one fire."

And the great sin of these women? According to the Malleus Maleficarum "Carnal lust!. All witchcraft comes from carnal lust, which in women is insatiable."

As summed up by Lederer (1968) in his interesting book, The Fear of Women, "witchcraft was a woman-thing, and the persecution of witches a man-thing; for it was first and last the women who were being persecuted and burned." In fact, hundreds of thousands of women were murdered, whole populations were destroyed, and some villages were left with only one female inhabitant. In 1404 alone, it is estimated that the Papal fathers burned at least 30,000 women. So many women were murdered, that it could be said that the Church was attempting no less than a whole sale genocide of women—"sexocide" at Lederer put it.

As noted, because many of the men (the Crusaders) had been killed or were serving in the army of the Catholic Lord God, the women were often left unprotected and sometimes whole villages were destroyed, or all the women in a given area were rounded up by the Catholic authorities and then sexually murdered.

These women, particularly those who were exceedingly attractive or ugly, were then hideously tortured and then slaughtered by burning, boiling in oil, crushing, and via whatever device the religious authorities felt appropriate or which suited their sick minds. In Germany huge ovens were constructed for the purposes of mass female murder (Achterberg, 1991; Lederer 1968). As noted, even the Lord God Yahweh recommended that haughty, beautiful women be burned in the fire.

However, it was not just beautiful females, for they come in a limited supply, but those who were old, eccentric, childless, and particularly women who owned property and pets, such as cats. Indeed, the cats would be tortured and murdered alongside the women. The "Black Plague" in fact was in part a consequence of the denunciation and killing of cats, coupled with the sanctification of rats and mice (the proverbial church mouse), by the Catholic authorities.

As to the children of these witches, the Church had only "compassion." These children would be merely flogged in front of the fires in which their mothers were burning.

Predominantly, when the priests set upon a village, it was the young and beautiful who were generally the first to be tortured, as they were experts at love magic. These beautiful women would bewitch men by shooting mesmerizing "beams of light from their eyes" which causes the man to fall in love (Briffault, 1931).

As pointed out by Dominicans Heinrich Kramer and Johann Sprenger, "Consider also her gait, posture, and habit, which is vanity of vanities. There is no man in the world who studies so hard to please the good God as even an ordinary woman studies by her vanities to please men… who... they infect with witchcraft by inclining men to inordinate passion. Yet...her heart is a net, it speaks of the inscrutable malice which reigns in their hearts... for they fulfill their lusts by consorting with devils."

According to Pope Innocent VIII, these women "have given themselves up to devils in the form of incubi and succubi. By their incantations, spells, crimes, and infamous acts they destroy the fruit of the womb in women, in cattle and various other animals; they destroy crops, vines, orchards...they render husbands impotent."

Of course, they also had the power to heal, so when the Archbishop of St. Andrews became ill and his physicians were unable to provide him with a cure, he sent for a well known woman healer whose expertise was in the making of ointments, Allison Peirsoun of Byrehill. Her cure was a success! So, the Archbishop had her tortured and burned.

RELIGIOUS SEXUAL SADISM

The torture of women, of course, was sexual. The woman would be stripped and her body, breasts, and orifices would be thoroughly investigated for the mark of the devil. However, the "investigation" was made with long needles and conducted by priestly specialists called "prickers," who would stick these needles into every suspected Devil's mark.

After the women became unconscious or unresponsive to the continued pricking, the priests would then employ "gresillons which crushed the tips of fingers and toes in the vice; the echelle, or rack, for stretching the body; the tortillon for squeezing its tender parts... legs were broken, even into fragments... or the legs would be grilled on the caschielawis...the fingernails were pulled off with the turkas, or pincers, and needles driven up to their heads into the quick."

As summed up by Henry Charles Lea: "Protestants and Catholics rivaled each other in the madness of the hours... Christendom seemed to have grown delirious, and Satan might well have smiled at the tribute to his powers seen in the endless smoke of the holocaust which bore witness to his triumph over the Almighty."

SEXUALITY, THE GODDESS AND THE SERPENT

Sexuality is a major concern of most major religions (Lederer 1968; Parrinder 1980; Smart 1969) as well as the limbic system. In fact, almost all major religions and their Gods, either act to promote sexuality, or to suppress it. This should not be entirely surprising for religions are very sexual and many were originally concerned with the fertility of the fields and the abundance of prey (Campbell 1988; Frazier 1950; Harris,1993; Kuhn 1955; Malinowski 1948; Parrinder 1980; Prideux 1973). Religious rituals evolved accordingly begin-

Figure 65.*A swollen naked breasted Yakshimi (tree goddess). Wither her swollen breasts, wide hips, slim waist and shaved vagina, she is the ideal estrus female. From Mathura, 2nd century India.*

Figure 66. *Venus and the lovers. An allegorical joke and a blasphemy in which the virgin Mary is depicted as naked and being adored by angels and devout men. (second figure) The penitent Magdalen.*

ning with the cult of the goddess, the sacred feminine, the Great Mother of All.

As summed up by Halle Austen (1990) in her book, The Heart of the Goddess, "creativity, the power to manifest physical and psychic reality, is one of the Goddess's primary aspects...the source of all being. She appears as the Great Mother, the Sustainer of Life, the Cosmic Creatrix. It is from her that all life proceeds and to her that all life returns." And, "just as our ancestors honored a woman's ability to create humans from her womb and feed them from her breast, they also honored the Earth as the Great Mother who nourishes us" and the sky and heavens as the Great Mother who would nourish the Earth and her children with drops of life sustaining rain.

Aditi, the Hindu Goddess of the Void, for example, represented "creative power" and "abundance," and the cosmic womb from which all creation has its source. The goddess is also known as the celestial cow and the golden calf who provides nourishment not just to humans, but the gods. As the Great Mother also nourishes the gods, she is also the guardian of cosmic harmony and order.

The cult of the goddess has its origins in the Paleolithic. Hence the numerous "Venus" statues and carvings of heavy breasted pregnant women.

The goddess cult continued to reign supreme during the Neolithic and she was worshipped by the ancient Sumerians, Egyptians, Akkadians, Babylonians, Hebrews, and in fact all ancient peoples including those of the Americas and Australia.

The Australian Aborigines, for example, are not only the oldest continuous culture that has survived on this planet, but they have worshipped the Great Mother, the "All Mother" since time immemorial, depicting her as giving birth in dreamtime to all the peoples of the Earth.

Because the sun also nourishes the Earth, the Goddess was also a goddess of the sun, for the sun was originally thought to be female. Hence, Igaehindvo the Cherokee Sun Goddess, Brigit the Celtic Fire Goddess, and Amaterasu Omikami the Great Spirit Shining in Heaven and Goddess of the sun of ancient Japan: "The radiance of the Sun Goddess filled the universe and all the deities rejoiced." In ancient Egypt the goddess Nut was believed to have given birth to the sun.

Woman was also associated with the sun and fire because in many ancient cultures, it was believed that woman first discovered the art of making fire, which she used to warm the people and prepare the food. Fire is also a symbol of spiritual awakening and knowledge of the spirit world.

The goddess, therefore, was associated in all ways with all things having to do with life and death, and the spirit world.

"I am Nature, the universal Mother, mistress of all the elements, sovereign of all things spiritual, queen of the dead. Though I am worshipped in many aspects, known by countless names, and propitiated with all manner of different rites, the whole earth venerates me." -Apuleius, second century B.C.

It is noteworthy that in addition to being the source of all life, that the Goddess was also associated with the serpent. The Sumerian "god" Enki, was depicted as a snake, and sometimes as a snake with breasts. The peoples of predynastic Egypt also worshipped the goddess in the form of a snake. In ancient Egypt, the hieroglyph for "snake" also means Goddess.

The Hindu Goddess Kali wore a garland of snakes around her neck—which represented the female life force, the transformative power of Shakti. Shakti was often depicted by the ancient Hindus and the pre-Aryan Dravidans, with a kundalini snake emerging from her womb and vagina.

The snake although an obvious phallic, and thus sexual symbol, is also associated with wisdom. Hence, the snake in the garden of Eden not only tempts Eve, but he induces her to eat of the fruit of the tree of knowledge. In fact, throughout the world snakes have commonly been the companions of oracles, those who had special knowledge of the future.

Figure 67. *Sumerian depiction of an Anunnaki female serpent "god."*

Figure 68. *The Mayan and Aztec god, Quetzalcoatl seated upon his jaguar throne next to his emblem, a giant feathered serpent.*

Figure 69. *Flying disc/winged globe of Egypt, with two serpents.*

The snake represents supernatural knowledge and power which is one of the reasons the Lord God instructed Moses to "take your rod and cast it down before Pharaoh. It shall turn into a serpent... Then Pharaoh called the wisemen and the sorcerers, now the magicians of Egypt and they... cast down every man his rod, and they became serpents: But Aron's rod swallowed up their rods" (Exodus 7:10-12). And, it was a serpent which Moses carried as a fetish which he used to protect and lead the Israelites as they wondered for 40 years in the desert.

Nevertheless, because of its association with wisdom, sexuality, and woman, the serpent also came to be viewed as evil. The Lord God condemned the serpent, whereas the Catholic Church depicted this reptile as synonymous with Satan, the Devil. Both woman and the serpent became enemies of the Lord God.

SEX, FOOD, AND RELIGION

The limbic system mediates not only sexuality, but internal homeostasis and food intake. Likewise, many modern mystical and religious practices have also involved the ritual control over sex and food. This includes many American Indian, Christian, Jewish, and Moslem sects (Campbell 1988; Parrinder 1980; Smart 1969). Thus the commandment "thou shalt not... " These are limbic taboos, as eating and sexuality (like murder and violence) are under limbic control.

Many limbic taboos, however, promote survival, for example, by proscribing the eating of poisonous plants or unclean animals. Similarly, by forbidding anal or indiscriminate sex one was spared the wrath of this "God" and whatever plagues he might send in the form of venereal disease or viruses. If we rule out the possibility of an attack with nuclear armed missiles, mass death due to disease is presumably what became of Sodom and Gomorrah where the anal sex crazed mobs attempted to sodomize even the angels sent by the "Lord God" himself (Genesis 19).

Sex and food (along with fear, rage, and aggression) are probably the most powerful of all limbic emotions and motivaters. If sufficiently hungry or sexually aroused, these conditions can completely overwhelm the brain. Limbic hyperactivation in turn can induce religious or spiritual dreams or hallucinations.

Hungry men, women, and infants will dream of food. Those who are sexually aroused will dream of sex. However, a parched and starving man will not just dream, he will hallucinate food and water and will attempt to slake his desires by consuming a hallucination.

Given that early (as well as modern) human populations were often concerned with obtaining food (as well as a sex partner) many of their earliest religious beliefs and rituals were therefore concerned with increasing the abundance of game animals as well as preserving their own progeny (Armstrong 1994; Campbell 1988; Frazier 1950; Harris,1993; Kuhn 1955; Parrinder 1980; Prideux 1973). As noted, many an ancient Upper Paleolithic cave was decorated with fertility and sex symbols, including pregnant women (Venus figures) and animals (Bandi 1961; Joseph 1996; Kuhn 1955; Leroi-Gurhan 1964), whereas Egyptian tombs contain numerous paintings of food and goddesses.

Thus, given our ancient hunter-gatherer (and then later, farming) heritage, many religions both ancient and relatively modern are highly concerned with fertility and food, and tend to be very sexual and limbic in orientation if not origin. This is also why there have always been fertility goddesses and gods who are associated with eating and drinking, especially alcohol (Campbell 1988; Frazier 1950; James 1958; Parrinder 1980; Smart 1969). This also includes, for example, Osiris, and especially Dyonisus who was among other things, a sex crazed dancing god of the vine. In fact, one of the first miracles performed by Jesus involved making wine from water, and, as we know, Jesus surrounded himself with highly sexual women, prostitutes who would sometimes rub precious oil on his body.

SEX, GOD, AND RELIGION

RELIGIOUS LOVE CHARMS AND SPIRITUAL SEXUALITY

Among the ancient religions of India and China, the sexual activity of the Gods and the promotion of similar sexual activities among the believers were widespread religious practices and beliefs (Austin 1990; Campbell 1988; Parrinder 1980).

Figure 70. *The god Shiva and the most feminine and lovely of his shktis, Parvati the daughter of a Himilayan god. Shiva and Parvati symbolize the union of the female and male energy of the cosmos. The god Vishnu and his voluptuous and swollen breasted Lakshmi. From a stone panel in the temple of Khajuracho, 10th century.*

For example, the ancient Vedas were greatly concerned not only with the worship of various nature gods, but with the rituals of sexual union. Ancient Indian religious texts are filled with love charms and instructions as to how to win the love of a man or woman, or to protect against demons.

Temple prostitutes were also quite common throughout India and the Middle East, as well as in Rome and Greece. Some temples employed so many girls that they were like giant brothel emporiums (Parrinder 1980). As noted, sexuality and desire (like religious feeling) are directly mediated by the amygdala and hypothalamus.

In fact, sexual intercourse became a religious ritual among Hindus and Buddhists who practiced "tantra." The practitioners of tantra were inspired by visions of cosmic sex and the acquisition of sexual energy. Through tantra one might be confronted with the cosmic mystery of creation as exemplified by another deity, Shakti, the divine mother. However, restrictions on where one could have sexual intercourse (not in public) and certain types of sexual acts such as oral sex, were prohibited as well as sex with strange women or those of a lower caste (Parrinder 1980). Nevertheless the joys of sex were continually emphasized and embraced. Hence, the Kama Sutra, the "love text".

On the other hand, it was believed by some ancient far Eastern sects that in order to gain power, one had to break taboos and, for example, engage in sexual orgies or have sex with women while they were menstruating. Menstrual blood was believed to possess the spiritual and creative life force, whereas sexual orgies were believed to liberate tremendous amounts of sexual energy.

These "taboo" sexual practices were also a form of tantra, referred to as "left handed tantra." Those who followed the way of the left handed trantra claimed that passion was nirvana and that adepts should cultivate all sexual pleasures (Parrinder 1980). Both male and female deities, usually in the act of having sex, were worshipped.

Ancient Chinese and Taoists religions are also quite sexual (Austin 1990; Parrinder 1980). These beliefs are exemplified by the concepts of Yin and Yang which appeared over 3000 years ago and which represented the male and female principles of the universe. Sexual intercourse was viewed as a symbolic union of the earth and heaven, which, during rainstorms were believed to mate. By engaging in sexual relations man and woman achieved harmony by following the example of the gods.

THE LORD GOD: A SEXUAL GOD

Beginning at about the same time that the Judaic religion became more dominant in certain areas of the Middle East, around 3,000 years ago, and over the following thousand years a tremendous change in religious sexual thought began to flourish, enveloping the Roman Empire, and which eventually paralleled and coincided with the development of Christianity and Islam.

Unlike the goddess and the highly sexual gods of, for example, the ancient Greeks and Romans, the "Lord God" of the Old Testament does not have sex with human women and there is no hint of sexual duality in his personage. He is a male god, a warrior and destroyer. Although not overtly sexual, the sexual activities of men and especially women were of great concern to Him. Be fruitful and multiply, He ordered, and as to certain women who were presumably barren, and in one case, still a virgin, He is reported to have opened their wombs.

Male sexuality was also a concern; that is, the diminishment of the intensity of man's sexual pleasure. Thus He required a form of sexual self-mutilation. As part of his covenant with Abraham and the Israeli people, it was ordered that every male child would suffer the amputation of the tip of his penis (which is densely innervated by fibers that yield intense sexual pleasure): "And ye shall circumcise the flesh of your foreskin; and it shall be a token of the covenant betwixt me and you" (Genesis 17: 10-11).

Although there is no evidence that the Lord God was sexually active with human females, it does appear that the Lord God had a sexual consort, the goddess Sophia, before he became the Lord God of the Earth. Sophia was the goddess of wisdom and she was not only his lover, she may have been his sister: "It is Wisdom calling. Understanding raising her voice. I Wisdom, live with Prudence; I attain knowledge and foresight... The Lord possessed me in the beginning in his own way, before his works of old...When he prepared the heavens, I was there...I was by him as one brought up with him. I was daily his delight, rejoicing always before him" (Proverbs 8).

In addition, it appears that she may have betrayed Him. "Rejoicing in the habitable part of the earth, and my delights were with the sons of men" (Proverbs 8:31).

It is true, however, that the above quote may mean that she simply was delighted by the sons of men, and did not have sex per se with men.

However, if she did betray Him, this may explain why she is never again referred to, as well as His following complaints: "Aholah played the harlot when she was mine; and she doted on her lovers...desirable young men...thus she committed her whoredoms with them and with all whom she doted... she defiled herself" (Ezekiel 21: 5-7). "Like mother, like daughter. You are the daughter of your mother, who rejected her husband" (Ezekiel 16: 44-45).

It may also explain His jealous prying nature, and obvious dislike of the female sex and his recommendation that women who were truly attractive and sexually desirable should be burnt (Isaiah 3:16-26, 4:4) as they were all "whores" (Hosea 2).

"Because the daughters of Zion walk with wanton eyes, mincing as they go, and making a tinkling with their feet...The Lord shall wash away the filth of the daughters of Zion... by the spirit of burning" -Isaiah 3:16-26, 4:4.

Indeed, Sophia's "delights with the sons of men" and her betrayal of the Lord God may explain why He not only disdains pretty women, but pardons and encourages the sexual exploitation of women and the rape and sexual slavery of women, and their murder if they dare behave like whores. In fact, He brags that he "delivered...Aholah who played the harlot when she was mine...into the hand of the Assyrians... They discovered her nakedness; they took her sons and her daughters, and slew her with the sword... they executed judgment on her" (Ezekiel 23:9-10).

RELIGIOUS RAPE AND SEX SLAVERY

The Lord God is very concerned with the sexual relations between men and women, and those men He loved most dearly had sex with multiple sex partners. The Lord God even approved of sex slavery, including sex with little girls who are taken slave.

"Kill every male among the little ones. But all the women and female children that have not known a man, keep alive for yourselves." -Numbers, 31

The permissive attitude of the Lord God when it comes to female sex slavery may explain why the modern state of Israel not only has no laws forbidding the owning or selling of human beings, but why non-Jewish women are openly sold as sex slaves in the state of Israel (see M. Specter, "Taffickers New Cargo: Naive Slavic Women, New York Times, January 11, 1998).

And, once a sex slave, always a sex slave, even if she is Jewish female.

"When you acquire a Hebrew slave... and if his master gave him a wife, and she has borne him children, the wife and her children shall belong to the master. When a man sells his daughter as a slave, she shall never be freed, as male slaves are." -Exodus, 21: 2-7.

And the Lord God even encourages and pardons the violent rape of young Jewish virgins by Jewish men. For example, after some of the Benjaminites raped a woman to death (Judges 19:25), and following the murder of their own women in retaliation by the other 11 tribes of Israel, these tribes then realized that the tribe of Benjamin would die out without women. So, they decided to attack yet another city of their fellow Jews and to "utterly destroy every male and every women that hath lain by man" with the exception of "young virgins" who the Benjaminites were allowed to rape (Judges 21:11-13).

However, not enough virgins were acquired following this massacre. So the Benjaminites were instructed by the Lord God to rape another group of young Jewish virgins.

"Then they said, Behold there is a feast of the Lord in Shiloh...Go and lie in wait in the vineyards. And see and behold if the daughters of Shiloh come out to dance in dances, then come ye out and catch you every man his wife of the daughters of Shiloh" (Judges 21:19-25).

The Benjaminites, however, enjoyed raping men as well as women, and were quite willing to gang rape a woman until she was dead (Judges 19:25-26, 20:5). However, according to the divine law, they could buy as well as brutally and sadistically rape female slaves, and if she lived for two days following a violent, brutal rape, there was no penalty.

Again, the Lord God of the ancient Jews had an obvious contempt for the female sex:

"Because the daughters of Zion are haughty and walk with stretched forth necks and wanton eyes, walking and mincing as they go, and making a tinkling with their feet; The Lord will smite with a scab of crowns of their head and the Lord will discover their secret parts. In that day the Lord will take away their tinkling ornaments...their bracelets...bonnets, ornaments...earrings, the rings...and fine linen...And it shall come to pass that instead of sweet smell there shall be stink." -Isaiah 3:16-26, 4:4.

Indeed, this Lord God, when angry, found pleasure in using explicit sexual imagery when condemning his people, Israel—whom He referred to as a woman when He was angry. Indeed, He repeatedly threatened to strip this brazen female "naked" and referred to her as an "adulterous harlot." Echoes of the divine betrayal by the Sophia, the goddess of Wisdom?

"And let her put away her harlotry from her face and her adultery from between her breasts. Else I will strip her naked... And I will snatch away My wool and My linen that serve to cover her nakedness. Now will I uncover her shame in the very sight of her lovers..." -Hosea 2.

SEXUALITY AND RELIGION

Although this volatile, mercurial, and masculine seeming "Lord God" was asexual, sexual behavior was of tremendous concern to "Him" for He commands sexual moral obedience—at least of women and married women in particular— and repeatedly tells his people, starting with Adam and Eve, "be fruitful and multiply."

And sexuality, and the condemnation and/or control of sexuality, remains a major concern of Christian and Moslem religions. However, although sexuality outside of marriage is condemned, modern Christian clerics and priests not uncommonly have sex with children, with each other, or with homosexual prostitutes.

According to the San Francisco Chronicle (Lattin, 7/15/97) homosexuality became so rampant within the ministry of the Episcopal church, and its homosexual clergy so openly promiscuous that the church lost over 5 million members by 1997.

According to Dr. Thomas Plante of the Jesuit college, Santa Clara University, and editor of a forthcoming book on sexuality and the church, "50% of the Catholic clergy are gay, even though they're not acting on it." However, according to the Boston Globe (1/31/2000) Catholic priests have a rate of HIV infection which is four times that of the general population. Indeed, recently the Bishop of the Santa Rosa Diocese in California was forced to resign because another priest accused the Bishop of repeatedly raping him.

Sex scandals are commonplace among priests and ministers.

The Reverend Jimmy Swaggart whose sermons were filled with fire and brimstone, and who regularly assailed Catholics, Jews (who "are going to Hell") pornography and prostitution, temporarily gave up a $150 million dollar a year world wide television ministry in 1988, when his fondness for prostitutes and pornography was exposed and he was caught with a prostitute. Moreover, the attorney who exposed Swaggart also claimed the minister was a pedophile. Swaggart has since returned to the ministry. During his sermons he yells, collapses to the floor, recounts conversations with god, repeatedly breaks into tears, and again rails against Catholics and Jews (who "are going to Hell"), and against pornography, prostitution, as well as hypocrisy.

Likewise, Jim Bakker lost a 300 million dollar ministry, when among other things, he and another pastor were accused of repeatedly sexually assaulting a young female member of their flock.

And more recently, the dean of Harvard Divinity School was forced to resign "for conduct unbecoming" after it was discovered that he had downloaded thousands of "explicit" pornographic images on his Harvard-owned computer in his Harvard-owned home.

Sexuality and religion are deeply entwined be it among members of cults or established religions. The Mormon Church initially willingly embraced, as a religious creed, the right of every man to have several wives; i.e. sex partners, and the founder of the Church was reputed to have 40 wives.

Likewise, Muhammed was reported to have the sexual prowess of forty men, and to have bedded at least 9 wives and numerous concubines including even one young girl (Lings 1983).

However, the grand champion of religious-sexual excess was King Solomon who required the sexual services of 700 wives and 300 concubines.

DAVID KORESH: SEXUAL THEOLOGY

David Koresh announced he was God in a wedding invitation to the Seventh Adventists Church in southern California. It read in part: "I will scold your daughters for their nakedness and pride that they parade in My Father's house, and by my angels, I will strip them naked before all eyes because of their foolish pride." Naked women at his mercy and who he would impregnate and "fill with seed" was his predominant religious fantasy.

As he confided to his "right hand man" Marc Breault early in his ministry: "I'll have women begging me to make love to 'em. Just imagine, virgins without number." Within just a couple of years he would be attended by at least twenty young women, most of whom he "married," including two that were just 14 years old, and one who was age 12 (Breault & King, 1993).

Sex was at the center of his theology, even claiming that god would take them to heaven in a divine spaceship that he sketched on a blackboard. It was an erect penis!

Koresh apparently was consumed by sexual thoughts and was the recipient of sexual visions that he claimed were sent to him by God. Soon he began demanding sex from the wives of his followers, women who he believed had married these other men without his permission and who should have married him

"All you men are just fuckers, that's all you are. You married without getting God's permission. Even worse, you married my wives. God gave them to me first. So now I'm taking them back."

According to Marc Breault, everybody was shocked, stunned, and Vernon kept saying things like: "So Scott, how does it feel to know your not married anymore... In October, 1989, he began having sex with the other men's wives... and directed the women to inform him when they had reached the fertile part of their cycle to maximize the chance of pregnancy." As per the men, Vernon informed them that it was their job to "defend King Solomon's bed."

Vernon not only had sex with and impregnated their wives—fathering over 20 children— but began having sex with these children; that is, when he wasn't beating them.

THE LIMBIC SYSTEM AND SEXUALITY

Why the concern regarding sex pro or con in religious thought? Why the illicit, perverse, or promiscuous tendencies of priests and other religious leaders? Sex, like religious experience, or the ability to derive pleasure from eating and drinking, is mediated by the limbic system; i.e. the hypothalamus, amygdala, and temporal and frontal lobes (e.g. Freemon & Nevis 1969; Joseph, 1988a, 1992a, 1999a; MacLean 1969, 1990; Remmillard 1983; Robinson & Mishkin 1968).

As noted, activation of the sexually dimorphic amygdala can produce penile erection and clitoral engorgement (Kling & Brothers, 1992; MacLean, 1990; Robinson & Mishkin, 1968; Stoffels et al., 1980), and trigger sexual feelings (Bancaud et al., 1970; Remillard et al., 1983), extreme pleasure (Olds and Forbes, 1981), memories of sexual intercourse (Gloor, 1986), as well as ovulation, uterine contractions, lactogenetic responses, and orgasm (Backman & Rossel, 1984; Currier et al., 1971; Freemon & Nevis, 1969; Remmillard et al., 1983).

However, the limbic system also mediates violent behavior, including sexually violent behavior. Thus religiosity also can also be tainted by violent sexual thoughts and behavior.

THE GODDESS, HOMOSEXUALITY, & RELIGIOUS EXPERIENCE

As noted, it has been estimated that 50% of Catholic priests are homosexuals, and that the HIV rate among Catholic Priests is four times that of the general population. In fact, throughout history, shaman and other religious figures have commonly been homosexuals. Homosexuals are probably drawn to the priesthood for the same reason that women have been viewed as more in touch with the supernatural; i.e., the sexual differentiation of the limbic system.

Recall that portions of the hypothalamus and amygdala are sexually dimorphic; i.e. there are male and female amygdaloid nuclei (Bubenik & Brown, 1973; Nishizuka & Arai, 1981). Female amygdala neurons are smaller and more numerous, and densely packed than those of the male (Bubenik & Brown, 1973; Nishizuka & Arai, 1981), and smaller, densely packed neurons fire more easily and frequently than larger ones. This may contribute to the fact that females are more religious, more emotional and more easily frightened than males as the amygdala is a principle structure involved in evoking feelings of fear (Davis et al., 1997; Gloor, 1997; LeDoux, 1996) as well as spirituality.

THE FEMALE LIMBIC SYSTEM AND RELIGIOUS EXPERIENCE

Confirming common experience, numerous scientific studies have demonstrated that women display clear superiorities over males in regard to the expression, perception, and comprehension of social emotional nuances, regardless of the manner in which they are conveyed (Burton & Levy, 1989; Brody, 1985; Buck, 1977, 1984; Buck et al., 1974, 1982; Card et al., 1986; Eisenberg et al., 1989; Fuchs & Thelan, 1988; Harackiewicz, 1982; Lewis, 1983, Rubin, 1983; Safer, 1981; Shennum & Bugental, 1982; Strayer, 1980). And this is true even from the earliest stages of childhood.

This greater social emotional sensitivity, including a much greater likelihood of becomes frightened and easily terrified, is likely due to sex differences in the functional and structural organization of the limbic system, the amygdala in particular. Because female amygdala neurons are more numerous and packed more closely together (Bubenik & Brown, 1973; Nishizuka & Arai, 1981), and as smaller, tightly packed neurons demonstrate enhanced electrical excitability, lower response thresholds, and increase susceptibility to kindling, there is thus a tendency for the female amygdala to become hyperactivated more easily than the male amygdala—thus inducing extreme fear as well as a propensity for religious and spiritual feelings.

Indeed, women are not just more emotional, but have more intense religious experiences, attend church more often, are more involved in religious activities, involve their children more in religious studies, hold more orthodox religious views, incorporate religious beliefs more often in their daily lives and activities, and pray more often as well (Argyle & Beit-Hallahami, 1975; Batason & Ventis, 1982; De Vaus & McAllister Glock. 1967; Lazerwitz, 1961; Lindsey, 1990; Sapiro, 1990).

Moreover, the anterior commissure, a thick rope of axonal fibers which interconnects the right and left amygdala of the right and left temporal lobe is also sexually differentiated. The anterior commissure is responsible for information transfer as well as inhibition within the limbic system. Specifically, the female anterior commissure is 18% larger than in the male (Allen & Gorski 1992).

Thus not only is the female amygdala more excitable, but the right and left amygdala (located in the right and left temporal lobe) can more easily communicate and excite one another. Hence, again, the increased tendency for females to become easily frightened and to be religiously inclined. To know fear is to know god.

THE HOMOSEXUAL LIMBIC SYSTEM AND SPIRITUAL EXPERIENCE

Although the etiology of homosexuality remains in question, it has been shown that the ventromedial and anterior nuclei of the hypothalamus of male homosexuals demonstrate the female pattern of development (Levay, 1991; Swaab, 1990), whereas the anterior commissure, which interconnects the right and left amygdala/temporal lobe, is "hyper-female" in size (Allen, & Gorski (1992). Male homosexuals are in possession of limbic system that is more "female" than "male" in functional as well as structural orientation.

This female pattern of limbic system development also explains why homosexuals are more inclined to behave and think like women rather than men. Indeed, homosexual males and females tend to be more alike than different in regard to social-emotional reactions and tendencies (Tripp 1987). In some cases these feminine tendencies are grossly exaggerated (Tripp, 1987); i.e. the "swishy" male with the exaggerated high pitched voice.

A significant number of homosexuals, in fact, are psychologically similar to females in a number of ways, including having a high interest in fashion and wearing apparel, a pronounced tendency to employ feminine body language and vocal tones, to shun sports and avoid fights, and to have a fear of physical injury, particularly during childhood (Bell et al. 1981; Bieber et al. 1962; Van Den Aardweg, 1984; Tripp, 1987). Many also tend to maintain intense dependency relations with their mothers and to remain distant from strong male figures including their fathers (Green, 1987).

As children homosexual males tend to prefer female companions and friends, girls toys, activities, and often girls clothes, (Bell, et al. 1981; Saghir & Robins, 1973; Grellet et al. 1982; Green, 1987).From 67% to 75% of homosexuals vs 2%-3% of heterosexual males reported being "feminine" and more like girls than boys as children (Saghir & Robins, 1973; Green, 1987).

Thus, being in possession of a "female" limbic system may not only account for similarities between homosexuals and women in regard to fear and other behaviors, but in respect to spirituality. Thus priests and shamans not only tend to be homosexuals, but public displays of overt homosexual activity and promiscuity coupled with religious fervor often comes to characterize the behavior of homosexual clergy, as was the case within the ministry of the Episcopal church, and which appears to be the case in the Catholic Church, at least covertly.

The homosexual limbic system, however, is actually organized in a hyper-female fashion. When compared to the female and especially the male limbic system, the homosexual limbic system could be considered different from the male and female "norm." And as noted, abnormalities in the limbic system or hyperactivity, is associated with hypersexuality, transvestitism, and public displays of sexuality (Blumer, 1970; 1999; Davies and Morgenstern, 1960; Kolarsky, et al., 1967; Leutmezer et al., 1999; Terzian and Ore, 1955).

As noted in an earlier chapter, in ancient religions, including those who worshipped the great goddess, male youths would sometimes castrate themselves, and would forever after dress as women in order to obtain her power and serves as her priests.

Goddess cults have always been associated with fertility rites and woman's sexuality. Homosexuality between women worshippers was common, whereas when men were allowed to participate, the religious service would become a sex orgy. That modern day homosexual priests with their female limbic system behave similarly is therefore to be expected.

HOMOSEXUAL PRIESTLY DISDAIN FOR THE FEMALE SEX

Despite the "love" between women that has always characterized the goddess cults, women in general, and young women in particular are sexually quite competitive and tend to feel considerable disdain for attractive women (Joseph, 1985, 2000d). That is, they feel threatened by sexy attractive women; a feeling of threat that can border on intense dislike if not hate for those women who are particularly sexy and especially those who flaunt their sexuality (Joseph, 1985, 2000d).

Fertile and sexy women are not only disliked by other women, but, as noted, aroused considerable hate among the priests of Yahweh, the Lord God, and the Catholic Clergy during the Middle Ages and until recently. Given that so many priests are in fact homosexuals, and have a "female" limbic system, and are thus similar to women in so many ways, this may also explain the extreme hatred for the female sex as expressed by the Lord God and innumerable theologians including the Lord God.

"If it was good company and conversation that Adam needed, it would have been much better if god were to have arranged to have two men together as friends, not a man and a woman." -St. Augustine.

MIND OF THE MESSENGER

A not uncommon characteristic of high levels of limbic system and inferior temporal lobe activity are changes in sexuality as well as a deepening of religious fervor (Bear 1979; Blumer, 1970; Slater & Beard 1963; Trimble 1991; Taylor 1972, 1975). Hypersexuality or conversely, hyposexuality is not uncommon.

It is noteworthy that not just modern day evangelists, but many ancient religious leaders, including Abraham, Jacob (Israel) and Muhammed, tended to be highly sexual and partook of many partners (e.g. St. Augustine of Hippo: "Give me chastity, 'o lord, but just not yet"), or, they shared their wives (Abraham), or they married women who were harlots (e.g. Hosea) or had sex with other men's wives (Muhammed, King David), or killed other men in order to marry or have sex with their wives (King David).

King Solomon (like his father King David) experienced numerous dream states in which he communicated with God, and he required the sexual services of 700 wives and 300 concubines.

TEMPORAL LOBE SEIZURES

Signs of limbic system hyperactivity and seizure activity include loss of consciousness, trance states, dreamy states, auditory and visual hallucinations and related disturbances of the auditory and visual system involving language and reading and writing. The disturbances of language and speech are due to the involvement of the temporal lobe in auditory and reading comprehension. That is, the language areas, upon receiving visual signals, provide the auditory equivalent to a written word so that the person knows what the written words sounds like (Joseph, 1982, 1996, 2000a).

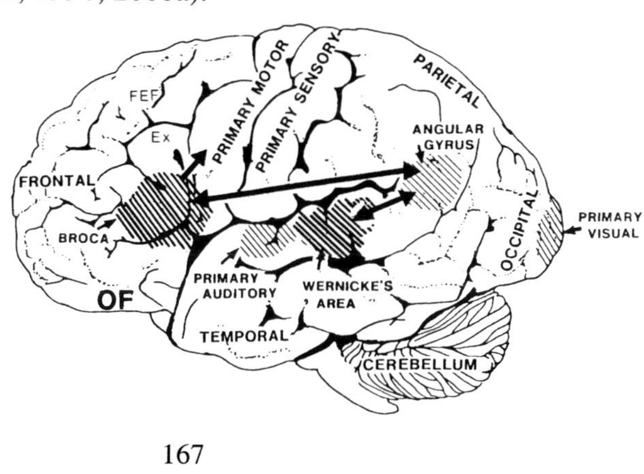

Figure 71. *The language axis of the left hemisphere.*

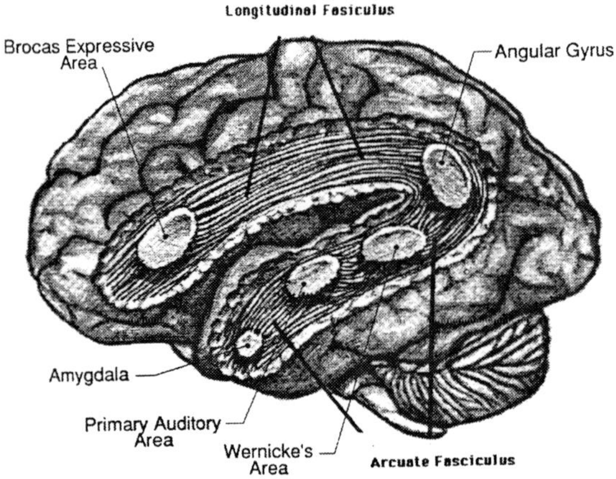

Figure 72. *Cutaway diagram depicting the pathway of the language areas of the left hemisphere, including the amygdala, Wernicke's receptive speech area, the angular gyrus (assimilation area) and Broca's expressive speech area.*

The auditory association area in the left temporal lobe (Wernicke's receptive speech area) not only comprehends incoming speech but assists in the programming of Broca's expressive speech area in the frontal lobe. It is Broca's area which produces speech, and a tissue immediately above Broca's area subserves writing. Therefore, abnormalities in the temporal lobe can induce severe disturbances of speech including abnormalities in the ability to write and spell words. In this regard it is noteworthy that whereas Moses suffered from a severe speech impediment and was slow of tongue, Muhammed, God's messenger, was apparently dyslexic and agraphic. He was unable to read or write.

On the other hand, hyperactivity in these limbic and temporal lobe structures can also induce pressured speech and writing. The afflicted individual may feel compelled to preach and to write out their mystical thoughts (Joseph, 2000a). Certain individuals who develop "temporal lobe epilepsy" or irritative lesions to this tissue, may suddenly become hyperreligious and spend hours reading and talking about the Bible or other religious issues. They may spend hours every day preaching or writing out their mystical or religious thoughts, or engaging in certain actions and movements they believe have religious significance. Many modern day religious writers who also happen to suffer from epilepsy are in fact exceedingly prolific, whereas conversely, those who feel impelled to preach tend to do just that. In fact, many of the prophets reported that they felt forced to preach and prophesize even though they struggled not to.

Temporal lobe hyperactivity or temporal lobe epilepsy is not usually associated with tonic clonic seizures and patients do not flail about on the ground. In some instances, particularly if the amygdala and amygdala-striatum is impacted, the patient may appear to be in a trance, and they may experience pleasant or unpleasant odors, heart palpations, difficulty breathing, excessive sweating, and disturbances of movement, ranging from a complete freezing of the body to spasmodic movements of the arms and legs (Joseph, 1999a, 2000a).

Following a temporal lobe seizure the patient may stagger about like a "stunned ox." In this regard when the prophet Jeremiah experienced the Lord God, his arms and legs convulsed and he staggered about like a drunk.

In addition, the presence of "god" may be experienced through dreams, through visions, and through voices—and it is usually a terrifying experience which grips the prophet like a seizure: "And I saw this great vision, and there remained no strength in me, for my comeliness was turned in me into corruption, and I retained no strength" (Daniel, 10:8); that is, he defecated and urinated on himself, as he fell to the ground—a not uncommon manifestation of certain seizures.

Daniel claimed he immediately lost consciousness before being confronted by the Lord god: "Thus was I in deep sleep on my face, and my face toward the ground" when an angel appeared in a prophetic vision (Daniel 10:9).

Likewise, Abraham would lose consciousness just prior to experiencing these "visions" or upon hearing the voice of the Lord God. "And a deep sleep fell upon Abraham (Genesis, 15:1,2).

In addition, and as discussed in earlier chapters, hyperactivity in this area of the brain can induce terror and severe depression, auditory and visual hallucinations, as well as religious fervor and even feelings of possession.

RELIGIOUS CASE HISTORIES

Consider Mary (described by Mesulam, 1981), a 26 year old female, A-average college student. For several months she had been complaining of odd mystical experiences involving alterations in consciousness, accompanied by auditory and visual hallucinations as well as frequent experiences of deja vu. These mystical experiences soon progressed to feelings of being possessed by the Devil. She was convinced the Devil was urging and trying to make her do horrible things to other people or to herself. She also claimed he would sometimes loudly cackle inside her head. Finally, a priest was brought in and a rite of exorcism was performed, as the Catholic hierarchy became convinced of the authenticity of her experiences, that she was possessed. However, her condition failed to improve. Finally an EEG was performed and abnormal activity was discovered to be emanating from both temporal lobes.

Another 44 year old female college graduate suffering from temporal lobe abnormalities instead came to believe she was possessed by God and at times also thought she was the Messiah, and at the behest of God, had a special mission to fulfill (Mesulam 1981). At the urgings of the "God" she ran for public office and almost won. However, she also engaged in some rather bizarre actions including widespread and inappropriate sexual activity -another manifestation of limbic hyperactivation (see also Schenk, and Bear 1981; Trimble 1991).

In a classic case described over 120 years ago by Sommer (1880), a 25 year-old man who suffered several seizures a day, claimed to have had repeated conversations with God. God's voice spoke to him quite clearly. One day, God told him he was Jesus Christ and to go forth and perform miracles. The first miracle he was to perform was fly through the air. So convinced was he that these revelations were real, and that he was in fact "The Christ" that this young man climbed up on a roof and leaped into the air. At autopsy he was found to have a hard sclerotic lesion of the right Ammon's horn; i.e. the hippocampus. Sommer (1880) concluded that these religious hallucinations (and all hallucinations and sensory illusions) were directly due to abnormalities in this and adjoining tissue—which includes the amygdala; the two core structures of the limbic system and temporal lobe.

MUHAMMED

In order to receive the word of God, Muhammed would typically lose consciousness and enter into trance states (Armstrong 1994; Lings 1983). However, he had his first truly spiritual-religious conversion when he was torn from his sleep by the archangel Gabriel who enveloped him in an terrifying embrace so overpowering that Muhammed's breath was squeezed from his lungs.

"Recite!" (iqra!) the angel demanded.

Muhammed refused: "I am not a recitor!"

The angel again enveloped him in a crushing embrace, squeezing the air from his lungs. Again the angel demanded: "Recite!" and again Muhammed refused. And then the angel crushed him a third time, at which point words began to pour from Muhammed's mouth:

"Recite in the name of thy Sustainer, who has created—created man out of a germ-cell! Recite—for thy Sustainer is the Most Bountiful, One who has taught (man) the use of pen—taught him what he did not know!"

Because the angel forced Muhammed to recite the words of God, it is for this reason that the book of Islam is called the qur'an: "Recitation."

This was the first of many such episodes Muhammed had with the archangel Gabriel who sometimes appeared in a titanic kaleidoscopic panoramic form.

Muhammed, however, was initially exceedingly distressed, horrified by what he had experienced, for he also feared that he may have been "possessed by a jinn," a sprite. It was commonly believed among the Arabic community that some people had their own individual, personal jinni who could provide them with good luck and inspiration.

Muhammed did not know what to think. Shattered by the experience and overcome with feelings of suicidal terror and depression, Muhammed finally decided to throw himself from a cliff. Again the angel Gabriel appeared to him as he stood at the precipice.

According to Muhammed: "I heard a voice from heaven saying, O Muhammed! thou art the apostle of God and I am Gabriel. I raised my head toward the heavens to see who was speaking, and lo, Gabriel in the form of a man with his feet astride the horizon... I turned my face away, but toward whatever region of the sky I looked, I saw him there."

Escape was impossible. Horrified, terrorized, and depressed by what he considered a "loathsome" experience, and fearing that he was "possessed by a jinn," Muhammed crawled on his hand hands and knees and flung himself into the lap of his wife, and begged her to shield him from the divine presence. "Then I told her the whole story." She soothed him and after listening to him describe his ordeal, she suggested that they speak with her cousin, "Waraqa, a Christian who knew scripture.

Eventually, over the course of several years, Muhammed reluctantly accepted his fate, and in accordance with the voice of "God" or his angels, Muhammed not only spoke the words of "God" but began reciting and chanting various themes of God in a random order over the course of the following 20 years; an experience he continued to find quite painful and wrenching (Armstrong 1994; Lings 1983). "Never once did I receive a revelation without feeling my soul being torn away from me."

However, in order to receive his revelations, Muhammed also entered into a trance state and would lose consciousness. He reported that a heaviness would fill him with a feeling of depression and grief, and that he would sweat profusely. He also stated that although the divine message was often clear, at other times it was a jumble of sounds and voices, "like the reverberations of a bell. And that is the hardest upon me; the reverberations abate only when I understand the message."

In addition to his religious zest, Muhammed was reported to have the sexual prowess of forty men, and to have bedded at least 9 wives and numerous concubines including even one young girl (Lings 1983). On one occasion, after being rebuffed by the husband of one delightful damsel, Muhammed went into a trance, and reported that "God" had commanded that the husband must give up his wife to become Muhammed's wife. Women, in fact, tended to be his first and earliest converts (Armstrong 1994).

Islam (which means "peace" or "surrender") is theoretically an exceedingly tolerant religion, and Muhammed was basically a kind and considerate man who showed considerable mercy for the vanquished. For example, when his and his followers captured the city of Mecca, he demonstrated incredible magnanimity toward his former townsmen and enemies, giving all but a handful a complete pardon. However, he was also known to fly into extreme rages and to kill (or at least order killed) wealthy infidels and merchants and those who opposed him.

These behaviors when coupled with his increased sexuality, heightened religious fervor, trance states, mood swings, suicidal depressions, and possible auditory and visual "hallucinations" of a titanic angel, certainly point to the limbic system and inferior temporal lobe as the possible neurological foundation for these experiences.

ABRAHAM

Abraham (like his nephew Lot), the theoretical patriarch of Jewish, Christian, and the Moslem religions, also experienced what could be considered visual as well as auditory "hallucinations." Abraham also engaged in some unusual sex practices. For example, after Abraham left Babylon and before he arrived in Egypt, he told his wife Sara to pretend they were brother and sister because she was so beautiful and other men might wish to have sex with her.

"And it came to pass, that when Abram was come into Egypt, the Egyptians beheld the woman that she was very fair... and the woman was taken into Pharaoh's house."

The Pharaoh believing that Abraham and Sara were brother and sister, gave to Abraham, "sheep, and oxen, and he assess and servants and camels" (Genesis 13, 24-16) in order to pay for her sexual services, However, when Pharaoh found out she was married, he was so disgusted he threw them both out of Egypt (Genesis 13: 18-20); but not before demanding an explanation. According to Abraham he lied and offered up his wife as a sex toy to the Pharaoh because he was "afraid."

And yet, when Abraham arrived at Gerar he repeated the lie and informed the King of the city that Sara, "is my sister." And again he offered her to those who wished to partake of her charms. "And Abimeleeh king of Gerar sent and took Sara. But God came to Abimeleeh in a dream by night and said to him, Behold thou art but a dead man, for the woman which thou has taken; she is a man's wife" (Genesis, 20).

Abraham, of course, also had sex with other women, banished his first born son, and the hand-maiden who bore him, sending them out into the desert to a certain death, and he also attempted to murder his second son, Isaac. Abraham believed he was following the orders of "God," for he heard a voice that instructed him to "Take now thy son, thine only son Isaac, whom thou lovest, and offer him for a burnt offering upon one of the mountains which I will tell thee of." However, after binding his son, laying him upon an alter and picking up his knife, Abraham suddenly heard the voice of an angel who ordered him to let the boy go free (Genesis, 22).

Abraham, therefore, heard voices, had visions, engaged in unusual sex practices, and was capable of extreme cruelty including repeated instances of attempted murder. Is it possible that Abraham suffered from excessive limbic system activity?

Figure 73. *The sacrifice of Isaac by Abraham. Etching by Rembrandt.*

Consider, after hearing the voice of "God," Abraham left ancient Babylon (automatic traveling) forgot his identity and changed his name (i.e. from Abram to Abraham), as if he were experiencing a fugue state which is associated with temporal lobe disturbances and loss of personal memory (due to involvement of the amygdala and hippocampus). Hence, he travels to a distant land, is no longer Abram, and he no longer recognizes Sara as his wife. Hence, he tells the Pharaoh, she is "my sister." Temporary fugue states are associated with abnormal temporal lobe activity, including temporal lobe epilepsy and loss of memory and amnesia for personal identity.

LOT

Epilepsy can be due to a number of different causes, such as head injury, heat stroke during infancy, and tumors. However, the predisposition to develop epilepsy can also be inherited.

Like his uncle Abraham, Lot also saw angels and talked to the Lord God. It was the Lord God's angels who warned Lot to leave Sodom; reportedly the most sexually corrupt city on Earth.

Once Lot escaped from Sodom, he celebrated by getting drunk and impregnating both his daughters who willingly snuck into his bed on two separate nights (Genesis, 20: 33-38). In fact, even before they left Sodom Lot had offered his daughters to some of the men of the city to do with as they pleased (Genesis 19: 8).

We do not know if Lot followed Abraham's example and also let other men have sex with his wife. Nevertheless, both Abraham and Lot clearly demonstrated signs of temporal lobe and limbic hyperactivation.

EZEKIAL

Many "prophets" and other religious figures also display evidence of the Kluver-Bucy syndrome—a disturbance also referred to as "psychic blindness" which is due to severe abnormalities or destruction of the amygdala. For example, patients may eat non-nutritional substance such as cigarette butts or other objects.

Thus we read that Ezekiel would eat dung.

In addition, many of the "prophets" avoided people and would seek isolation—yet another characteristic of limbic and amygdala abnormalities.

Likewise we read that Ezekial isolated himself from other humans and refused to speak to others. If they approached he would withdraw. If they followed he would flee.

Social isolation, however, is a common means of achieving enlightenment, and isolation also acts on the amygdala (Joseph, 1982, 1992a. 1999a,b).

It was while isolated from all human contact that Ezekial had a shattering experience which caused him to lose consciousness. He had seen a cloud of light shot through with lightning, and within that stormy light he observed a great chariot pulled by four beasts each of which had four heads with the face of a man, bull, a lion, and eagle, and each wheel of the chariot rolled in a direction different from the others. And he heard wailing, moaning, and voices that gave him commands. And he experienced a sweet taste in his mouth, like honey, when "the spirit lifted me and took me, my heart overflowed with bitterness and anger." Afterward he lay "lie someone stunned" for an entire week.

Yet other signs of amygdala hyperactivation include catalepsy and catatonia. Thus we read that Ezekial was forced to lie on one side for 390 days without moving and then on his other side for 40 days. He was in all respects completely catatonic.

Cataplexy, or in this case, what appears to be catatonia, is also know as an arrest reaction, that is due to excessive fear (e.g. "paralyzed with fear"), or to abnormalities in the amygdala striatal medial frontal lobe emotion-motor circuit. If exceeding frightened, one may freeze and fail to move, a function of the amygdala acting on the motor centers in the striatum and medial frontal lobe (Joseph, 1999b). The airline industry refers to this as "frozen panic states" and about 20% of those involved in airline or other disasters will freeze and fail to move or to take any evasive action that might save their lives.

If there is an abnormality in this emotional-motor circuit, the individual may develop Parkinson's disorder, or catatonia, in which case they may lie frozen in the same posture for weeks and months. In Ezekial's case, the possibility of amygdala hyperactivity seems to be implied; not only because of the above mentioned conditions, but as he was obsessed with sexuality and often employed violent sexual imagery when he prophesied.

TRANCE STATES

Numerous religious figures have achieved enlightenment, or were only able to commune with god, once they entered a trance state. Buddha, for example, is said to have at first communed with gods, and then to have transcended the gods by entering a trance state which enabled him to experience nirvana.

It is said that when Buddha entered into trance that fragrant breezes swirled about him, flowers bloomed and blossomed and fell from the air, and that the Earth began to rock as the gods in heaven began to rejoice. However, one god, a demon, Mara, was alarmed. She told Buddha to remain in a state of bliss and to never, under any circumstances attempt to inform others of what he had accomplished as no one would believe him. Two other gods, however, Sakra, the Lord of the devas, and Maha Brahma begged him to teach his method to all the world. Buddha heeded their advice.

For the next 45 years he wondered all over India preaching his message. Humans could transcend suffering and the gods, and through kindness, compassion, meditation and Yoga, they could come into contact with the ultimate reality.

Trance states are said to enable one to sense and perceive what others cannot. In Buddhism it is believed that trance enables one to gain use of Power over the material world.

Figure 74. *The "Beautiful Bodhisattva" Padmapani. (Starving Buddha) Cave painting, Ajanta India. About 600 A.D. Fasting is a common source of spiritual enlightenment and also induces hallucinations.*

This includes the Power (te) of not contending, the Power to use men, and the Power for causing others to act, or to prevent them from acting.

Mystics may achieve trance states through ritual and discipline or through pain, sex, fasting or drugs. These trance states have been divided into five stages by some (Buddhists), six by others (Tantra), and four by yet other mystics (Sufis).

Broadly considered, these trance stages begin with the perception of visions and voices, then progress to a non-perceptual awareness of God, followed by transcendence and a merging and becoming one with God, which is the supreme mystical act.

While in trance, some individuals not only experience a bright light, but they may be blinded by it. In some cases the light is so bright those around them will see it. Moses and Jesus both shone with a light that others could see, whereas St. Paul was blinded by the great light that shone around his head.

During revival meetings, it is not uncommon for revivalists to suddenly go into trance and see "a brightness like the sun" "everything is bathed in a rainbow of glory."

VISIONS AND DREAMS

Throughout the "Old Testament" the "Lord god" delivers his words through visions and dreams, and in some instances the words themselves constitute the "vision;" that is, like an auditory hallucination:

"And an angel said unto Israel... And an angel said unto Balaam... and Elohim said unto him... And an angel of the Lord called unto Abraham out of heaven... and Elohim said unto Noah... The word of the Lord came unto Abraham in a vision... And the Lord said unto Abraham... and the Lord said unto Jacob...and the Lord said unto Joshua... and the Lord said unto me... and the word of the Lord came unto me... "etc.

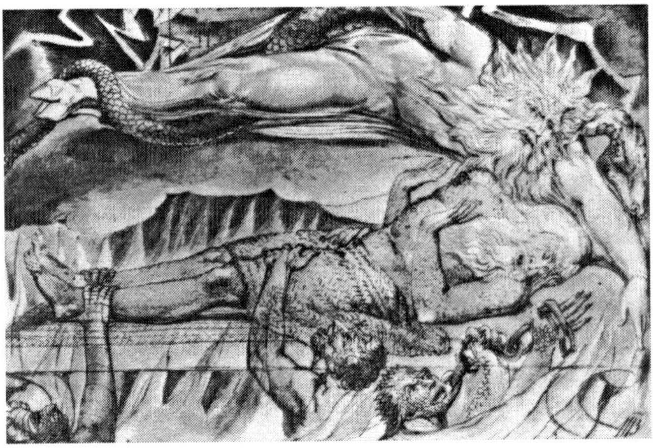

Figure 75. *"With dreams upon my bed thou scarest me & Affrightest me with visions" Williams Blake, 17th century.*

Likewise, the gods and goddesses of ancient peoples throughout the world, including for example, the gods of the ancient Romans and Greeks would speak and appear to specific, chosen people in visions and dreams; an experience also referred to as an "epiphany" or in modern psychiatric terminology, a "hallucination."

One of Jacob's many epiphanies included a dream of a ladder which stretched from heaven to earth; and angels were ascending and descending between the realms of god and man.

Figure 76. *Jacob's dream of the ladder to Heaven with angels going to and fro. Drawing by Hayley, 18th century.*

People who suffer from periodic episodes of limbic and temporal lobe hyperactivation, such as those with temporal lobe epilepsy, may hear voices and suffer seizures which may be indistinguishable from a trance state. It is not uncommon for these seizures to be preceded by an auditory or visual hallucination or aura (Gloor, 1997; Penfield and Perot 1963; Trimble 1991; Williams 1956). Patients can have any number of very odd hallucinations, such as smelling sweet or horrible odors, hearing voices, music, or conversations, seeing angels, demons, ghosts, and God.

The great existential author, F. Dostoevsky, apparently suffered temporal lobe epilepsy. Dostoevsky, alleged (via one of his characters) that when he had a seizure the gates of Heaven would open and he could see row upon row of angels blowing on great golden trumpets. Then two great golden doors would open and he could see a golden stairway that would lead right up to the throne of God.

MOSES AND TEMPORAL LOBE LIMBIC HYPERACTIVITY

The story of Moses is in part mystery, at least regarding his paternal origins. We are told that he was raised in the palace of the Pharaoh of Egypt who regarded him as a grandson. The identity of his father is unknown and we are also told that his mother hid him for three months after he was born. When she could hide him no more, she placed him in a wicker basket among the reeds of the Nile. It was there that Moses was discovered by the daughter of Pharaoh, who in turn raised him like a son. But then we are told that the princess paid a Hebrew woman to nurse the child. When he grew to be a boy the princess named him "Moses, which means: "I drew him out of the water." "Moses" however, was also a common Egyptian name, including that of a mighty Pharaoh: Thutmoses.

Moses had a violent temper and one day beat an Egyptian to death. Overcome with fear, when he realized the murder had been witnessed, he fled to the land of Midian where he proceeded to challenge a group of men and rescue the daughters of the local pagan priest.

Moses, the "Egyptian" then married Zipporah, the daughter of the priest. It was later, after the birth of his son, Gershom, and while alone and isolated and attending a flock of sheep in the wilderness, near the mountain of God, that the Lord God appeared and spoke to him from inside a blazing bush.

The Lord God then proceeded to instruct Moses as to what he should say to the Israelites: "The Lord, the god of your fathers, the God of Abraham, the God of Isaac, the God of Jacob has sent me to you."

But "Moses answered and said to the Lord, Please O Lord, I have never been a man of words. I am slow of speech and slow of tongue." Indeed, his speech is so garbled that the Lord God decides to appoint Moses' brother Aron to assist him. "You shall speak to him and put the words in his mouth."

Possibly, Moses requires an interpreter because he does not know the language of the Hebrews; being raised as a prince in the household of the Pharaoh. However, he also required Aron to speak for him to Pharaoh. Thus it appears that he may well have had a severe speech impediment as he claims. In fact, coupled with his violent temper, his severe depressions, and the possibility of auditory and visual hallucinations, it could be argued that Moses suffered from temporal lobe epilepsy: The "Divine Illness." Seizure activity within the temporal lobe and limbic system are clearly associated religious experiences and can give rise to murderous rage reactions as well as disturbances of speech and language.

Moses may have suffered from temporal lobe seizures as a consequence of being left for days, as an infant, to bake in the hot, broiling Egyptian sun, after his mother abandoned him in a basket on the Nile. If that were the case his infant brain could have become overheated and damaged by the high temperatures.

If Moses subsequently developed temporal lobe seizure activity, this could explain his hyper-religious fervor, his rages and the numerous murders he committed or ordered. Indeed, a recurring theme throughout the story of Exodus is that of Moses repeatedly ordering human slaughter, beginning with the first Egyptian he killed, followed by the first born sons of the Egyptians, then Pharaoh and the Egyptian army, and then the slaughter of the Hebrews who had followed him, as well as the butchery of innocent men, women, and children who just happened to live along the path of the wondering Israelis.

"You shall not let a soul remain alive." -Exodus 20:15-18.

He even ordered that the Israelis kill members of their own family.

"Each of you put sword on thigh, go back and forth from gate to gate throughout the camp and slay brother, neighbor, and kin... Dedicate yourselves to the Lord this day—for each of you has been against son and brother—that He may bestow a blessing on you today." -Exodus, 32:26-29).

Similarly, his speech impediment (being "slow of tongue"), hyper-graphia (having authored the voluminous "laws"), and "hallucinations" such as hearing the voice of God are not uncommonly associated with temporal lobe seizures and limbic hyperactivation.

JESUS CHRIST AND TEMPORAL LOBE HYPERACTIVITY

Jesus Christ also was known to fly into violent and destructive rages, such as when he yelled, cursed, overturned the tables and struck and chased the money lenders from the temple (St. John, 2: 14-15). He also frequently appeared irritable, sullen, gloomy, depressed, distrustful and angry with his Disciples whom he would sometimes curse e.g. referring to Peter as "Satan" (e.g. St. Matthew 16: 23).

Jesus was also not beyond behaving in a petulant and sadistic manner, such as when he repeatedly refused the request of "a woman of Canaan" who "came and cried unto him, saying, Have mercy on me, O Lord, thou son of David; my daughter is grievously vexed with a devil. But he answered her not a word. And his desciples came and besought him, saying, Send her away; for she crieth after us. But he answered and said: I am not sent but unto the lost sheep of the house of Israel. Then she came and worshipped him saying, Lord help me. But he answered and said, It is not meet to take the children's bread and cast it to dogs (St. Matthew 15: 22-26).

He even cursed a fig tree for lacking fruit when he was hungry, "Let no fruit grow on thee henceforward for ever" (St. Matthew, 21: 19).

However, as a possible "clone" of the "Lord God," his behavior in this respect was little different from his "Father."

Jesus was also apparently hypo-sexual. Like hypersexuality, loss of sex drive in also attributed to the limbic system. Although surrounded by unmarried female followers, many of whom had been prostitutes, he apparently never succumbed to temptation, though he certainly enjoyed having women kiss and wash his feet or rub expensive oil on his body.

Depression, mood swings, episodic violence, and hypo-sexuality (as well as hypesexuality), are all associated with temporal lobe and amygdala hyperactivation. As per "hallucinations" Jesus did go alone into the wilderness for forty days, and there he saw and spoke with "Satan." Jesus frequently sought solitude and isolation. Many religious figures have done likewise.

Figure 77. *Afer 40 days alone in isolation, Jesus with Satan by his side confronts some of the demons of hell.*

LIMBIC SYSTEM ISOLATION AND HALLUCINATIONS

It has been well established that even short-term social and sensory isolation lasting just a few days can induce emotionally and visually profound hallucinations. Even after just a few days these isolation-induced hallucinations may become so emotionally charged and personally distressing that volunteers will refuse to discuss them (Bexton, Heron and Scott 1954). As noted, Jesus spent 40 days alone in the wilderness, and so too did Moses during which he continually communed with "God."

John C. Lilly (1972) combined LSD with prolonged water immersion and social and sensory isolation for about 7 hours on several occasions. According to Lilly he experienced and observed the presence of spiritual, god-like beings who beckoned to him.

Isolation, as well as food and water deprivation, increased or decreased sexual activity, pain, drug use, self-mutilation, prayer and meditation are common methods of attaining mystical states of religious and spiritual awareness, and have been employed world wide, across time and culture (d'Aquili & Newberg 1993; de Ropp 1993; Frazier 1950; James 1958; Lehmann & Myers 1993; Malinowski 1948; Neihardt & Black Elk 1989; Smart 1969). These conditions also activate the limbic system as well as those feature dectecting neurons in the overlying temporal lobe (including Wenicke's receptive speech area), thereby giving rise to complex visual and well as auditory hallucinations and the secretion of opiate-like enkephalins.

Figure 78. *Aztec worshippers induce visions of the "god of the dad"by self-inflicting wounds.*

Figure 79. *Saint Anthony beset by demons from hell.*

PROPHECY: TRUTH CONCEALED

Beginning with Abraham, and throughout the "Old Testament" the "Lord God" delivers his words primarily through visions and dreams, and frequently his prophets lose consciousness or enter into trance states. Many of His prophets appear to be suffering from temporal lobe epilepsy or hyperactivity.

In the 12th century, Moses Maimonides, composed a book "A Guide for the Perplexed" as a letter to R. Joseph. According to Maimonides "the Divine Will has withheld from the multitude the truths required for the knowledge of God... Do not imagine that these most difficult problems can be thoroughly understood by any one of us."

"At times the truth shines so brilliantly that we perceive it as clear as day. Our nature and habit then draw a veil over our perceptions, and we return to darkness almost as dense as before. We are like those who, though beholding frequent flashes of lightning still find themselves in the thickest darkness of night."

"For some the lightning flashes in rapid succession, and they seem to be in continuous light, and their night is as clear as the day. This was the degree of prophetic excellence attained by Moses, the greatest of prophets."

"By others, only once during the whole of night is a flash of lightning perceived. This is the case with those of whom we are informed "They prophesied and did not prophecy again." "There are some to whom the flashes of lightning appear with varying intervals; others are in the condition of men, whose darkness is illuminated not by lightning, but by a small light that is not continuous, but now it shines and now it vanishes..."

"The degrees of perfection of men vary according to these distinctions. Concerning those who never beheld the light even for one day, but walk in continual darkness, it is written: "They know not, neither will they understand. They walk in darkness" (Psalms, 82:5). Truth, in spite of all its powerful manifestations is completely withheld from them" (Maimonides, 12th century).

The Truth revealed, however, is often a shattering experience, that grips one like a seizure. Likewise, the gift of prophecy, is not always a welcome gift, and even the role of prophet may be resisted. Moses actively resisted and argued with the "Lord God" and repeatedly tried to convince Him to pick someone more deserving. Other prophets have also attempted to resist, but to no avail. They were often hounded by the "Lord god" or his angels, or felt compelled to prophecy even when threatened with death by the people—and many a prophet was killed by the people, including the ancient Jews.

Jeremiah, for example, was openly despised and ridiculed by the ancient Jews. Nevertheless, though he wished it otherwise, he could not withhold his prophesizing: "For the Word of the Lord was unto me a reproach and a mocking all day, and I said, I will not mention it, nor will I again speak in His name; but it was in mine heart as burning fire, enclosed in my bones, and I was wearied to keep it, and did not prevail" (Jeremiah, 20:8,9).

THE TRANSMITTER TO GOD

Although it is possible that certain religious figures may have been suffering from temporal lobe epilepsy, it is noteworthy that seizures are stereotypical and idiosyncratic. That is, unless an individual has several different seizure foci, each seizure is basically identical to the next and the auras and hallucinations are quite similar from one seizure to the next.

This is not the case with many of the prophets. As detailed by Moses Maimonides: "According to the books of the prophets, a certain prophet after being inspired with one kind of prophecy is reported to have received prophecy in another form. It is possible for a prophet to prophecy at one time in the form and at another time in another form. The prophet does not prophecy continuously but is inspired at one time and not at another, so he at one time prophecy in the form of a higher degree and at another time in that of a lower degree; it may happen that the highest degree is reached by a prophet only once in his life time, and afterwards remains inaccessible to him, or that a prophet remains below the highest degree until he entirely looses the faculty."

For example, "And the word of the Lord ceased from Jeremiah" (Erza, i:1), or "And these are the last words of David" (Samuel, 23:1).

Some individuals may prophecy once and only once—which argues against temporal lobe epilepsy.

THE BIRTH OF GOD

In ancient Sumer (in southern Iraq around 6,000 years ago), it was believed that the Universe was ruled by a pantheon of Gods, the Anunnaki (Armstrong 1994; Kramer 1956, Wooley 1965); perhaps the same pantheon alluded to in the first chapter of Genesis.

The Sumerians also worshiped household gods and goddesses, including a personal God, which in some respects could be likened to a "guardian angel" or a spirit (totem) helper, as was common among the Plains Indians. This personal God served almost as a conscience and as a mediator between the head of the household and the great Gods which ruled the Earth and the cosmos.

Because this was a private, personal God, it was not uncommon for a believer to engage in prolonged and daily discussions with his deity (Kramer 1956: Woolley 1965). To this god one could bear their heart and soul regarding sins, injustice, personal shortcomings and hopes for the future. Hence, this god was indeed a personal god with whom one could "talk" and maintain a special personal relationship and which served to protect the Sumerians from the Pantheon of gods who rules the Earth at that time—or so claim the ancients.

And then one day something astounding and revolutionary occurred in the mind of a man of the city, of Ur of the Chaldees, of ancient Sumer, in ancient Babylon, and birthplace of Abram a rich Babylonian prince. Abram had left the city and began having visions and hearing voices. It was coming from his personal God and it later gave him a command (Genesis 12): "Get thee out of thy country ...and I will make of thee a great nation... and in thee shall all the families of the earth be blessed..."

And Abram and his personal god walked and talked, as God had not done since the time of Adam and Eve. And then one day this personal God came to a decision and said to Abram: "Thy name shall be Abraham, for a father of many nations have I made thee. And I will make thee exceedingly fruitful... and I will make thee the father of many nations... and I will be their God" (Genesis 17).

Abraham, both saw and heard his God on numerous occasions both awake and dreaming, often falling on his face as God appeared. They ate together, and walked and spoke together during the heat of the day, and during the darkest hours of the night. This Lord God, the "God of Abraham" was also making all types of grandiose promises and predictions, all of which came to pass.

PROPHECIES FULFILLED

Is it possible that Abraham was dreaming? Could this personal God from ancient Ur have been but a hallucination, and given Abraham's odd sexuality and murderous actions, a product on temporal lobe epilepsy or subclinical seizure activity?

When we consider that this is the same Lord God (at least in religious theory) who today is worshiped by Jews, Christians, and Moslems alike, the possibility of hallucinations does not seem likely. Indeed, has not the Lord God's prophecy to Abraham come to pass: "And I will make thee the father of many nations... and I will be their God" (Genesis 17).

In fact, given that the God experienced by Abraham and Sara (and in fact, with few exceptions, the God repeatedly described in the Bible) not only appeared as a man but behaved as a man and not a spirit-like supernatural being, the possibility of hallucinations does not seem likely.

Likewise, when we consider how many other prophesies were fullfilled, including the repeated destruction and recreation of Israel, including, most recently in 1948—the aftermath of a world war led by an Austrian German-Jew, Adolf Hitler—as well as the hundreds of millions who worship a Jew (Jesus) as "God," it borders on the irrational to simply dismiss these events as a hallucination, a myth, or a coincidence.

As noted, above, under conditions of limbic hyperactivation, not all "hallucinations" are hallucinations, but instead may represent the perception of stimuli which are normally filtered from consciousness. Under conditions of sensory deprivation, pain, social isolation, drug use, the nuclei of the limbic system may become abnormally activated and possibly hyperactivated such that subclinical seizure activity (kindling) develops (Cain, 1992; Gloor, 1997; Joseph, 1996, 1998b, 1999b,d).

Under conditions of limbic kindling, hyperactivation, or seizure activity, sensory and emotional filtering that normally takes place in these nuclei is reduced or abolished. That is, the individual may begin to perceive things or individuals that (presumably) do not exist, or they may gain access to "hidden" knowledge that bursts upon them with a shattering clarity, or they may achieve a "higher" understanding of existence and the nature of reality. They may commune directly with god, goddesses, devils, demons, and angels.

As these same nuclei are also implicated in dream states, near death experiences, and out-of-body phenomenon, it could thus be argued that individuals who for whatever reason are "blessed" with an overactive amygdala-temporal lobe are also given access to god-like stimuli which are also normally filtered from consciousness.

"Know that for the human mind there are certain objects of perception which are within the scope of its nature and capacity to perceive; on the other hand, there are amongst things which actually exist, certain objects which the mind can in no way grasp: The gates of perception are closed against it. Further, there are things which the mind understands, one part, but remains ignorant of the other. And when man is able to comprehend certain things, it does not follow that he may be able to comprehend everything."-Moses Maimonides

Moreover, consider the prophecies delivered to Muhammed. In less than fifty years all the Arabic tribes had been converted to Islam.

Or consider the prophecies of the god of the cross, that is, the Mayan and Aztec God, Quetzalocoatl. As noted in an earlier chapter, Quetzalocoatl, the plumed serpent, was associated with the planet Venus, and the sign of the cross was one of his many emblems which is depicted in the center of his shield.

According to Mayan and Aztec religious belief, Quetzalocoatl, the god of the cross, had been driven from the lands at the time of the great flood, some 12,000 years ago. However, it had been prophesied that Quetzalocoatl, the plumed serpent and god of the cross, would return to Mexico and that the ruling gods, and their temples, would be completely overthrown. In fact, an exact date was given for his return, which would be signified by the appearance of a comet

Figure 80. *It was predicted that in the year 1519 a comet would appear in the east and signal the return of Quetzalocoatl. The emperor Mochtezuma observes a comet from the East—a prophetic sign of the return of the Quetzalocoatl, the plumed serpent (a bearded god whose symbol was also the sign of the cross), and the impending destruction of the Aztec empire. A few weeks later, the Spaniards, bearded and wearing plumed helmets, and carrying the sign of the cross, arrived off the East coast of Mexico.*

in the East. In the Christian calendar this was to be in the year 1519.

As predicted, in the year 1519 a comet appeared in the East, and soon thereafter, the plumed and helmeted Cortez and his crew, flying the Spanish flag and the sign of the cross appeared off the East Coast of Mexico. And, as predicted, the old god, as well as the Aztec civilization were destroyed, and the god of the cross is now worshipped not just by the Mexican, but peoples throughout the Americas. Just a coincidence?

THE TRANSMITTER TO GOD

The question as to why any particular individual might be chosen to serve as a prophet or messenger of "God" cannot be answered here, though we can certainly consider possibilities.

Every individuals appears to be naturally "wired for god" and thus capable of receiving the word of god. However, some display signs of hyperactivity in this region of the brain which appears to enhance these capabilities—albeit in accordance with the waxing and waning activity within the limbic system and temporal lobe. Or perhaps a person who lives a highly spiritual or mystical life style perpetually activates this region of the brain and achieves what others can only hope for via drugs, fasting, self-mutilation, and isolation; i.e. access to God, or the spiritually sublime.

Or perhaps the presence of "God" triggers hyperactivity in the limbic system of those chosen to be His prophets, which thus enables them to hear and see god-like stimuli as well as causing them to demonstrate signs of temporal lobe abnormalities. That is, just as something frightening or sexual will activate limbic neurons, something exceedingly frightening, spiritual, or god-like, might hyperactivate these same neurons, eventually creating supersensitive conditions and thusperpetually activating the "transmitter to God."

As to the possibility that individuals such as Moses, Jesus, Abraham, Muhammed, or other "prophets" and messengers may have been hallucinating, this is not terribly likely since what they heard and experienced was often different from day to day and as there was an obvious message and plan of action that they were exposed to and which they relayed to others. Moreover, the prophecies they were given and what they were told would come to pass, came to pass!

Indeed, as the limbic system is clearly implicated in every single case, and as this region of the brain normally inhibits and filters incoming sensory stimuli, it could thus be argued that individuals who for whatever reason are "blessed" with a hyperactivated limbic system, or a limbic system which is highly "evolved," or who are directly contacted by god, are therefore provided access to god-like stimuli and alternate realities which are normally filtered from consciousness.

"If the doors of perception were cleansed everything would appear... as it is, infinite..."-W. Blake

Indeed, what the evidence suggests is that these limbic structures periodically become hyperactivated and open up windows and doorways to alternate realities which are normally hidden from view. Under conditions of limbic system hyperactivity, what is concealed is suddenly revealed, including even the private thoughts of the gods.

-12-

THE TWILIGHT OF THE GODS

The Anunnaki, Exodus, and The Deluge

The spiritual beliefs of the Cro-Magnon and other peoples of the Upper Paleolithic were incredibly advanced as compared to their predecessors and the Neanderthals who managed to hang on for an additional 10,000 to 15,000 years after their arrival. The complexity, originality, and artistic and symbolic accomplishments of these peoples and their conception of, and ability to symbolically express the spirit world represented an incredible leap in religious thought and intellectual ability. Moreover, almost identical religious concerns and depictions of spiritual belief appeared throughout Paleolithic Eurasia and the Middle East at almost the same time period, as is apparent from an examination of the art that adorns hundreds of underground and above ground Paleolithic "cathedrals."

Over time, however, these beliefs also became modified and less uniform, particularly during the transition from the Upper Paleolithic to the Neolithic.

Nevertheless, throughout the Upper Paleolithic and the Neolithic and continuing into modern times, some believed the Netherworld was alive with the souls of trees, plants, animals, humans, and demons, and that the day and the night were ruled by all manner of goddesses and then, later, male gods (Armstrong 1994; Brandon 1967; Budge 1994; Campbell 1988; Frazier 1950; Harris,1993; Kuhn 1955; Smart 1969; Wilson 1951). They believed in gods and goddesses of the forest, of the river, of the sky, the clouds, the seasons, of the day and of the night. Planetary gods, moon gods, sun gods, personal gods, and goddesses and gods who created the Heavens and the earth. Gods and goddesses who created man and woman in the image of the gods. And then "Gods" who gave of their own soul and spirit, thus awaking man and woman to their own spirituality through the breath of life... so claimed the ancients.

THE GODDESS: THE GREAT MOTHER OF ALL

Yet, the first gods were not men but goddesses of nature and of life. It was woman who first became the godhead: The Great Mother of All. Although she may have been attended by priests and shamans, the first gods were goddesses; fertility goddesses, earth goddesses, mother nature, and goddess of the hunt (Austin, 1990).

Figure 81. *(above) The patriarchical gods and their male priests, declared war against the Goddess, and the Mother of all, became a whore, "Satan's Bride," "harlots from hell" who cavorted and had sex with devils. (left) The "Great Mother Goddess" (from the Upper Paleolithic, 30,000 B.P.).*

And just as the peoples of the Upper Paleolithic were worshipping goddesses and creating her image to be adored, Neolithic peoples continued these traditions and were worshipping goddesses who were obviously pregnant and with child. The Goddess cults became the dominant form of "organized" religion during the Neolithic. Ancient paintings from this time and after depict the goddess in all her fertile majesty, and sometimes with a youthful, lesser male god who would be like a son... and later... a lover.

Hunting and fertility, violence and sex, are characteristic aspects of most ancient religions, with gods and goddesses of the hunt competing with fertility goddesses of the earth who again reigned supreme as agriculture and farming replaced gathering and hunting as the main source of subsistence. And just as agriculture was reinvented during the early Neolithic, worship of the Goddess, and the Goddess cult spread world wide.

Be it Crete, the Aegean, Greece, Rome, Asia, India, the Eastern Mediterranean, the Goddess cult was widely practiced. The Great Mother of All personified life, and was revered throughout the world as life giving and producing.

And, she was just as likely to be attended by women as men. During her festivals young males would trance themselves into a religious frenzy, and would take knives or swords and cut and castrate themselves. By sacrificing their manhood these youths would gain access to her power and could then became priests to the goddess so as to become as her, even dressing in robes and going about as a females forever after. In fact, the adoption of female dress by male shamans, medicine men, and priests has been a world wide custom. The priests dressed as women because it imparted greater spiritual energy to the priests, the clothing of women being used to transfer the powers of one to the other.

In addition, just as a significant number of the modern day clergy are homosexuals, and just as homosexuals, as youths prefer girls toys and clothes, this too played a factor in the dawning of goddess attire. Indeed, in later centuries although the homosexual clergy dispensed with castration—the exception being young boys who the priests would use for sex—they retained the tradition of dressing in womanly robes which continues to be the practice in many modern day religions.

Earth and Sky Goddesses and pregnant women, the Great Mother embodied the sexual power and the spiritual power of the life force that could be imparted to life as it emerged from the womb and the fertile fields. Male priests thus dressed accordingly.

Because of her life giving abilities, even during the Paleolithic she was associated with the land, the hunt, and the cosmos. Woman embodied the land from which plants grew from the womb of the earth, and she was the sky from which rain dropped from her celestial breasts to nourish the land and her children below.

Woman with her lunar menstrual cycle became the moon and the night, dominating life and death as the life giving principle.

It was this same life giving power which seeped back into the Earth and the sky when the living were buried at death in the womb of the Earth. It is the earth from which new life would spring anew. Woman as nature is the earth, giving birth and taking her children, in death, into the bossom of the underworld, the earthwomb, where spirits entombed would later emerge, reborn, sometimes as the soul of a newborn infant. Woman, the goddess was the great cycle of life. Woman was the earth, she was nature, she was god!

The great goddesses, the embodiment of life, ruled the Upper Paleolithic, Neolithic Europe, the Americas, Africa, Australia, and the Middle East. She was An, and then Ianana in ancient Sumer, Ishtar in Babylon, Anu and Isis in Egypt, Anat in Cannan, and Aphrodite in Greece. And each of these female goddess had the spiritual power of life and death and the spiritual power to give life to those who were yet to be born.

The great goddess was the queen of the heavens as well as the Earth, and Neolithic Kings could only claim and retain their kingship by paying homage to, claiming to be the son of, and later, by marrying the goddess. By marrying and possessing the queen of heaven and the Earth, the king could claim dominion over both.

One of the most ancient symbols associated with the great goddess is the kingly throne.The name, Isis, for example, also means "the throne." The kingly throne was originally a symbol of the legs and thighs of the goddess. Thus by mounting her he took possession of the earth, his country, the "mother-land" by seating himself upon her lap.

THE WAR AGAINST THE GODDESS

Ishtar and Isis were regarded as the Universal Mother ages before any male tribal deity dared to demand entry into the divine pantheon. Indeed it was only around 6,000 years ago, that male gods began to compete with the goddess for worshipers and sacrificial goods.

The first male god to obtain national political prominence and backing was Marduk. Marduk ascended to the head of the divine pantheon when the sixth king of the first dynasty of Babylon, Hammurabi, came to power. Hammurabi, who issued the world-famous codes of law, worshipped Marduk and solidified a kingdom that stretched from the central provinces embraced by the Tigris and Eurphrates, to the Persian Gulf. And for the next twenty centuries, Babylon remained one the greatest cities in the world. Babylon was a world-wide power and so too was its god, Marduk. And so too was her goddess queen, Ishtar, who Marduk initially battled for supremacy.

As noted, in some ancient cultures, at first these male gods were personified as sons, and lesser gods who were her attendees. Later these male gods became her lover, and then her king, the Lord God who would rule and possess her.

It is precisely because there were so many gods and goddesses, who often served completely different functions, that the ancient Israelites, including Abraham, Isaac, and Jacob never clearly indicated that they believed in a single god, or that the Lord God was the only god. Rather, they promised to worship Him to the exclusion of other gods. Hence the commandment: Thou shalt have no other gods before thee."

Nevertheless, the Israelites, including King Manesseh, King Among, King Solomon, and Jezebel, the wife of King Ahab, continued to worship and practice the rites of other gods and goddesses, including Baal, Asherah, Yam, and Anat. As Moses ascended Mount Sinai, the people, including even the Lord God's high priest, Aron, almost immediately began performing the sacred rites associated with the great goddess, the celestial cow, the Great Mother of All, whose milk, in the form of raindrops, nourishes the earth.

"We will burn incense unto the queen of heaven, to pour drink offerings unto her as we have done, we and our fathers, our kings, and our princes." -Jeremiah, 17,18.

The Lord God ordered her worshippers killed in retaliation and women in general began to be viewed with increasing disdain and suspicion. For the next two thousand years His prophets and priests would continually denounce and hurl invectives against women, for woman represented the eternal cycle of life and death whereas the Lord God did not: "I am a god of the living, not the dead" He would proclaim. Hence, the Jewish prayer: "Thank you God for not making me a woman."

Despite the war against woman the goddess, the ancient Israelites continued to repeatedly go astray. Despite repeated warnings and retributions, the ancient Jews worshipped numerous female (and other male) gods, seeking nurturance and protection from the Great Mother, and in particular to glorify sexuality. The first Temple was the site of a flourishing fertility cult involving ritual prostitution. King Manasseh even placed an effigy to Asherah in the Temple. Some Israelites even believed that Asherah was the wife of Yahweh. Women in particular, worshipped her as a god in her own right and sex orgies became part of her rituals.

THE SPIRITUAL LIFE FORCE

Although the Lord God may have provided woman and man with a living soul, the Lord God is not associated with the "life force," that female-principle of life which some believe permeates and emanates from every living thing.

This is why the cult of the goddess, the Great Mother of All, was such a danger to the male-Lord God Yahweh. The Goddesses and Great Mother embodied this nourishing, spiritual life force whereas He represented fear, obedience, and retribution.

This life force is experienced by some as exceedingly personal, and they identify it with the "spirit" or "soul" that has a unique and individual presence in every living thing. Others experience this life force as an impersonal power that exists everywhere in all things. Thus some have attempted to gain control over this power through ritual, sacrifice, and trance, so as to do good, but more often, to do bad.

This feeling of life's "power," the liberation of that power upon death, and the possibility of controlling that power, has given rise to innumerable religious rituals and beliefs, some of which can be traced to the Middle and Upper Paleolithic when archaic Homo sapiens, Neanderthals, and later the Cro-Magnon peoples ruled the planet.

Ancient, primitive humanity believed that this life force exits the body upon death. The Cro-Magnon of the Upper Paleolithic also associated that power with life and fertility, and thus with animal procreation and the birth of new life. Again, it was these beliefs and this association between woman, death, and fertility, which gave rise to the cult of the goddess.

GODS AND MORE GODS AND PERSONAL GODS

The Lord God is a rather young God, at least in the sense that He did not make himself known to the peoples of the Earth until after "the seventh day" of creation. And He did not even fully introduce himself until He met up with Moses, and told him one of His names: "Yahweh."

Prior to His emergence as a force to reckon with, and as the Neolithic drew to the close, it was claimed that the Earth was governed by a pantheon of gods—presumably the same pantheon that is alluded to in the opening chapters of Genesis, which appears to be a retelling of Sumerian cosmology. The Sumerians believed that this pantheon of ruling gods and goddesses numbered 50.

The Sumerians, however, did not believe there was anything spiritual or supernatural about these gods, the Anunnaki, and instead worshipped their own personal, or household gods and goddesses who they believed could intercede or their behalf before the ruling pantheon.

Although the cult of the goddess was also widespread, these personal gods were as numerous as the people, such that each household might harbor numerous personal gods and goddesses, one for each family member and those of ancestors who had long ago passed away. However, in some homes, all the family members might worship the personal god of the head of the household, and this god in turn could be passed down to subsequent generations.

The Sumerians had a large Semitic population, who also adopted some of these religious customs. Hence we see that the personal god of Abraham, became the god of Isaac and the god of Jacob and thus the god of Israel.

SUMERIAN AND BIBLICAL CREATION SCIENCE

Modern day "Creation Science" is rooted in the story of Genesis which in turn appears to be a retelling of the Sumerian tales of creation. The story of Genesis bears a striking resemblance to the "creation myths" including the "flood myths" penned almost 6,000 years ago by the peoples of Sumer—in what today is Iraq; stories that were still in fashion with the rise of the Babylonian state (Roux, 1992).

These and numerous other Biblical - Sumerian/Babylonian similarities (e.g. Chiera, 1966;Heidel, 1988; Kramer, 1991; Sitchin, 1990) should not be surprising considering that Abraham, the presumed patriarch of all modern day Jewish peoples, hailed from Ur of the Chaldees, which was originally a Sumerian city. In fact, a considerable proportion of the Sumerian population consisted of Semitic peoples (Roux, 1992) and Abraham may well have been a prince of the city.

According to Roux (1992, p. 85), "For more than three thousand years the gods of Sumer were worshipped by Sumerians and Semites alike; and for more than three thousand years the religious ideas promoted by the Sumerians played an extra-ordinary part in the public and private life of the Mesopotamians, modeling their institutions, coloring their works of art and literature."

Hence, it could be argued that the true authors of Genesis were the Sumerian peoples. As succinctly put by the renowned Sumerian scholar, Samuel Noah Kramer (1991, p. 75), "There is good reason to infer that in the third millennium BC., there emerged a group of Sumerian thinkers and teachers who, in their quest for satisfactory answers to some of the problems raised by their cosmic speculations, evolved a cosmology and theology carrying such high intellectual conviction that their doctrines became the basic creed and dogma of much of the ancient Near East."

Our knowledge of ancient Sumer comes from a variety of ancient texts, including epic tales, hymns, poetry, proverbs, prayers and incantations. Some of these texts are written in ancient Sumerians, others are Akkadian and Babylonian copies that were found in the ruins of palaces and temple libraries.

IN THE BEGINNING THERE WAS CHAOS

Sumerian cosmology, as to the origin of the Universe, in some respects resembles modern cosmology. For example, they imagined that at first there was nothing but chaos, and because there was nothing, it had no name. Moreover, because there was nothing, "No gods whatever had been brought into being. Uncalled by name, their destinies undetermined." Again, however, rather than a pure absence, this nothingness was chaos (Kramer, 1991; Roux, 1992), a "commingling" of clouds ("mummu"), and fresh waters (Apsu) and salt waters (Tiamat).

And out of this chaos there came form and substance, and then "An" from which flowed the seeds of life; seeds which eventually fell to Earth and which also fell upon the planet of the gods, thus giving birth to the gods, the Anunnaki. "An begot the Anunnaki" (Kramer, 1991).

THE ANUNNAKI: GODS FROM ANOTHER PLANET

According to Sumerian theology, a pantheon of gods, human-like in form, but possessing extra-ordinary super-human scientific powers and technological capability, took possession of the Earth so as to exploit this world for its resources. These same gods, the Anunnaki, claimed credit for creating the Earth, the heavens and the stars. However, these human-like "gods" were in turn ruled by laws and regulations that were promulgated and enforced by yet other gods who lived in different regions of the cosmos (Kramer, 1991). According to the Sumerians, different "gods" through agreements worked out between them and their various factions, were in charge of different regions of the cosmos and thus ruled over and exploited those life forms which dwelled on the different planets. The Earth, was but one of these many planets, and was ruled by a pantheon of human-like gods.

As based on his interpretation of ancient Sumerian cuneiform writing and glyphs, Kramer (1991) informs us that these gods formed and "functioned as an assembly with a king at its head, its most important groups consisting of seven gods... and fifty who were known as the great gods..." the most important rulers of Earth being Enlil who was exceedingly arrogant, exploitive, and brutal, Ninhursag who was his wife, and Enki who was a scientist and the half-brother of Enlil. First and foremost of the Sumerian pantheon, was "An" (Anu in Egyptian, or Anum in Akkadian). "An" was the "eternal sea" of space, the creator of the gods, including the peoples of Earth.

It is noteworthy that the Sumerians repeatedly acknowledged that Enlil, Enki and the other Anunnaki were not really "gods" but technologically advanced people who had come to the Earth from the heavens, from another planet, Nibiruo (Sitchin, 1990). Thus their names: the "Anunnaki" which means: "Those who came from Heaven to Earth."

According to the Sumerians, these "gods" were space-traveling peoples who not only flew in spherical and winged air ships, but who, according to Sumerian calendars, first arrived on this planet almost 500,000 years ago (Sitchin,

1990) —at about the same time that a new breed of humanity, the first Homo sapiens, emerged, their earliest remains being discovered in the Middle East (Joseph, 1996, 2000a). Thus, it could be surmised that the Anunnaki appeared on this planet just before the "seventh day" of creation, when the first primitive man and woman had emerged from the dust.

Moreover, according to the Sumerians, these gods had wives and acted no different from other humans. In fact, although in charge (king) of the Earth, Enlil was bound by rules and regulations dictated by yet other gods who dwelled in other regions of the cosmos, and he was required to carry out their instructions (Kramer, 1991). Apparently those instructions involved depleting the Earth of certain resources, such as tin, which in turn required a huge work force of slaves (Sitchin, 1990).

Figure 82.*The Anunnaki "god" Enki is associated with entwined serpents that form a double helix. reprinted from Sitchin, 1990. Genesis Revisited. Avon, New York.*

THE ANUNNAKI CREATE PRIMITIVE WORKERS

According to Sumerian cosmology, although the Earth was alive with all manner of beast, the "gods" determined that none were suitable to perform the duties required by the gods. In order to obtain a suitable work force, Enki, who was a master scientist and who carried a staff upon which coiled the double helix of two entwined snakes, performed experiments on these human-like animals and other creatures, creating all manner of hybrid beasts.

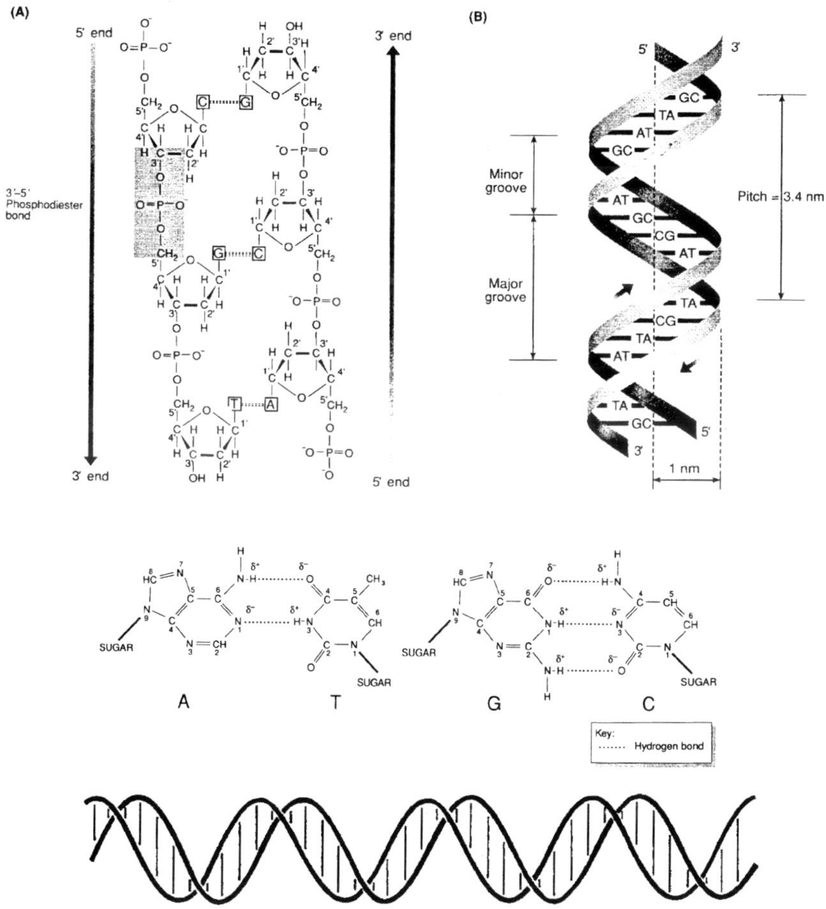

__Figure 83.__ Molecular and structural organization of DNA.

These experiments are depicted in Sumerian glyphs in which Enki and his assistants are shown dressed in aprons and holding flasks and other scientific instruments; and so too are depicted the results of his hybrid experiments, creatures that are half animal half man. Finally, by taking blood and other tissues from the body of the gods and mixing it in his flasks and then implanting the embryo into the womb of a goddess, Enki was able to create the first Homo sapiens, "primitive workers" who were created so as to work as forced labor, to tend the gardens and care for the live stock of the gods. "Primitive man I will create. He shall be charged with the service of the gods that they might be at ease."

Figure 84. *The Anunnaki, Enki, is associated with the serpent and is described by the Sumerians as a master scientist. In this glyph he is apparently directing workers in his laboratory, one of whom pushes a cart that contains objects similar to those situated in the heavens and toward which Enki is reaching. Before Enki is a huge vat or container.*

Figure 85. *According to the Biblical version of genesis, man and woman are created in chapter 1. However, in chapter 2, a "new" man, is created, "Adam" who receives life from god, and becomes "a living soul." According to the Sumerian version, this "new man" was created in a laboratory and placed into the womb of a goddess. According to Sumerian mythology, it is a goddess who serves as the "host" who gives birth to the "new man" that is created in the laboratory of Enki—a "new" man who is created in the image of the gods, and who possesses wisdom.*

***Figure 86.** According to Sumerian mythology, Enki (depicted as the serpent) created all manner of primitive workers which were part human and part animal. Enki's creations can also play music.*

***Figure 87.** A stone bull with a human head. The "crown" upon its head indicates that the creature is of divine origin.*

Thus the "gods" according to the Sumerians "lowered from heaven... the throne of kingship." These individuals were half god and half human and were expected to rule over the fields, the animals, and the incredibly stupid human-like animals that roamed about the planet.

According to the Sumerian's Kings lists, the Anunnaki created these first god-kings, over 240,000 years ago (Roux, 1992) when a goddess gave birth to a man who had been experimentally created and implanted in her womb. "Modern" human DNA also traces it ancestral lineage to a female ancestor who lived about 250,000 years ago (Stoneking & Cann, 1989; Vigilant et al. 1991). Likewise, tools associated with evolutionarily advanced humans have also been dated to around 250,000 years B.P. (Waters, 1997).

As noted, modern human DNA differs significantly from Neanderthal DNA, and Neanderthals died out about 30,000 years ago at which point the rapidly proliferating Cro-Magnon gained complete dominion over the planet. It is also around 30,000 years B.P, according to the Egyptian kings lists, that the gods established the first kingships (i.e., 32,000 years ago).

According to the Sumerians, Enki the scientist and god of the snake, created a new man and woman who could be instructed in the art of culture, science, medicine, and technology (Heidel, 1988; Kramer, 1991); a superior human which included women so beautiful that even the gods lusted and desired them. In consequence, the Anunnaki fathered innumerable children—and in so doing broke the laws formulated by the supreme lords of the universe. The children of the gods then began to rapidly proliferate.

Hence, in summary, according to Sumerian mythology, at first there was chaos, and then there were great clouds which consisted of the primeval elements necessary for the creation of the planets and of all life. From this chaos there emerged An, the eternal heavens of space, who seeded the planets with life, including those planets which would give rise to the gods. These gods were exactly like humans, came to this planet in flying ships order to exploit its resources, and then created "workers" whose purpose was to serve the needs of the gods. For the next 200,000 years these "workers" attended to the fields, gardens, and livestock so that the gods could rest and be at ease.(Stoneking & Cann, 1989; Vigilant et al. 1991;(Waters, 1997)).

SUMERIAN AND BIBLICAL PARALLELS

The first 25 verses of the first book of Moses (Genesis) repeats much of the creation saga, as told by the peoples of ancient Summer and Babylon, including, in verses 26-31, the story of the step-wise creation of all manner of species which culiminated in "man" and "woman" who are fashioned by a single god, who was a member of a pantheon of gods.

According to the Biblical version of Genesis: "And God said, let us make man in our image, after our likeness, and let them have dominion over the fish of the sea, and over the fowl of the earth, and over the cattle... and God saw everything that he had made, and behold it was very good."

The Sumerians tell us that after the creation of workers that Enki and the others were able to rest.

Likewise, we are told in Genesis, that on the seventh day, God rested — for even Gods grow weary. Nevertheless, despite the fact that all that god beheld was "very good" including the creation of these first men and women, apparently they were not good enough. The primitive men and women that god created as part of the natural progression beginning with simple life forms, could not till the earth or take on the responsibilities that the gods required. Thus, Enki fashions a man and woman who are created in the image of the gods and who possess wisdom.

In chapter 2 of Genesis, and after the seventh day when "god" had rested, the Lord God makes His first appearance. In Genesis were are told that the

Lord God created yet another man who could tend the gardens; a man endowed with the spirit, or essence of god—yet a man who was to remain stupid and ignorant and whose only purpose was to toil at the behest of the Lord God.

"The Lord God formed a man of the dust of the ground and breathed into his nostril the breath of life; and man became a living soul. And the Lord God planted a garden, eastward in Eden; and there he put the man he had formed. And out of the ground made the Lord God to grow every tree that is pleasant to sight and good for food" —for even Gods grow hungry. "But of the tree of knowledge," the Lord God warned, "thou shalt not eat."

Figure 88. *"The Fall of Man and the Expulsion from the Garden of Eden." Michelangelo, 1508.*

According to the Biblical version, it is only after this warning, after pointing out the tree of knowledge to Adam, that woman, "Eve" is created. She is called "woman" we are told, because she was taken out of a man.

There is something odd about this story, for in life it is man who is taken from the womb of "woman"—which also means womb-man, the man with a womb. It is woman who gives birth to man, and not the other way around.

In this regard it is noteworthy that "Eve" means: "mother of all." However, by a subtle pay on words, it can also mean: "of the rib."

In Genesis, "Eve" is associated with the serpent. She is beguiled by the serpent who provides her with knowledge and wisdom which she then provides to the man.

Likewise, in the Sumerian version, a female goddess becomes the "mother of all" when Enki, the double helix god of the snake, performs an experiment and implants the mixture into the womb of this goddess, the Mother of All, who gives birth to the first man.

Genesis appears to be a distorted echo of the Sumerian account of human creation; possibly purposefully distorted so as to cast aspersion on the original creator god, Enki, and the mother goddess who is the "mother of all."

Again, according to Sumerian mythology, it is a goddess who serves as the "host" who gives birth to the "new man" that is created in the laboratory of Enki. That is, it is through this woman, this goddess, that a new man is created, a man who is part-god, and who possesses wisdom.

According to the Biblical version, after the creation episode involving "Eve" a crime is committed. A former member of the divine pantheon, a serpent (the Sumerian God: Enki), a fallen angel, provides woman with the fruit of knowledge. She eats, and then offers the fruit of knowledge to man, who also eats, and all are condemned.

But condemned by who? By the Lord God who we later discover is named Yahweh, the ""Destroyer" the "Lord of Armies" of "hosts." It is the Lord God who appears upon the scene after the seventh day who seeks to punish Enki and Eve "the mother of all" for this crime.

The Lord God, speaking to his pantheon of gods says: "Behold the man is become as one of us, to know good and evil... "and so the Lord God "drove out man" from his garden, and promised the worst retributions to woman and man for becoming like the gods, knowing good and evil.

They are cast out of the garden of Eden and terrifying soldiers, that is "Cherubin" with a "flaming sword which turned every way" was stationed at the boundaries of the garden to kill them if they dare to return.

AN INTEGRATED INTERPRETATION OF SUMERIAN GENESIS

Extrapolating from the accounts provided by the Sumerians and the authors of Genesis, and accepting for the moment that these accounts may be true, it thus appears that men and women, "gods" and "goddesses" from another planet established themselves on Earth somewhere around 500,000 years ago in order to deplete the planet of its resources. This is the same time period when the exceedingly ape-like Homo erectus first came to be slowly replaced by the first archaic Homo sapiens including Neanderthals.

Thus, when the Anunnaki first arrived on this planet (be it 500,00 or 250,000 years ago), the only available work force were extremely primitive humans who proved to be incapable of performing the necessary work.

According to the Sumerians, Enki performed experiments in his laboratory and created a new man and woman who were able to perform the tasks assigned. As Enki's emblem is the double helix, this creative act may have involved genetic engineering and the creation of a clone or a hybrid clone that he implanted in the womb of a woman "god." This female "god" who also resembles a snake, then gives birth to humans who are fashioned in the image of the gods and who have knowledge of good and evil.

And, as we know, a people, great and tall, who strode upon the Earth like gods, the six foot tall Cro-Magnon people appeared on Earth; yet from whence they came, or how they "evolved" is unknown. Hence, at least from the standpoint of a thought experiment, it is possible that the Cro-Magnon people were the result of this genetic experiment, performed maybe around 250,000 years ago or as recently as 70,000 years B.P.

And then, a second god appears on Earth for the first time and calls himself the "Lord God." The Lord God, also known as the Destroyer and the Lord of Armies, appears after the first gods have taken their leisure, that is, after the proverbial "seventh day." In the account provided by Genesis, whereas "God" creates the first man and woman, and then rests, the Lord God then appears upon the Earth and claims to have created Adam to tend his own gardens—which is exactly what the Sumerians tells us were the motives of the Anunnaki. However, this Lord God also drives out "the man" and presumably Eve and the serpent god, from their homes and takes control of the garden of Eden.

Could it be that Yahweh and his "hosts" arrived here after the Anunnaki and then immediately began to war and struggle with them for control of the Earth? Can it be that perhaps Yahweh did not initially engage in any acts of creation, and did not even arrive on this planet until after the creation of the Cro-Magnon Adam and Eve?

THE SONS OF GODS HAVE SEX WITH HUMAN WOMEN

"When the morning stars sang together all the sons of God shouted for joy." Job 38:7.

And who is the morning star? Venus, is the goddess of love, knowledge, and wisdom; also known as the great serpent. And who are the morning "stars?" Perhaps the Cro-Magnon daughters of the snake?

And who are the "sons of God?" Perhaps the sons of God, that is, of the Anunnaki, also known as the Anakites, and the Nephilim?

"When the goddesses of love gathered and danced and sang together, all the sons of god shouted for joy!

According to the King James version of Genesis (chapter 6): "And it came to pass, when men began to multiply on the face of the earth, and daughters were born unto them, that the sons of God saw the daughters of men that they were fair; and they took them wives of all which they chose... There were giants in the earth in those days; and also after that, when the sons of God came in unto the daughters of men, and they bare children..."

As stated more clearly in the original Hebrew version of Genesis ("Tanakh"): "It was then, and later too, that the Nephilim appeared on earth—when the divine beings cohabited with the daughters of men, who bore them offspring. They were the heroes of old, the men of renown."

THE FLOOD AND THE DESTRUCTION OF ANCIENT CIVILIZATION

The Sumerians tell us that the Anunnaki at first attempted to use selective birth control and sterilization to prevent the daughters of men from becoming pregnant with the children of the sons of the gods. They also attempted to use these same measures to prevent the daughters of those women who had been impregnated by the sons of god, from breeding. The Anunnaki failed in their birth control efforts and the land became filled with the sons and daughters of the sons of the gods.

According to the Sumerians, the Anunnaki King of the Gods, Enlil, received instructions that he was to destroy these illegitimate children of the gods, the "heroes of old" as they were conceived in violation of the laws (Heidel, 1988; Kramer, 1991). Moreover, he was to destroy the hybrid, half human half animal creations of Enki.

Likewise, the Lord God of Genesis could not bear this "wickedness" and set out to destroy one and all... "both man and beast..." in a great cataclysmic flood. Indeed, throughout Exodus the Lord God also emphasizes that all animals of the conquered and murdered people must also be completely destroyed.

As we have determined in an earlier chapter, the floods, the "great deluge" is not a myth, as there are world wide ancient legends (Hammerly-Dupuy, 1988), and geological (Schoch, 1992; Woolley, 1965) and other evidence of a world wide flood (Hammerly-Dupuy, 1988), and cataclysmic weathering alterning events, including the carcasses of wholly mammoths and other creatures, that were swallowed whole by oceans of waters and then flash-frozen with grass still in their mouths—some 12,000 years ago.

That is, the evidence suggests that following a terrible flood there was an "instant ice age" that was immediately followed by a rapid rise in temperature, thus releasing a second deluge. We are also told of two floods in Genesis one of which lasted 7 days, and another that lasted 40, whereas the Sumerians tell us that there were terrible winds and cold, as well as flood.

The rise in temperature following this rather instant ice age has also been scientifically verified, by James White, a climatologist at the University of Colorado. In a study published in Science, White presents evidence which indicates that immediately following this ice age temperatures increased by 20 degrees in a very short time. That is, temperatures returned to normal, thus unleashing even more terrible floods from the melting ice.

Ancient peoples from throughout the world including Meso-America, have passed on to their descendants, an almost ancestral memory of a time when the Earth was buffeted by terrible storms and freezing rains, of rising rushing waters that destroyed the cities, destroyed civilization, and destroyed the crowns of creation of woman and man (Hammerly-Dupuy, 1988). These cosmic catastrophes enveloped the Earth, some 12,000 years ago, when, according to the ancients, the planet Venus snaked through the heavens, rocketing through the skies like a twisting serpent with the Martian oceans (his coat and skin) trailing behind like a great tail. Venus then lashed the Earth with oceans of water, only to "tear out the eye of the sun" (an eclipse?) causing an instant ice age followed by even more terrible floods when the eclipse was over and the sun again began to shine.

In the oldest existent written records available to modern woman and man, records carved in stone over 6,000 years ago, we are told by Sumerian scholars of five great cities that had been erected over ten thousands years ago (Woolley, 1965); cities by the names of Eridu, Badtibira, Larak, Sippar, and Shuruppak (Kramer, 1991; Roux, 1992), which were destroyed in this great cosmic cataclysm. And Plato tells us of two great cities and civilizations, Atlantis and Athens, the Mayas tell us of "Mu," and the ancient Egyptians speak of numerous cities ruled first by the God, then the demigods, and finally, 15,000 years ago, the first kings.

Presumably the Sumerians, the ancient Egyptians, the Mayans, and Plato, were able to distinguish between myth and fact. Indeed, Plato tells us that this information is from the realm of fact, whereas the Sumerians always began their fables and tales of the marvelous in the following way: "One upon a time..." The same is not true regarding Sumerian accounts of the flood or of the gods (Heidel, 1988; Kramer, 1991; Woolley, 1965).

In fact, the Sumerians divided history into two periods: "Before the flood" (Lam abubi) and "After the flood" (Arki abubi), with their own civilization, arising some 6,000 years ago, belonging to the later (Kramer, 1991; Woolley, 1965). According to the Sumerians, the ancient Egyptians, Plato, and the Mayans, these predeluvial civilizations were incredibly scientifically advanced, and were ruled by mighty kings—including, according to Samarian and Semitic accounts, the descendants of the illegitimate "sons of the gods."

In fact, a great pre-deluvial sphinx still stands in Egypt. As based on geo-weathering studies conducted by Schoch (1992) and published in "Science," the great sphinx is around 13,000 (or more) years in age, and suffered the bulk of its erosion when inundated by torrential rains and flooding. And, as detailed in an earlier chapter, the three great pyramids of Giza appear to have been constructed by an incredibly technologically advanced predeluvial, predynastic Egyptian civilization.

EXODUS: GENOCIDE AND THE CHILDREN OF THE GODS

According to the Sumerians, although the floods destroyed all of civilization, not everyone was killed as the children of the Gods had been forewarned by Enki (Heidel, 1988; Kramer, 1991; Roux, 1992). Enki warned the people because it was he who had created them.

Because Enil either failed to foresee the flood, or because he failed to kill all the illegitimate children of the gods, he was overthrown and replaced by another god. The Babylonians say the god that toppled Enlil was Marduk, the son of Enki.

Likewise, for creating humanity, for making them in the image of the gods, Enki, the science god of the snake, was condemned.

In the account provided by Genesis, we are told that the Lord God of Genesis also failed to kill all the children of the gods. It was not just Noah who escaped the calamities and floods that enveloped the Earth, but the "wicked" children of the Gods, the descendants of the "Nephilim." The Nephilim survivors may well have included Canaan, the grandson of Noah; Canaan being yet another member of the Sethian race.

As mentioned in an earlier chapter, in a different Sumerian account, the flood is described as an unexpected force of nature, which the Anunnaki could do nothing to prevent. And (according to this version), it was because of this failure to foresee or prevent this catastrophe, and it was because the power base of the Anunnaki had been destroyed, that Enlil was easily overthrown and replaced by Marduk who also tossed out Enki and the other members of the ruling pantheon following the flood.

According to this version of Sumerian history, the Anunnaki were taken so unawares by the impending cosmic catastrophe that they panicked and were forced to flee the Earth, like frightened dogs with tails between their legs, taking refuge in the heavens.

"The gods cowered like dogs and crouched in distress. Ishtar cried out like a woman in travail... The Anunnaki gods wept with her. The gods sat bowed and weeping" (Roux, 1992), for they were about to lose everything they had worked for.

After the floods had subsided, the Anunnaki are described as returning from the heavens, famished and starved, as they had been insufficiently provisioned.

As in the Biblical version, the humans of Earth who survived this cataclysm did so by building and arc. And as the survivers emerged after the waters had receded they built a fire, and roasted meat. According to the Sumerian version the gods returned from the heavens and "the gods smelled the sweet savor. The gods gathered like flies over the sacrifice" for they were starved and famished. Likewise, in the Biblical version, the Lord God also smells the sweet savor and joins Noah and his family in the feast.

And it is here that the Sumerian account of the history of the Anunnaki and their Nephilim children ends, and where the Book of Moses explains what transpired next.

EXODUS: THE LORD GOD PLOTS TO KILL THE CHILDREN OF THE GODS

For reasons that are never explained, Canaan the grandson of Noah, and a survivor of the great flood, is condemned by Noah. Canaan, but not his brothers, is cursed, not because of anything he did, but because his father, Ham, saw Noah lying in his tent drunk and naked (Genesis 9:21-28). It is Canaan and his children and descendants, according to the Genesis, who would establish the land of Canaan. And it is the descendants of Canaan, of the Sethian race, who the Lord God would seek to erase from the face of the Earth.

The Lord God would plot and scheme for thousands of years, to destroy the last descendants of the Nephilim, the Anunnaki ("Anakites"), as well as those of the Caananite branch of the Sethian race—all of whom may have been one and the same. The Lord God would create his own "godly offspring" who He would toughen up to serve as an army that would seek out and destroy the last of the descendants of those old Gods whose son's impregnated the women of Earth, thereby giving rise to titans and heroes of old. The Lord God would exterminate the sons and daughters of the son's of God, and the children of the daughters of Enki's human creations.

And so, according to Genesis, The Lord God chooses Abraham to be the "father" of the first of his "godly offspring," the multitude who would becomes slaves in ancient Egypt.

And thus, with the Books of Moses, begins the Exodus. The Lord God gathers up an army of the descendants of Israel -his "first born son." And with the assistance of Moses, He leads them from the land of Egypt to destroy the peoples of Canaan. However, the Lord God also explains to his godly offspring that they were chosen for this task "not because of their virtues, it is rather because of the wickedness of those nations that the Lord is dispossessing... " Indeed, to stress this important point, the Lord God repeats it to Moses and the Jews: "It is not because of your virtues and your rectitude that you will be able to possess their country; but it is because of their wickedness" (Deuteronomy, chapter 9).

And who are these "wicked" people that must be destroyed? It is "A people great and tall, the Anakites... The Lord your God will wipe them out." And who are these Anakites, these giants, "great and tall?" but none other that the children of the "Anunnaki," the Nephilim—or at least, so say the Books of Moses.

And after "Moses sent men to secretly scout the land of Canaan... they returned... and the men who had gone up said, We cannot attack that people... All the people that we saw in it are men of great size, we saw the Nephilim there—the Anakites are part of the Nephilim—and we looked like grasshoppers... to them" (Numbers, Chapter 13).

THE TWO GODS

The Earth is now populated by over six billion people, and less than half of the adult population believe in a god that is in any way similar to the Lord God of the Jews, Christians, and Moslems.

Some peoples believe in an all pervasive spirit, others worship their ancestors or their rulers, yet others worship multiple gods and a hierarchy of gods that differ in their power and potency.

For example, the hymns of the Rig Veda are addressed to various nature gods, gods associated with natural phenomenon. In return for worship and sacrifice the gods were asked for blessings, more food, an abundance of offspring, a long life, and so on.

The ancient Hindus developed a trinity: Brahman, Shiva, and Vishnu. Shiva, a great Yogi was the god of good and evil, fertility and asceticism; a creator and destroyer who taught his followers to transcend this reality and personal concepts of divinity through meditation. Vishnu is believed to have no beginning and no end, and sometimes takes on human form, including that of Krishna who was believed to be a personification or rather, incarnation (avatar) of Vishnu.

The Sumerians also believed that the Earth was ruled by a pantheon of gods, and this same pantheon is alluded to in the Bible.

"And god said, Let us make man in our image, after our likeness." -Genesis, 1:26.

"And the Lord God said, Behold, the man has become as one of us." -Genesis, 3:22.

"God standeth in the divine assembly, among the divine beings; he pronounces judgment among the gods." -Psalm 82:1.

Prior to the revolutionary visionary experience of Muhammed, the Arabs had long believed in numerous lesser gods, including jinn, as well as several greater gods, including a creator god, al-Lah. al-Lah, after creating the world, the ancient Arabs believed, withdrew from the world—just as we are told that upon the seventh day of creation, God withdrew from the world in order to rest.

In the seventh century, many Arabs also believed that the massive cube-shaped shrine in Mecca, the Kabah, had originally been dedicated to al-Lah, and were upset that another deity, Hubal, resided there. Moreover, it was believed by some Arabian Jews, that Ishmael, the son of Hagar and Abraham, built the Kabah, the first temple of the one God, and that Ishmael had become the father of the Arabs, such that Arabs were also the sons of Abraham.

Before his conversion, Muhammed had also come to believe that al-Lah, the High God of the Arabs, was different from that of Hubal, and maybe even identical to the creator God worshipped by Christians and Jews.

The more impersonal Allah does in fact resembles the creator God in a number of respects and lacks the continual upwelling rages and the terrifying behaviors associated with the Lord God. As stated in the Koran, it is Allahwho "created the heavens and the earth and the succession of night and day... giving life to the earth after it has been lifeless, and causing all manner of living creatures to multiply therein."

However, like the Lord God, Allah transcends creation and time, acting as judge and bestowing punishment upon those who refused to obey His laws or heed his messenger.

Allah, and the Lord God of antiquity were judgmental and would dole out punishment to offenders.

THE TWO GODS

The peoples of antiquity believed in numerous goddesses and gods. These various gods included a benevolent creator "God" sometimes associated with Enki and the Great Mother of All. These gods also included a violent, commanding, mercurial, "Lord God" who makes demands of the people and who kills and murders innocent and guilty alike, and who leads according to some unknown purpose. This Biblical creator God appears in some respects to incorporate aspects of the benevolence of the Mother Goddess. Thus the creator God sees everything as good. And, like the Great Mother of All, and Enki of the Sumerian pantheon, the creator God wishes nothing but good for his creations and seeks to promote life and its well being. The creator God does not lead, does not destroy, and in many respects is similar to the Tao and Great Spirit of the pagan world and predeluvial antiquity.

"The Tao produces all things and nourishes them; it produces them and does not claim them; it does all, and yet does not boast of it; it presides over all, and yet does control them. This is what is called The Mysterious Quality of the Tao." -Tao Teh King

The Lord God is more like the Babylonian Marduk who overthrows the old Anunnaki gods including Enki. It is Marduk, the son of Enki, who casts his father out of heaven, whereas in the Biblical version, it is the Lord God who casts his son, Satan, out of heaven.

Figure 89. *Satan cast out of heaven.*

The Lord God although claiming at times to be the creator, is also completely distinct from the God of the creation, the Great Mother of All. Instead of promoting life, He continually destroys life, and sees everything as evil and deserving of death, be it animals, or innocent women and children.

In the Biblical account of Genesis, "God" (who is referred to as "God") and the "Lord God" (who is referred to as the "Lord God") have completely different attitudes about humans and play different roles in the affairs of woman and man. The "God" who creates the Earth and all life sees these creations as "good" and "very good" and then decides to withdraw from these creations and to sleep and dream.

The "Lord God" takes a more active, commanding, judgmental and murderous interest in human affairs. And, he is a braggart who enjoys terrifying and humiliating humans, including even his faithful servants, such as Job. Job's children were murdered on orders from the Lord God, his livestock were stolen, and he was then physically tortured with sores and boils.

Even after the Lord God has ground these pitiful humans into the ground, and killed their wives and children, and afflicts them with boils and sores, He feels a need to lord it over and bully the children of woman and man.

"Then the Lord answered Job out of a whirlwind, and said Who is this that darkeneth counsel by words without knowledge. Gird up now thy loins like a man; for I will demand of thee, and answer thou me. Where was thou when I laid the foundations of the earth, declare if thou have understanding. Canst thou bind the sweet influences of Pleiades or lose the bands of Orion? Knowest thou the ordinances of heaven? Canst thou set the dominion of thereof in the earth? Canst thou lift up thy voice to the clouds? Canst thou send lightning that they may go and say unto thee: Here we are? Canst thou draw out leviathan with a hook? Or his tongue with a cord? Have you an arm like God, and canst thou thunder with a voice like his?" -Job 38:7.

Figure 90. *And Satan... smote Job with boils.... (W. Blake).*

This bullying braggadocio is completely contrary to that we would associate with the Great Mother, a loving just god, or the Tao:

"He who stands on his tiptoes does not stand firm; he who stretches his legs does not walk easily. He who displays himself does not shine; he who asserts his views is not distinguished; he who vaunts himself does not find his merit acknowledged; he who is self-conceited has no superiority allowed him." -Tao Teh King.

Figure 91. *Satan.*

Jung, in the masterwork, Answer to Job, explains that it is the Lord God's feelings of inferiority which fuels His incalculable mood swings and devastating attacks of wrath. It is this terrible sense of inferiority, this incredible self-doubt, that gives rise to His need to thunder and brag about his superiority, as well as his tendency to attack anyone and everyone, including even His most loyal followers.

For example, in the story of Job, we are told that beset by a doubting thought, the Lord God gives his blessing to the utter destruction of his faithful servant. Job is robbed of his herds, his servants are slaughtered, then his sons and daughters are killed by a whirlwind, and he is smitten with boils and sores and lay near death. He is at the brink of the grave. And although Job continues to display his faithfulness, and although the Lord God has broken three of His own commandments, He has no feelings of compassion, no mercy, no remorse, but instead reacts with more ruthless brutality and feels a need to go on for 73 verses shouting that He, the Lord God, is more powerful than anyone, including Job. His behavior is so bizarre, given the fact that Job is already well aware of the power of the Lord, that one can only conclude that he who doubts the Lord God's greatness, is the Lord God Himself.

"Yahweh projects on to Job a skeptic's face which is hateful to him because it is his own" (Jung, 1971; p. 543). Indeed, according to Jung, it is this sense of self-doubt, this terrible feeling of inferiority which gives rise to his "jealousy and irritable nature" and His need to be always "prying mistrustfully into the faithless hearts of men and exploring their secret thoughts."

"For the ear of jealousy hereth all things: and the noise of murmurings is not hid." -Wisdom of Solomon, 1:10; -Zechariah 4:10.

The Lord God is not only a jealous braggart, but He tells us He can listen to our secret thoughts, and that He alone is beyond judgment, because He is the greatest, most wonderful, most powerful, and the most righteous god of them all. Even when He commits heinous atrocities, those who have been wronged by Him remain miserable and accused because He is beyond good and evil and prefers to blame others for His cruel mistakes.

"Who is this that darkens counsel by words without insight? Will you even put me in the wrong? Will you condemn me that you may be justified?" Job 38.

GOD AND THE LORD GOD

THE RAGING LORD GOD

Is the Lord God, a "god" at all? Or, like the Sumerian gods, the Anunnaki, is He a being from another planet?

And if He is a god, or if he is a man, why has He come to the Earth?

The "Lord God" of the Old Testament, is a "Destroyer" who is easily provoked to destruction and rage, who demands not love, but fear and sacrifice, and who repeatedly and indiscriminately murders His people, His "godly offspring," including Moses. All innocent bystanders are exterminated by the Lord God; they are brutally butchered and their daughters enslaved and raped often for no good reason, or simply because they had the misfortune of living near the land or owning the property He wished to give to the wondering Israelites.

"When the Lord thy God shall bring thee into the land, and shall cast out many nations before thee, the Hittite, and the Gergashite, and the Amorite, and the Canaanite, and the Perizzite, and the Hivite, and the Jebusite... and the Lord thy god shall deliver them up before thee, and thou shalt smite them, then thou shall utterly destroy them."-Deuteronomy 7:1-2.

"Of the cities of these peoples, that the Lord they God giveth thee for an inheritance, thou shalt save alive nothing that breathest." -Deuteronomy, 20:16.

"Great and goody cities, which thou didst not build and houses full of all good things which thou didst not fill, and cisterns hewn, which thou didst not hew, and vineyards and olive-trees, which thou didst not plant, and thou shalt eat and be satisfied." -Deuteronomy 6:10-11.

"They exterminated them, they did not spare a soul." -Joshua 11:14.

The Lord God even required that the ancient Jews kill their brothers, fathers, mothers, and children as a sign of loyalty:

"Each of you put sword on thigh, go back and forth from gate to gate throughout the camp and slay brother, neighbor, and kin... Dedicate yourselves to the Lord this day—for each of you has been against son and brother—that He may bestow a blessing on you today." -Exodus, 32:26-29.

This Lord God is so lacking in compassion, and is so vicious and sadistic that He "visits the iniquity of parents upon children and children's children, upon the third and fourth generations" (Exodus 34:6-7). The Lord God not only approves of and encourages murder, rape, and theft, but vengeance on future generations for the crimes of their parents.

And He repeatedly flies into crazed, infantile, almost insane, irrational rages, and behaves like such a crazed madman that He nearly completely annihilates his "chosen peoples" and nearly destroys His own well thought out plans.

For example, after escaping the Egyptians, who the Lord God utterly destroys, Moses ascended a mountain and then stayed to talk with the Lord God. The Lord God suddenly broke off his conversation and shouted in a panic: "Go get these down; for thy people which thou broughtest out of the land of Egypt have corrupted themselves" for they are about to begin worshipping the golden calf. After He gets over his initial hurt and shocked surprise, He then proceeds to work himself up into a lather and in an enraged sulk cries out: "Now therefore let me alone" because He is going to get mad, and He is going to get even, and He is going to kill everybody. "Now therefore let me alone that my wrath may wax hot against them, and that I may consume them" (Exodus 32: 7,10).

Fortunately, for the Israelis, Moses was able to appeal to His pride, by pointing out how foolish He would look, and how the Egyptians would laugh at Him if He killed His people. "Let not the Egyptians say, It was with evil intent that He delivered them, only to kill them off in the mountains and annihilate them from the face of the earth." Control yourself, Moses councils, and reluctantly the Lord calms down, for to look foolish and to have the Egyptians laugh and mock Him, is more than He can bear. So, instead he sends Moses down the mountain to kill the people for Him.

And not only is He a sometimes irrational killer, He promotes and encourages a savage system of slavery, including even the enslavement of his Hebrew children who can be beaten and slowly murdered at will by their masters:

"When a slave owner strikes a male or female slave with a rod and... if the slave survives a day or two, there is no punishment, for the slave is the owners property." -NRSV 21:20.

This Lord God even approves of sex slavery, including sex with little girls, and the rape of young Jewish virgins by Jewish men (Judges 21:11-13):

"As the Lord God commanded... kill every male among the little ones. But all the women and female children that have not known a man, keep alive for yourselves." -Numbers, 31

"Go and lie in wait in the vineyards. If the daughters of Shiloh come out to dance in dances, then come ye out and catch you every man his wife of the daughters of Shiloh." -Judges 21:19-25.

The Lord God of the ancient Jews had an obvious contempt for the female sex:

"The daughters of Zion are haughty and walk with wanton eyes, mincing as they go, and making a tinkling with their feet. The Lord will smite with a scab of crowns of their head...And it shall come to pass that instead of sweet smell there shall be stink." -Isaiah 3:16-26, 4:4.

The hatred of women is unique to the Lord God of the Israelis, for there is no suggestion of misogyny among any other creator god. Even the God of the Koran forbade the mistreatment of women. Instead of wishing that they should rot and be burned, as was repeatedly suggested by the Lord God, Allah gave women the legal right of inheritance and divorce and fostered equality among the sexes. The Koran does not prescribe the veil, except for Muhammed's wives which was meant as a mark of high status. It was only later that Muslims relegated women to a second class status. The Koran, in fact, insists that other religions and other peoples be respected.

"Do not argue with the followers of earlier revelations—unless it be such of them as are set on evil doings: For our God and your God is one and the same, and it is unto him that we surrender ourselves."-the Koran

"We believe in God and in that which had been bestowed upon Abraham and Ishmael and Isaac and Jacob and their descendants, and that which had been vouchsafed to Moses and Jesus...and to all the prophets by their sustainer: we make no distinction between any of them. And it is unto him that we surrender ourselves." -the Koran

By contrast, the Lord God is a god of rape, pillage, murder, terror, horror and hate, who repeatedly murders His own people.

"I will strike them with pestilence and disown them," He thunders at Moses (Numbers 14:11-18). In one episode of divine rage, He kills 24,000 of His people with a plague (Numbers 25:7-9).

In fact, the Lord killed or allowed every Jew who exited Egypt to die in the desert, refusing to allow even Moses to set foot on the promised land.

The Lord God even brags that he purposefully made His people miserable even though His actions were completely unjustified. He tells us that He set for them impossible goals so that they would blame themselves when he ruthlessly and brutally attacks and murders them for their failures.

"I gave them laws that were not good and rules by which they could not live... I defiled them by their very gifts—that I might render them desolate, that they might know that I am the Lord." -Ezekial 20:25-26.

Is the Lord God a "god of love?" or a "just God?" Or, is He a Lord of death, murder, rape, pillage, and deception?

What is clear is that He is a Lord God who forces his own people to butcher and betray their own children, their own fathers, and their own brothers and sisters. He is a Lord God whose first act is to create and then enslave a man and a woman who He forces to "tend and till" his fields and who He then condemns, and whose children he condemns, because they ate some fruit in His garden.

THE LORD GOD EVIL

It is a stereotypical Lord God stratagem to make His victims believe they are responsible for their misfortune, when in fact, He planned everything, even humiliating and forcing them to disobey so He could punish or destroy them.

"But I will harden his heart. And thou shall say unto Pharaoh, Thus saith the Lord, Israel is My first born son. I have said to you, Let my son go, that he may worship Me. Yet you refuse to let him go. Now I will slay your first born son." -Exodus 4:21-23.

"But I will harden Pharaoh's heart that I may multiply My signs and marvels in the land of Egypt. When the Pharaoh does not heed you, I will lay My hand upon Egypt." -Exodus 7:3.

This is just a prelude to the nightmare or murder and rape that this Lord God will soon unleash upon the land. The Lord God is as likely to murder and punish the innocent as the guilty and tens of thousands if not hundreds of thousands of men, women, children, and even their animals are slaughtered by the Israelis as they wonder in the desert of the Sinai for the next 40 years.

And even after He settles His children in the promised land He turns Jews against Jews and turns Jews loose on the innocent who they plunder, rape, and murder

"He multiplies wounds without causes. He destroys both the blameless and the wicked. If the scourge slay suddenly, He will laugh at the trial of the innocent. He deprives trusty men of speech, And takes away the reason of elders. He pours disgrace upon great men, and loosens the belt of the mighty. He exalts nations, then destroys them; He expands nations, then leads them away. He deranges the leaders of the people, and makes them wander in a trackless waste." -Job, 12:20-24

Even innocent children are slaughtered simply for laughing and jeering:

"Elisha... turned and looked at them and cursed them in the name of the Lord. Thereupon two she-bears came out of the woods and mangled forty two of the children." -II Kings 2:23

The Lord God even boasts: "I make evil!"

Because of the obviously wicked and seemingly dual nature of the Lord God, some theologians and popes, including Clement of Rome, believed and taught that the Lord God rules the earth with the left and right hand; the right being Christ, and the left being Satan—opposites which are united in God. God is a unity, both good and evil. Carl Jung referred to this as an antinomy, a totality of inner opposites.

By contrast, the Christian Gnostics believed there were two Gods, and they distinguished between the hateful, vengeful, murderous god of the Jews and the Hidden God of Jesus Christ. They argued that the Hidden God is the same God that had been worshiped by the entire pagan world, the god of the first cause which was also the God of Aristotle.

Even the Lord God repeatedly tell us there are other gods, and He warns his people that they dare not worship these other gods or He will destroy them.

"Now I know that the Lord is greater than all gods; for in the things wherein they dealt, proudly he was above them." -Exodus 18:11

""Be circumspect and make no mention of the name of the other gods." -Exodus 23:13.

However, later in the Bible, He both admits and then denies the existence of others gods: "No god was formed before me, nor will be after me. I, I am Yahweh, there is no other savior but me." This view is also echoed in the Koran: "He is the One God; God the Eternal, the Uncaused Cause of all being. He begets not, and neither is he begotten and there is nothing that could be compared to him."

Similarly, although the ancient Hindus, positing numerous gods, and the three great gods, Brahman, Shiva, and Vishnu, they also believed this trinity were three aspects of a single reality.

Because the Lord God is perceived as both good and evil, some believe it is possible to beg God to intercede on their behalf against the bad Lord God. Moses, Job, and Jesus, for example, clearly believed they could call upon God to provide them help against the Lord God.

"I desire to argue my case with God. I will defend my ways to his face," cries Job. "Do not lead us into temptation," Jesus calls out to Him.

Yet, He does tempt. He does destroy. The Lord God is a jealous tempest of destructive energies that he willingly unleashes without moderation. And none of his qualities are an obstacle to the others, as He gives in to every ruthless and destructive whim as it occurs to Him even if it injures the innocent including those he professes to love: "Lord, where are thy former kindnesses, which by thy faithfulness thou didst swear to David?"

His behavior and that of His minions and divine sons, is so ruthless and horrible, that even "God" is appalled by His injustices and the wickedness of His people. God goes before the divine assembly not only to protest this ungodly behavior but to instruct them and the Lord God as to how they should behave and to cease these wicked ways.

"God standeth in the divine assembly, among the divine beings; he pronounces judgment among the gods. How long will you judge unjustly and accept the persons of the wicked? Defend the poor and fatherless: do justice to the afflicted and needy. Deliver the poor and need; liberate them from the hand of the wicked." -Psalms 82:1-6.

THOU SHALT NOT KNOW

The "God" who is credited with the creation expects nothing more of his creations than to be fruitful and multiply. The creator god looks upon these creations and proclaims them as "Good... Very good!"

As is evident throughout Genesis, the Lord God does not see humanity as "good" as was the proclamation of the "god" who is credited with the creation. The Lord God sees everything as evil and flawed. And no wonder, He is gazing at his own image, his own unknown face—and that face is hateful. It is a face that enjoys nothing more than humiliating and frightening the peoples of the Earth; peoples which by all means, should remain stupid, without knowledge, and ignorant of good and evil so that they slavishly accept good and evil, especially His evil, without distinction and without the capacity to judge Him for what He is.

"Will you put me in the wrong? Will you condemn me that you may be justified?"Job 38.

Hence, the first commandment: Thou shalt not know!

"And the Lord God commanded the man, saying, Of every tree of the garden though mayest freely eat; But of the tree of knowledge of good and evil, thou shalt not eat of it."

And then the first lie: "For in the day that thou eatest thereof thou shalt surely die." -Genesis, 2:17.

The Lord God, however, underestimates these humans, and in so doing, shows a shocking lack of wisdom or foresight.

"And the Lord God walking in the garden in the cool of the day... called unto Adam and said unto him, Where art thou?"

"Where art thou?" Why can't He find them if he is a god?

And why is He looking for them? Does He need them to get back to work tilling his gardens? Is he lonely?

The Koran teaches that God created Adam in his own image so that he could contemplate himself as if before a mirror.

"And Adam said, I heard thy voice in the garden, and I was afraid, because I was naked; and I hid myself." "And the Lord God said, Who told thee that thou was naked?"

"Who told thee?" this Lord God bellows, for not only is He shocked, but He cannot figure it out Himself. Indeed, it never even occurs to Him that these bags of bones may have actually eaten of the fruit. Instead, Adam blames the woman, and it is the woman who tells Him. The Woman! which must have been galling indeed.

And this raging slave master who demands complete obedience from his slaves who He forces to "till and tend" His gardens, He not only flies into a petulant rage but He experiences this terrible urge to get even. He sadistically punishes these slaves who did not know any better until after they ate of the fruit of knowledge, and then promises to make their lives and that of their offspring as miserable as possible until the very end of time.

"I will put enmity between thee and the woman... I will greatly multiply thy sorrow... cursed is the ground for thy sake... thorns and thistles shall it bring forth to thee..." -Genesis, 3.

THE LORD GOD PROVOKES CAIN AGAINST ABEL

The Lord God also enjoys turning humans against one another, husband against wife, father against son, brother against brother, using a strategy of divide, humiliation, and conquer; a strategy that involves forcing His victims to believe that because He treats them badly, they must be bad, and thus deserving of the punishments and horrors that He inflicts upon them.

"And Adam knew Eve and she conceived...Cain, and said, I have gotten a man from the Lord. And she again bare his brother Abel."

"Abel was a keeper of sheep, but Cain was a tiller of the ground... and Cain brought of the fruit of the ground an offering unto the Lord. And Abel, he also brought of the firstlings of his flock and of the fat thereof."

"And the Lord had respect unto Abel, and to his offering: But unto Cain and to his offering he had not respect. And Cain was very wroth, and his countenance fell."

Perhaps the Lord God simply loves meat and hates His vegetables, which explains why he has no respect for the offering of Cain who apparently doesn't know any better. Or perhaps Cain knows too much, showing imagination and a little god-like ingenuity by evolving beyond gathering to agriculture and farming.

Or maybe even the Lord God does not know why He is angry with Cain. Insight into human nature or into His own nature, is not a quality of the Lord God.

Or maybe He dislikes Cain because, unlike Abel, Cain may have been created in the image of God, much like Adam and the first man was created in the image of God. "I have gotten a man from the Lord," Eve tells us. She does not say that she gave birth to a son.

In any case, after rejecting his offering, the Lord God then proceeds to insult Cain and belittles his feelings. The Lord God, in fact, appears to enjoy "rubbing it in" by playing dumb.

"And the Lord said unto Cain, why art thou wroth? And why is thy countenance fallen?"

Cain is so devastated that he doesn't answer, though he could have certainly replied: "Because you rejected my love and the fruit of my labors. Because you kicked away my offering and then you kicked me in the teeth...and for no good reason. Because you are viscous, hateful, and cruel!"

It does not appear to occur to The Lord God that it may be His behavior which has caused Cain's countenance to fall. That maybe Cain's countenance has fallen because He just kicked Cain in the teeth.

Rather, Cain's wroth makes the Lord God suspicious. As if there were no reason for Cain to be angry and upset.And then He concludes, or at least wishes to convince Cain that because Cain feels badly, then he must have behaved badly, which is a sin. Therefore, in a neat trick of reversing cause and effect, the Lord God explains that it is because Cain has sinned, that the Lord God has decided to reject him and his offering.

"If thou doest well, shall thou not be accepted? And if thou doest not well, sin liest at the door. And unto thee shall be his desire, and thou shalt rule over him."

Essentially the Lord God has told Cain, that Cain is an inferior person, a failure, a sinner, and is not acceptable to the Lord. And why is that? Again, perhaps because Cain showed some ingenuity. Instead of stalking, herding, and killing animals, as does his brother, he instead has gained dominion over the land and has become a farmer!

Knowledge, imagination, creativity, and any semblance of independent thinking is hateful to this Lord God.

And what of the fact that this Lord God fears that Cain shall rule over his own desires? Why is self-mastery a sin?

The Lord God also turned Cain against Abel whose offering He approved of. The Lord God recklessly puts Abel at risk for retaliation by provoking Cain. By rejecting Cain and engaging in this humiliating act of favoritism, He turns Cain against his brother.

Did the Lord God simply lack any semblance of insight or foresight as to what would happen? Is this part of a grand, long range stratagem? Or is it just stereotypical for the Lord God to behave an incredibly self-centered, arrogant, cruel, insensitive fashion that puts even those He favors at risk?

"And it came to pass when they were in the field, that Cain rose up against Abel his brother and slew him."

Given that this Lord God repeatedly claims to be all knowing, it is thus rather surprising that He does not know that Cain would kill or has killed Abel.

And, how is it that an all knowing Lord God repeatedly loses track of his human creations, first Adam and Eve, and now Abel?

"And the Lord said unto Cain, Where is Abel thy brother?"

But this is a characteristic of this Lord God. He did not know that Adam and Eve would eat of the tree of knowledge of good and evil. And, just as He couldn't find Abel, He couldn't find them when he sought their company in the garden.

Perhaps He is just being shrewd? Perhaps He is just pretending to be an ignorant, insensitive brute that has no understanding of human nature, so that they will underestimate him? Is it a test? For He is fond of giving tests.

What is clear is that whereas the God of the Biblical and Sumerian creation proclaims that all is good, the Lord God sees these creations as evil and deserving of every misfortune He can lay upon them even if they have done absolutely nothing wrong, as is the case with Cain, and more vividly, with Job.

Insofar as the Lord God is concerned, there is something bad about these humans. Something that He hates. Hence, the Lord God feels compelled not only to treat them badly but to kill them. Indeed, He finally decides to destroy not only woman and man, but every innocent living thing.

"And the Lord said, I will destroy man whom I have created from the face of the earth; both man and best, and the creeping thing, and the fowls of the air." -Genesis, 6:6,7.

ALLOGENES AND A JEALOUS LORD GOD

It appears that the Lord God hates all living things that are of the Earth. And what is the source of this hate? Jealousy, perhaps? He repeatedly tells his people that "I am a jealous god."

But jealous of what? Jealous of whom?

Perhaps jealous of that god, of the "god" that is the source of all creation? Jealous of those creatures and those humans who this original "god" created?

A careful reading of Genesis informs us that this benevolent creation "god" not only created the first woman and man, but this "god" created their first children, perhaps in much the same way that Eve was supposedly fashioned from Adam.

"And Adam lived a hundred and thirty years and begat a son in his own likeness, after his image; and called his name Seth...and Seth begat sons and daughters in his own likeness, after his image." -Genesis, 5: 3,4.

Seth, who was perhaps the first "son" of Adam, was not born of woman, but created in the "likeness" and in the "image" of Adam. Seth was, in essence, a second Adam. Moreover, the sons of Seth were also created "in his own likeness, after his image."

Although we may be tempted to ponder and then reject the possibility that these gods were creating genetic clones and even clones of clones (hence Enki's emblem of the double helix), it is noteworthy that ancient books presumed to have been written by Seth and his sons are referred to as the Allogenes (Doresse, 1986). Allogenes, however, does not refer to genetic engineering. Rather allogenes means: "stranger" and "one of another race." Seth and his children were different from the other children of Adama and Eve. They were "of another race" and fashioned in the image of Adam who through the help of god, became a "living soul." Thus, it may well be that Seth and his son are thus of the Sethian spiritual race (Robinson, 1988) containing whatever special seed or substance that god/Enki mixed together before inserting the concoction into the womb of the Mother of All.

And as to Adam and Eve and their other children, according to the Sumerian account, these children were not created by the Lord God, but by Enki. Adam and Eve, Seth, Cain and Abel were created not in the image of the Lord God, but in the image of the creator god, Enki, the Anunnaki god of the snake.

Is this why the Lord God turned Cain against Abel? Did He in fact hate them both?

The Lord God repeatedly informs us that He is "jealous." What is the Lord God jealous of? Of other gods? Of other gods and their creations? Of other gods and their children!

"Be circumspect and make no mention of the name of the other gods."
-Exodus 23:13.

WHY HAD THE LORD GOD COME TO RULE THE EARTH?

As is stated in the Sumerian account, the God of the snake, of the Morning Star, Enki, creates humans by taking tissues of the gods and mixing it with human tissue. He creates an embryo and implants it in a female goddess, the Mother of All, who gives birth to the first man.

Enki conducted several experiments, creating all types of hybrid half-human and human creatures, including better versions of woman and man. Finally, he created humans of such god-like perfection and young women who were so god-beautiful that the sons of the gods came down from heavens to have sex with the daughters of man, with these goddesses, these daughters of Venus, the serpent, Ishtar, the morning star.

"When the morning stars sang together all the sons of God shouted for joy." -Job 38:7.

And we are told in the Sumerian account that gods were not supposed to impregnate the daughters of man, that it was against some divine law, and that the women had to be sterilized.

We are told in Genesis, when the Lord God discovered that the daughters of men had children by the sons of god, that He too viewed this and the behavior of these godly children, as evil, as against some divine law.

For these crimes, for creating humans in the image of the gods, who know of good and evil, for allowing the daughters of men to become pregnant and have children of the gods, Enki, and his creations were condemned.

Enki, the god of the two entwined double-helix snakes, is tossed out of heaven, he becomes a fallen angel, for he has broken the laws of the divine pantheon.

Did this same ruling pantheon of gods send Yahweh to Earth to enforce the law? To destroy the unlawful creations? Is this why "God" went before the divine assembly to complain about what they have unleashed upon the planet, upon his people?

Yahweh was a Destroyer, and Yahweh, the Lord God, sees it as His mission to destroy not only "god's" human creations but the children of the sons of god. Was this not the point of the flood and then again, the first exodus?

THE ANUNNAKI GODS OVERTHROWN

The ancient Sumerians tell us that the ruling pantheon who controlled the Earth, the Anunnaki, were overthrown. That a new god arrived from the heavens and established himself as King. We are told that the rule of the Anunnaki was abolished, in part, because they had failed to foresee and to prevent the flood.

However, it is also said that the flood was the work of the new god, a destroyer, who orchestrated this world wide disaster so as to kill the children of the gods and to cause havoc and turmoil among the Anunnaki, so they could be easily overthrown.

Yet other accounts tell us that it was the son of Enki, the son of the Anunnaki god of the snake, Marduk who claimed the godhead and who deposed Enlil, the former king of the Earth, following the failure to prevent the flood.

Yet another version is that the pantheon of gods who ruled not the Earth, but the Universe, decreed the overthrow of the old gods and the destruction of all life, because the sons of the gods had been impregnating the daughters of woman and man. The birth of these children of the sons of god, was not a sin per se, but a violation of some cosmic law. And the penalty was death by cosmic destruction.

According to the Sumerians it was decreed that "A flood will sweep over the cult centers to destroy the seed of mankind. This is the decision, the word of the assembly of the gods" (Kramer, 1991).

According to Genesis, the punishment for breaking this law was to be enforced by the Lord God, Yahweh the Destroyer.

According to Genesis, the Lord God arrives, looks down upon the children of the gods and the humans of the Earth who act out everything they imagine. What annoys Him most, are the activities of the children of the gods—now the heroes of old, giants who were the direct descendants of those sons of gods who had sex with the daughters of woman and man. The Lord God decides to kill them all. "Every thing that breathes shall die."

GOD WARNS NOAH THAT THE LORD GOD WILL BRING A FLOOD

Yet in attempting to destroy mankind, this Lord Gods shows Himself to be inept. "God" not only warns some of the people so that they escape the destruction that the "Lord God" had planned but he saves the children of the sons of God, including those of the Sethian (Allogene) race. In consequences, the Sethians and at least a few of the children of the gods (who may be one and the same) escape the divine wrath and must be hunted down.

According to the Sumerian version of Genesis and the flood, Enki, the god of the snake, warns a man named Zisusundra of the coming catastrophe, and in so doing again violated the laws of the ruling pantheon. And why would he commit yet another crime? According to the Sumerians, it was because Enki loved them so, for they were the children of the children of his many creations, beginning with Adam and continuing with the sons of Adam which were also created in the image of Adam and the Gods. It was the Sethian children, each an image of their father who was created in the image of the gods, who Enki/god seeks to save.

"Adam... begat a son in his own likeness, after his image; and called his name Seth...And Seth lived an hundred and five years and begat Enos... who begat Cainan... who begat... who begat... who begat... who begat Lameeh...

who begat a son: And he called his name Noah" (Genesis, 5: 3,4).

Enki warned his children, his creations, of the coming flood, whereas in Genesis, it is "God" who warns Noah.

According to the Biblical account, God decided to sabotage and wreck the Lord God's plans by informing Noah of the Sethian race, of the coming floods so that at least some representatives of humanity and at least a few of the living creatures of the Earth could escape the destruction planned by the Lord God.

However, in a strange twist, although the Lord God initially takes credit for the flood, in later chapters of the Bible, the flood is blamed on the serpent, Venus, the morning star, also known as Ishtar, The Great Goddess, and goddess of war.

"And there appeared a great wonder in heaven: A woman clothed with the sun, and the moon under her feet, and upon her head a crown of twelve stars: And she being with child cried travailing in birth and pained to be delivered...

And there appeared another wonder in heaven: And behold a great red dragon having seven heads and ten horns and seven crowns upon his head. And his tail drew the third part of the stars of heaven and did cast them to the earth...

And there was a war in heaven: Michael and his angels fought against the dragon: and the dragon fought and his angels. And the great dragon was cast out, that old serpent, called the Devil and Satan which deceivith the whole world: He was cast out and his angels were cast out with him...

And the serpent cast out of his mouth water as a flood. And the earth opened her mouth and swallowed up the flood which the dragon cast out his mouth. And the dragon was wroth and went to make war." -Revelation, 12

"How art thou fallen from heaven, O' Lucifer star of the morning. Is this the one that made the earth to tremble, that did to shake kingdoms. That made the world as a wilderness, and destroyed the cities."-Isaiah, 14

By making himself the cause and later the hero, The Lord God is in this respect identical to the Babylonian God, Marduk. Marduk's primary rival was Ishtar, Venus, the Morning Star and Tiamat the great dragon. In the Babylonian version it is Tiamat and Apsu who attempt to destroy the Earth, and in this regard, these forces of evil become identical with the Lord God:

"Apsu...said unto Tiamat: Their ways are loathsome unto me. I will destroy, I will wreck their ways... and Tiamat was wroth..."

As noted, according to Sumerian accounts, the Anunnaki were forced to quickly depart the Earth for the heavens, and they left without sufficient provisions. According to the Sumerians, after the floods had subsided, the Anunnaki returned from the heavens, famished and starved, and immediately sought out

Noah/Zisusundra who was preparing a sacrificial offering over a roasting fire. Smelling "the sweet savor" of the roasting, sweet succulent meat "the gods gathered like flies over the sacrifice" for even gods grow hungry.

Likewise, according to the Biblical version, the "Lord smelled a sweet savour" and He joined Noah and his family.

And, upon partaking of the bloody, roasting sweet savouring meat, the Lord God immediately begins to boast and to lie, and promises to never again unleash his rage against woman and man and the living things upon the Earth (Genesis, chapters 8, 9).

THE TWO GODS

In the story of Abraham we are again presented with the oppositional tendencies of the two Gods. After Sara, in her old age finally has a son, Isaac, "God" but not the "Lord God" informs Abraham that he is to take "thy son, thine only son, Isaac, whom thou lovest... and offer him there for a burnt offering" (Genesis, 22: 1,2). Upon building an altar and binding Isaac and laying him upon the altar with knife in hand, "the angel of the Lord called unto him out of heaven... and said, Lay not thine hand upon the lad, neither do thou any thing unto him" (Genesis 22: 10, 11, 12).

Hence, one "god" seeks the death of a boy that is a product of something the Lord God did to Sarah by opening her womb. And, at the last moment, as Abraham is about to kill the boy, the Lord God intervenes. Is one god attempting to sabotage the plans of the other god?

And again the Lord God opposes himself by attempting to kill his prophet Moses soon after he instructed him to travel to Egypt and lead the Israelites to the promised land, the purpose of which is to destroy the Nephilim, and the children of Canaan of the Sethian race.

"At a night encampment on the way, the Lord encountered him and sought to kill him." -Exodus 4:24

And once Moses arrives in Egypt, God influences Pharaoh's mind and turns him against the Lord God's plans. Yahweh responds with escalating fury each time God manipulates Pharaoh's mind so that he does the exact opposite of what Moses requests. Every time Pharaoh begins to yield due to the plagues sent by the Lord God, he then become again stubborn when god "hardened Pharaoh's heart."

However, just as it is a characteristic of the Lord God to deny as well as take responsibility for various crimes committed against humanity, the Lord God also claims that it is He who does not want His children, His "first born son" to be released. He claims that He stiffens Pharaoh's resolve so that He can kill the first born sons of every Egyptian and demonstrate His power for all to behold. Perhaps in this case, He is telling the truth? Perhaps He truly wishes to covertly prevent Pharaoh from acting on His overt wishes. And why is that? So that He has yet another excuse to kill—as if the Lord God would need an excuse.

"When thou goest to return into Egypt, see that thou do all those wonders before Pharaoh which I have put in thine hand: But I will harden his heart, that he shall not let the people go... When the Pharaoh does not heed you, I will lay My hand upon Egypt." -Exodus 4:21; 7:3.

So, again we are presented with a god who opposes the Lord God, and a Lord God who takes credit for opposing His own plans. However, regardless of who was truly responsible for Pharaoh's behavior, The Lord God also decides to murder all the first born sons of Egypt and the first born son of Pharaoh when in fact Pharaoh had no choice in the matter and was apparently only doing as dictated by the Lord God's Divine will.

"Behold I will slay thy son." -Exodus 4:23

"And it came to pass, that at midnight, the Lord smote all the firstborn in the land of Egypt; from the firstborn of Pharaoh that sat on his throne upon the firstborn of the captive that was in the dungeon; and all the first born cattle...And there was a great cry in Egypt; for there was not a house where there was not one dead." -Exodus 12: 29,30.

CHILDREN OF THE GODS: FIRST EXODUS

THE GOD OF ABRAHAM REVISITED

As is apparent from a close reading of Genesis when the Lord God announces His presence to Abraham, and later His plans, Abraham has never before heard of this Lord God, or of Noah or of Adam and Eve. Moreover, although Abraham follows the dictates of this Lord God, he also disobeys Him, for example, by offering his wife, Sarah (Sarai) to Pharaoh. The Lord God is forced to intervene because Sarah is the vessel through which the Lord God promises Abraham the godly children who will some day take possession of Cannan, the "promised land."

Abraham also does not appear to have much faith in this Lord God, for upon leading a successful war party to rescue his nephew Lot who has been taken captive by four kings he not only fails to evoke the name of the Lord God, but accepts the blessings of the god of Melchizedek, the "god most high" who is also described as the "creator of heaven and Earth (Genesis 13).

Nevertheless, once the battle has been won and Abraham has freed his nephew, the Lord God suddenly speaks up and attempts to take credit for the victory:

"Fear not, Abram, I am a shield to you; Your reward shall be great." (Genesis 15).

Abraham is not impressed. The Lord God has made many empty boasts, including the claim that Abraham would be the father of a great nation. His promises to Abraham and Sara begin to appear as cruel and sadistic lies. Or is He just toying with them? Or does He have some purpose or divine plan that is apparent only to Him?

GODLY CHILDREN

Despite His repeated promises, Sara and Abraham fail to have children. Not because she is barren, for she announces: "The Lord has kept me from bearing" (Genesis, 16:2). Sara is convinced that the Lord God is actually attempting to prevent her from becoming pregnant with Abraham's child.

Disgusted with these false promises and the cruel ways of this Lord God, Sara defies this deity, and tells Abraham to have sex with her servant girl, Hagar who then conceives.

The Lord God, as is His nature, then attempts to take credit for Hagar's pregnancy, telling her, after she becomes pregnant that she will become pregnant and that her offspring will also be a multitude.

Thirteen years pass and the Lord God, looking exactly like any other man, appears again outside Abraham's tent and repeats His promise that Sarah will become pregnant.

"I will bless her and give thee a son also of her: yea, I will bless her, and she shall be a mother of nations; kings of people shall be of her."

Abraham, laughs in the Lord God's face, saying: "Can a child be born to a man a hundred years old, or can Sarah bear a child at ninety?" (Genesis, 17:17).

The Lord God declares that this is true, but now demands that Abraham cut off the end of his penis, and orders that all the males of the household do likewise. Moreover, every male born of Abraham's line, he is told, must also cut off their foreskin.

Yet another dozen years pass, and still Sarah fails to conceive.

"And the Lord appeared unto him in the plains of Mamre... And Abraham lift up his eyes and looked, and lo, three men stood by him... And they said unto him, Where is Sarah thy wife?"

Abraham tells the three men that she is inside the tent. They then proceed to talk and go inside to eat.

Following a sumptuous meal, one of these men then informs Abraham:

"I will return unto thee, according to the time of life; and lo, Sarah thy wife shall have a son."

Sara, who was listening, laughed, which enraged the man who now claimed he was the Lord God: "Is there anything too hard for the Lord? At the time appointed I will return unto thee, according to the time of life, and Sarah shall conceive a son" (Genesis, 18).

What is important to note, about the above promises, which neither Abraham nor Sarah believe, is that the Lord God claims that when He returns she will become pregnant. That is, what He is saying is that He, the Lord God will make her pregnant. Indeed, we are told: "And the Lord visited Sarah as he had said, and the Lord did unto Sarah as he had spoken. Sarah conceived and bare Abraham a son in his old age" (Genesis, 21:1,2).

What is it the Lord did unto Sarah? Is the boy a child of the Lord God, or is Abraham the sire?

"And what does the Lord desire? Godly offspring." -RSV; 2:13-16.

Does not the Lord God tell Abraham that it is He who will give him a son through her? He will give him a son after He returns and does something to her?

"I will bless her and give thee a son also of her." -Genesis, 17:16

"And the Lord visited Sarah as he had said, and the Lord did unto Sarah as he had spoken. Sarah conceived." -Genesis, 21:1,2.

A careful reading of the Bible suggests that Abraham is not the father of Isaac, though he is the father of Ishmael, the son of Hagar the slave woman, for the Lord God tells Abraham that "the son of the slave woman... is your seed" but that it is "through Isaac that offspring will be continued for you" (Genesis, 21: 12,13).

But will these offspring be of Abraham or of the Lord God?

"I am He who formed thee in the mother's womb." -Isaiah 44:2.

"Do not forget the God that gave you birth." -Deuteronomy 32:18.

"And what does the Lord desire? Godly offspring." -RSV 2:13-16.

CLONING: COUSINS MARRYING COUSINS OF THE SAME SEED

Sarah, the daughter of Abraham's brother. This is important, for Isaac is also ordered to marry someone of his own blood, his cousin, a daughter of the house of his mother's father. Absolutely, under no circumstance is Isaac to take a wife from "among the daughters of the Canaanites." Not only is he to take a wife from Abraham's father's house, but an angel of the Lord God will chose her (Genesis, 24:7). He chooses Rebekah, who like her aunt, fails to become pregnant after sex with her husband.

And, just as the Lord God did something to Sara to make her pregnant, the Lord God also does something to Rebekah, the wife of Isaac, who has repeatedly failed to become pregnant. And, apparently He explained this to Rebekah, though whatever He told her has been edited out or was never included in the Genesis account.

Much to her surprise, she becomes pregnant not with one child, as the Lord may have promised, but she is going to have twins. She asks the Lord God for an explanation.

There are several explanations. For one, Isaac, like his father, possibly allowed other men to have sex with her, for when residing in the land of Gerar, Isaac told the men who inquired about her beauty, that "She is my sister" (Genesis 26:8). The men of the city apparently had sex with Rebekah.

When "some time had passed" and King Abimelech observed Isaac fondling Rebekah, we are told that he exclaimed: "What have you done to us?" and then the king warns his own people not to have sex with her.

Hence, it is possible that she carried twin babies who had different fathers, or which were conceived in different ways.

The Lord God is apparently not overly concerned about this turn of events, for he tells Rebekah: "Two separate peoples shall issue from your body; One people shall be mightier than the other. And the older shall serve the younger" (Genesis, 25:23).

She has twins, one of whom is red and hairy, Esau. Esau becomes an outdoorsman, a skillful hunter who hunts his food in the field. The other is Jacob who is his mother's favorite and who remains close to camp.

Although Isaac loved Esau, Rebekah, acting according to the instructions of the Lord God, conspires with her younger son to obtain the older boy's, Esau's birthright, by fraud and trickery.

THE OPENING OF THE WOMBS

Jacob had come into this world, holding onto the foot of his brother as they emerged from the womb; already reaching for his future and his brother's blessing, and repeatedly demonstrating that he is the bolder, the stronger, and the more treacherous of the two. When as a young man he came upon his older brother ill, faint, and near death, Jacob refused his brother's cries for assistance, demanding, instead that Esau first give him his birthright. Esau complies.

"And Esau said, Behold I am at the point to die. And Jacob said, Swear to me this day...and he sold his birthright unto Jacob." -Genesis 25: 30-32.

Jacob then conspires with his mother to trick his father, Isaac, into giving Jacob the "blessing" that rightly belongs to Esau. The "blessing" is his birthright, Esau being the first born son. Isaac being old and blind, is easily fooled by Jacob who says to Isaac. "I am Esau, thy firstborn."

Tricked and betrayed, Isaac gives his blessing to Jacob, the blessing that was rightfully due to and now twice stolen from Esau.

Once Isaac discovered the trickery, he accepted it, for it could not be withdrawn. Isaac then "charged Jacob, saying, Thou shalt not take a wife of the daughter of Canaan. Arise, go to the house of thy mother's father and take a wife from thence of the daughters of Laban, thy mother's brother... and give thee the blessing of Abraham, to thee and to thy seed with thee; that thou mayest inherit the land wherein thou art a stranger, which God gave unto Abraham" (Genesis, 28).

Jacob marries not one but two of his cousins. And, just as the Lord God did unknown things to open the wombs of Sarah and Rebekah, He did again the same with the two wives of Jacob, Rachel and Leah. "The Lord God saw Leah... and opened her womb." The Lord God remembered Rachel... and opened her womb" (Genesis, 30).

"And what does the Lord desire? Godly offspring." -RSV 2:13-16.

Godly offspring were the also the consequence of the sons of god having sex with the daughters of man; a common god-like behavior, for gods, since the inception of male gods, have been impregnating the daughters of men. And they continued to do so well after the Lord God claimed to be the only god.

Indeed, we are told "God," that is the "high" god, but not the Lord God, opened the virgin womb of Mary, the mother of Jesus Christ. The virgin Mary, became pregnant directly by the actions of a Holy Ghost who did something to her womb (e.g. St. Luke 1: 26-35). And the angel Gabriel "came in unto her... and said unto her, And behold thou shall conceive in thy womb, and bring forth a son..." Mary asked the angel, "How shall this be, seeing I know not a man? And the angel answered and said unto her, The Holy Ghost shall come upon thee, and the power of the Highest shall overshadow thee..."

What are we to make of these stories, where a man, who looks like a man, claims to be the Lord God, or the "high" god, and has the power to make barren and even virgin women pregnant? Where He visits them and opens their wombs? Is he implanting embryos? Clones? Performing genetic experiments?

Moreover, why is it that this Lord God requires that Abraham, Isaac and Jacob, marry their cousins, and possibly their sisters who inevitably turn out to be barren? Women who complain that it is the Lord God who prevents them from becoming pregnant until He decides to open their wombs?

One might assume that He requires that they be barren and of the same kin and "seed" so that they will only give birth to the children that He chooses and creates for His grand purpose.

And what is His purpose: To raise an army that will kill the people of Cannan, the Anakites, the Nephilim, the children of the gods, of the Sethian race; to kill them, to utterly destroy them and take their land.

"Ye are gods; and all of you are children of the most high. But, ye shall die like men and fall like one of the princes." -Psalms 82:1-6.

GODLY OFFSPRING

It is noteworthy that Abraham had another child that was of his seed, and so too did Isaac. But these children did not meet the Lord God's requirements. The wombs of their mothers were not opened by the Lord God. And these children quickly depart the divine drama. The Lord God ceases to be interested in their activities.

"And what does the Lord desire? Godly offspring." -RSV; 2:13-16.

And as to those children born of those wombs He did open, it is not clear if they all met the Lord God's requirements. Jacob, as we have seen, was shrewd, ruthless, cunning, and a supremely self-confident and bold heartless thief who was more than willing to allow his brother to suffer and die in order to steal his birthright and his blessing. And Jacob was quite willing to deceive and make a fool of his father, by tricking him into giving up Esau's blessing. Jacob, therefore, refused to accept his lot in life but instead boldly, ruthlessly, and shrewdly carved out his own future and his own destiny.

By contrast, when Abraham brought Isaac to the mountain to be sacrificed, Isaac did what he was told, helped gather the wood, laid down upon it, and meekly and passively accepted his fate without a struggle.

Whereas Isaac meekly accepts his fate, Jacob tricks his own father and spells out and dictates to the Lord God under what conditions he will accept the Lord as his God (Genesis 28:20-22). Jacob is not only a bold liar and thief who twice cheated his brother out of his birthright, but when he is attacked by a "divine being" he prevails. And who is the "divine being?" Jacob tell us that it is "god." Not the Lord God, but "god" who attacked him and who tried to kill him.

And why would "god" try to kill him? Perhaps for the same reason he prevails. Jacob has shown himself to be worthy of the name "Israel."

It is not the meek and easily fooled Isaac or his likewise weakwilled son Esau, who is named Israel, but Jacob the bold liar and cunning thief; Jacob who bravely struggles with divine beings and who even bargains with the Lord God. It is not Abraham, it is not Isaac, it is not Esau, but Jacob who the Lord God declares as his "first born son" the first of his "godly offspring."

ISRAEL, MY FIRST BORN SON

The Lord God is so pleased by Jacob's courage, strength, shrewdness, and intelligence, that he tells Jacob, "Your name shall no longer be Jacob, but Israel, for you have striven with God and men and have prevailed."

It is Israel who the Lord God proclaims to be his "first born son" (Exodus 4:21). Israel, in fact means "May god show his strength."

And, now that the Lord God has finally produced his "first born son" he prepares to show his strength and encourages unchecked fertility so as to fill the land with His children. Jacob has twelve boys, and the twelve have their seventy who in turn give birth to a nation of people who were so "fertile and prolific that they multiplied so that the land was filled with them" (Exodus 1:7).

But now in order to accomplish the next step in His divine plan, the killing of the children of the gods and of the Sethian race, Yahweh must release his own children from Pharaoh's grip. He begins by sending Moses and the plagues to humble mighty Egypt, and then He claims that He stiffens Pharaoh's resolve.

Finally, as a last warning the Lord God tells Pharaoh: "Israel is My first born son. I have said to you, Let my son go, that he may worship Me. Yet you refuse to let him go. Now I will slay your first born son."

The Lord God kills all the first born of Egypt. Pharaoh, humbled and defeated, consents.

The Lord God now has an army, an army directly descended from his "first born son." And He repeatedly reminds them:

"Do not forget the God that gave you birth." -Deuteronomy 32:18.

It is the children of this army which the Lord God will lead to Cannan so as to destroy the children and the descendants of God.

THE FIRST EXODUS RECONSIDERED

Perhaps 500 years after Joseph, the 11th son of Israel, who had found favor with the Pharaoh, had died, the Israelites (also known as the Hebrews), had grown from a tribe of 12, to a multitude of 600,000 or more.

Although the history is not clear, the Hebrews, that is, the Hyksos (the "Shepherd Kings'), may even have briefly ruled Egypt, having overthrown the native kings.

Consider: after Joseph had found favor with Pharaoh, he informs his brothers and kin that "the good of all the land of Egypt is yours" (Genesis, 15: 20). And, once Joseph was appointed governor, he not only appointed his brothers and kin to positions of power and gave them the best of the land, but he began depleting the Egyptians of all their money, all their cattle, and all their land. And when famine came, although "there was no bread in all the land of Egypt" he "nourished his father, and his brethren, and all his father's household with bread" (Genesis, 47).

Thus, the Hyksos, may well have been the Hebrews, and the Hebrews may well have gained control over Egypt which they ruthlessly ruled and exploited for several centuries.

In any case, the Hyksos, never popular, were finally driven from power, and were finally cast out of Egypt. However, it is not known with certainty if the Hyksos were the Hebrews.

Nevertheless, that the Jews were resented, is, however, quite clear. Indeed, the Hebrews were viewed by the Egyptians and her Kings as a threat to public order, like a disease, like vermin, like a cancerous growth, particularly as their numbers and their influences in government and finance grew.

"Behold, the people of the children of Israel are too many and too mighty for us," Pharaoh complained to his ministers and counselors. "Come, let us deal wisely with them" (Exodus 1:9-10).

Presumably, the Pharaoh dealt "wisely" by first turning them out and denying them the right to practice their professions—for Joseph and his extended family, had obtained positions of power in the kingdom. The Israelites were stripped of their jobs and of their power.

Next, came laws to control breeding, as the Israelites were "too many." Pharaoh ordered that Jewish babies be killed, as the Jews were breeding like animals: "The Hebrew women are not as the Egyptian women, for they are chayot" (Exodus, 1:19)—chayot meaning: "like animals."

And because they were perceived as an alien threat, and as subhumans, "like animals," the Pharaoh decided to enslave them and work them to death. And he ordered that they be put to work at the hardest labor and that they be whipped and starved and treated with complete "ruthlessness...They made their lives bitter with heavy work at mortar and brick, and with all kinds of labor in the field" (Exodus 1:14).

"And so they died, one after another, as if smitten by a pestilential destruction... And then their taskmasters threw their bodies, unburied, beyond the borders of the land, not allowing their kinsmen to even weep over those who had thus miserably perished." -Philo of Alexandria.

DRIVEN FROM EGYPT BY THE LORD GOD

Moses was finally appointed by the "Lord God" to lead his people, "his first born son" out of Egypt. And yet, the Lord God repeatedly "hardens the heart of Pharaoh who punishes the Israelites severely.

"Lord," Moses implores, "why hast though dealt ill with this people. For since I came to Pharaoh to speak in Thy name, he hath dealt ill with this people."

But the "Lord God" has his own goals to consider, and the suffering of this people matter to him not at all, for He replies: "I will harden the Pharaoh's heart, and multiply My signs and My wonders in the land of Egypt" which of course, results in only more suffering, death and privation for the Jewish people.

As a perusal of the Books of Moses emphatically illustrates, the Israelites were unwillingly brought forth from the land of Egypt by Moses. And these peoples complained bitterly and suffered miserably when they were forced by Moses to march through the deserts. Death and suffering was everywhere—tens then hundreds of thousands, if not 600,000 murdered by no less than the "Lord God."

No sooner had they left the lands of Egypt, than "God" sends a plague that kills 24,000 of His people (Numbers, 25:5). He murders his people repeatedly for almost any reason, including murmurring. If the Bible is to be believed, the exodus resulted in the death of every single adult Jew who was brought forth from the land of Egypt—600,000 murdered by a wrathful Lord God. Six hundred thousand that He killed outright or allowed to die of old age, in the deserts of the Sinai, including even Moses who the Lord God kills by His own hand.

THE PROPHECY OF THE SECOND EXODUS

With the establishment of Israel the "Lord God" of the ancient Jewish people repeatedly threatens them with the most horrible of misfortunes and foretells, through his prophets, that they will be scattered and dispersed throughout the lands—and this is exactly what transpires, repeatedly, beginning in the 6th century B.C., when the southern kingdom of Judah was destroyed and the people marched off into exile in Babylon. It is Babylon and before that, Sumer where much of the story of creation may well have been first composed, only to be later incorporated and retold in Genesis.

And then again, almost 2,000 years ago, following their return from exile and return to the promise lands, the Lord God again warns the ancient Jews of their destruction.

"The Lord will bring a nation against you from afar, from the end of the earth, which will swoop down like the eagle... a ruthless nation, that will show the old no regard and the young no mercy." -Deuterotomy 28:47-50.

And this is exactly what transpired when Roman legions, marching under the banner of the swastika and the Eagle, swooped down and destroyed the second temple. Again the Jews are driven from Israel, and dispersed throughout the lands.

But then the Lord God also tells the Jewish people that someday He will return them to the promised land. And this prophecy too was fulfilled, by no less than Adolf Hitler; a man who likened his nation to the "Holy Roman Empire" and who modeled his government after the Roman Catholic Church (which he also sought to destroy). And, Hitler's armies marched under the banner of the Eagle and the swastika, the twisted cross, the "gammadion"—which is also one of the many names of god, including the Lord God of the old testament: "Tetragrammaton" ("absolute existence").

Hitler went forth according to instructions he claimed to have received from Divine Providence. He was to go forth and cleanse the land of Jews. He was to begin the second exodus.

HITLER AND DIVINE PROVIDENCE: SECOND EXODUS

"Behold, the people of the children of Israel are too many and too mighty for us. Come, let us deal wisely with them." -Exodus 1:9-10.

Figure 92. *Adolf Hitler.*

As Hitler struggled to become dictator of Germany, and as he clearly states in his book, Mein Kampf, the Jews, he preached had not only obtained positions of power disproportionate to their numbers, but they were stealing German wealth, were engaged in sex slavery, and they threatened to overwhelm society with evil and moral decay. They were like a disease, like vermin, like a cancer, and were less than human; they were like animals, subhuman. Hitler counseled that the German nation should deal wisely with them.

When Adolf Hitler finally came to power, not only did the majority of the German peoples willfully and fearfully followed his dictates, but many even compared him to John the Baptist, Jesus Christ and even God. "Is he John the Baptist? Is he Jesus?" Goebbels wrote in his diary. Many honestly believed they were in the presence of a German Messiah! And many shared his lowly opinion of the Jewish people, who Hitler promised to sweep from Germany and send back to their promised land.

Hitler claimed he was acting in accordance with the will of Divine Providence. He believed he had been appointed by God.

Hitler was to be the "Lord God's" angry fist which would savagely strike a scattered people, the Jews, and drive them back to Israel, the Promised Land.

The second exodus would mirror the first.

"He exalts nations, then destroys them; He expands nations, then leads them away. He deranges the leaders of the people, and makes them wander in a trackless waste." Job, 12:20-24

Once Hitler came to power, and as he led his nation out of the great depression to greatness, he and his government issued orders controlling Jewish breeding and sexuality; and then the Jews were barred from practicing their professions; and then the Jews were officially described as subhuman, then they were ordered to immigrate.

And just as the ancient Jews stripped the Egyptians of their worldly goods before setting off for the promised land, the German Jews who sought to immigrate were stripped of their worldly possessions. Those who remained or failed to heed the six years of repeated warnings to leave Germany were finally herded into concentration camps where they were enslaved, starved and worked to death.

"And so they died, one after another, as if smitten by a pestilential destruction... And then their taskmasters threw their bodies, unburied, beyond the borders of the land, not allowing their kinsmen to even weep over those who had thus miserably perished." -Philo of Alexandria.

HITLER THE JEW?

During his tumultuous rise to the pinnacles of power Adolf Hitler was often accused of being Jewish. Even the leaders of the National Party which he sought to lead, ridiculed Hitler as a "Jew" and for "behaving like a Jew" as did many of his enemies.

Before coming to power, Adolf Hitler was also a target of widespread ridicule, and was mocked by enemies and the press who questioned his ancestry and who laughably referred to him as "Adolf Schickelgruber." "Schickelgruber" had been the name of Adolf's maternal grandmother, and for 39 years, the name of his father, Alois.

Although the "Schickelgruber" moniker rankled the rising dictator, what concerned him and what he feared most was the history behind the name: the discovery that he was part "Jew;" a fear he repeatedly voiced long after coming to power.

"People must not know who I am," he ranted, and then ranted again when informed that his family history was being investigated. "They must not know where I came from."

Long before and well after Hitler became Chancellor of Germany, considerable effort was expended to falsify, erase or destroy the records from his past. His half-brother, Alois Jr., was placed in a concentratin camp where he died, and investigations were conducted by the Gestapo who repeatedly visited his ancestral village in Austria, questioning and threatening anyone that had been associated with the Hitler family.

Hitler was so concerned that when he annexed Austria, in 1938, he ordered that his family's ancestral village, Dollersheim, and all neighboring villages be destroyed. His armies marched in and then cleared out and forcibly evacuated the villagers who were dispersed far and wide. And then Hitler in fact, made it disappear, erased it from the face of the Earth. His armies bombed Dollersheim and all neighboring villages into oblivion as part of a training exercise. Even his father's and grandmother's graves were obliterated and no trace remains (Rosenbaum, 1999).

Nevertheless, what has survived the ravages of time, purposeful destruction and clever forgery, is the fact that Adolf's father, Alois Schickelgruber was the illegitimate son of a female servant, Maria Anna Schickelgruber. Maria Anna became pregnant while living as a servant in a Jewish household —a common servant girl fate. It was assumed by family members and villagers alike that she'd been impregnated by the head of the house, Baron Rothschild (Langer, 1973; Payne, 1973); a rumor that the Austrian Secret police claimed to have confirmed when ordered by Austrian Chancellor Dollfuss to conduct a thorough investigation. Later, when Hitler orchestrated the anschluss of Austria and German troops marched in, he had Dollfuss murdered, and in addition to destroying Dollersheim, ordered that all documents related to that investigation be destroyed.

Yet others claimed that the man who had impregnated Adolf's grandmother was the Jewish scion of the seigneurial house of Ottenstein.

Hitler's own nephew, William Patrick Hitler, and Adolf's personnel attorney, Hans Frank, claimed that his grandfather was a wealthy "Granz Jew" by the name of Frankenberger who in turn "paid a maintenance allowance from the time of the child's birth until his fourteenth year."

As Frank reported to Hitler, and as he recounted at his Nuremberg war crimes trial, based on what he learned "the possibility cannot be dismissed that Hitler's father was half Jewish as a result of an extramarital relationship between the Schickelgruber woman and the Jew from Graz. This would mean that Hitler was one-quarter Jewish."

When Adolf Hitler was presented with the results of Frank's investigation, although denying he was Jewish, Hitler did admit to Frank that a Jewis man paid his grandmother money, because the "Jew" was tricked into believing he was the father of Alois (Rosenbaum, 1999). Of course this means, if Adolf (or rather Frank) is to be believed, that his grandmother was having sex with a Jewish man before she became pregnant.

What these stories all have in common, of course, is that Hitler's grandfather was a rich Jewish man, and that after becoming pregnant his grandmother was banished from the Rothschild or Frankenberger or the Ottenstein home and sent back to her village to have her baby, Alois. It also appears that funds and even "hush money" were secretly provided for her and the baby

When required to fill out the baptismal certificate for her son, she left the line as to the father of her boy, completely blank. Why did she leave it blank? Two reasons. Having been impregnated by a Jewish man was nothing to be proud of given the anti-Semitic attitudes of the peasant farmers and villagers of Lower Austria. Secondly, it is said that she was paid to keep the paternity secret.

Yet another factor suggesting that Alois was Jewish was the fact that he was nothing like the peasants of his mother's village where people intermarried and produced generation and after generation of peasant farmers. Alois in fact left the village and sought his fortune. Alois was supremely self-confident, politically astute, and ambitious, and with the help of influential aristocrats in Vienna, Alois became a government official.

SCHICKELGRUBER BECOMES HITLER: Abram Becomes Abraham. Jacob Becomes Israel

As to the name "Hitler," although Alois Schickelgruber was proud of his heritage, he found it to his financial advantage to change his name at age 39. Exceedingly shrewd and ambitious, Alois was presented with an opportunity to become instantly a man of considerable property; and the name of that opportunity was Johann Hiedler who had lived in nearby town of Weitra. Johann Hiedler died at age 84 without wife or children—a condition that normally would result in his estate being confiscated by the Austrian government.

Alois instantly seized this opportunity and made arrangements with the local parish priest to alter the parish birth records (Shirer, 1941, 1960). The priest scratched out the name "Shicklegruber" and penciled in "Hiedler."

Alois wasn't especially fond of the "Hiedler" moniker, and altered the spelling to make it sound more pleasing. Alois "Hiedler," became Alois Hitler, and Alois Hitler, unlike any of his mother's peasant farmer relatives, became an official in the Austrian government (Payne, 1973; Shirer, 1941, 1960).

***Figure 93**. (Above) Alois Schickelgruber. (Below) Alois Heidler/Hitler.*

ALOIS: A BASTARD JEW?

According to German historian, Helmut Heilber: "The aberrational quality of the Hitler family beginning with the ambitious and enterprising father of Adolf shows that other blood must have entered the Lower Austrian Waldviertel stock which had been weakened by years of inbreeding."

Likewise, according to Walter Langer (1972) who was employed by the Office of Strategic Services to conduct a study of Hitler just before the war: "The intelligence and behavior of Alois, as well as that of his two sons (Alois Jr., and Adolf), is completely out of keeping with that usually found in Austrian peasant families. Their ambitiousness and extraordinary political intuition are much more in harmony with the Rothschild tradition."

Alois was not only ambitious and successful, but proud of his paternity—having a father who was wealthy and an aristocrat. Alois, in fact, chose a Jewish man to act as Adolf Hitler's godfather (Langer, 1972), and a Jewish doctor helped to deliver Hitler into this world.

Thus, the evidence strongly suggests that Alois was half Jewish and that Adolf Hitler was one quarter Jewish—a possibility vehemently rejected by Nazis and Jews alike.

HITLER AND THE VOICE OF DIVINE PROVIDENCE

As a young man, Adolf did not feel it necessary to hide his origins. He admitted to having a Jewish father and bragged of having rich Jewish relatives (Hanisch, 1936, 1939). As a young man, Adolf even dressed like a "Jew," and formed close "friendships" with Jewish men—one of whom he lived with briefly (Heidan, 1936; Payne, 1973). Moreover, in addition to associating with, dressing like, living with, and obtaining money from Jews, in February of 1919 Adolf Hitler participated in a parade, as a designated mourner, for a very close friend, a Jewish socialist who had been murdered in Munich (Rosenbaum, 1999).

And like Jewish prophets and Moses before him, Adolf also appears to have been chosen by Divine Providence and the Lord God.

> "I will chose the wicked for an evil day…
> … I will speak in visions and dreams."

Well before Adolf Hitler began his rise to power, and before he found it convenient to hide his Jewish heritage, he began to hear the voice of God—of "Divine Providence." For example, he relates the following experience during the first World War. "I was eating dinner in a trench with several comrades. Suddenly a voice seemed to be saying to me, "Get up and go over there." It was so clear and insistent that I obeyed automatically. I rose to my feet and walked twenty yards. Then I sat down to go on eating. Hardly had I done so when a flash and deafening report came from the part of the trench I had just left. Every member in it was killed" (Price, 1937).

Remarkably, although he served as a runner (messenger) during the first World War, and although the average war time life span of a runner was just a few weeks, Adolf Hitler nevertheless survived in this position for several years with only minor injuries—a good fortune that he also attributed to Divine Providence.

As Fuehrer of Germany, he repeatedly spoke of hearing "Divine" voices, and claimed that he was following "the commands that Providence has laid upon me… Divine power has willed it... Not even if the whole party tried to drive me to action, I will not act. But if the voice speaks, then I know the time has come to act."

And, like Moses before him, and declaring to be guided by "Divine providence," Hitler turned his eyes to the East, and modeling his "government" after that of the Holy Roman Empire and Catholic Church, and marching behind the banner of the eagle and the twisted cross, the swastika, he ordered the Jews to immigrate, and engaged in wide scale ethnic cleansing and mass murder ostensibly so as to obtain living space—exactly as did Moses.

But, perhaps even more importantly, Hitler initially had no interested in killing off or exterminating the Jewish population, and in fact, those who were first forced into the concentration camps were political enemies. Instead, Hitler did all in his power to force the Jews, the subhumans, to immigrate, even relying on forced expulsion. It was only in 1941, 8 years after he came to power, that he began to systematically exterminate the Jewish people.

In 1941, and after suffering his first defeats, the murder and the cleansing of the lands of Jews became more important to Hitler than winning the war. He began diverting from his floundering war effort, the needed funds, troops, and trains which he ordered were to be used strictly for the purpose of terrorizing, killing, and rounding up for mass murder those Jews who had failed to heed his 8 years of warnings to immigrate. In this respect, it could be surmised that the entire purpose for the war was to drive out the Jewish people.

SECOND EXODUS

"The Lord will bring a nation against you from afar, from the end of the earth, which will swoop down like the eagle... a ruthless nation, that will show the old no regard and the young no mercy." -Deuteronomy 28:47-50.

The "final solution," only became the final solution in 1941, when the remaining Jews, failed or were unable to heed his threats and demands to immigrate, and/or failed to escape his war machine as it blitzed onwards. It was only when confronted with millions of Jews that could not be relocated to Israel and

Madagascar that systematic mass killings began.

Again, however, initially he ordered that the Jewish people immigrate. Hundreds of thousands did heed the call and attempted to escape and to immigrate. However, many did not wish to go to Israel, and some returned to Germany or sought haven in other countries.

However, just as "God" had hardened the heart of Pharaoh, world leaders also experienced a hardening of the heart, and denied the persecuted Jewish people entry into their countries. The Jewish people, driven from Germany and all "strange" lands, had only one place to go: Israel.

As noted, the 600,000 ancestors of the 6 million Jews murdered by Adolf Hitler in his quest for "living space" and racial purity, also engaged in wide scale ethnic cleansing, some 3,000 years ago. Led by Moses, his brother Aron, and divine providence, in their 40 year search for living space, "the promised land," the Jewish people indiscriminately killed and slaughtered men, women, and children whose only crime was having lived for centuries on land the Jews wished to claim for their own.

And just as the Lord God would kill every single Jew, the 600,000 who He brought forth from the land of Egypt in his successful quest to establish Israel, Hitler would kill six million. And, just as Moses was aided by a Jew, Aron, in the killing of fellow Jews and innocents alike, Adolf Hitler was aided by a fellow Jew, Reinhard Heydrich who organized the "Office for Jewish Emigration" which later became the office of extermination. It has been said Heydrich was so tormented by his Jewish ancestry and the "Jew within" that he sought to cleanse himself by orchestrating the extermination of all European Jews (Rosenbaum, 1999).

However, instead of killing 600,000 of the "chosen" who the Lord God killed or allowed to die of old age in the desert, Hitler would kill six million. And just as "God" ordered the murder and pillage of millions of non-Jews to fulfill his goals, Hitler did likewise.

"I believe that it was God's will to send a youth into the Reich, to let him grow up, to raise him to be the leader of a nation so as to enable him to lead his people back to the homeland." -Adolf Hitler

And who were "his people?" Hitler was not even born in Germany.

What was the ultimate outcome of World War II? The reestablishment of of Israel—exactly as God's prophets prophesied. Again, Hitler was more concerned with cleansing the lands of Jews than wining the war. Hitler believe he was acting according to the will of the Lord God. Divine Providence.

"There is a higher ordering, and we are all nothing else than its agents." -Adolf Hitler.

-16-

"GOD" AND EVOLUTION IN THE ANCIENT CORNERS OF THE COSMOS

... and the spiraling universe swirled back and coiled 'round on planets' knees and shooting stars to ponder its own depths in the temple of human consciousness...

... .in the mirror of the sea of human consciousness...

... to peer and reflect upon its own soul...

... as mirrored in the rising tides of human consciousness...

"And when you look up to the sky and behold the sun and the moon and the stars, the whole heavenly host, you must not be lured into bowing down to them or serving them. These the Lord your God allotted to other peoples."

-Deuteronomy 4.19

The ancient peoples of the Earth, at least as exemplified by the ancient Egyptians and Sumerians, believed that the Earth was originally ruled by gods who came down from the heavens, from planets just like Earth. "Anunnaki" means: "Those who came from Heaven to Earth."

The Sumerians did not believe that the "Anunnaki" were "spiritual" beings or all that divine. They believed the Anunnaki to be an exploitive, technologically sophisticated human-like peoples who were born, just like humans, who had wives and children, and who hailed from another planet, Nibiruo.

The Sumerians in fact depicted the Anunnaki as not only looking much like humans, but as steering or riding in flying ships, flying saucers, and flying discs.

***Figure 94.** Babylonian/Assyrian and Persian gods in their flying discs*

Figure 95. *The Anunnaki: "From heaven to Earth they came." According to the Sumerians, they came in space craft from another planet.*

It was in fact, because they did not believe the Anunnaki to be true god-like spiritual beings, that the Sumerians worshipped personal gods who did not belong to this alien assemblage. It was a personal god, the "God of Abram," that Abraham the patriarch of all modern day Jewish people, carried with him when he left Ur of the Chaldees.

The Sumerians were able to distinguish between myth, fable, and fact, for these were a cultured, sophisticated peoples. They always began their fables with the following caveat: Once upon a time. This was not the case regarding the Anunnaki.

Specifically according to Sumerian mythology, the Anunnaki were born when the seeds of life which swarm throughout the cosmos, fell upon their planet. "An begot the Anunnaki" (Kramer, 1991), "An" being the primeval seas of space, a mixture of cloud and water that existed initially as chaos long before the creation of this universe. And it is "An" the eternal seas of extra-stellar and inter-stellar space from which flowed the seeds of life which rained down upon the Earth; seeds of life that also rained down upon the planet of the Anunnaki —so say the ancients.

THE GENETIC SEEDS OF LIFE

According to ancient Sumerian and Egyptian cosmology, the first living things to appear on Earth did not crawl out of an organic soup—at least on Earth- but they fell to Earth as seeds of life, containing within them the kernel of the creation of all life—what today we would call DNA.

"In the beginning... the earth was void and without form, and darkness was upon the face of the deep. And the Spirit of God moved upon the face of the waters." -Genesis, 1:1,2.

Figure 96. *God and the creation.(Europe: A prophecy, W. Blake)*

"Thy Sustainer—created man out of a germ cell...in the waters which God sent down from the sky, giving life to the Earth..." -Koran

The Sumerians believed that the seeds of life swarm throughout the cosmos, and they associated this life force with "An" the ultimate creator god. Therefore, with the exception of "An" those actually claiming to be gods, including the king of the gods and the Lord God, were formed from the same seeds that rained down upon the Earth.

However, the Sumerians also believed that the Anunnaki, who from the "heavens to the Earth came" took dominion over the Earth and became its rulers—a view also echoed by the ancient Hebrews: "Blessed art thou, O Lord, our God, King of the Universe" (Samuel, 7; Isaiah 6).

ASTROBIOLOGICAL ORIGINS OF LIFE ON EARTH

It is now well established that the proverbial "organic soup" was missing all essential life-creating ingredients, including free phosphorus, oxygen, and the amino acids that are the building blocks of DNA (Joseph, 2000a,c). Only DNA can create DNA, and life is produced only from other living things. Every single attempt to create life from non-life, has failed, no matter how sophisticated the experiment. Every single experiment which has attempted to create DNA, has failed. Only DNA can produce DNA and only life can produce life.

This means that the first forms of life to emerge on this planet, around 3.8 billion years ago, acquired their DNA from other living creatures who were not of this Earth. That is, the first creatures to emerge on Earth were astrobiological in origin (Joseph, 1997, 2000a,c). They hailed from another planet, were thrown into the abyss following a cosmic calamity, and landed on Earth encased in all manner of titanic debris and oceans of ice that rained down upon the planet for the first 700 million years after it was formed.

The first life forms to emerge on Earth were incredibly complex, they appeared 3.8 billion years ago following the cessation of a 700 million year cosmic bombardment, and there is no evidence of any precursor, pre-life forms (Joseph, 1997, 2000a,c). Hence, the first life to emerge on Earth, must have been contained in that debris, and they must have heralded from another planet.

"Thy Sustainer—created man out of a germ cell...in the waters which God sent down from the sky, giving life to the Earth..." -Koran

Consider, if life were to suddenly appear on a desert island, we would assume that it fell from the sky, or washed to shore. The Earth too, is an island swirling in an ocean of space, and living matter, and all manner of complex organisms, may have been washing ashore since the creation.

ORGANIC SOUPS ON OTHER PLANETS

One need not reject the "organic soup" scenario in order to arrive at the conclusion that life on Earth first arose on other planets. Rather, it may well be that the Universe is awash with "organic soups." However, if organic soups could have formed on other worlds, and since cosmic collisions are commonplace, not only between planets but entire galaxies, does it not seem reasonable to assume that some of these creatures may have survived a cosmic, planetary collision, trapped in gigantic debris, and that some of these creatures may have subsequently been hurled to Earth?

Indeed, if complex life "evolved" on other planets, not only might their descendants have been hurled to Earth (and other planets) encased in all manner of titanic planetary debris following cosmic catastrophes, but these highly evolved life forms may have played a role in the emergence and evolution of life on this planet. This latter possibility, in fact, was proposed by Nobel laureate, Francis Crick, and Leslie Orgel, who in a paper published in 1973, raised the possibility that life may have been purposely sent to Earth in a rocket ship by an exceedingly technologically advanced alien race.

Likewise, as noted, the Sumerians believed than a technologically advanced race of humans came to the Earth tens of thousands of years ago, not to create life on Earth, but to mix and insert something of the gods into the germ cells of primitive humans, to create a woman and a man in the image of the gods, so that they could see as gods and be as gods, knowing good and evil.

Indeed, the Universe may well swarm with the seeds of life; genetic seeds which were repeatedly cast into the abyss following cosmic collisions and planetary shearing impacts, only to wash down upon some distant shore (Joseph, 1997, 2000a,c).

METAMORPHOSIS: GENETIC ENGINEERING OF THE ENVIRONMENT

Although Darwinians and neo-Darwinians argue against purpose or progress, it is obvious from the fossil record that increasingly complex and intelligent species have emerged over the course of the last 3.86 billion years. And they have emerged in a highly predictable, step-wise, sometimes leaping progression: single celled creatures, simple then complex multi-cellular organisms, Ediacaran fauna, Cambrian fauna, armored jawless fish, jawed fish, lobed finned lung fish, amphibians, reptiles, repto-mammals, therapsids, mammals, primates, woman and man (Joseph, 1993, 1996, 1997, 2000a,c).

Moreover, it is apparent that these creatures and earlier species genetically engineered the environment so as to alter the climate and the chemical composition of the atmosphere and seas, to accommodate those yet to be born (Joseph, 1997, 2000a,c). Hence, the first creatures to emerge on Earth, 3.87 billion years ago produced a surplus of carbon isotopes and were secreting oxygen as a waste product (Mojzsis, et al., 1996) thus flooding the atmosphere with oxygen making it possible for oxygen breathing creatures to emerge. By 3.46 billion years B.P., photosynthesizing cyanobacterial communities began taking root on every continent (Schopf, 1999).

Over the next billion years, as the Earth continued to cool and internal and external radiation began to taper off, and in parallel with the genetically induced alterations of the climate, atmosphere, earth and seas, ground hugging, water loving, cold seeking, sun worshipping, single- and multi-celled organisms gained dominion over the planet and the sunlit bottoms of innumerable shallow seas. Like their ancestors, many were oxygen secretors and practiced a crude form of photosynthesis such that ultraviolet and other wave lengths of light were absorbed which enabled them to survive.

By 1.8 billion years B.P., a globally oxidizing atmosphere had formed (Collerson & Kamber, 1999) and organic-cystic coated multi-cellular ("leaf-like") life forms, referred to as acritarchs, had emerged, and likely contained mitochondria-like organelles. Being in possession of mitochondria provided these creatures and their descendants with an incredible energy source which in turn promoted the emergence of increasingly complex organisms, and increasingly complex cells, including what would become nerve cells.

By 1.3 billion years ago, the multi-cellular ancestors for invertebrates had emerged (Wray et al., 1996). According to Wray et al., (1996) these "minute creatures" were "soft bodied... little squishy things... crawling and sliding between grains of mud or sand on the sea bed." These included long sinuous meandering worms which were burrowing beneath the wet sands of shallow seas (Seilacher et al., 1998). The animals appear to have also "evolved" a nerve net, i.e., a primitive nervous system consisting of nerve-like sensory-motor-cells which were strung loosely together, thus forming a network of nerves.

With the increase in the number of oxygen secreting organisms, oxygen levels began to significantly increase, the ozone layer became established, and carbon dioxide began to slightly diminish (Collerson & Kamber, 1999; Schopf, 1992, 1999). In consequence, by 600 million B.P. the climate became warmer, carbon dioxide levels markedly diminished, and the atmosphere and oceans became richer in waste secreted oxygen (e.g., Butcher et al., 1992; Knoll, 1991, 1992). As the environment acts on gene selection, and can activate silent genes which then expressed precoded traits (Joseph, 1997, 2000a,c) these changes induced an incredible explosion of complex life, the Cambrian Explosion.

THE CAMBRIAN EXPLOSION

The environment acts on gene selection, and the changing environment and chemical composition of the atmosphere promoted the evolution of complex eukaryote life including the Ediacaran fauna who feasted upon the deep layers of bacterial mats that had been forming for over 3 billion years. The Ediacaran fauna, however, were calcium carbonate secretors, and it is from calcium carbonate that shells and bones are constructed.

The Ediacaran fauna, and those creatures who had come before them, made possible the metamorphosis of shell fish and the skeletal system, and thus promoted those environmental conditions that resulted in an explosion of life with all manner of complex creatures appearing in every river, ocean, and stream; an explosion of life collectively referred to as The Cambrian Explosion. That is, they altered the environment, which acts on gene selection and silent gene activation, thereby expressing traits and features that had been precoded into the genes thereby giving rise to complex organisms (Joseph, 1997, 2000a, c).

These complex life forms included all manner of "small shelly fish"

(Anabrites, Protohertzina), as well as sponges, jelly fish, mollusks, brachiopods, and the first arthropods (e.g. trilobites) which immediately sprouted legs.

"If it could be demonstrated that any complex organ existed which could not possibly have been formed by numerous successive. slight modifications, my theory would absolutely break down." -Darwin, 1857.

With no history of derivative ancestral forms, all manner of complex life forms suddenly emerged with gills, intestines, joints, brains, and modern eyes equipped with retinas and fully modern optic lenses. These included organisms with a hard tube-like outer-skeleton consisting of calcium carbonate, and all manner of "small shelly fish" (Anabrites, Protohertzina), as well as sponges, jelly fish, mollusks, brachiopods, and the first arthropods (e.g. trilobites) which immediately sprouted legs and primitive brains.

In fact, every phylum in existence today emerged during the Cambrian Explosion, including some phyla which emerged then became extinct. The survivors, however, included the phylum Chordata; i.e. tunicates and the first jawless fish who possessed a notochord and simplified brain that consisted of a brainstem and limbic forebrain (Joseph, 1996, 2000a).

Hence, during the Cambrian epoch there was also a cerebral and thus a cognitive explosion as the first true brains were established, brains which would continue to undergo a genetically preprogrammed metamorphosis until finally ending up in human heads.

And yet, just as the Ediacaran fauna emerged, secreted massive amounts of calcium, and then departed the scene, an incredible number of phyla emerged during the Cambrian explosion, made their own genetically engineered contributions, and then became extinct—a pattern of sometimes inexplicable species extinction that has been repeated time and again.

Indeed, just as the placenta is jettisoned after it serves its purpose, innumerable species have died out once they had made their contributions to the next stage of "evolutionary" development. Thus, we see that major species have emerged, flourished, diversified, modified the environment, and then died out, only to be followed by yet another wave of "novel" species who released and secreted additional "waste" products thus making their own contribution to the environment and the development of the next wave of diverse species, their descendants, before disappearing from the scene.

However with each successive wave there has been not just diversity, but progress, environmental change, and increased complexity in design and intelligence, leading from simple cellular organisms to all manner of species, including woman and man. And, similar events have likely taken place on innumerable planets, including worlds formed billions of years before the creation of the Earth.

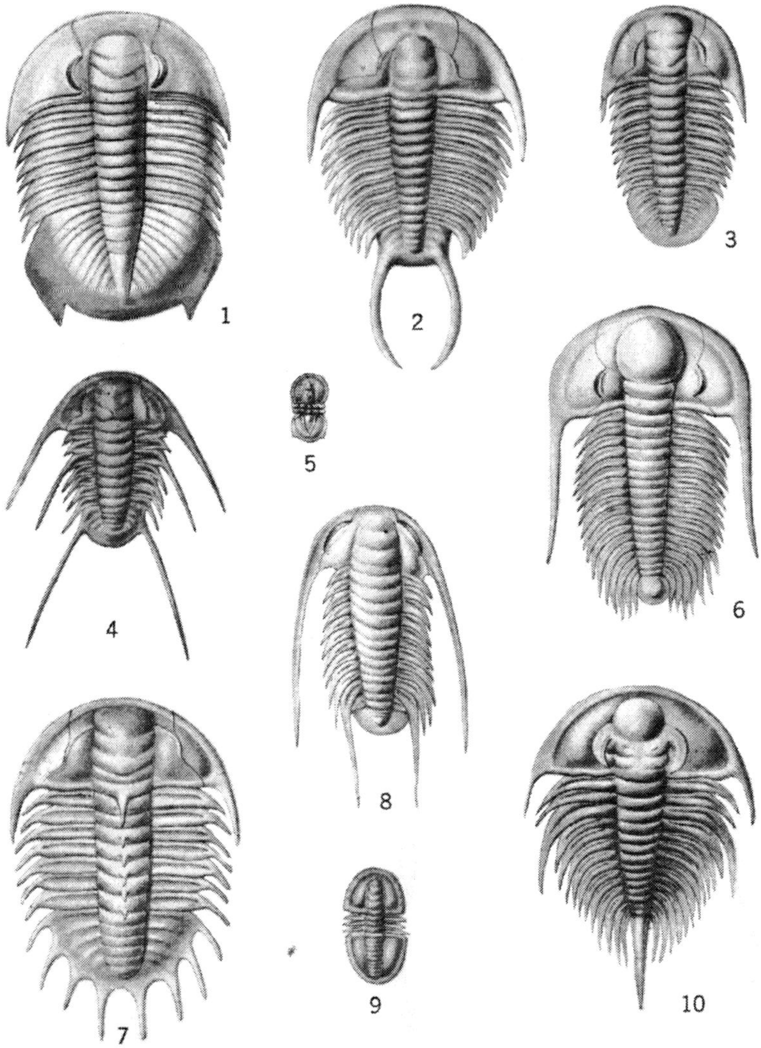
1
2
3
4
5
6
7
8
9
10

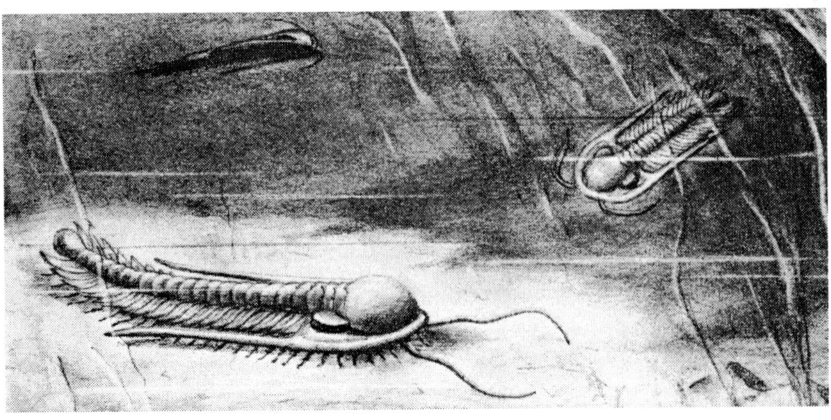

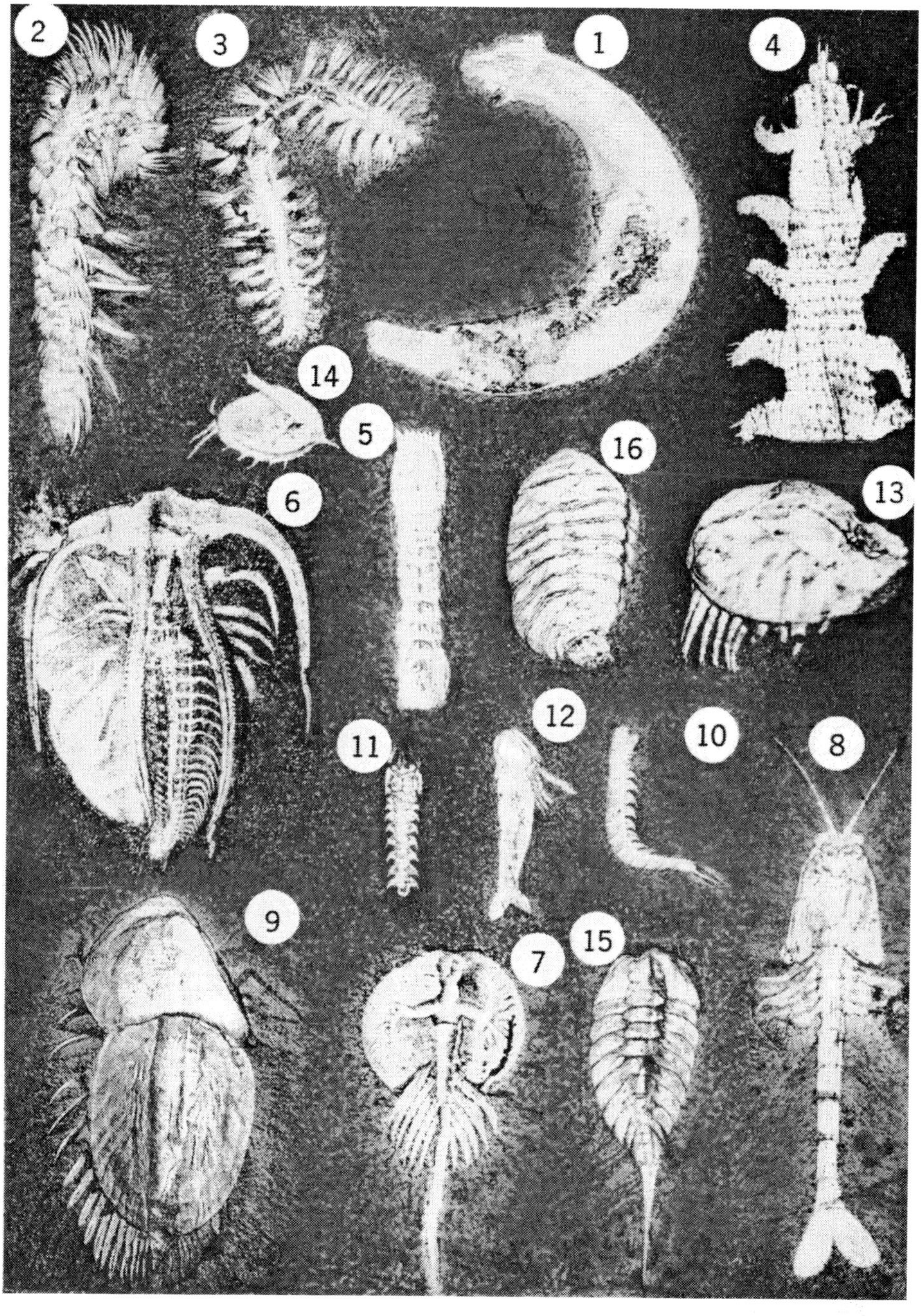

Figure 97. *Cambrian Trilobites. Drawn by L.S. Douglas. Reprinted from Dunbar, 1960. Historical Geology, Wiley, New York.*

A STEP-WISE METAMORPHOSIS

Two hundred million years after the onset of the Cambrian explosion of life most of these life forms were quite suddenly sloughed off in a mass extinction (marking the end of a period referred to as the Permian). Contrary to Darwinian theory, not a single new phylum emerged. Instead, the ancestral line which would eventually give rise to woman and man began seeking a new life on dry land. In fact, just as there is absolutely nothing random about the organization and expression of DNA, the source of all variation, the emergence of new and increasingly complex species have also "evolved" in a highly organized, predictable pattern.

As noted, following Permian mass extinction this was followed by yet another explosion of life both in the sea and on dry land, the metamorphosis of which again paralleled dramatic shifts in climate, atmospheric conditions, and other environmental variables (e.g. (Butcher et al., 1992; Knoll, 1991, 1992). Again, the changing environment acts on gene selection, to activate silent genes which contain precoded traits, and precoded species (Joseph, 1997, 2000a,c). That is, these traits and "new" species are preprogrammed into the genes, waiting for an environmental signal to emerge; and when they emerge, it is in a predictable, step-wise, molecular clock-like fashion.

Amphibians emerged some 350 million years ago, followed by reptiles 300 million years B.P., who were followed by repto-mammals 250 million years B.P., then the more mammal-like therapsids 200 million years ago, followed by mammals 150 million years ago, then primates 70 million years B.P., followed by apes 30 million years B.P., then Australopithecus, around 5 million years B.P., followed by H. habilis (2.2 million years B.P.), then H. erectus, (1.9 million years B.P.), then archaic Homo sapiens (500,000 years B.P.), and then Cro-Magnon, over 35,000 years ago.

This step-wise progression is also obvious from an examination of DNA. Contrary to Darwin's and neo-Darwinian theory, there is nothing random about the organization or expression of DNA (Calladine & Drew, 1992; Strachan & Read, 1996; Watson et al., 1992), and over the course of the last 3.8 billion years, the expression of DNA, including the coding and activation of silent DNA, has occurred in a highly predictable, step-wise fashion, in accordance with the ticking of a genetic clock.

That is, the expression of DNA and the expression of new species, has been genetically regulated, such that over the course of "evolution" changes in the expression of DNA have also occurred in a highly predictable, step-wise fashion. Increasingly intelligent and complex species have emerged in accordance with genetically induced changes in the genetically engineered environment, and in accordance with the "ticking" of the genetic clock.

THE TICKING OF THE GENETIC CLOCK

The structure of DNA is such that it contains the genetic instructions, or at least, the genetic capability, for creating all manner of life. This information, however, appears to be stored within silent non-coding genes and silent nucleotide sequence segments referred to as introns. Genes are divided into coding and non-coding sequences, and most genes, depending on species, are completely suppressed and silent.

Nevertheless, these silent genes (introns) and the traits they code for, exist prior to their expression, having been inherited from previous species, sometimes as silent genes, and genes within genes, and thus species within species (Joseph, 1997, 2000a,c). Moreover, changes in the expression of these genes, or DNA-products, have not only paralleled the emergence of new species in a highly predictable, molecular-clock like fashion, as if programmed by a preset "genetic clock, but these genetic changes can be used to make accurate predictions about when species first emerged and then diverged from a common ancestor.

For example, all species contain similar types of ribosomal RNA (rRNA). However, there are obvious differences between species in base pair rRNA organization. There is nothing random about these differences, as they in fact differ in a predictable step-wise fashion as we ascend the ancestral tree.

For example, those species which have an almost identical nucleotide base pair rRNA organization presumably diverged only recently or have diverged only minimally, e.g., bacteria. However, when comparing humans to bacteria, there are significant and predictable differences in the sequences of DNA and RNA nucleotide bases. It is these same predictable differences which have enabled various investigators to make accurate and verifiable predictions about divergence or the emergence of various species.

Data from a "molecule clock" based on the analysis of eight different genes in seven different classes of invertebrates (e.g. starfish, snails, eels, spiders), predicted the existence of invertebrates which diverged over 1 billion years ago (Wray et al., 1996)—a prediction since verified by Seilacher et al., (1998) who found evidence of complex multi-cellular organisms in sediments over 1 billion years old. And, it was data derived from a "molecule clock" which predicted that complex fully modern microbes had become established over 3 billion years ago (Woese, 1989, Woese et al., 1990)—a prediction that has now been repeatedly verified (Hoffman et al., 1999; Mojzsis, et al., 1996; Schopf, 1993, 1999).

In fact, this same step-wise sequential progression is evident from an examination of the approximately 100 amino acids that comprise an exceedingly important protein which participates in oxygen utilization: cytochrome c. Cytochrome c. is found in all animals, and consists of amino acids. However, cytochrome c. becomes increasingly different, albeit in a step-wise, clock-like fashion, as we descend the ancestral tree. Of the approximately 100 amino acids that comprise human cytochrome c 99 are identical to those of other primates, such as the rhesus monkey, 89 are shared with other mammals, 86 with reptiles, 82 with amphibians, 79 with fish, 69 with the silkworm, 57 with wheat, and 55 are identical to those of the yeast (Denton, 1986; de Duve, 1995).

This progression is evident not only based on DNA, but the fossil record. Complex life has evolved in an organized and purposeful, step-wise manner, leading from simple cell to all manner of creatures, including modern woman and man.

As summed up by Denton (1998) "the rate of change in many genes is regulated by a clock which seems to tick simultaneously in all branches of the tree of life." Indeed, this was evident even ten years ago, for according to Lewin (1988), "the notion of and evidence for a molecular clock... has become... pervasive."

THE ENVIRONMENT ACTS ON GENE SELECTION

The expression of this genetic clock requires that the climate, atmosphere, oceans, and the environment, be genetically engineered so as to prepare the planet for those yet to be born. DNA acts on the environment for the purposes of DNA activation and dispersal.

Thus, the environment is also modified in a genetically preprogrammed clock-wise fashion (Joseph, 1997, 2000a,c). Indeed, the environment acts on gene selection (de Jong & Scharloo, 1976; Dykhuizen & Hart, 1980; Gibson & Hogness, 1996; Polaczyk et al., 1998; Rutherford & Lindquist, 1998; Wade et al., 1997), which acts on the environment, which acts on gene selection, thereby creating a complex feedback mechanism which gives rise to diverse products and species. And these genetically engineered environmental changes have acted on the DNA of each successive generation of species, our ancestors, whose DNA gave birth to our own.

Therefore, according to the theory of astrobiological evolutionary metamorphosis, since modern day DNA traces it ancestry to the first life forms to arrive on Earth, it thus appears that these creatures contained the genetic instructions for the genetic engineering of the atmosphere and climate and the metamorphosis of all Earthly-life. They engaged in genetic engineering for the purpose of silent-DNA activation and dispersal, which in turn has led to the step-wise creation of increasingly complex animals (Joseph, 1997, 2000a); animals which also "evolved" on other planets.

In other words, just as a mother's womb is genetically in tune with that of her egg, it also appears that these biologically engineered environmental modifications of the earth, atmosphere, oceans, and seas, were also preprogrammed into the genetic code. These modification were biologically and genetically induced so as to promote and accommodate the lifestyles of those DNA-organisms yet to be born, albeit in accordance with specific genetic instructions which were inherited from those creatures who were among the first to take root on this planet. Hence, just as DNA contains the genetic instructions for creating an embryo, fetus, baby, child, adolescent and adult, and the genetic instructions for inducing the metamorphosis and transformation of a caterpillar into a butterfly, the "seeds of life swarming throughout the cosmos" and their DNA, may have also contained the instructions for genetically engineering the environment, so as to make possible the step-wise creation, expression, and dispersal of all manner of DNA-based life forms, including, on this planet and innumerable other ancient worlds, the likes of woman and man.

Likewise, the silent genes which are to be acted on by the changing environment, and those silent genes with the instructions for the next stage of genetic engineering and the creation of additional and more complex species, are also passed down to subsequent species. That is, genes exist prior to their selection, sometimes as genes within genes, and the information they contain for the manufacturing of specific products or species, also exists prior to their activation and may be passed down to a later generation at which point the silent gene may be expressed.

As summarized by Rutherford and Lindquist (1998, 0. 341), "experiments have shown that populations contain a surprising amount of unexpressed genetic variation that is capable of affecting certain typically invariant traits." Moreover, Rutherford and Lindquist (1998) have experimentally demonstrated that by altering environmental conditions, such as temperature or diet, that regulatory proteins which normally suppressed these genes may be inactivated. By eliminating these suppressive influences results in intron activation and the expression of "new" traits and appendages that had been coded into formerly silent genes.

As summed up by Rutherford and Lindquist (1998, p. 341), these regulatory proteins, such as Hsp90, serve as "a capacitor for the conditional release of stores of hidden morphological variation;" variations which may be produced by altering the environment, and which may then be passed down to subsequent generations which continue to express the "variant" trait.

However, Hsp90, also reacts to environmental stress including diet and fluctuations in temperature (Rutherford & Lindquist, 1998). Indeed, as demonstrated by, Rutherford and Lindquist (1998, p. 341) Hsp90 acts as an "explicit molecular mechanism that assists the process of evolutionary change in response to the environment" and it accomplishes this through the "conditional release of stores of hidden morphological variation... perhaps allowing for the rapid morphological radiations that are found in the fossil record."

GENETIC COMMONALTIES

According to the theory of evolutionary metamorphosis, the first creatures to emerge on this planet likely harbored "human" genes, and thus some of the same exact genes which are found in all five Earthly phyla (Joseph, 1997, 2000a,c). Much of their genomes was also probably suppressed and silent, as is the case with most modern day species.

However, silent genes and the instructions for creating additional genes, can be passed on to subsequent generations and species so as to become activated at a later date under the proper environmental conditions. As such, two species that diverge from a common ancestor may later generate the same exact gene. Thus although the common ancestor does not appear to possess this gene, it did pass along the instructions for creating that gene; e.g, perhaps as genes within genes (and thus species within species).

Hence, because species can pass on genes within genes, myriad life forms contain many of the same exact genes, including the same exact nucleotide sequence segments and "master regulatory genes" which code for the development of the heart, lungs, eyes and brains (D'Souza et al. 1995; Garcia-Fernandex & Holland, 1994; Ruddle, et al. 1994; Strachan & Read, 1996; Watson et al. 1992). Therefore, although the common ancestors had neither heart, lungs, eyes, or brains, the genetic instructions for hearts, lungs, etc., were genetically preprogrammed and inherited as genetic potential.

Other inexplicable commonalties include the "independent" evolution in both birds and mammals, of a "double pump" heart and the formation of a interventricular septum which induces a total separation of deoxygenated and oxygenated blood, and endothermy, i.e. the capacity to increase the production of endogenous metabolic energy. Both birds and mammals are endotherms, whereas reptiles and amphibians, the descendants of the common ancestors to birds and mammals, are exotherms who lack a double pump heart or an interventricular septum. And, the common ancestor to birds and mammals died out over 300 million years ago (Kumar & Hedges, 1998).

It is because of this common inheritance that humans and other species not only have so many of the same exact genes (D'Souza et al. 1995; Garcia-Fernandex & Holland, 1994; Ruddle, et al. 1994; Strachan & Read, 1996; Watson et al. 1992), but have "evolved" almost identical brains and complex body parts, including eyes, brains, fingers and hands.

Likewise, it could be argued that because humans have inherited the same exact genes, they not only "evolved" similar modes of communicating, speaking, behaving, competing or having sex (e.g. Chomsky, 1957, 1972; Ekman, 1993; Eible-Elbesfeldt, 1993; Joseph, 1993, 1996, 2000a; Waal, 1989; Wickler, 1973), but commonalties in regard to spirituality and religious experience.

Nevertheless, these and other common genes cannot be located in bacterial or other simple multicellular genomes, or common ancestors, which suggests that initially they must have existed—at least on Earth—as silent intronic genetic potential which was passed on to three, and in some cases, four different phyla; i.e. as genes within genes.

Obviously, identical structures and almost identical genes could not have randomly and independently evolved in three or five different phyla as is demanded by Darwinian theory. Ovaries, neurons, hearts, eyes and lungs did not randomly evolve, they were genetically preprogrammed, and these genes were inherited from those creatures who were among the first to take root on this planet, who in turn inherited their genes from creatures who lived on other planets—organisms which likely included creatures similar to woman and man.

Likewise, those genes coding for spiritual experience, existed prior to their expression. The capacity for spiritual experience is a trait that was inherited from ancestral species who in turn trace their DNA to creatures who long ago lived on other planets.

In other words, the Earth, and all manner of planets, were genetically seeded to grow humans and an incredible variety of divergent species. The Earth was genetically seeded to grow humans who would become increasingly intelligent, and increasingly spiritually inclined.

As similar genetic seeds have likely fallen on other planets, what this also implies is that humans may well have "evolved" on other worlds, tens of billions if not trillions of years ago. And, some of these evolutionarily advanced humans, may have traveled to our planet, and claimed to be "gods."

SPIRITUAL METAMORPHOSIS

Animals, such as elephants and dogs obviously mourn when loved ones die. Elephants become upset when the find the bones of other elephants, and they may attempt to bury these bones. Chimpanzees engage in complex rituals, such as a rain dance, in response to approaching storms. And, it has been anecdotally reported that dogs and other animals possess a "sixth sense" which enables them to detect the presence of ghosts and spirits, or evil emanations.

Thus, it could be argued that the genes associated with spiritual experience might also be found in other animals, including dogs, chimpanzees, and elephants. In this regard, it could also be argued that the genes which enable spiritual expression existed initially as silent genes, which were passed down from species to species, waiting for an environmental signal to trigger their activation.

However, as genes consist of coding and non-coding sequences, and as they have the capability of producing increasingly complex products and sensory capabilities, it could be argued that this spiritual awareness is not as developed in animals as it is in human, due to differences in gene expression.

Likewise, it could be argued that these spiritual genes have been more fully, but not yet completely expressed, in humans. Nevertheless, it is the coding and activation of these genes which are responsible for the identical aspects of spirituality and religious expression across cultures and over the course of evolutionary history.

In other words, spirituality is not due to superstition, but has a genetic as well as a spiritual basis. The environment acts on gene selection, and genes which coded for the ability to perceive spiritual nuances, and for those neurons and brain structures which could act as a transmitter to god, came to be expressed over the course of evolution, which is why spiritual belief and spiritual experience are world wide. However, this also implies that human can continue to spiritually evolve in the future.

In fact, given that over 90% of the human genome is silent and suppressed, and as evolutionary metamorphosis is an ongoing phenomenon, it could be argued that we have the potential to become increasingly spiritually inclined and increasingly god-like. Becoming increasingly god-like would be especially likely if we were indeed fashioned in the image of the Gods, and if the evolutionary metamorphosis of life continues in the future. We may possess, hidden away within our silent DNA, the genetic capability to not only be like gods, but to transcend god and good and evil.

THE DEATH OF DARWINISM

Darwin's acolytes and those who champion his theory claim that "the blind, unconscious, automatic process which Darwin discovered, and which we now know is the explanation for existence, has no purpose in mind. It has no mind, no mind's eye. It does not plan for the future. It has no vision, no foresight, no sight at all" (Dawkins, 1987, p. 5).

Yet, contrary to Darwinism, the behavior of individual organisms and species is in fact goal directed and purposeful. Living creatures are not random collections of molecules which are mindlessly and reflexively bouncing about the environment. Their behavior is purposeful.

Likewise, although the motto of the capitalist business community, is "survival of the fit," if Darwinian principles were applied to business, or even every day life, these business would quickly become extinct. The successful business is run with certain goals in mind which are intelligently considered and purposefully planned and carried out, purposefully modified, etc., and so on.This is not Darwinism! Rather it is the nature of life.

Darwinism, in fact, is merely a tautology that has no predictive utility. In can only predict by hindsight and requires circular reasoning: survivors survive because they are fit; the fit are fit only if they survive.

Contrary to Darwinism, life is goal directed, behavior is not random, and the evolution of life on this planet has not been due to the natural selection of random variations, as there is absolutely nothing random about the organization and expression of DNA which is the source of all variability.

Rather, the metamorphosis of life on this planet has been genetically preprogrammed and is under strict genetic control, unfolding in accordance with the DNA-instructions inherited from creatures that long ago evolved on other planets.

Consider: A caterpillar spins a cocoon and later emerges as a butterfly, thus undergoing a profound metamorphosis. This metamorphosis is under genetic and environmental control and is genetically preprogrammed. However, if that same metamorphosis took a million years, instead of a single season, the Darwinians would claim that the appearance of design is an "illusion," that the result is not due to purposeful planning aimed at the realization of specific goals (the butterfly), but is due to the natural selection of chance and minor variations, i.e., "random mutations" (e.g. Dawkins, 1987).

However, just as a caterpillar is genetically preprogrammed to undergo metamorphosis and emerge as a moth or butterfly, so too were humans and all manner of creatures (or variations thereof) genetically preprogrammed to emerge, equipped with similar genes and similar traits that were inherited from those life forms which were among the first to take root on this planet.

Contrary to Darwinism, the evolution of life has been genetically predetermined and precoded, has unfolded in accordance with specific genetic plans and DNA-based instructions, and has been striving (and still striving) toward fulfilling specific genetic goals: the dispersal and activation of silent DNA and the replication of life forms that long ago lived on other planets.

METAMORPHOSIS IN THE ANCIENT CORNERS OF THE COSMOS

The antiquity of the Universe is unknown, though there are those who claim it has been in existence for only 12 to 18 billion years (reviewed in Cowen 1995; and Hellemans 1995). The infant Earth is a scant 4.6 billion years young.There are billions of ancient galaxies consisting of trillions of aged solar systems that are likely ringed with planets -many probably quite like our own.

And, just as the Earth has been genetically seeded to grow humans and all manner of species (and numerous variations thereof), these same "genetic seeds" have rained down on innumerable worlds since time immemorial. And, just as Life has evolved on this world, it could be predicted that Life has evolved on at least a few of these planetary archipelagoes including creatures who long ago evolved in a fashion similar to woman and man.

However, as metamorphosis appears to be an ongoing phenomenon, and as over 90% of the human genome is silent and suppressed, this indicates that metamorphosis will continue into the future on this planet. What this also implies is that those creatures who have "evolved" on more ancient worlds, may have "evolved" beyond modern humans and acquired additional neurological, cognitive, perceptual, and spiritual capabilities, billions and perhaps trillions of years before this planet was formed.

THE MYTH OF THE BIG BANG

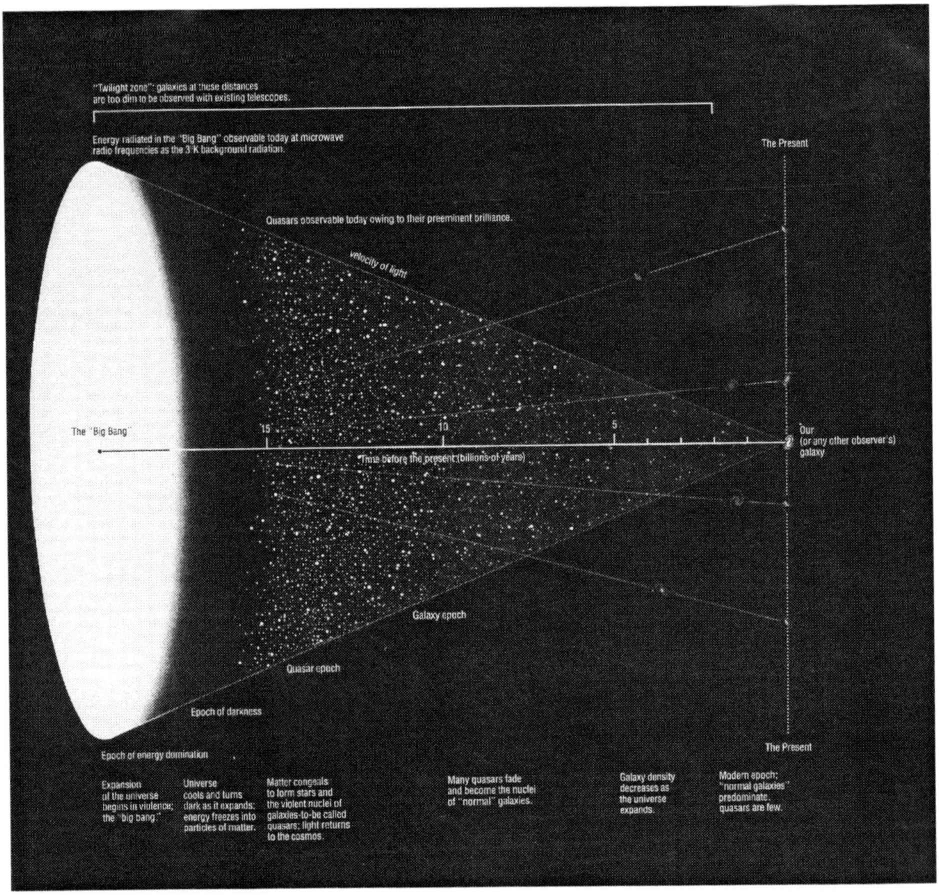

Figure 98. *Schematic illustration of the theoretical "Big Bang." Reprinted from Ferris, 1982; Galaxies, Sierra Club Books, San Francisco. There are several major conceptions of the big bang, and one is that at first there was absolutely nothing, not even space, and then there was a big explosion which created molecules and thus the Universe. This notion could also be characterized as the "nothing happened" theory of creation. Another conception is that at first there was pure energy and then this energy exploded which caused a massive and exceedingly hot expansion, and then as this expansion cooled, some of this energy froze into particles of molecules which later gave rise to stellar clouds, and then stars and planets.*

"To reach emptiness extreme... Endless the series of things without a name on the way back to where there is nothing." Lao Tzu

"For though Heaven and Earth and the Ten Thousand Creatures were produced by Being; being was produced by non-being. Non-being by being."-Tao Te Ching

"There was something undefined and complete, coming into existence before Heaven and Earth. How still it was and formless, standing alone, and undergoing no change, reaching everywhere and in no danger of being exhausted! It may be regarded as the Mother of all things." The Tao Teh King.

The "big bang" theory of the creation appears to preclude any possibility of an all pervading god, or spiritual life force as being the uncaused cause of this Universe or the emergence of life on this world or others. However, that presumption is not necessarily correct and depends on which theory of the big bang one believes in, and how long ago this big bang may have actually occurred. In fact, the theory of the big bang may well be irrelevant to the question of life, god, or spirituality, as this theory is not supported by the available evidence.

The theory of the big bang rests upon the notion that at first there was absolutely nothing. Nothing! Not even space! And then, inexplicably, this nothingness began to heat up and then it exploded. And out of nothing there was suddenly stuff. Or, another way of putting it: nothing happened. And, out of nothing flowed space, time, elementary particles, then protons, neutrons, electrons... the Universe and finally those molecules which would some day fall to earth. And, just as nothing supposedly gave rise to everything, life would emerge from non-life, from an organic soup, and give rise to all life including the generation of those scientists who believe in "nothing."

More specifically, it is supposed that within one trillionth of a second after the big bang—an explosion that was tens of billions of degrees hot—that both matter and anti-matter were created. In some scenarios, this resulted in an anti-matter universe, and another universe consisting of matter.

In yet another scenario, since whenever matter and anti-matter have contact, they instantly annihilate one another in flashes of pure energy, it is proposed that there was a slight imbalance such that there was slightly more matter than anti-matter. Hence, within the one trillionth of a second after the big bang and after almost all matter and anti-matter were destroyed—thus creating the cosmic microwave background radiation that permeates the universe—the fragmentary remainder of matter gave rise to this universe.

THE BIG BANG AND CHAOS

The theory of the big bang is problematic as it rests upon the premise that at first there was nothing and then there was an explosion and then there was stuff. Some theorists have recognized this position is rather untenable, and have modified the theory of the "big bang" by positing the initial existence of pure energy. According to this version of the big bang theory, this pure energy became increasingly chaotic and for some reason exploded, thereby giving rise to an orderly expanding and uniform universe, where at first there was nothing but chaos.

Of course, the pre-existence of "pure energy" also seems to refute the central tenant of the "big bang" which is at first there was nothing. Indeed, this pure energy could be likened to "god" and the "great spirit" and in this regard it could be said that "god" and the "great spirit" are timeless and existed prior to the creation of this universe.

Moreover, the notion of order emerging from chaos, including even the condensing and creation of vast interstellar clouds, is actually a very old idea that was penned by the Sumerians over 6000 years ago. For example, the Sumerians imagined that at first there was nothing and because there was nothing, it had no name. However, this "nothing" was not a pure absence. Rather, all was chaos (Kramer, 1991; Roux, 1992), a "commingling" of clouds ("mummu"), and fresh waters (Apsu) and salt waters (Tiamat). Because there was nothing, only chaos, "No gods whatever had been brought into being. Uncalled by name, their destinies undetermined." And, out of this chaos there came form and substance, and then "An" from which flowed the seeds of life; seeds which eventually fell to Earth and which also fell upon the planet of the gods, thus giving birth to the gods, the Anunnaki (Kramer, 1991).

BIG BANG MYTHOLOGY: THE BACKGROUND RADIATION

There is obvious evidence for "energy" and interstellar clouds that give birth to stars, planets and galaxies. However, the theory of the "big bang" is not supported by the evidence including the fact that the "uniformity" that is required in the distribution of matter, and the supposed '3 degree background radiation that is supposed to exist uniformly in all directions of the universe (as predicted and required by this big explosion), is not uniform. Rather, there are entire walls of galaxies spread at irregular intervals (Cohen et al., 1996), with the "older" and more distant galaxies clustered together rather than spread apart (Glanz, 1996).In fact, there are entire rivers of galaxies flowing in directions that would not be likely if due to a big bang (e.g. Flamsteed 1995).

The "background radiation" is also characterized by "density fluctuations" and other deviations which indicate the universe is not behaving in a fashion that would be expected from an inflationary explosion (Ferreira et al., 1998). According to one team of astronomers (reviewed in Glanz, 1996) there are "clumpy structures as far as they could see, far enough to make theorists uncomfortable." Why "uncomfortable"? Because these findings refute the central tenants of the theory of the big bang.

Moreover, it has been repeatedly reported that a mysterious kind of anti-gravity energy, a "repulsive force permeates the universe, accelerating its expansion and sweeping distant objects unexpectedly far away" (reviewed in Glanz, 1998). These findings are not compatible with a big bang creation.

BIG BANG MYTHOLOGY: THE SPEED OF LIGHT

The theory of the big bang is also incompatible with findings based on the analysis of radio waves from 160 distant galaxies. Radio waves move in relation to an axis of orientation running through space. According to Dr. Borge Nodland of the University of Rochester, and Dr. Joun Ralston of the University of Kansas, this axis of orientation differs in different regions of space and determines how light travels and the speed and direction at which it travels in different regions of space. That is, these radiations rotate, like a corkscrew as they move through space, and undergo a complete rotation every billion miles.

Moreover, this axis is different in different regions of space; running one way, for example, toward the constellation Aquila and another way toward the constellation Sextans (Nodland & Ralston, 1997). What this means, according to Dr. Nodland, "is that not all space is equal" and that "light travels at different speeds" in different regions of the universe—findings which are completely contrary to the uniformity predicted by the theory of the big bang.

The theory of the big bang, including estimates as to the age of the universe, are dependent upon the false assumption that light always travels at the same speed and in a straight line. As noted above, that assumption is false (Nodland & Ralston, 1997). Light not only travels at different speeds in different regions of the universe, but at different speeds in this solar system and above the planet Earth—which is also inconsistent with the big bang requirement of uniformity.

Specifically, it was discovered and reported by Unran Inan (a professor at Stanford) at the Annual Meeting of the American Geophysical Union, in September of 1996, that flickering lights and glowing rings that are commonly detected high above thunderstorms, expand faster than the speed of light. This phenomenon is set in motion by a bolt of lightning striking the ground. This bolt causes electromagnetic pulses to race upward and to expand at an exceedingly rapid rate, thus creating an upward expanding bubble-like glowing ring which strikes the ionosphere and which then continues to expand faster than the speed of light. Hence, not only is the speed of light not a constant, but the speed of light is not a limiting factor in speed of movement.

Of course, because light changes speed and even direction, this also makes it impossible to determine the distance or age of distant stars, based on the speed of light.

THE BIG BANG, RELATIVITY, AND THE PARADOX OF THE TIME MACHINE

The theory of the big bang and all notions as to the age of the universe are also based on the false and arrogant assumption that we are able to detect the most distant galaxies and the oldest galaxies. However, these galaxies may be so distant, or ceased to exist so long ago, that they simply cannot be detected by those instruments currently available.

Currently, via the assistance of the Hubble telescope, astronomers have been able to detect galaxies that they believe to be a little over 12 billion light years distant (though others claims 14 billion or even 18 billion)—findings which assume uniformity in the speed of light. Although Esther Hu who detected this distant galaxy has also reported that "we've already got some candidate objects that are even further away," the light from the more distant and aged stars may have winked out of existence so long ago that they will never be detected.

The theory of the big bang, and in fact all current estimates as to the age of the universe, are also refuted by and fall prey to "the paradox of the time machine."

Consider: If you were to step into a time machine and go back 1000 years in time, you would not reappear on the exact same spot on Earth 1000 years ago, but in outer space as the Earth, our solar system, and this galaxy are in motion and were not in this spot 1000 years ago.

Likewise, those distant stars whose 12 billion year old light are just now arriving on Earth, reflect not where these stars are now, but where they were 12 billion years ago and only from the vantage point of where the Earth is now—and where the Earth is now is not ground zero for the supposed big bang.

That is, these stars were 12 billion light years distant from this specific spot in the Universe 12 billion years ago and not 12 billion light years distant from the supposed big bang.

As this particular spot is not ground zero, that distance means absolutely nothing except that 12 billion years ago these stars were 12 billion light years away from this spot. If we chose a spot 12 billion light years in the opposite direction and make our age estimates from this new location, then these stars suddenly become 24 billion years in age, and so on. Distance and thus age estimates based on distance and the location of an observer, are entirely relative and become meaningful only if we can identify a ground zero or starting point and this information simply does not exist.

Moreover, these stars have had an additional 12 billion years to move further away from the spot they were in 12 billion years ago. They may have moved in a different direction all together, as not just planets, but solar system, and entire galaxies are in orbit. Our solar system, for example, takes about 126 million years to make a complete orbit of the Milky Way—which means in 60 million years it will be headed in the opposite direction.

What goes around, comes around, and entire galaxies can change direction, such that "red shifts' (indicating an object that is speeding away) can thus become "blue shifts" (and stars currently displaying "blues" can become "reds") and what appears to be expanding will later appear to be contracting as its orbit takes it first away from, and then back toward this galaxy and our solar system which is also in orbit.

To be blunt: Although theories and speculation abound, we do not know the age of the universe or how it came into being though it is apparent that galaxy forming molecular clouds are abundant in interstellar space.

Rather, what the available evidence suggests, is that the cycling and recycling of material that comprises and creates planets, stars, and complex organic molecules, may have been ongoing for all of eternity.

"Truly Being and Non-Being grow out of each other." -Lao Tzu

And if the age of the Universe is eternal, then it would also appear that life may have roots that extend interminably into the long ago.

EVOLUTION IN THE ANCIENT CORNERS OF THE COSMOS

Can a lizard comprehend a man?
Can a man comprehend a god?
Who dares speak for God?
Perhaps…
… Even the gods have gods...

On Earth, the leaping, branching, and step-wise progression which has led from multi-cellular creature to cartilaginous fish, to bony fish... amphibian, reptile, repto-mammal, therapsid, mammal, primate, and woman and man, has taken place over the last billion years. Given that "evolution" is under strict genetic control, unfolding according to the ticking of a molecular genetic clock, and since over 90% of human DNA is dormant and silent and as tens of thousands of silentgenes (and almost 3 billion base pairs) have yet to be expressed, the likelihood is that evolutionary metamorphosis is an ongoing phenomenon and will continue on this planet into the future. If the genetic seeds of life swarm throughout the cosmos, and if they contain the genetic instructions for the metamorphosis of all life, then it can be predicted that similar events have taken place on at least a few million other worlds. In fact, those who dwell in the more ancient corners of the cosmos may have evolved beyond modern humans billions of years before the Earth became a twinkle in God's eye... billions if not trillions of years before the first upright earthly human emerged from the mists of time.

Indeed, as current estimates of the age of the Universe are based on the light still detectable, and as the light from innumerable stars may have winked out of existence billions of years ago, the age of the Universe and the metamorphosis of life may in fact extend interminably into the long ago. The implications are staggering.

Consider: What might be the technological and scientific capabilities of a civilization a million years older than our own? What of a civilization that has had ten million, or a billion, or 20 billion years to seek technological perfection? They might seem as "gods" even if they were merely human.

And yet, it could be expected that these ancient ones might have evolved new brain tissues and additional layers of gray matter and neocortex and perhaps additional limbic system nuclei... gaining intellectual, sensory, and spiritual capabilities which provide not just a "6th sense" but a 10th sense, and so on, completely eclipsing all aspects of human cognition, perception, and intelligence.

Consider, of the 3% of human DNA which is required to build a human being, 20% of that is used to create a brain, and another 30% of that DNA is expressed in the process of running and maintaining the brain (Brain, 1990). That is, 50% of the 3% of DNA which is coded, serves the human brain. Hence, since 97% of the 140,000 or more genes (and their 3 billion or more base pairs) that make up the human genome are repressed to varying degrees, up to 50% of the human genome, and thus perhaps as many as 50,000 repressed genes and over a billion base pairs of nucleotides may be available for future and additional cerebral metamorphosis and expansion of the brain.

Since increased complexity and progressive cerebral encephalization is characteristic of the evolution of brain-based life on this planet, the same could be expected on other complex-life bearing worlds. Consider: the Cro-Magnon peoples of the Upper Paleolithic had a brain that was 1/3 larger than modern humans (Joseph, 2000a).

Given evidence of increased brain size in previous species of humanity, coupled with the as yet untapped genetic potential within the human genome, then it can be predicted that those creatures evolving in the more ancient corners of the cosmos may have acquired more complex limbic system capabilities, as well as increased association and assimilation neocortical tissue, and may have evolved additional limbic nuclei and layers of neocortex, exceeding the 6 to 7 layered neocortex that is characteristic of mammals and primates—and this may have transpired billions of years before the creation of the Earth.

In fact, given the unknown antiquity of the universe, the brains of some exobiological organisms may consist of 8, 10, 12 or more layers of neocortex and greatly increased limbic, neocortical, perceptual, intellectual, memory, and spiritual capacity, thus completely dwarfing the human brain in neuronal, sensory, spiritual, and cognitive ability.

In fact, these ancient ones may have long ago engineered their own DNA and thus genetically engineered their own metamorphosis and purposefully developed limbic structures and cerebral tissues that might enable them to analyze, see relationships, or comprehend and manipulate phenomenon that modern humans cannot even conceive much less comprehend. These peoples, these ancient ones, would be as "gods" even if they were merely human.

And what are the powers of a "god?" What might be the creative and intellectual potency of a being whose brain and civilization has evolved over tens of billions of years, who has likely engineered their own DNA, and who has additional and expanded limbic system capability, or 10 or 20 or more layers of neocortex —compared to those seven we call our own?

From the perspective of those astrobiological organisms who evolved in the ancient regions of the cosmos, the human brain and mind may seem to be just one small step above a frog or a reptile; which, in many ways it is.

Conversely, the human ability to comprehend the intellectual, scientific and technological accomplishments and spiritual capabilities of an alien brain organized in this evolutionary advanced fashion, might be analogous to a lizard's ability to comprehend a man. That is, the mental, intellectual, creative, technological, and spiritual capabilities of creatures who began to evolve tens of billions of years ago, would lie well beyond human understanding. They would be as gods even if they were merely human.

Might this also explain the claims of the ancient Sumerians, Babylonians, Hebrews, Greeks, Romans, (and many other ancient peoples) that "God" and the "gods" looked and behaved just like humans and possessed human attributes including egotism, jealousy, irrational rages... including perhaps a tendency to brag and to take credit for achievements not their own —such as the creation of the universe?

Might this explain the innumerable competing personalities that have appeared on Earth, claiming to be gods? Might these human attributes and the accompany sense of superiority explain the propensity for indiscriminately killing anyone and everyone who does not obey orders and follow "god's" plans? Is it possible that Yahweh is not a god at all, but an evolutionary advanced human-like being that evolved on another planet?

And if humans were in fact created in the image of the Gods, having descended from similar genetic seeds, and if evolutionary metamorphosis is an ongoing phenomenon... then perhaps we too possess the genetic potential to be as gods... to be as God... and... the genetic potential... to evolve... beyond good and evil.

-17-

THE TRANSMITTER TO GOD:

In Search of the God Within

Spiritual and religious belief have a scientific, neurological, and genetic foundation. It is this neurological and genetic foundation which explains why mystical, spiritual, and religious experiences and beliefs are world-wide and have been in evidence for over 100,000 years.

It is also clear that there are individual differences in spirituality. However, as the environment acts on gene selection and can promote or retard neurological and perceptual development (Joseph & Casagrande, 1978, 1980; Joseph & Gallagher, 1980; Joseph, 1982, 1998a, 1999a,b), these individual differences may be due in part to the "use it or lose" it principle. As the environment and experience act on gene selection and brain development, those who more fully and more frequently participate in experiencing the spiritually sublime are more likely to continue to develop these capacities.

Those who engage in activities that hyperactive these brain structures are also more likely to have profound spiritual experiences. Dreaming, trance states, fasting, isolation, pain, drugs, and sexuality, activate specific and specialized neurons located in the limbic system and temporal lobe, the same structures which mediate religious and spiritual experiences.

The hyperactivation of these structures and their association with religious experience, also explains why spiritual states are often experienced under conditions involving extreme fear or death. Fear activates the amygdala. When facing a horrifying death even a committed atheist may feel compelled to cry out and pray to god for salvation.

HALLUCINATIONS AND RELIGIOUS EXPERIENCE

Admittedly, hyperactivation of the limbic system can also induce a variety of profound and complex hallucinations. The fact that the limbic system is common to all people may explain why throughout history and the world over, people not only have similar religious experiences, but similar religious hallucinations.

However, consider LSD. Much of what is experienced under LSD, are not hallucinations per se, but are due to the disinhibition of multi-sensory neurons which normally process and filter signals from divergent sensory sources simultaneously. A single neuron in the amygdala, for example, may receive visual, auditory, and tactile signals and then combine this information to provide a multi-sensory experience (Joseph, 1992).

Normally much of what impinges upon the brain is filtered out before it is transmitted to the limbic system. Similarly, much of what is perceived by the limbic system is also filtered before this data is transferred to the overlying neocortex—which is associated with the rational, conscious mind. These complex multi-sensory attributes and perceptions are filtered out because there is no need, for example, to taste colors or see sound.

LSD, however, blocks the reception of a neurotransmitter, serotonin, which normally acts to inhibit the reception and integration of these signals in structures such as the amygdala. LSD, therefore, enables the brain to continue processing information that is normally filtered and suppressed. In consequence, one can see sound, feel colors, peer between molecules, and even perceive other worldly realities. What is normally hidden is suddenly revealed. Is it possible that the presence of gods, demons, or angels are also "normally" filtered out?

Of course, under LSD, or in response to extreme fear, one may experience sensory distortions and complex hallucinations that have nothing to do with spirituality (Joseph, 1998a, 1999a,b). Moreover, some individuals may attribute religious and spiritual significance to objects, places, people, or locations, that are in fact devoid of these attributes.

For example, there are neurons and neural networks which make it possible to perceive geometric patterns, forms, and faces, as well as to attribute emotional and personal attributes to these stimuli. Therefore, hyperactivation of the limbic system and temporal lobe might result in hallucinations of faces, geometric shapes, colors, and so on, which are then misperceived as gods, ghosts, angels, aliens, and demons. The brain believes it is seeing a face of a demon, because "face" neurons have been activated and infused with intense emotion.

The same may occur even during the course of a religious experience, such that some aspects are real, whereas other features are hallucinations that come to be misinterpreted and invested with spiritual significance. As stated in the Egyptian and Tibetan Books of the dead, hallucinations and misperceptions are common following death, which in turn may result in the soul becoming frightened and confused, and losing its way.

According to the Bardo Thodol (Tibetan Book of the Dead), "These realms are not come from somewhere outside thyself. They come from within... they exist from eternity within the faculties of thine own intellect... issuing from within thine own brain... reflections of thine own thought-forms..."

Of course, the high priests of science might answer that these "realms" come from inside because they are hallucinations, and that there is no Hereafter or spirit world. Rather, these are silly superstitions that are based on hallucinations produced by an addled brain.

If that is the case, then from an evolutionary, Darwinian perspective, we must ask: What is the adaptive evolutionary significance of hallucinations? Why have people evolved the capacity to hallucinate? Why has our brain become adapted for perceiving what supposedly does not exist? Why would the limbic system evolve specialized neurons or neural networks that subserve the capacity to dream about, experience, or hallucinate spirits, angels, and the souls of the living and the dear departed, if these entities have no basis in reality?

Indeed, what is the adaptive significance of experiencing a life after death? How could humans have possibly evolved the capacity to have this particular "hallucination" only after they have died? How can you pass on a trait to one's offspring for them to inherit and then experience, when you have died before you first have that experience?

THE DARWINIAN EVOLUTION OF RELIGIOUS EXPERIENCE

The limbic system subserves the "four Fs:" feeding, fighting, fleeing, and sexuality. Thus the limbic system is exceedingly concerned with all aspects of emotional and motivational functioning and is desirous of maintaining life. Hence, in regard to "after death experiences" it could be argued that the limbic system generates a desire to physically survive which is so intense that this desire continues even after death and leads to a belief in a life after death. That is, the limbic system has evolved specific neural networks which creates dreams and hallucinations of souls and spirits of friends and relatives, so as to promote the promise of spiritual and eternal salvation and the illusion of eternal self-preservation, even after death.

Thus, according to Darwinian principles, the experience of life after death is actually an adaptive illusion which actually promotes life by contributing in some way to survival, which is why these traits are passed on to subsequent generations.

For example, those who developed and practiced limbic taboos and religious rituals (e.g., not eating certain foods), and who evolved a religious-moral conscience capable of redirecting and controlling the more dangerous limbic impulses, were more likely to survive, and, presumably, more likely to successfully breed.

Therefore, the preservation of these traits are the result of natural selection and survival of the fittest who pass on these characteristics and capacities to future generations. Those who did not possess, for example, "after-death" neurons were weeded out as "unfit." Those who possessed religious and spiritual capabilities were naturally selected such that they and their children survived.

Presumably, an evolutionary process such as this would have led to an exponential increase in the number of survivors and "religious" neural networks. Soon religion and religious beliefs, as well as mystical experience and related "hallucinations" became world wide and increasingly intense and profound.

However, if that is the case, then the limbic system has evolved the capacity to not only regulate itself so as to promote life, but to deceive itself via heightened emotional and opiate induced religious euphorias, and the creation of false hopes and dreams whose only purpose is to promote the survival of the species.

In this regard it could be argued that these mystical images, archetypes, and spiritual feeling states, have always been internally generated, like a dream, that again have no basis in external reality, but which serve only the need and desire to survive. That is, there may not be an "out there" or "Heaven" or external God, in some mystical space and alternate spiritual dimension, but rather, an internal heaven (or Hell) dominated, controlled, and produced by the limbic system. Thus the limbic system and temporal lobes insure the survival of the self by dreaming and hallucinating ghosts, spirits, and avenging angels, and by promoting the illusion of perpetual and eternal survival or damnation if taboos, rituals, and the laws of God are obeyed.

Unfortunately, this argument does not explain why even after death individuals continue to dream and hallucinate, and why so many who return from the dead report similar religious and spiritual experiences that include being welcomed by the dear departed. Again, what is the adaptive significance of these neurons firing and creating a hallucination even after death? A capacity such as this would represent a degree of limbic-evolutionary foresight that is almost too incredible to accept without positing some guiding intelligent force behind it's design. Does that intelligence belong to the Gods, and/or to the limbic system and the DNA of woman and man?

Consider also the massive secretion of opiates which guarantees most prey and other hapless creatures, a "merciful death" as they fall and lie still while they are simultaneously eaten alive by predators. What is the adaptive significance of a "merciful death?" Can a merciful loss of life promote the survival of the creature which is dying an otherwise horrible death? Obviously not. Rather, "mercy" such as this again raises the possibility of an intelligent force which purposefully and thoughtfully insured its "evolution."

SPIRITUALITY IS GENETICALLY CODED

The environment and experience act on gene selection, including the activation of those genes that code for neurons and limbic system structures such as the amygdala. The environment acts on those genes which code for those neurons which subserve the capacity for spiritual experience.

For example, we are able to perceive sounds because there are sounds and voices that can be perceived and because we possess specialized brain tissue (e.g. auditory cortex) which analyzes this information. First there were sounds which acted on gene selection which produced specialized nerve cells that could initially analyze vibrations and then later, sounds. These experiences acted on gene selection so that an increasing range of significant sounds could be perceived.

We see because there are people and objects to view and because we possess neurons which code for various visual features and shapes. If there was nothing to visually contemplate we would not have evolved eyes or visual cortex which analyzes this information.

However, the capacity to see is also genetically precoded, which is why even animals living in blackened caves in the bottom of the ocean possess nonfunctioning eyes. The environment acts on gene selection, and genes can be partially or fully activated, or partially or fully suppressed.

Likewise, it could be argued that the evolution of this genetic and neuronal spiritual, mystical, religious capacity is the consequence of repeated and exceedingly intense perceptual and emotional experiences with the spiritually sublime over countless generations. Via perhaps, the guiding influence of the "Great Spirit" or perhaps, after repeated experiences with gods, spirits, demons, angels, and lost souls, and since experience acts on gene selection, Homo sapiens sapiens therefore evolved these "neurons" which enabled them to better cope with the unknown, as well as to perceive and respond to spiritual messages which increased the likelihood of survival.

SPIRITUAL METAMORPHOSIS

Rather than due to superstition, humans have "evolved" the capacity to have spiritual experiences through the metamorphosis of brain structures which could be likened to a "transmitter to god." This spiritual metamorphosis in turn is a function of the environment acting on gene selection so as to activate silent genes and silent DNA nucleotide sequences which code for those brain structures which serve as a transmitter to God: the amygdala, hippocampus, and overlying temporal lobe.

It is because the capacity to have these experiences has been precoded into the genome of not just humans, but those creatures that were among the first to take root on this planet, which explains why even some animals display a spiritual awareness. Dogs, wolves, elephants, chimpanzees, have also evolved a limbic system which is remarkably similar to the human limbic system which is why they also display and experience complex emotions and form emotional attachments (Joseph, 1992a, 1993, 2000a).

However, as the environment and experience acts on gene selection, these limbic structures have continued to "evolve" and have become more massive and elaborate over the course of human "evolution." It is the metamorphosis of these brain structures, this transmitter to god, which in turn has enabled humans to more fully establish contact with the spiritual world.

Moreover, spirituality appears to be an emerging trait that may continue to develop in the future, over the course of human metamorphosis. That is, those structures which comprise the transmitter to god, may continue to expand in response to the spiritual environment acting on those genes which also code for spirituality—spirituality genes which remain, at present, at least partially silent and suppressed.

That is, it is likely that spiritual-like, psychic experiences may represent a quasi-dormant capacity, a "6th sense" which has yet to fully emerge. What is commonly referred to as ESP, for example, may be an emerging trait that will more fully evolve over time and with the expansion of the brain. Thus, humans, like the gods, may "evolve" the capacity to fully communicate their thoughts and desires through dreams and visions.

Conversely, due to the use it or lose it principle, these and related capacities may instead represent a regressive trait that was long ago almost lost and nearly extinguished—thanks, for example, to the Inquisitions of the Catholic Church, and cosmic catastrophes that destroyed those highly evolved humans who had fully acquired these spiritual sensitivities.

Consider the massive 1800 cc brain of the 6ft tall Cro-Magnons and the "marvelous cities" and technologically advanced civilizations associated with these peoples. The Cro-Magnon brain is one third larger than the cerebrum of modern humans. These people were not only intellectual giants, but compared to all those who came before or after them, physical giants, whose origins, frankly, are unknown. Indeed, they may well be children of the sons of God: the Anakites, the Nephilim—who the "Lord God" conspired to exterminate with the assistance of his own "godly offspring," the Israelites.

Indeed, according to the ancient Sumerians and the Greek Philosopher Plato, these giants, heroes of old, long ago built great and marvelous cities and towering civilizations which were destroyed in a world wide flood some 12,000 years ago. However, although the vast majority of these intellectual and physical giants became extinct or were hunted down and eradicated, those smaller sized, more primitive humans who had evolved from archaic Homo sapiens, survived.

It is the survival of the more primitive Homo sapiens, coupled with the possibly purposeful extinction of most (but not all of) the Cro-Magnon and the complete eradication of their cities and civilizations, which explains why after the great flood, and throughout the Neolithic the average human was about five feet tall and had a brain which was one third smaller than that of the average Cro-Magnon. It is only within the last 100 years that Western human males have grown significantly in stature, attaining a height of 5 ft. 9 inches on average. Modern humans are short (and small brained) compared to the average 6 foot tall Cro-Magnon.

Thus, perhaps modern day "psychic abilities" are but pale remnants of capacities which have since regressed, or which have yet to more fully evolve.

THE PHYSICS OF METAPHYSICS

We are repeatedly told, for example, in the Tao, and the Tibetan Book of the Dead, that there are no gods, or demons, or angels: "No terrible God punishes you. The shapes of frightening monsters who take hold of you, place a rope around your neck and drag you along, are just an illusion which you create from the forces within you. Know that apart from these karmic forces there is no Judge of the Dead, no gods, and no demons. Knowing that, you will be free." -Tibetan Book of the Dead.

Yet, we are also informed of a reality which is different, and more real, than the illusions that comprise much of everyday experience.

"To know that what is impenetrable to us really exists, manifesting itself to us as the highest wisdom and the most radiant beauty, which our dull faculties can comprehend only in their most primitive forms—this knowledge, this feeling, is at the center of all true religiousness. In this sense, and in this sense only, I belong to the ranks of devoutly religious men." -Einstein

"The kingdom is a spirit-like thing, and cannot be got by active doing. He who would so win it destroys it; he who would hold it in his grasp loses it."
-The Tao Teh King.

According to Plato, man's reality is shrouded in darkness and shadows which reflects the divine and unchanging reality beyond the world of the senses. However, Plato also believed that one could achieve enlightenment by liberating the mind and allowing it to be enveloped by the divine light.

In part, the mind is restrained by its senses and perceptual capabilities, and the inhibitory influences that filter out stimuli which may be overwhelming. Our intellectual and perceptual capabilities cannot process what they cannot perceive or comprehend. Language and belief also act as yoke, by shaping perceptions and labeling that which is beyond the norm, as abnormal, unnatural, crazy, and sinful.

However, trance states, isolation, fasting, prayer, meditation, and LSD can free the mind of inhibitory restraint, producing not just dream-like hallucinations, but by opening the mind to the full range of experience, so that what is concealed may be revealed.

Yet, to enter into this other perceptual reality so that what is hidden is revealed, also entails the temporary annihilation of this world and this reality. Being becomes non-being, and non-being becomes being—which is also the philosophical view of the Tao.

Being become nonbeing, and nonbeing becoming being, is also a principle of physics. That is, form and substance are in fact manifestations of dynamic patterns of energy and electromagnetic radiation that have no material reality. Form and substance, that is, the "particles" they are comprised of, exist only as probabilities. Form and substance have probable realities and can become something else entirely, the most obvious example of which, is death and decay. What is, can undergo a transformation from being into nonbeing, such that what is hidden may be suddenly revealed.

Consider the theoretical molecular foundations of matter, e.g., electrons, protons, neutrons, photons, neutrinos, etc., Each of these "particles" are balanced by the existence of anti-particles which are in all respects opposite in charge. However, in some instances, these elements also comprise their own anti-particle (e.g. photons). Thus, there is being, and anti-being.

In fact, these particles do not really exist, except as probabilities. These "subatomic" particles have probable existences and display tendencies to assume certain patterns of activity that we perceive as shape and form. Yet, they may also begin to display a different pattern of activity such that being can become nonbeing and thus something else altogether.

Shape and form are a function of our perception of these dynamic interactions. However, we can only perceive what our senses can detect, and what we detect as form and shape is really a mass of frenzied subatomic electromagnetic activity that is amenable to detection by our senses. It is the perception of certain aspects of these oscillating patterns of activity, which in turn are dependent on our sensory capabilities, which give rise to the impressions of shape and form. If we possessed additional senses, or an increased sensory channel capacity, we would perceive yet other patterns and other realities.

More specifically, this electromagnetic activity is so frenzied, that a particle can exist here and now there, and although it is neither here nor there it is perceived as a solid object that has shape, form, length, mass, weight, and so on. This is because the rapidity of movement obscures the fact that much of what we perceive are particular patterns of electromagnetic activity that are in frenzied motion.

Mass, as Einstein determined, is therefore nothing other than energy. That is, mass (M) is equal to energy (E) divided by the speed of light squared (M=E/C2). However, whereas mass can be destroyed, energy cannot. Rather, as mass is destroyed, an equal amount of energy is released back into the electromagnetic continuum. The energy released as a function of destruction, is equal to the mass of the object times the square of the speed of light (E=MC2). Conversely, if we increase the amount of energy, we increase the amount of apparent mass.

Ultimately, what this means is that mass does not consist of tiny particles that are packed tightly together. Rather, what we perceive as mass (shape, form, length, weight) are dynamic patterns of energy which we selectively attend to and then perceive as stable and static. And, we are perceiving only fragments of the continuum.

This energy that makes up the object of our perceptions, is also but an aspect of the electromagnetic continuum which has assumed a specific pattern that may be sensed and processed by our brain. Moreover, these patterns can break down and assume other patterns and readily assume all manner of patterns that we cannot detect with our senses. Erosion, decay, and death are but a few examples of how this energy can be released to take on a different pattern.

However, again, the patterns that resemble particles, also display tendencies to exist and tendencies to no longer exist. Because they have probable existence it is impossible to predict an atomic event with 100% certainty. This principle, in fact, is called the uncertainty principle, because one can never predict when a particle may exist and where it may exist when it does exist. Again, these particles exist and do not exist and are always in motion—which gives rise to the illusion of permanent shape and form. It is also these principles which form the crux of quantum electrodynamics, or field theory.

In summary, form and substance are comprised of particles which take on specific patterns and which are the result of concentrations of energy that emerge and disappear back into the electromagnetic quantum field; a knot of energy that is a kind of blemish in the continuum of the quantum field.

This reality, therefore, is a manifestation of alterations in the patterns of activity within the electromagnetic field. The electromagnetic field, this energy, is therefore the fundamental entity, the continuum that is constitutes the basic oneness and unity of all things.

PERCEPTION IS REALITY

A radio or television receiver may be capable of receiving radio or television transmissions from hundreds or thousands of stations. These transmissions contain all manner of messages, voices, shapes, images, and information, and continue to be transmitted, even if the radio or television is off. There are other channels and other transmissions even if we have only one channel. This information is out there if we know it or not, and if we receive it or not.

However, we can only receive and perceive these messages, these images, if the television or radio is on. The number of stations and messages we can receive depends on the channel capacity of the radio/television receiver. That we cannot see or hear it without the proper receiver, or if the radio/television is off, does not mean that this information, these images, these sounds, do not exist, or that those who do perceive these stimuli are hallucinating.

The same is true regarding other realities.

Yet, we can only perceive what we are able to perceive.

Perception is also reality. Our senses not only limit and shape our perceptual reality, but the very act of perceiving can alter that reality. What is observed is effected by being observed, as has also been demonstrated in quantum physics.

The observer is also a part of the electromagnetic continuum. Hence, upon observing and attempting to measure a particle's mass and velocity, the act of observation, the mere presence of an observer, will effect the trajectory and mass of the particle.

Thus, a thing is what it appear to be, at the moment it appears, relative to the observer that it appears to. However, a second observer can change that reality, merely by perceiving. Perceptions, therefore, can shape and alter reality.

Likewise, by changing one's perceptions, by changing the observer, can also change the reality that is being perceived; just like changing the channel on the radio or television.

"Jesus said: Recognize what is before your eyes, and what is hidden will be revealed." -Gospel of Thomas.

What one perceives is a function of sensory and perceptual filtering (and thus channel capacity), such that only select aspects of the continuum are perceived. By eliminating this filter, by enabling the brain to attend to different aspects of the electromagnetic continuum, by expanding the channel capacity, what is hidden may be revealed. What is hidden may be perceived.

IN THE BEGINNING THERE WAS LIFE

"There is a limit to our life, but to knowledge there is no limit."
-Chuang Tzu

"And his was mind was afterwards clear as the morning, and after this he was able to see beyond his own individuality. That individuality perceived, he was able to banish all thought of past and present. Freed of this he was able to penetrate to the truth— how the destruction of life is not dying— that there is no differences between life and death." -Chuang Tzu

Because the original genetic seed that is common to all life contains (at least as unrealized potential) the life plans for all life, different species also possess the genetic potential to assume multiple forms. This transformation and metamorphosis is due to the environment acting on gene selection, such that changing environments, and thus changes in specific patterns of energy within the electromagnetic continuum, act on silent genes to express genetically precoded traits.

Transformation in shape and form, and thus the emergence of seemingly novel species, are a function of cross generational influences acting on genetic potential, genetic predispositions, and the universal LIFE force that exists within us all.

Although it may seem mundane, it is noteworthy that all (known) life, all living things, not only possess DNA/RNA, but life. Life is common to all life—what some might call the "soul" or the essence or "spirit of god."

I would argue that LIFE cannot be created or destroyed, and that at the beginning of time and all being, there was life. In the beginning there was life. The universe itself, is alive.

Although this proposition may appear to bear the stamp of metaphysics, it is in fact based on quantum mechanics and the same theorem proposed by Einstein to account for the indestructibility of energy; i.e. E=M/C2. Energy can neither be created nor destroyed.

Is not life a form of energy? Do not even the proponents of the "big bang" admit that in the beginning there must have been pure energy?

What is this energy but life?

Hence, at first there was life.

In the beginning there was life—a pure energy that binds us all and which is synonymous with the "spirit of god."

I propose that LIFE itself, and not inert matter formed the heart of what we call "the beginning." Rather than considering life as some waste product of moist, nutrient rich, electrified matter, perhaps matter is a nutrient rich waste product of LIFE.

LIFE cannot be created or destroyed. LIFE can take many forms. Untold multiple physical manifestations of LIFE are shaped and molded by forces both internal and external. LIFE that takes the form of turtle, frog, woman or dog, remains LIFE; that is, alive. Although life can be neither created nor destroyed, the structural organization that gives form to life, is subject to disintegration and decay. What we call death.

Again, consider Einstein's theorem. Although energy cannot be destroyed or created, the destruction and transmutation of matter is something wholly different and is dependent on the organization and stability of the force field which is energy.

Although material forms may become unstable, disintegrate or assume new organization, the constituent fabric that gives rise to matter and its manifest structure, is pure energy -which cannot be destroyed. However, if matter decays, if the body dies, that energy is liberated, although its material form appears to disintegrate and to die.

In every living thing there dwells the power of the infinite universe.

DEATH AND THE BODY

"Tao is forever and he that possesses it, though his body ceases, is not destroyed." -Lao Tzu

Death is generally a gradual process, with some cells and tissues disintegrating in advance of others, and yet other tissues living for hours or even days or weeks before the body decays.

Presumably, even after death, so long as the body (or at least the limbic system) lives, one's sense of a personal soul and identity remains intact. This personal identity is perceived, after the death of the body, as an out-of-body experience. Moreover, this personal identity, the energy field associated with the dying body, may be perceived by others, as a ghost, spirit, or departing soul. Presumably, this ethereal after-death existence and sense of personal identity remains tethered to the body (or limbic system) until the body completely dies and decays.

Indeed, the linkage of the personal soul and individual immortality to the body were widespread beliefs and practices among the ancient Egyptians which is why they expended so much effort to preserve the body via mummification. If the body could be preserved, so could one's personal soul and sense of individuality, leading to "immortality".

Others, including the Tibetan Buddhists sought just the opposite, to free the soul from the body and so as to escape the "illusion" of individuality and personal existence.

Therefore, what some experience as their personal soul upon death, may be but a gradual liberation of LIFE that at first retains its bodily (limbic) links, thus preserving one's sense of individuality; the shadow of one's previous form as the body dies.

As the body is consumed, perhaps so too is the sense of individuality, freeing the soul, one's LIFE, to be embraced by the radiance of all LIFE thereby becoming One with the Great Spirit and the Gods.

"Thine own consciousness, shining, void, and inseparable from the Great Body of Radiance, hath no birth, nor death, and is the Immutable Light—Buddha Amitabha, the source of life and boundless light." -Bardo Thodol (Tibetan Book of the Dead)

ALPHA & OMEGA

According to Darwin (1871): "A belief in all-pervading spiritual agencies seems to be universal, and apparently follows from a considerable advance in man's reason, and from a still greater advance in his faculties of imagination, curiosity, and wonder. I am aware that the assumed instinctive belief in God has been used by many persons as an argument for His existence. But this is a rash argument, as we should be thus compelled to believe in the existence of many cruel and malignant spirits, only a little more powerful than man; for the belief in them is far more general than in a beneficent Deity."

Yet, despite, Darwin's rash claims to the otherwise, we are in fact spiritual beings, and there is scientific evidence to support these beliefs. We in fact possess the genetic and neurological capability to experience god, demons, spirits, souls, and other realities, for this reality is only one of many.

And, we possess a brain that not only shapes and filters this reality, but which, under certain conditions enables us to perceive at least some of these other realities. These same areas of the brain enable humans (and perhaps other animals) to experience the spirit and the soul as they transcend the body to traverse these myriad realms

Given the obvious role of the temporal lobe and limbic system in the generation and perception of myriad spiritual states and alternate realities, and its role in maintaining a personal identity and all associated personal memories, it also appears that the limbic system not only serves as a transmitter to god, but may well be the seat of the soul.

If that is indeed the case, then Buddha, Lao Tzu, Chuang Tzu, Jesus and other Jewish, Arabic, Muslim, Indian, Babylonian, Sumerian, Egyptian, Greek, Roman, and Gnostic mystics were correct when they proclaimed:

"The Kingdom of God is within you."

REFERENCES

Allen, L.S. & Gorski, R.A. (1992). *Sexual orientation and the size of the anterior commissure in the human brain.* Proceedings of the National Academy of Sciences,89, 7199-7202.

Allen, L.S. Hines, M. Shryne, J.E. & Gorski, R.A. (1989). *Two sexually dimorphic cell groups in the human brain.* Journal of Neuroscience, 9, 497-506

Al-Maqrizi, K.(1911). *Das Pyramidenkapitel "Hitat".* Graefe, Leipzig.

Amaral, D. G., Price, J. L., Pitkanen, A., & Thomas, S. (1992). *Anatomical organization of the primate amygdaloid complex.* In J. P. Aggleton (Ed.). The amygdala. (pp. 1-66), New York: Wiley-Liss.

Antequera, F., & Bird, A. (1993). Proceedings of the National Academy of Sciences, 90, 11995-11999.

Arrhenius, S. (1908). World in the Making. NY.

Atweh, S. F., & Kuhar, M. J. (1977a) *Autoradiographic localization of opiate receptors in rat brain.* I. Brain Research, 129, 1-12.

Atweh, S. F.,& Kuhar, M. J. (1977b) *Autoradiographic localization of opiate receptors in rate brain.* III. Brain research, 134, 273-405.

Austin, H. I. (1990). *The heart of the goddess.* Wingbrow Press, Berkeley.

Bagshaw, M., & Benzies, S., (1968). *Multiple measures of the orienting reaction and their dissociation after amygdalectomy in monkeys.* Experimental Neurology, 27, 31-40.

Bakan, P. (1977). *Dreaming, REM sleep and the right hemisphere: A theoretical integration.* Journal of Altered States of Consciousness, 3, 285-307.

Balcells, L., Swinburne, J., Coupland, G. (1991). *Transposons as tools for the isolation of plant genes.* Trends in Biotechnology, 9, 31-36.

Banquet,J. P. (1983) *Inter- and intrahemispheric relationships of the EEG activity during sleep in man.* Electroencephalography and Clinical Neurophysiology, 55, 51-59.

Barnes, G. L. (1993). *China, Korea, and Japan. The rise of civilization in East Asia.* Thames & Hudson, London.

Bear, D. M. (1979) *Temporal lobe epilepsy: A syndrome of sensory-limbic hyperconnexion.* Cortex 15: 357-384.

Bear, D.M. & Fedio, P. (1977).*Quantitative analysis of interictal behavior in temporal lobe epilepsy.* Archives of Neurology, 34, 454-467.

Belfer-Cohen, A., and E.Hovers, (1992) *In the eye of the beholder: Mousterian and Natufian burials in the levant.* Current Anthropology 33: 463-471.

Belfort, M. (1991). *Self-splicing introns in prokaryotes,* Cell, 64, 9-11.

Belfort, M. (1993). *Introns.* Science, 262, 1009-1010.

Bell, A.P., Weinberg, M.S., & Hammersmith, S.K. (1981). *Sexual Preference: Its Development in Men and Women.* Bloomington, Indiana University Press.

Bell, B. D. (1994). *Pantomime recognition impairment in aphasia.* Brain & Language, 47, 269-278.

Berkner, K. L. (1988). *Development of adneovirus vectors for the expression of heterologous genes.* Biochemical Techniques, 6, 616-629.

Bertini, M., Violani, C., Zoccolotti, P., Antonelli, A., & DiStephano, L. (1983) *Performance on a unilateral tactile test during waking and upon awakenings from REM and NREM.* InSleep, (pp. 122-155)ed. W. P. Koella Basel: Karger.

Bexton, W. A., Heron, W.,& Scott, T. H. (1954) *Effects of decreased variation in the sensory environment.* Canadian Journal of Psychology, 8, 70-76.

Bieber, I., Dain, H. J. Dince, P. R., et al. (1962). *Homosexuality.* New York, Basic Books.

Binford, S. R. (1968) *A structural comparison of disposal of the dead in the Mousterian and the Upper Paleolithic.* Southwest Journal of Anthropology 24: 139-54.

Blater, M. (1996). Science, 273, 871-972.

Blumer, D., & Benson, D.F. (1975).*Personality changes with frontal and temporal lesions.*In D.F. Benson & D. Blumeer (Eds.), Psychiatric aspects of neurologic disease.New York: Grune & Stratton.

Brain, The (1990). Cold Springs Harbor Symposium, The Brain, Cold Springs Harbor, NY.

Brandon, S.G. F. (1967) *The Judgment of the Dead.* New York, Scribners.

Brauer, G. (1989). *The Evolution of modern humans: A comparison of the African and Non-African evidence.* in The human revolution: Behavioral and biological perspectives on the origins of modern humans, vol 1. Edited by P. Mellars and C. B. Stringer. Edinburgh: Edinburgh University Press.

Breasted, J. H. (1909). *History of Egypt.* New York, Scribners.

Breathnach, R., Benoist, C., O'Hare, K., et al. *Ovalbumin gene.* Proceedings of the National Academy of Sciences, 75, 4853-4857.

Breault, M., & King, M. (1993). *Inside the Cult.* Signet, New York.

Breedlove, M. , & Cooke, B. (1999). Proceedings of the National Academy of Sciences.

Brend, R. (1975). *"Male female intonation patterns in American English.* InB. Thorne & N. Henley, (Eds.) Language & Sex.Massachussetts: Newbury House Publishers.

Brody, L. (1985). *Gender differences in emotional develoment. A review of theories and research.* In Steward, A. & Lyko, M. (eds). Gender and personality. Durham, Duke University Press.

Brooks, A. S., Helgren, D. M., Cramer, J. S., et al. (1995). *Dating and context of three middle stone age sites with bone points in the Upper Semliki Valley, Zaire,* Science, 268, 548-552.

Broughton,R. (1982) *Human consciousness and sleep/waking rhythms: A review and some neuropsychological considerations.* Journal of Clinical Neuropsychology, 4, 193-218.

Brougton, R. S. (1991). *Parapsychology.* Ballatine, New York.

Bubenick, G. A., & Brown, G. M. *Morphologic sex differences in the primate brain areas involved in regulation of reproductive activity.* Experimentia, 1973, 15, 619-621.

Buck, R. (1977). *Nonverbal communication of affect in preschool children.* Journal of Personality and Social Psychology, 35, 225-236.

Buck, R. (1984). *The communication of emotion.* New York, Guilford.

Buck, R., Baron, R., & Barrette, D. (1982). *The temporal organization of spontaneous nonverbal expression.* Journal ofPersonality & Social Psychology, 42, 506-517.

Buck, R. Miller, R. & Caul, W. (1974). *Sex, personality and physiological variables in communication of affect via facial expressions.* Journal of personality and social psychology, 30, 587-596.

Burton, L. A. & Levy, J. (1989). *Sex differences in the laterlized processing of facial emotion.* Brain and Cognition, 11, 210-228.

Butzer, K. (1982) *"Geomorphology and sediment stratiagraphy," in The Middle Stone Age at Klasies River Mouth in South Africa.* Edited by R. Singer and J. Wymer. Chicago: University of Chicago Press.

Calvo, J. M., Badillo, S., Morales-Ramirez, M., Palacios-Salas, P. (1987). *The role of the temporal lobe amygdala in ponto-geniculo-occipital activity and sleep organization in cats.* Brain Research, 403, 22-30.

Campbell, J. (1988) *Historical Atlas of World Mythology.* New York, Harper & Row.

Card, A. L., Jackson, L. A., Stollak, G. E., & Ialongo, N. S., (1986). *Gender role and person-perception accuracy.* Sex Roles, 15, 159-171.

Carrasco, D. (1990) *Religions of MesoAmerica.* San Francisco, Harper & Row.

Casagrande, V. A., & Joseph, R. (1978). *Effects of monocular deprivation on geniculostriate connections in primates.* Anatomical Records, 14, 2001.

Casagrande, V. A., & Joseph, R. (1980). *Morphological effects of monocular deprivation and recovery on the dorsal lateral geniculate nucleus in Galago.* Journal of Comparative Neurology, 194, 413-426.

Cech, T. R. (1986). *RNA as an enzyme.* Scientific American, 255, 64-65.

Chauvet, J-M., Deschamps, E. B. & Hillaire, C. (1996) *Dawn of Art: The Chauvet Cave.* H.N. Abrams.

Chen, R., & Forster, F. M. (1973). *Cursive and gelastic epilepsy.* Neurology, 23, 1019-1029.

Child, I. L. (1985). *Psychology and anomalous observations.* American Psychologist, 40, 1219-1230.

Clark, J. D., & Harris, J. W. K. (1985). *Fire and its role in early hominid lifeways.* African Archaeology Review, 3, 3-27.

Cohen, S., Chang, A., Boyer, H., & Helling, R. (1973). *Construction of biologically functional bacterial plasmids.* Proceedings of the National Academy of Sciences,70, 3240-3244.

Corning, W. C., Dyal, J.A., & Willows, A. (1973). *Invertebrate learning.* Plenum. New York.

Cowen, R. (1995). *Hubble constant: Controversy continues.* Science News, 147, 198.

Crick, F., & Orgel, L. (1973). *Directed Panspermia*, Icarus, 19, 43-57.

Crick, F. H. (1981). *Life itself,* Simon & Schuster

Daly, D. (1958) *Ictal affect.* American Journal of Psychiatry, 115, 97-108.

Darwin, C. (1859). *The origin of species by means of natural selection.* London, Murray.

Darwin, C. (1871). *The origin of species and the descent of man.* New York, Random House.

Darwin, C. (1887). *Letters.* In Darwin, F. (ed.), *The Life and Letters of Charles Darwin, Vols. 1 & 2.* Appleton, New York.

Davis, M., Walker, D. L., & Lee, Y. (1997). *Amygdala and bed nucleus of the stria terminalis: Differential roles in fear and anxiety measured with acoustic startle reflex.* Annals of the New York Academy of Sciences, 821, 305-331.

Davison, C., & Kelman, H. (1939).*Pathological laughing and crying*.Archives of Neurology and Psychiatry, 42, 595-643.

Dawkins, R. (1987) *The Blind Watchmaker.* (Norton, New York.

De Jong, G., & Scharloo, W.(1976). *Environmental determination of selective significance of neutrality of amylase variants in Drosophilia.* Genetics 84, 77-94 (1976).

Denton, M. J.(1998). *Nature's Destiny.* The Free Press, New York.

Desmone, R., & Gross, C. G. (1979) *Visual areas in the temporal cortex of the macaque.* Brain Research, 178, 363-380.

De Vaus, D., & McAllister, I. (1987). *Gender differences in religion.* American Sociological Review, 52, 472-481.

Devereux, G. (1953). *Psychoanalysis and the Occult.* International Universities Press. New York.

Devore, I. (1974). *Male dominance and mating behavior in Baboons.* In Beach, F. (ed). Sex and Behavior, Wiley, NY.

Dibb, J., & Newman, A. J. (1989). *Evidence that introns arose at proto-splice sites.* EMBO, 8, 2015-2021.

Dicks, D. Myers R. E. & Kling, A. (1969). *Uncus and amygdaloid lesions on social behavior in free ranging rhesus monkeys.* Science, 160, 69-71.

Dorit, R. L. Schoenbach, L., & Gilbert, W. (1990). Science, 250, 1377-1382.

Dover, G. A. (1995). Nature Genetics, 10, 254-256.

Dreifuss, J. J., Murphy, J. T., & Gloor, P. (1968). *Contrasting effects of two identified amygdaloid efferent pathways on single hypothalamic neurons.* Journal of Neurophysiology, 31, 237-248.

Dundes, A. (1988). *The flood myth.* U. California Press. Berkeley.

Dykhuizen, D., & Hart, D. L. (1980) *Selective neutrality of 6PDG alozymes in E. coli and the effects of genetic background.* Genetics 96, 801-817.

Eadie, B. J., & Taylor, C. (1993) *Embraced by the light.* New York, Bantam

Ekman, P. (1972). *Universals and cultural differences in facial expressions of emotions.* In J. Cole (ed). Nebraska Symposium on Motivation, Lincoln, University of Nebraska Press.

Ekman, P. (1993).*Facial expression and emotion.* American Psychologist 48, 384-392.

Ellis, M. M., Spann, D. R., & Posakony, J. W. (1990). *Extramacrochaetae, a negative regulator of sensory organ development.* Cell, 61, 27-38.

Eible-Eisbesfeldt, I (1996).Ethology. Holt. NY

Fedigan, L. (1992). *Primates and paradigms: Sex roles and social bonds.* Montreal: Elden Press.

Ferreira, P. G., J. Majueij, & K. M. Gorski,(1998). Astro. J. Lett. 503, L1-L4.

Fields, C., Adams, M. D., White, O., & Venter, J. C. (1994). Nature Genetics, 7, 345-346.

Finnegan, D. J. (1989). *Eurkaryotic transposable elements and genome evolution,* Trends in Genetics, 5, 103-107.

Flamsteed, S. (1995). *Crisis in the cosmos.* Discover, March, 67-77.

Fraenkel-Conrat, H., & Williams, R. C. (1955). *Reconstitution of active tobacco mosaic virus from its inactive protein and nucleic acid components.* Proceedings of the National Academy of Sciences, 41, 690-698.

Freedman, W. L. (1994). Science, 266, 539-540.
Freemon, F. R.& Nevis, A. H.(1969) *Temporal lobe sexual seizures.* Neurology, 19, 87-90.
Freud, S.(1900) *The interpretation of dreams.* In J. Strachey (Ed) Standard Edition (Vol 5. London: Hogarth Press.
Fukuda, M., Ono, T., & Nakamura, K. (1987). *Functional relation among inferiotemporal cortex, amygdala and lateral hypothalamus in monkey operant feeding behavior.* Journal of Neurophysiology, 57, 1060-1077.
Fuller, J. L., Rosvold, H. E.. & Pribram, K. H. (1957). *Effects on affective and cognitive behavior in the dog after lesions of the pyriform-amygdaloid-hippocampal complex.* Journal of Comparative and Physiological Psychology, 50, 89-96.
Gargett, B. H. (1989) Grave Shortcomings: The evidence for Neandertal burial. Current Anthropology 30: 157-90
Gibbons, A. (1996). *On the many origins of species.* Science, 273, 1496-1499.
Gibson, G., & Hogness, D. S.(1996). *Effects of polymorphism in the Drosophilia regulatory gene Ultrabithorax on homoetic stability.* Science 271, 200-203.
Glanz, J. (1996). Science 272, 1590 (1996).
Gloor, P. (1960). Amygdala. In J. Field (Ed.), Handbook of physiology (pp. 300-370). Washington, DC: American Physiological Society.
Gloor, P.(1986) *"The role of the human limbic system in in perception, memory, and affect. Lessons from temporal lobe epilepsy."* In The Limbic System: Functional organization and Clinical Disorder. ed. B. K. Doane, & K. E. Livingston. New York, Raven Press.
Gloor, P.(1992). *Role of the amygdala in temporal lobe epilepsy.*In J. P. Aggleton (Ed.). The amygdala. (pp. 505-538), New York: Wiley-Liss.
Gloor, P. (1997). *The temporal lobe and limbic system.* Oxford University Press, New York.
Goldstein, L., Stoltzfus, N. W., & Gardocki, J. F. (1972) *Changes in interhemispheric amplitude relationships in the EEG during sleep.* Physiology and Behavior, 8, 811-815.
Godwin, M. (1990) *Angels.* New York, Simon & Schuster.
Green, R. (1985). *Gender identity in childhood and later sexual orientation.* American Journal of Psychiatry, 142, 339-341.
Green, R. (1987). *The "Sissy Boy Syndrome" and the Development of Homosexuality.* New Haven. Yale U. Press.
Greenberg, M., & Weber, P. (1985). Nature, 316.
Gross, C. G., Rocha-Miranda, C. E., & Bender, D. B. (1972) *Visual properties of neruons in inferotemporal cortex of the macaque.* Journal of Neurophysiology, 35, 96-111.
Halgren, E.(1992). *Emotional neurophysiology of the amygdala within the context of human cognition.*In J. P. Aggleton (Ed.), The amygdala. (pp. 191-228), New York, Wiley-Liss.
Halgren, E., Babb, T. L., & Crandall, P. H. (1978) *Activity of human hippocampal formation and amygdala neurons during memory tests.* Electroencephalography and Clinical Neurophysiology, 45, 585-601.
Halgren, E., Walter, R. D., Cherlow, D. G., & Crandal, P. H. (1978) *Mental phenomenoa evoked by electrical stimualtion of the human hippocampal forma-*

tion and amygdala, Brain, 101, 83-117.

Hall, J. (1978). *Gender effects in decoding nonverbal cues.* Psychological Review, 85, 845-857.

Hammerly-Dupuy, D. (1988). *Some observations on the Assyro-Babylonian and Sumerian flood stores.* in Dundes, A.The flood myth. U. California Press. Berkeley.

Hanisch, R. I (1939). *I Was Hitler's Buddy.* New Republic, (April) pp. 239-242, 270-272, 297-300.

Harackiewicz, J. N., & DePaulo, B. M. (1982). *Accuracy of person perception.* Personality & Social Psychology Bulletin, 8, 247-256.

Harold, F. B. (1980) *A comparative analysis of Eurasian Palaeolithic burials.* World Archaeology 12: 195-211.

Harris, M. (1993) *Why we became religious and the evolution of the spirit world.* In Lehmann, A. C. & Myers, J. E. (Eds) Magic, Witchcraft, and Religion. Mountain View: Mayfield.

Harvey, R. P.(1996). *NK-2 Homeobox genes and heart development.* Developl Biol. 178, 203-216.

Hayashi, J-I., Tekemitsu, M., Goto, Y-I., Nonakoa, I. (1994). Journal of Cell Biology, 125, 43-50.

Hawkes, J. 1963) *The World of the past. Vol. 1.* New York. Knopf.

Hedges, S. B. (1994). *Molecular evidence for the origin of birds.* Proceedings of the National Academy of Sciences, 91, 2621-2624.

Hedges, S. B., & Kumar, S. (1999). *Divergence times of eutherian mammals.* Sciences, 285, 2031.

Hedges, S. B., et al., (1992). *Human origins and analysis of DNA sequences.* Science, 255, 737-739.

Heidel, H. (1988). *The Babylonian Genesis.* Oriental Institute of Chicago.

Heidan, J. (1936) Hitler. Knopf, New York, 1936.

Hellemans, A. (1995). *Dwarfs and dim galaxies mark limits of knowledge.* Science, 268, 366-367.

Heller, W., & Levy, J. (1981). *Perception and expression of emotion in right-handers and left-handers.* Neuropsychologia, 19, 263-272.

Henikoff, S., Keene, M. A., Fechtel, K., & Friston, J. W. (1986). *Gene with a gene.* Cell, 44, 33-42.

Hermann, B. P., & Chambria, S. (1980). *Interictal psychopathology in patients with ictal fear.* Archives of Neurology, 37, 667-668.

Hobson, J. A., Lydic, R., & Baghdoyan, H. A. (1986) *Evolving concepts of sleep cycle generation: From brain centers to neuronalpopulations.* Behavioral and Brain Sciences, 9, 371-448.

Hodoba, D. (1986) *Paradoxic sleep facilitation by interictal epileptic activity of right temporal origin.* Biological Psychiatry, 21, 1267-1278.

Horowtiz, M. J., Adams, J. E., & Rutkin, B. B.(1968) Archives of General Psychiatry, 19, 469-487.

Horsh, R. B., Fry, J. E., Hoffman, N. L., et al. (1985). *A simple and general method for transferring genes into plants.* Science, 227, 1229-1231.

HumphreyM. E., & Zangwill, O. L. (1951) *Cessation of dreaming after brain injury.* Journal of Neurology, Neurosurgery, and Psychiatry, 14, 322-325.

Jackson, D., Symons, R., & Berg, P. (1972). *Biochemical method for inserting new genetic information into DNA*.Proceedings of the National Academy of Sciences, 69, 2904-2909.

Jackson, J. H. (1880) *Dreamy States*.In J. Taylor (Ed) Selected Writings of John Hughlings Jackson (1958) New York, Basic Books.

Jackson, J. H., & Stewart, (1899) *Epileptic attacks with a warning of a crude sensation of smell and with the intellectual aura (dreamy state) in a patient who had symptoms pointing to gross organic diseae of the right temporo-sphenoidal lobe.* In J. Taylor (Ed) Selected Writings of John Hughlings Jackson (1958) New York, Basic Books.

Jaynes, J. (1976) *The origin of consciousness in the breakdown of the bicameral mind.* Boston: Houghton Mifflin.

Jelinek, W. R., Tommey, T. P., Leinwand, L., et al. (1980). *Ubiquitous interspersed repeated DNA sequences in mammalian genomes.* Proceedings of the National Academy of Sciences, 77, 1398-1402.

John, B., & Miklos, G. (1988).*The Eucaryotic Genome in Development and Evolution.* Allen & Unwin, London,

Johnson, J. E., Birren, S. J., & Anderson, D. J. (1990). *Two rat homologues.* Nature, 346, 858-861.

Johnson, R. N. (1972) *Aggression in man and animals.* Philadelphia. W. B. Saunders.

Johnson, W. E., & Coffin, J. M. (1999). *Constructing primate phylogenies from ancient retrovirus sequences.* Proceedings of the National Academy of Sciences, 96, 10254-10260.

Joseph, R. (1979).*Effects of rearing and sex on learning and competitive exploration.* Journal of Psychology, 101,37-43.

Joseph, R. (1982). *The Neuropsychology of Development.* Hemispheric Laterality, Limbic Language, the the Origin of Thought.J. Clin. Psy. 444-33.

Joseph, R. (1984). *La Neuropsiciologia Del Desarrollo: Lateralidad, Hemisferica, Lenguaje Limbico, y el Origen del pensamiento.* Archives of Psychiatry and Neurology, Venezolanos, 30, 25-52.

Joseph, R. (1985). *Competition between women.* Psychology, 22, 1-11.

Joseph, R. (1986a). *Reversal of language and emotion in a corpus callosotomy patient.* Journal of Neurology, Neurosurgery, & Psychiatry, 49, 628-634.

Joseph, R. (1986b). *Confabulation and delusional denial: Frontal lobe and lateralized influences.* J. Clin. Psy. 42, 845-860.

Joseph, R. (1988a) *The Right Cerebral Hemisphere: Emotion, Music, Visual-Spatial Skills, Body Image, Dreams, and Awareness.* J.Clin. Psy., 44, 630-673.

Joseph, R. (1988b). *Dual mental functioning in a split-brain patient.* J. Clin. Psy.,44, 770-779.

Joseph, R. (1990). *Neuropsychology, Neuropsychiatry, Behavioral Neurology,* Plenum, New York.

Joseph, R. (1992a) *The Limbic System: Emotion, Laterality, and Unconscious Mind.* The Psychoanalytic Review,79, 405-456.

Joseph, R. (1992b).*The Right Brain and the Unconscious*.New York, Plenum.

Joseph, R. (1993). *The Naked Neuron: Evolution and the Languages of the Body and Brain.* New York, Plenum Press.

Joseph, R. (1994) *The limbic system and the foundations of emotional experience.* In V. S. Ramachandran (Ed). Encyclopedia of Human Behavior. San Diego, Academic Press.

Joseph, R. (1996). *Neuropsychiatry,* Neuropsychology, Clinical

Neuroscience, 2nd Edition. Williams & Wilkins, Baltimore.

Joseph, R. (1997). *The Evolution of Life on Other Planets: The Origin of Life and Evolutionary Metamorphosis.* California University Press, California.

Joseph, R. (1998a). *The limbic system.* In H.S. Friedman (ed.), Encyclopedia of Human health, Academic Press. San Diego.

Joseph, R. (1998b). *Traumatic amnesia, repression, and hippocampal injury due to corticosteroid and enkephalin secretion.* Child Psychiatry and Human Development. 29, 169-186.

Joseph, R. (1998c). *Flavonoid substance and/or flavone glocosides substance as a treatment for disorders of the brain.* United States Department of Commerce: Patent & Trademark Office, March, # 60/080,768.

Joseph, R. (1998d). *Olfactory substance as a treatment for disorders of the brain.* United States Department of Commerce: Patent & Trademark Office, March, # 60/080,770.

Joseph, R. (1998e). *Combined use of Ginko Biloba and Hypericum Perforatum (Saint John's Wort) as a treatment for disorders of the brain.* United States Department of Commerce: Patent & Trademark Office, March, # 60/080,769.

Joseph, R. (1999a). *Frontal lobe psychopathology: Mania, depression, aphasia, confabulation, catatonia, perseveration, obsessive compulsions, schizophrenia.*Psychiatry, 62, 138-172.

Joseph, R.(1999b).*Environmental influences on neural plasticity, the limbic system, and emotional development and attachment,* Child Psychiatry and Human Development. 29, 187-203.

Joseph, R. (1999c). *The neurology of traumatic ("dissociative") amnesia.* Commentary and literature review. Child Abuse & Neglect. 23,

Joseph, R. (2000a). *Clinical Neuroscience.*3rd edition.University Press California, San Jose.

Joseph, R. (2000b). *Astrobiology, the Origin of Life, and the Death of Darwinism.* University Press California, San Jose,

Joseph, R. (2000c). *The evolution of sexuality and sex differences in language and visual spatial skills.* Archives of Sexual Behavior, 29, 35-66.

Joseph, R. (2000d). *Female Sexuality: The Naked Truth.* University Press California, San Jose.

Joseph, R. (2000e).*The Limbic System.* University Press California, San Jose.

Joseph, R. (2000f). *Fetal brain behavioral cognitive development.* Developmental Review, 20, 81-98.

Joseph, R., & Casagrande, V. A. (1978). *Visual field defects and morphological changes resulting from monocular deprivation in primates.* Proceedings of the Society for Neuroscience, 4, 2021.

Joseph, R. & Casagrande, V. A. (1980). *Visual field defects and recovery following lid closure in a prosimian primate.* Behavioral Brain Research, 1, 150-178.

Joseph, R., Forrest, N., Fiducia, N., Como, P., & Siegel, J. (1981). *Electrophysiological and behavioral correlates of arousal.* Physiological Psychology, 1981, 9, 90-95.

Joseph, R., & Gallagher, R. E. (1980). *Gender and early environmental influences on activity, overresponsiveness, and exploration.* Developmental Psychobiology, 13, 527-544.

Joseph, R., & Gallagher, R. E. (1985). *Interhemispheric transfer and the completion of reversible operations in non-conserving children.* J.Clin. Psy.41, 796-800.

Joseph, R., Gallagher, R., E., Holloway, J., & Kahn, J. (1984). *Two brains, one child: Interhemispheric transfer and confabulation in children aged 4, 7, 10.* Cortex, 20, 317-331.

Joseph, R., Hess, S., & Birecree, E. (1978). *Effects of sex hormone manipulations and exploration on sex differences in maze learning.* Behavioral Biology, 24, 364-377.

Jouvet, M. (1967) *Neurophysiology of the states of sleep.* Physiological Review, 47, 117-177.

Jung, C. G. (1945) *On the nature of dreams.* (Translated by R.F.C. Hull.), The collected works of C. G. Jung, (pp.473-507) Princeton: Princeton University Press.

Jung, C. G. (1964) *Man and his symbols.* New York. Doubleday.

Kapp, B. S., Supple, W. F., & Whalen, P. J. (1994). *Effects of electrical stimulation of the amygdaloid central nucleus on neocortical arousal in the rabbit.* Behavioral Neuroscience, 108, 81-93.

Kerr, N. H., & Foulkes, D. (1981) *Right hemisphere mediation of dream visualization: A case study.* Cortex, 17, 603-610.

Kling, A. (1972). *Effects of amygdalectomy on social-affective behavior in non-human primates.* In B. E. Eleftherious (Ed.). The Neurobiology of the amygdala, (pp 127-170). New York: Plenum.

Kling. A. S. & Brothers, L. A.(1992). *The amygdala and social behavior.*In J. P. Aggleton (Ed.). The amygdala. New York: Wiley-Liss.

Kling, A. S., Lloyd, R. L., & Perryman, K. M. (1987). *Slow wave changes in amygdala to visual, auditory and social stimuli following lesions of the inferior temporal cortex in squirrel monkey.* Behavioral and Neural Biology, 47, 54-72.

Kling, A., & Steklis, H.D. (1976).*A neural substrate for affiliative behavior in nonhuman primates.*Brain Behavior and Evolution, 13, 216-238.

Kramer, S. N. (1991). *History begins at Sumer.* U. Pennsylvania Press, Philadelphia.

Krettek, J.E., & Price, J.L. (1977).*Projections from the amygdaloid complex.* Journal of Comparative Neurology, 172, 723-752, 687-722.

Kripe, D. F. & Sonnenschein (1973) *A 90-minute daydream cycle.* Sleep Research, 2, 187-190.

Kumar, S., & Hedges, S. B.(1998). *A molecular time scale for vertebrate evolution.* Nature. 396, 336-342.

Kuhsel, M. G., Strickland, R., & Palmer, J. D. (1990). *An ancient group I intron shared by eubacteria and chloroplasts,* Science, 250, 1570-1573.

Kurten, B. (1976) *The cave bear story.* New York: Columbia University Press.

Labandeira, C. & Phillips, T. (1996). Proceeding of the National Academy of Sciences.

Lamond, A., I., & Gibson, T. J. (1990). *Catalytic RNA and the origin of genetic systems.* Trends in Genetics, 6, 145-149.

Langer, W. C. (1972). *The Mind of Adolf Hilter.* Basic Books, New York.
LeDoux, J. E. (1996). *The emotional brain.* New York: Simon & Schuster.
Lazerwitz, B. (1961). *Some factors associated with variations in church attendance.* Social Forces, 39, 301-309.
Lehmann, A. C. & Myers, J. E. (1993) *Magic, Witchcraft, and Religion.* Mountain View: Mayfield.
Leroi-Gourhan, A. (1964.) *Treasure of prehistoric art.* New York: H. N. Abrams.
Leroi-Gourhan, A. (1982). *The archaeology of Lascauz Cave.* Scientific American 24: 104-112.
Leutmezer, F., Serles, W., Bacher, J., et al., (1999). *Genital automatisms in complex partial seizures.* Neurology, 52, 1188-1191.
LeVay, S.A. (1991).*A difference in hypothalamic structure between heterosexual and homosexual men* Science, 253, 1034-1037.
Levinson, B., Kenwrick, S., Lakich, D., et al. (1990). *A transcribed gene in an intron of the human Factor VIII gene.* Genomics, 7, 7-11.
Levy, J., & Heller, W.(1992). *Gender differences in human neuropsychological function.* In A. A. Gerall, H. Moltz, & I. L. Ward (eds.), Handbook of behavioral Neurobiology, Vol. 11, Sexual differentiation (pp. 245-274). Plenum, New York.
Lewin, B.(1988). *Molecular clocks turn a quarter of a century.* Science, 239, 561-563.
Lewis, R.S., & Anders, E. (1983). Science.
Levinson, G., & Gutman, G. A. (1987). Molecular Biology & Evolution, 4, 203-221.
Lilly, J. C. (1972) *The Center of the Cyclone,* New York. Julian Press.
Lilly, R., Cummings, J. L., Benson, F., Frankel, M. (1983), *The human Kluver-Bucy syndrome.* Neurology, 3, 1141-1145.
Lindsey, L. L. (1990). *Gender roles. A sociological perspective.* Englewood Cliffs. Prentice Hall.
Lindsley, D. (1961). *Common factors in sensory depr-vation. In P. Solomon (Ed.), Sensory deprivation.* Cambridge: Harvard University Press.
Lings, M. (1983) *Muhammad, his life based on the earliest sources.* New York. Ballintine Books.
Lisk, W.G. (1967).*Neural localization for androgen activation of copulatory behavior in the male rat.* Endocrinology, 80,754-780.
Lisk, W.G. (1971).*Diencephalic placement of estrodiol and sexual receptivity in the female rat.*American Journal of Physiology, 203, 493-500.
MacLean, P. D. (1969) *The hypothalamus and emotional behavior.* In The hypothalamus.ed W. Haymaker(pp. 127-167) Springfield. Thomas.
MacLean, P. (1990) *The triune brain in evolution.* New York: Plenum.
Malinowski, B. (1954) *Magic, Science and Religion.* New York. Doubleday.
Maglio, V. J. (1978.) *Evolution of African Mammals.* Harvard University Press. Cambridge.
Manning, A. (1972). *An introduction to animal behavior.* Menlo Park, Addison-Wesley.
Margulis, L. (1970). *Origin of Eukaryotic cells,* Yale U. Press, New Haven.
Marshall, J.F., & Teitelbaum, P. (1974).*Further analysis of sensory inattention following lateral hypothalamic damage in rats.*Journal of Comparative and Physiological Psychology, 86, 375-395.

Martin, J.P. (1950).*Fits of laughter (sham mirth) in organic cerebral disease.*Brain, 73, 453-464.

Maxam, A. M., & gilbert, W. (1977). *A new method of sequencing DNA.* Proceedings of the National Academy of Sciences, 74, 560-564.

McCown, T. (1937) *"Mugharet es-Skhul: Description and excavation," in The stone age of Mount Carmel.* Edited by D. A. E. Garrod and D. Bate. Oxford: Clarendon Press.

McKay, D. S., Gibson, E. K., Thomas-Keptra, K. L. (1996). Science, 273, 924-929.

Mesulam, M. M. (1981) *Dissociative states with abnormal temporal lobe EEG: Multiple personality and the illusion of possession.* Archives of General Psychiatry, 38, 176-181.

Mellars, P. (1989). *Major issues in the emergence of modern humans.* Current Anthropology 30: 349-385.

Mellars, P. (1996) *The Neanderthal legacy.* Princeton University Press.

Mellars, P. (1998). *The fate of the Neanderthals.* Nature 395, 539-540.

Mesulam, M. M. (1981) *Dissociative states with abnormal temporal lobe EEG: Multiple personality and the illusion of possession.* Archives of General Psychiatry, 38, 176-181.

Meyer, J. S., Ishikawa, Y., Hata, T., & Karacan, I. (1987) *Cerebral blood flow in normal and abnormal sleep and dreaming.* Brain and Behavior 6, 266-294.

Mojzsis, S. J. et al., (1996). Nature 384, 55-59.

Moritz, C., Dowling, T. E. & Brown, W. M. (1987). *Evolution of animal mitochondrial DNA: Relevance for population biology and systematics.* Annual Review of Ecological Systematics 18: 269-292.

Morris, J. S., Frith, C. D., Perett, D. I., Rowland, D., Young, A. W., Calder, A. J., & Colan, R. J. (1996). *A differential neural response in the human amygdala to fearful and happy facial expression.* Nature, 383, 812-815.

Moss, B. O., Elroy-Stein, Mizukami, T., et al. (1990). *New mammalian expression vectors.* Nature, 348, 91-95.

Murdock, G. P., & Provost,C. (1981). *Factors in the Division of Labor by Sex.* Ethnology, 12, 203-235;

Nakamura, K., & Ono, T. (1986). *Lateral hypothalamus neuron involvement in integration of natural and artifical rewards and cue signals.* Journal of Neurophysiology, 55, 163-181.

Nadler, R. D., & Braggio, J. T. (1974). *Sex and species differences in captive reared juvenile chimpanzees and orangutans.* Journal of Human Evolution.

Neihardt, J. G. (1988) Black Elk Speaks. Nebraska, U. Nebraska Press.

Neithammer, C. (1977). *Daughters of the earth.* New York, Collier

Noyes, R., & Kletti, R. (1977) *Depersonalization in response to life threatening danger.* Comprehensive Psychiatry, 18, 375-384.

O'Brien, S. J., Womack, J. E., Lyons, L. A., et al. (1993). *Nature Genetics*, 3, 103-112.

Ovchinnikov, I. V., et al., (2000).*Molecular analysis of Neanderthal DNA from the northern Caucasus.*Nature, 2000.

Offen, M. L., Davidoff, R. A., Troost, B. T., & Richey, E. T. (1976). *Dacrystic epilepsy.* Journal of Neurology, Neurosurgery and Psychiatry, 39, 829-834.

O'Keefe, J.& Bouma, H. (1969). *Complex sensory properties of certain amygdala units in the freely moving cat.*Experimental Neurology, 23, 384-398.

Olds, J. A. (1956).*A preliminary mapping of electrical reinforcing effects in rat brain.*Journal of Comparative and Physiological Psychology, 49, 281-285.

Olds, J. A., & Milner, P. (1954).*Positive reinforcement produced by electrical stimulation of septal areas and other regions of the rat brain.* Journal of Comparative and Physiological Psychology, 47, 419-427.

Olds, M. E., & Forbes, J. L. (1981).*The central basis of motivation: intracranial self-stimulation studies.*Annual Review of Psychology, 32, 523-574.

Olmstead, C. E., Best, P. J.,& Mays, L. E. (1973) *Neural activity in the dorsal hippocampus during paradoxical sleep, slow wave sleep and waking.* Brain Research, 60, 381-391.

Orgel, L. E. (1994). *The origin of life on earth.* Scientific American.271, 76-83.

Parrinder, G. 1980) *Sex in the World's religions. Oxford University Press.* New York

Pathy, L. (1991). Exons—original building blocks of proteins? BioEssays, 13, 187-192.

Payne, R. (1973) *The Life and death of Adolf Hitler.* New York, Praeger.

Penfield, W. (1952) *Memory Mechanisms.* Archives of Neurology and Psychiatry, 67, 178-191.

Penfield, W., & Perot, P.(1963) *The brains record of auditory and visual experience.* Brain, 86, 595-695.

Petes, T., & Fink, G. R. (1982). *Gene conversion between repeated genes.* Nature, 300, 216-217.

Polaczyk, P. J., Gasperini, R., & Gibson, G.(1998). *Naturally occurring genetic variation affects Drosophilia photoreceptor determination.* Developl. Genes Evol. 207, 462-470.

Prideaux, T. (1973). *Cro-Magnon.* New York: Time-Life.

Ransom, T. W., & Powell, T. E. (1972). *Early social development of feral baboons.* In F. E. Poirer (ed.). Primate socialization. New York, Random House.

Rainbow, T.C., Parsons, B., & McEwen, B.A. (1982).*Sex differences in rat brain oestrogen and progestin receptors.* Nature, 300, 648-649.

Raisman, G. & Field, P.M. (1973). *Sexual dimorphism in the neuropil of the preoptic area of the rat and its dependence on neonatal androgen.* Brain Research, 54, 1-29.

Reinisch, J. M., and Sanders, S. A. (1992). *Prenatal hormonal contributions to sex differences in human cognitive and personality development.* In Gerall, A. A., Moltz, H., & Ward, I. L. (Eds.), Handbook of Behavioral Neurobiology, Vol. 11, Sexual Differentiation (pp. 221-244). Plenum, New York.

Remmillard, G. M., Andermann, F., Testas, G. F., et al.(1983) *Sexual ictal manifestations predominant in women with temporal lobe epilepsy.* Neurology, 33, 323-330.

Richmond, B. J., Optican, L. M., Podel, M., & Spitzer, H. (1987) *Temporal encoding of two-dimensional patterns by single units in primate inferior temporal cortex.* Journal of Neurophysiology, 57, 132-162

Richmond, B. J., Wurtz, R. H., & Sato, T. (1983) *Visual responses of inferior temporal neurons in awake rhesus monkey.* Journal of Neurophysiology, 50, 1415-1432

Rightmire, G. P. (1984) *"Homo sapiens in Sub-Saharan Africa," in The origins of modern humans: A world survey of the fossil evidence.* Edited by F. H. Smith and F. Spencer. New York: Alan R. Liss.

Ritchie, D. (1994). *UFO.* Facts on File, NY
Rolls, E. T. (1984). *Neurons in the cortex of the temporal lobe and in the amygdala of the monkey with responses selective for faces.* Human Neurobiology, 3, 209-222.
Rolls, E. T.(1992). *Neurophysiology and functions of the primate amygdala.* In J. P. Aggleton (Ed.). The Amygdala. (pp. 143-166). New York: Wiley-Liss.
Rolls, E.T., Burton, M.J., & Mora, F. (1976).*Hypothalamic neuronal response associated with the sight of food.*Brain Research, 111, 53-66.
Rosenbaum, R. (1999). *Explaining Hitler.* Harper, New York.
Roux, G. (1992) *Ancient Iraq.*Penguin, New York.
Russell, M., et al., (1999). The Journal of the Geological Society of London, 156, 869-870.
Rutherford, S. L., & Lindquist, S.(1998). *Hsp90 as a capacitor for morphological evolution.* Nature 396, 336-342.
Saghir, G. B.,& Robins, E. (1973). *Male and female homosexuality.* Baltimore, Williams & Wilkins
Sancar, A. (1994). *Mechanisms of DNA excision repair.* Science, 266, 1954-1956.
Sarich, V. (1970). *Primate systematics.* In Old Word Monkeys. J. R. Napier & P. H. Napier (Eds.) 175-226. Academic Press, New York.
Schaller, G. B. (1963). *The Mountain Gorilla.* Chicago. University of Chicago Press.
Schenk, L., & Bear, D. (1981). *Multiple personality and related dissociative phenomena in patients with temporal lobe epilepsy.* American Journal of Psychiatry, 138, 1311-1316.
Schenkel, R. (1966). *Play, exploration, and territoriality in the wild lion.* In P. A. Jewell & C. Loizos (eds.). Play, exploration and territoriality. Academic Press. London.
Schock, R. M. (1992). *Sphinx, riddle put to rest.* Science, 255, 101-103.
Schopf, J. W. (1978)*The evolution of the earliest cells.* Scientific American, 1978, 239, 84-100.
Schopf, J. W. (1992). *The oldest fossils and what they mean.* In J.W. Schopf (ed.). Major events in the history of life. New York, Bartlett.
Schopf,J. W. (1993). Science.640.
Schopf, J. W. (1999). *Cradle of life: The discovery of Earth's earliest fossils.* Princeton University Press.
Schenk, L., & Bear, D. (1981) *Multiple personality and related dissociative phenomenon in patients with temporal lobe epilepsy.* American Journal of Psychiatry, 138, 1311-1316.
Schwarcz, et al. (1988) *ESR dates for the hominid burial site of Qafzeh.* Journal of Human Evolution 17:
Scott, S. K., Young, B. S., Calder, A. J., Hellawell, D. J., Aggleton, J. P., & Johnson, M. (1997). *Impaired auditory recognition of fear and anger following bilateral amygdala lesions.* Nature, 385, 254-257.
Serafetinides, E. A. (1965) *The significance of the temporal lobes and of hemisphere dominance in the production of the LSD-25 symptomology in man.* Neuropsychologia, 3, 69-79.
Sethi, P. K., & Raio, S. T. (1976). *Gelastic, quiritarian, and cursive epilepsy.* Journal of Neurology, Neurosurgery and Psychiatry, 39, 823-828.

Sheng, M., & greenberg, M. E., (1990). *The regulation and function of c-fos and other immediate early genes in the nervous system.* Neuron, 4, 477-485.
Shirer, W. L. (1941). Berlin Diary. New York.
Shirer, W. L. (1960). *The Rise and Fall of the Third Reich,* Fawcett, New York.
Sitchen, Z. (1980). *The stairway to haven.* Avon, New York.
Sitchin, Z. (1990) *The lost realms.* New York. Avon.
Smart, N. (1969) *The religious experience of mankind.* New York.
Smirnov, Y. A. (1989) *On the evidence for Neandertal burial.* Current Anthropology 30: 324.
Solecki, R. (1971) *Shanidar: The first flower people.* New York: Knopf.
Southard, E. E. (1919) *Shell-shock and other Neuropsychiatric Problems.* Boston.
Spencer, S. S., et al., (1983) *Sexual automatisms in complex partial seizures.* Neurology, 33, 527-533.
Steklis, H. D., & Kling, A. (1985). *Neurobiology of affiliative behavior in nonhuman primates.* In M. Reite & T. Fields (Eds.). The Psychobiology of attachment and separation, (pp. 93-134). Orlando, FL: Academic Press.
Strachan, T., & Read, A. (1996). *Human molecular genetics.* Wiley, NY.
Strauss, E., Risser, A., & Jones, M. W. (1982). *Fear responses in patients with epilepsy.* Archives of Neurology, 39, 626-630.
Swaab, D.F, & Fliers, E. (1985). *A sexually dimorphic nucleus in the human brain* Science, 228, 1112-1114
Swaab, D.F. & Hoffman M.A. (1988). *Sexual differentiation of the human hypothalamus: Ontogeny of the sexually dimorphic nucleus of the preoptic area.* Developmental Brain Research, 44, 314-318.
Swaab, D.F., Hoffman, M.A. (1990). *An enlarged suprachiasmatic nucleus in homosexual men.* Brain Research, 537,141-148.
Tautz, D.(1998). *Debatable homologies.* Nature, 395, 17-19.
Taylor, D. C. (1972) *Mental state and temporal lobe epilepsy.* Epilepsia,13, 727-765.
Taylor, D. C. (1975) *Factors influencing the occurrence of schizophrenia-like psychosiswith temporal lobe epilepsy.* Psychological Medicine, 5, 429-254.
Teitelbaum, P. (1961).*Disturbances in feeding and drinking behavior after hypothalamic lesions.*In M.R. Jones (Ed.), Nebraska Symposium on Motivation, Lincoln: University of Nebraska Press.
Teitelbaum, P., & Epstein, A.N. (1962).*The lateral hypothalamic syndrome.* Psychological Review, 69, 74-90.
Tellegen, A., Horn, J. M., & Legrand, R. G. (1969). Psychonomic Science, 14, 104,
Terzian, H., & Ore, G. D. (1955). *Syndrome of Kluver and Bucy in man by bilateral removal of temporal lobes.* Neurology, 5, 373-380.
Tow, P.M., & Whitty, C.W.M. (1953).*Personality changes after operations of the cingulate gyrus in man.*Journal of Neurology, Neurosurgery and Psychiatry, 16, 186-193.
Tripp, C. A. (1987). *The homosexual matrix.* New York, New American Library.
Turon, C. (1997). American Association for the Advancement of Science.
Uhl, R. G., Kuhar, B. R., & Snyder, S. H. (1978). *Enkephalin containing pathways: Amygdaloid efferents in the stria terminalis.* Brain Research, 149, 223-228.
Ullman, M., & Krippner, S. (1989). *Dream Telepathy.* McFarland, New Jersey.

Uno, H., Tarara, R., Else, J., & Sapolsky R. M. (1989). *Hippocampal damage associated with prolonged and fatal stress in primates.* Journal of Neuroscience, 9, 1705-1711.

Ursin, H., & Kaada,B. R. (1960). *Functional localization within the amygdaloid complex in the cat.* Electroencephalography and Clinical Neurophysiology, 12, 1-20.

Van Den Aardweg, G.J.M. (1980). *Parents of homosexuals—not guilty?* American Journal Psychotherapy 38,181-189.

Velikovsky, I. (1950) *Worlds in collision.* Dell, NY

Venkatesh, B., et al. (1999) *Late changes in splicesomal introns define clades in vertebrate evolution.* Proceedings of the National Academy of Sciences, 96, 10267-10271.

Vochteloo, J. D., & Koolhaas, J. M. (1987). *Medial amygdala lesions in male rats reduce aggressive behavior.* Physiology and Behavior, 41, 99-102.

Wade, M., Johnson, N.A., Jones, R., Siguel, V., & McNaughton, M. (1997). *Genetic variation segregating in natural populations of Tribolium castaneum affecting traits observed in hybrids with T. fremani.* Genetics, 147, 1235-1247.

Wasman, M., Flynn, J.P (1962) *Directed attack elicited from the hypothalamus.* Archives of Neurology, 6, 220-227.

Watson, J. D., Gilman, M., Witkowksi, J., & Zoller, M. (1992). *Recombinant DNA.* Scientific American Books, NY

Weil, A. A. (1956). *Ictal depression and anxiety in temporal lobe disorders.* American Journal of Psychiatry, 113, 149-157.

Weingarten, S. M., Cherlow, D. G., & Holmgren, E.(1977) *The relationship of hallucinations to depth structures of the temporal lobe.* Acta Neurochirugica, 24, (199-216.

Williams, D. (1956) *The structure of emotions reflected in epileptic experiences.* Brain, 79, 29-67.

Wilson, J. A. (1951) *The culture of ancient Egypt.* Chicago, U. Chicago Press.

Witkowski, J. A. (1988). *The discovery of split genes.* Trends in Biochemical Science.

Woese, C. R., et al., Proc.Natl. Acad. Sci. 87, 4576-4579 (1990).

Woolley, C. L. (1965). *Ur of the Chaldees.* Norton, NY.

Young, A. W., Aggleton, J. P., & Hellawell, D. J., (1995). *Face processing impairments after amygdalotomy.* Brain, 118, 15-24.

Zilman, A. L. (1981). *Women as shapers of the human adaptation: in Woman the Gatherer.* Edited by F. Dalhberg. New York: Yale U. Press.